HELLFIRE PASS

At 04.00 hours the alert went up. The British armies were in sight, and they had no idea how close they were to the barrels of the German guns. A deafening explosion tore the air. The 88 mm. had spoken . . . the British Mark II tank was no match for it.

Now a hail of death spat from the German positions, rapid fire from every battery. Hell had broken loose. A dozen burning British tanks lay shattered before the German lines. The 88 mm. fired into the close-formation infantry columns. The effect was murderous. From this moment on Halfaya was known as Hellfire Pass—and Erwin Rommel as the man to be reckoned with.

THE BANTAM WAR BOOK SERIES

This series of books is about a world on fire.

The carefully chosen volumes in the Bantam War Book Series cover the full dramatic sweep of World War II. Many are eyewitness accounts by the men who fought in a global conflict as the world's future hung in the balance. Fighter pilots, tank commanders and infantry captains, among many others, recount exploits of individual courage. They present vivid portraits of brave men, true stories of gallantry, moving sagas of survival and stark tragedies of untimely death.

In 1933 Nazi Germany marched to become an empire that was to last a thousand years. In only twelve years that empire was destroyed, and ever since, the country has been bisected by her conquerors. Italy relinquished her colonial lands, as did Japan. These were the losers. The winners also lost the empires they had so painfully seized over the centuries. And one, Russia, lost over twenty million dead.

Those wartime 1940s were a simple, even a hopeful time. Hats came in only two colors, white and black, and after an initial battering the Allied nations started on a long laborious march toward victory. It was a time when sane men believed the world would evolve into a decent place, but, as with all futures, there was no one then who could really forecast the world that we know now.

There are many ways to think about war. It has always been hard to understand the motivations and braveries of Axis soldiers fighting to enslave and dominate their neighbors. Yet it is impossible to know the hammer without the anvil, and to comprehend ourselves we must know the people we once fought against.

Through these books we can discover what it was like to take part in the war that was a final experience for nearly fifty million human beings. In so doing we may discover the strength to make a world as good as the one contained in those dreams and aspirations once believed by heroic men. We must understand our past as an honor to those dead who can no longer choose. They exchanged their lives in a hope for this future that we now inhabit. Though the fight took place many years ago, each of us remains as a living part of it.

THE FOXES OF THE DESERT

PAUL CARELL

Translated from the German by Mervyn Savill

BANTAM BOOKS

TORONTO · NEW YORK · LONDON · SYDNEY · AUCKLAND

THE FOXES OF THE DESERT

A Bantam Book / published by arrangement with
E. P. Dutton & Co., Inc.

PRINTING HISTORY

First published in the German language as
DIE WÜSTENFÜCHSE
by Henry Nannen Verlag, 1958.
© 1958 Nannen Verlag GmBH, Hamburg.

E. P. Dutton edition published January 1961

Bantam edition published January 1962
2nd printing . . . . January 1967
3rd revised printing / November 1987

Maps by Alan McKnight.
Illustrations by Greg Beecham.

ISBN 0-553-26591-1

Published simultaneously in the United States and Canada

PRINTED IN THE UNITED STATES OF AMERICA

O   0 9 8 7 6 5 4 3 2 1

CONTENTS

ACKNOWLEDGMENTS

The publishers would like to express their thanks to Messrs. Cassell for permission to quote extracts from Sir Winston Churchill's War Memoirs, and to Messrs. Hamish Hamilton for permission to quote extracts from Alan Moorehead's *African Trilogy*.

PREFACE

This book could never have been written had not more than a thousand soldiers, N.C.O.'s, junior and senior officers come to my aid. They placed at my disposal intelligence reports, battle reports, sketches, photographs and accounts of their experiences. To all of them I am inordinately grateful.

My special thanks for advice and help are due to the last C.-in-C. of the Army Group Afrika, Colonel-General von Arnim, to the former Commander of the Afrika Korps in Libya and Egypt as well as of the 90th Korps in Tunisia, General Nehring, and the gallant Chief of Staff of the Afrika Korps, Lieutenant-General Bayerlein.

A single idea has dominated the mind of the author, his collaborators and advisers: to give a true and accurate account of the North Africa Campaign. I dedicate this book to the memory of the fallen of both sides and trust that it may serve as a warning to the living.

PAUL CARELL

NORTH AFRICAN DESERT

Miles

0   50 100   200   300

--=≈ Wadis   ⌁⌁ Escarpment
⊂⊃ Sand   o Wells & Tombs
----- Motorable Tracks   ⊂≈⊃ Marshes

"We have a very daring and skilful opponent against us and may I say across the havoc of war, a great General."

SIR WINSTON CHURCHILL
in the House of Commons, January 1942

1

"THE JERRIES ARE COMING"

A silent, pitch-black night shrouded North Africa. It was past midnight of the 31st March, 1941.

In a depression among the sand dunes before El Agheila, on the western frontier of Cyrenaica, lay a British reconnaissance patrol. From the top of the dunes the two officers observed a fort through their night field glasses. For a long time they watched the enemy position in silence. Lieutenant Fred Miller, known to his friends as "Dusty," cocked his ear attentively in the direction of the Italian positions. He nudged his friend, Lieutenant James Clark. "I'll tell you something, Nobby, the war has stopped breathing." It was in fact, deathly still and the great silence of the night lay over the desert. It certainly seemed as though the war had come to a standstill—at least temporarily. No shouts from the sentries, no rattle of weapons, no noise of some rumbling truck, not a sound from the enemy lines.

Clark and Miller, with the driver and the wireless operator, formed the crew of a green-and-yellow camouflaged British armoured scout car which stood hidden among the high dunes. The rear right mudguard bore the emblem of the 7th British Armoured Division, a red jerboa in a white circle. The wits among the 11th Hussars, at the *thés dansants* at the Continental in Cairo, used to say to the ladies: "Graziani's quarter of a million Italians took to their heels like a woman who has seen a mouse." They had run from the Egyptian frontier to Tripolitania, from Sollum to El Agheila, to the very spot where the scout car stood waiting to see whether the Italians would venture to fight back.

The 11th Hussars, who had exchanged horses for tanks,

1

and with whom Clark and Miller were serving, was now attached to the 7th Armoured Division. "The glorious 7th" was no longer at the front. It had been sent back to Cairo for a rest. Since the hurried transfer of British front-line troops from North Africa to Greece had very much weakened the reconnaissance units, "Nobby" and "Dusty," both well-trained intelligence officers, had joined the 2nd Armoured Division which was in the front line at that time facing the routed Italians. It was easy to see by Miller's lobster red face that he had not been very long in the sand and the sun. The 19-year old lieutenant had arrived a few days before by air in Cairo from the reserve battalion of the 11th Hussars. He was delighted to find his friend, James Clark, there.

Felton, the driver, had prepared their supper over a little fire in a sandhole. He had thrown long strips of spaghetti from a blue packet into boiling water and opened a tin of preserved cherries with his bayonet. The four men proceeded to eat this diet which was strange indeed for the British. The noodles, parmesan cheese and preserved fruit were the loot with which they had stuffed their car on the 7th of February, the day Benghazi fell.

While Clark, Felton and the wireless operator, Corporal Farquhar ate in silence, Miller began to ask questions. He confessed how much he regretted not having been present during the pursuit of Graziani's Italians between December 1940 and February 1941. In this hectic, victorious British advance in the North African Desert ten Italian divisions were routed; 130,000 prisoners were taken, 400 tanks and 1200 guns captured. What a war! What a victory! And to have missed it!

As soon as the men had wrapped themselves in their overcoats and crept under the truck, Clark stuck a Players in his mouth and began to tell a story which was common knowledge throughout the whole Army. The story of "Electric Whiskers" whom he had captured and for which feat he had won the M.C.

"Electric Whiskers" was the subject of countless anecdotes in Cairo and London. It was the nickname given to the wiry little Italian Corps Commander, General Bergonzoli, in the Spanish Civil War and it had stuck to him here in Africa. His soldiers had christened him "Barba Elettrica" because his red beard apparently gave off red sparks. No one really knew why this General had become popular on both sides of the line, but it was so. During the victorious British campaign in Cyrenaica it had become a sporting issue to capture "Barba Elettrica." After every victory, after each conquered town, the question was asked among the staffs and in the British newspapers: "Have they caught 'Electric Whiskers'?" But the little Italian General seemed to enjoy a charmed life. He lost every battle and in due course his entire Army Corps, but he himself escaped—from Sollum, from Bardia, from Tobruk and from Derna.

"But I got him in Benghazi," said Clark. "When I stuck my tommy-gun through the window of his Fiat, he said to me: 'You got here a bit too quick today'. He looked tired. I took him to General O'Connor and was present at the interrogation. I shall never forget it. We asked him how he managed to escape so many times. Barba Elettrica replied: 'When you surrounded Bardia in December I slipped through your lines at night with a few of my officers. During the day

Rolls Royce Scout Car

we hid in caves and it took us five days to reach Tobruk. When Tobruk fell, I managed to make my way to Derna. But when that stronghold was besieged by the Australians I drove along the coastal road to Benghazi. But now you've got me. You were too quick, that's all.'"

In Benghazi, apart from him, the British had captured half a dozen generals. The Bersaglieri General Bignani, the Artillery General Villanis, the Sapper General Negroni, the tank General Bardini, General Cona and his chief of Staff, General Giuliano. They simply waited for them. "I haven't seen so many Italians since the 1911 Durbar," General O'Connor remarked.

The British were confident. Before long they would be in Tripoli. It would be fun. The "Eyeties" always had good bases, they were said to go to war with every possible comfort. In Benghazi the British claimed to have captured a whole truck full of girls "For Officers only."

What a lovely war! The armoured car crew wrapped themselves up tightly in their overcoats for the desert night was cold. Clark rolled over on his side. "Keep your eyes skinned, Dusty, that the Eyeties don't grab us." Then half-asleep he added: "And take care that the war doesn't start breathing again."

Lieutenant Clark certainly did not realise that in another couple of hours the war would start to breathe again with a vengeance.

While this "recce" crew at El Agheila were sleeping beneath their truck, in a damp dark room in the Hotel d'Italia in Benghazi Lieutenant-General Neame, V.C., C-in-C Cyrenaica, was studying the map with General Gambier-Parry, Commander of the 2nd Armoured Division which had recently been sent from England to North Africa. On the table lay the message which Clark had radioed a few hours before. "Nothing to report at El Agheila. Everything quiet."

Perhaps the generals felt they should not have halted in the Bay of Sirte a couple of months ago, but should have pushed on another 500 miles to Tripoli. Nevertheless, 500 miles was a long way and the tanks were not in the best trim and having to send troops to Greece and Crete had cost the African army three divisions. And then there were the Germans. They would certainly have flown their reserve airborne divisions across from Southern Italy. Every day in Benghazi showed what the men of the 10th Fliegerkorps could do. The British had had great trouble unloading ships in the harbour. Most things would have to be sent by truck from Tobruk. Hitler could not afford and would not allow his friend Mussolini to leave North Africa and expose the soft underbelly of Europe. That he was prepared to make sacrifices could be seen by the arrival of the 5th Light Division in Tunis. They called themselves the German Afrika Korps—a high-faluting name. They were "kicking up quite a dust" in Tripoli and making a song and dance about the fact that their 3rd

Reconnaissance Unit recaptured the advance fort of El Agheila on the 24th March. The name of their Commander was Rommel—Erwin Rommel. He was thought to be an aggressive type.

General Gambier-Parry called into the adjacent room and after a moment a major of the Intelligence Corps came in with a red folder. He read out: "Rommel, Erwin. Born November 15th, 1891, at Heidenheim, Württemburg. 1910, Officer Cadet in a Württemburg Infantry Regiment. After attending the War Academy at Danzig in January 1912, promoted to Lieutenant. Fought in the First World War in the Battle of the Argonne. Served in Roumania and Italy. Twice wounded. Decorations: Iron Cross, 1st Class, and Pour le Mérite. Between the two wars, regimental commander and commandant of a Kriegsschule. On the outbreak of war, in command of the Nazi Headquarters in Poland. Later O.C. 7th Panzer Division of the 15th Korps."

At this juncture General Neame commented that 7th Panzer was the 'ghost division' which broke through on the Maas.

"On the 21st May, 1940," the major went on, "Rommel was nearly captured during our counter-attack at Arras. He led his division through La Bassée to Lille. Awarded the Knight's Cross to which recently he is believed to have added the Oak Leaves. Has probably been with his staff in Tripoli since the 12th February." The report told the generals little enough.

Neame walked over to the window. One thing seemed certain. Rommel and his troops were nothing more than stiffening for the Italians. Rommel was there to give them a bit of backbone. The British Secret Service in Berlin had this on the best authority. They had no reason to fear a German-led offensive in Africa. A division would not be enough for that purpose, particularly since they were troops with no experience of desert warfare. The Secret Service in the Italian zone was not always reliable, but it was known for certain that so far only the 5th Light was there. It was also known that they were intended as a more or less psychological tonic for the Italians. Three days ago in Cairo, General O'Connor and General Wavell, on the basis of a secret message received from London, were satisfied that a German-Italian offensive of limited dimensions could not be expected before the end of May. Moreover, Hitler must send at least another two divisions. This fitted in with the reports of reconnaissance patrols.

The calculations of the two generals that night of the 31st March, 1941, were far from irresponsible. General Wavell, C-in-C Middle East, had received agents' reports from Berlin that Hitler had given orders forbidding Rommel to undertake any large-scale offensive operations. Although the British did not know the exact wording of these orders, the information from Berlin and Rome was so emphatic that they relied upon it.

But sometimes the best Secret Service reports from the enemy camp can lead to fatal errors. This happened twice to the British in North Africa. The agents' reports were correct. They referred in fact to the Führer's orders Nos. 18 and 22 which revealed Hitler's plans. The British took the necessary counter-measures. But in Africa a certain general did not follow his Führer's plans and the result was a German victory that could easily have resulted in the defeat of Great Britain.

The attitude of Hitler and the German High Command towards the African map in German grand strategy is revealed in the Führer's secret orders and the military conferences at Headquarters.

On the 12th November 1940—i.e. before the Italian defeat in Africa—Hitler declared in his Führer's Order No. 18: "The engagement of German forces in Africa, if at all, is to be envisaged only when the Italians have reached Mersa Matruh. In this event it will primarily be the engagement of German air forces if the Italians can place the necessary flying base at their disposal. Preparations by the three services of the Wehrmacht for this or any other campaign in the African theatre of war are to be made within the following framework. Army: A Panzer division to be kept in readiness for service in North Africa. Navy: The refitting of German ships lying in Italian harbours suitable for transport to carry the greatest possible number of troops either to Libya or to North-West Africa. Luftwaffe: Preparations to be made for offensive operations against Alexandria and the Suez Canal in order to close the latter to the British Command."

It can be seen that Hitler's calculations were based on the possibility of a break-through to the Egyptian border. He was of the opinion that only then would the Italians need the help of German armour and air support in order to put the Suez Canal out of action. What a mistake!

A month later the position looked completely different. No more thought now of an Italian offensive. On the contrary, since December 8th, 1940, the British in North Africa had been advancing steadily towards the west.

On the 10th December Hitler had to revise his earlier decisions and order the Luftwaffe: "To operate as rapidly as possible in North Africa from Southern Italy. Their task is to attack the British fleet in Alexandria, in the Suez Canal and in the straits between Sicily and the North African Coast."

At the same time Hitler ordered preparations for the transport of the Panzer Division destined for North Africa.

All his dispositions, however, were overshadowed by the planned invasion of Russia. For Hitler, North Africa was a minor theatre of war. He did not believe in a decisive victory in this area, nor did he anticipate any great danger from this quarter.

Three weeks later the Italian disaster was apparent. Now, on the 11th January, 1941, the Führer's Order No. 22 announced: "The position in the Mediterranean on strategical, political and psychological grounds demands German aid. Tripolitania must be saved." Despite this resolute decision it must not be overlooked that in North Africa Hitler was thinking only of defence measures. In his opinion there was no hope of using the Mediterranean Zone to bring about actions decisive to the war. The man who proposed to bring Russia to her knees in six months did not believe that he could win a speedy victory in North Africa. On the 8th January, 1941, Hitler still insisted: "It is not possible either for the Italians or for ourselves to launch an offensive against Egypt." If at all, he considered that the earliest date would be the winter of 1941. What was the reason? Because he hoped that by then he would have destroyed Russia. His confidence in a victory in the East was so great that at the beginning of February he still declared that the loss of North Africa could be borne from a military point of view but must have a strong psychological effect on Italy. "We must make every effort to prevent this. The Luftwaffe must be engaged and a containing force sent to Africa." Hitler's "containing" force meant the first contingents of the German Afrika Korps at divisional strength. "There is no question of sending a second Panzer Division," Hitler declared. Once more he had to change his mind. The speed of the British advance, which reached Benghazi on the 6th February, 1941, forced him to reinforce the German troops sent to the aid of the Italians. The 5th Light Division should be reinforced by the 15th Panzer Division. Erwin Rommel was appointed General-in-Command of the German troops in Africa. Field-Marshal von Brauchitsch confirmed his appointment as commander of the Afrika Korps on the 6th February, 1941. The father of the "Desert Foxes" entered the stage of World War II history. But Hitler raised a warning finger, saying that until autumn 1941 no large-scale operations were to be carried out in North Africa.

On the 18th March Rommel was still at the Führer's headquarters. He was told expressly that the German High Command momentarily planned no decisive action against the British in North Africa. On the arrival of the 15th Panzer Division at the end of May he could launch limited attacks in the Agedabia region. Later, possibly, he could take Benghazi. Rommel was to submit his plans to G.H.Q. by the 20th April. This was Hitler's timetable. Chief of the General Staff Halder considered the whole Afrika Korps a political issue to keep the Italians in the saddle.

Lieutenant-General Rommel was a good soldier. He knew that orders had to be carried out. But he also knew that the "top brass" sitting at their desks in Berlin did not always have a clear picture. Rommel was not the man to pass up any chance of winning a victory. He soon realised that the British adversary behind the dunes of El Agheila had been decisively weakened by the despatch of strong forces to Greece. Churchill had become so certain of victory in the desert that he had compelled General Wavell to occupy the positions in Cyrenaica with reduced forces. In addition to this the supply lines from Cairo to Bardia and Tobruk and from there to Benghazi and finally to El Agheila were too long for the transport available to the weak British divisions.

Rommel soon discovered this. Naturally he also discovered that the British were making every effort to fortify their weak positions—above all, the strategically important narrows of Mersa el Brega. Was he supposed to wait? To wait until his opponent had built up a strong defence position against which an attack in May might fail or succeed at the cost of

Erwin Rommel

enormous sacrifice, simply because Hitler and the German High Command in Berlin had a completely false concept of the desert war and because Mussolini and his generals in Rome were still quaking with fear after the devastating "sixty-two days campaign"? No. Mersa el Brega and perhaps even Agedabia must be taken at once and he must certainly not wait until the end of May.

If victories could be calculated there would never be defeats. War in the desert differs from war on classical land terrain. The desert is like the sea. There are huge expanses for bold surprise actions against decisive strong points, the capture of which can cause the collapse of an entire front. The Italians had experienced this. In two months they were chased 650 miles across North Africa by three British assault divisions comprising 31,000 men, 120 guns and 275 tanks. This small force conquered and destroyed ten Italian divisions totalling more than 200,000 men. Great Britain was proud of her achievement. The Italian army, for the most part, fought bravely but their armament was wretched and they were completely outclassed by the motorised British divisions. In actual fact the British had only envisaged a local five-day attack with purely local objectives. But as we have said, the desert is like a sea. As soon as a strong point yields a vast space lies ahead and anyone who gives ground in the desert finds little foothold for consolidation. This happened to the Italians. Strange that the British generals in Benghazi and Cairo did not think that a German general might possibly exploit this law. But General Wavell had his agents' reports on the plans of Hitler and Mussolini. According to these plans and according to the classic rules of warfare Rommel should not have opened his offensive with his division at the end of March, 1941. The offensive was subject to the orders of the Italian general staff, to which Rommel was subordinate, and was certainly not due now. And because General Wavell knew this and reckoned on an orthodox, submissive Rommel he retired to bed in Cairo on the 30th March, 1941, to sleep in peace.

General Neame and Gambier-Parry also retired to rest on their camp-beds in the Hotel d'Italia in Benghazi.

Lieutenant Fred Miller dozed in the silent night near El Agheila. All he could hear was the snoring of his comrades. And at that moment the war began to "breathe" again.

The clank of tank tracks... Then silence and an oath. Fred Miller was on the alert, but there was no need for him to wake the others. Clark, too, was peering out from under the scout car. They lay on their bellies and stared ahead at mighty shadows which rattled as they moved. They heard shouts. "Tanks," whispered Miller, "German tanks." The monsters drove past 30 yards away in a southerly direction. "One, two, three, four, five..." Clark stopped counting. The sixth veered and made directly for them. The commander was standing in the turret. He had spotted them. "Move off," yelled Clark. The driver and wireless operator were already in the car. The self-starter hesitated. "Get cracking, man!" At last. The rattling shadow was almost on them as they drove off. The desert suddenly sprang to life, the shadows coming from all directions.

They reached the Mersa el Brega road, sped towards the Arab village with the white mosque on the heights. Dawn began to break on an historic morning.

"German tanks to the south and on the coastal road," James Clark shouted to the commander of a reconnaissance unit of the 2nd Armoured Division, which lay in front of Mersa el Brega.

The news ran like wildfire through the unit.

They drove off in their Bren carriers but they did not get very far. Rommel had begun his first battle.

At 09.44 hours on 31st March, 1941, the "recce" cars of the Stahnsdorf 3rd Reconnaissance Unit off Mersa el Brega ran into an advanced "recce" unit of the 2nd Armoured Division. At 09.50 hours the first shells burst... The opening shots in Rommel's wild ride for Tobruk.

After the duel between the reconnaissance units which ended with the retreat of the British, the tanks of the 5th Panzer Regiment from Berlin-Wünsdorf under Lieutenant-Colonel Albrich attacked the actual Mersa el Brega position. Eight days before, during the storming of the desert fort El Agheila, the regiment had suffered its first casualties when one of its tanks drove over a mine, the first casualties of the Afrika Korps.

That day they attacked again. Corporal Gerhard Klaue of No. 8 company from his turret spotted his first enemy, a camel which rushed like a wild thing towards the German armour. Was this some devilish stratagem of the "Tommy"?

Presumably not. The beast sheered off and disappeared in a cloud of dust. The Panzers continued to advance but they could make no headway against the strongly held British position.

At 17.30 hours two German Stuka attacks on the British lines followed in swift succession. Heavy flak was brought to bear on the British artillery positions. The thermometer registered a hundred degrees. The infantry slowly felt its way through the undulating sand dunes. Then the first mines went up. "Sappers forward!" They planted their black flags and swept a path through the field. These black flags, waving in the bright sunlight, pointed the way to the motorised infantry and the men of the 8th Machine-gun Battalion. They attacked. The first men fell, but Mersa el Brega was taken— the desert gate to Cyrenaica.

In this way the first objective sanctioned by the Italian High Command had been reached, but Rommel saw that the British were weak. The British C-in-C had not reckoned with a German attack and his divisions were not equipped for it. Rommel ordered his troops to continue the advance. The tank tracks rattled in the sand. The tyres of the "recce" trucks and armoured cars crunched through the blue-grey fields of mussel shells, the Sebka, between Mersa el Brega and Benghazi. They were lucky that during those days no spring rain fell, for the dusty clay can change within a few minutes to a morass into which vehicles sink like a spoon into porridge.

Throughout 2nd April, Rommel's "wild chase" continued. Reconnaissance aircraft reported that the British were still retreating. Rommel gave orders to attack Agedabia. It fell. With Agedabia in his hands his troops now possessed the good fresh water springs in this part of the desert. The British continued to retire. They still refused to give battle. Wavell sent his desert specialist, General O'Connor and Brigadier-General Combe, the Commanding Officer of the 11th Hussars, to General Neame. According to their information Rommel could not launch an offensive. What was going on? General Neame pointed to the reports of his units. The Germans had overrun the 3rd Armoured Brigade. A gap had been pierced in the front.

And Rommel's orders were: "Continue to advance."

Together with the cheering reports of the rapid retreat of the British that piled up on Rommel's table, which he had erected beside his Commander tank, came S.O. S.s. from his units. "No more juice!" "Run out of petrol!" Supplies informed the General that they needed at least four days to bring up enough fuel for all the vehicles. But Rommel showed them the meaning of organisation. He ordered all the division's light trucks to be unloaded and formed into columns. They were sent back to the west to fetch fuel and ammunition. Rommel gave them twenty-four hours for this action—a dangerous twenty-four hours during which the division was immobile. But General Neame did not exploit this chance.

The Germans pulled it off. Within twenty-four hours fuel and ammunition were up at the front. The 5th Light Division could tank up and continue its chase.

Meanwhile the chaos on the British side was almost incredible. Conflicting orders brought the commanding officers at the front to the pitch of despair. Their regiments were being defeated but the C-in-C in Cairo did not believe in Rommel's power to stage an offensive with a single division. Wavell sent out orders from his headquarters which conflicted with the orders of the General Commanding Cyrenaica. Sir Richard O'Connor went over the head of Lieutenant-General Neame in command of the troops in Cyrenaica and addressed himself direct to the Divisional Commanders Gambier-Parry and Morshead.

As a result of the contradictory reports from the front lines, Wavell lost sight of the position and finally flew to Cyrenaica. His feelings are easy to imagine, since a few days before in Cairo he had assured Foreign Minister Anthony Eden and the British Chief of the General Staff, Sir John Dill, that the Germans could not possibly attack before the middle of May.

On his arrival at Neame's headquarters Wavell, who was normally such a great strategist, committed another blunder. He did not believe that the Germans would advance into the desert. He was convinced that the "inexperienced" Rommel would advance along the broad tarred coastal road, the Via Balbo. "Try to pierce Rommel's flank when he advances along the Via Balbo towards Benghazi. Benghazi will not be defended, but the plateau"—here Wavell pointed to Er Regima—"must be held."

What did the word "must" mean? The generals were off

balance. They had under-estimated Rommel and his soldiers. They would continue to make mistakes and these would prove very costly.

Wavell asked to see the list of supply dumps in the desert. These well-supplied dumps were the modern fortresses in motorised warfare. The largest of these was at Msus, where the British fuel supplies had been stored in underground tanks. Then there was Mechili, the age-old caravan centre, known as the "heart of Cyrenaica." These were the British supply islands in the desert sea.

But Wavell's calculations were based on an error of judgement.

Firstly, Rommel, contrary to expectations, advanced through the desert to Mechili. Secondly, the German general had worked out a new tactic. It was based on the knowledge that the major problem of desert warfare is petrol supplies. The Luftwaffe was ordered to make the destruction of the British supply columns its main objective. The old-fashioned idea of piling up fuel in desert dumps proved fatal to the British.

On the morning of 4th April the news broke in Msus that German tanks were attacking the position. The garrison in the village blew up the gigantic dump. The Germans were not approaching, however. The clouds of black smoke hid the tanks of the British 2nd Armoured Division which had come to refuel. All they now saw of the fuel they so badly needed was a monstrous blue-black mushroom which spread out over Msus, temporarily blotting out the sun. Most of the tanks had to be abandoned.

Rommel himself in the leading "recce" truck of the 3rd Reconnaissance Unit, commanded by Lieutenant-Colonel Freiherr von Wechmar, sped to Benghazi. He reached the harbour in the early hours of 4th April. The British had had no time to destroy the harbour installations.

Nor had Rommel time to make an inspection. He did not even glance at the beautiful broad market place where white-robed Arabs stood in idle curiosity, greeting each tank with cries of delight. He paid no attention to the groundnut and lemon merchants who, despite the war, continued to hawk their wares. He merely smiled at the lemonade merchant seller who approached his car with a humble gesture to offer him some turgid concoction. He had only one thought in his head: to advance.

Combat groups were forced to penetrate far into the broad valleys of Cyrenaica.

From Agedabia Major-General Streich's Combat Group with the 8th Machine-gun Battalion under Lieutenant-Colonel Ponath, and Lieutenant-Colonel Graf Schwerin's Combat Group with the Italian contingents were despatched in a wide sweep to Mechili.

Lieutenant-Colonel Albrich, with the main body of his 5th Panzer Regiment, the 2nd Machine-gun Battalion, and 40 tanks of the Italian Ariete Division, made a simultaneous attack on Mechili via Msus.

Major-General Kirchheim marched out of Benghazi with elements of the Brescia Division along the Via Balbo to Derna, and a contingent was sent south to Mechili. The spurt towards Mechili through the broiling desert of sand and stone would never be forgotten by the men of the Afrika Korps who took part in it.

In the whole of Cyrenaica there was one single man who, swift as lightning, saw through Rommel's strategy. This was Lieutenant-General O'Connor, the wiry little Irishman who was acknowledged throughout the British army as the greatest expert on desert warfare. He was the brains of the British North Africa campaign. Wavell had sent him on 2nd April from Cairo to the front to give Neame a hand. He was determined to save Cyrenaica. Neame and O'Connor left Maraua on the evening of 6th April. They drove straight through the abandoned Italian settlements where the grapes were already green and the corn already high. Their destination was Tmimi, their new headquarters, but they lost their way and reached the Derna road.

And then it happened.

The staff car in which the two weary Generals were sitting was caught up by German motorised infantry. They were men of the Ponath Group. The driver of the British Humber recognised the Germans and immediately grabbed for his rifle. The man in the side-car of the first motor-cycle was killed, but from the second vehicle a sub-machine gun spat and the British driver collapsed. General Neame and the desert expert Sir Richard O'Connor stared in horror into the barrels of German machine-guns. They raised their hands...

On 7th April the Streich and Schwerin Combat Groups invested Mechili. For the second time the "heart of Cyrenaica," the desert fortress with the towers, was called upon to surrender. Twice the Tommies refused. As darkness fell the British units tried to break out. General Gambier-Parry and Brigadier-General Vaughan were captured, and with them a great part of an Indian motorised brigade, a company of the famous Rajputana Artillery and Divisional Headquarters—in all 2,000 men. The Germans took considerable booty. A third crack British general in North Africa, Gambier-Parry, was also out of the contest.

On the day that Mechili fell the Ponath Group took Derna. In the little town thousands of swallows had assembled for their yearly migration north to the homeland of the Afrika Korps. But Rommel left the 5th Light Division no time to admire the swallows. He hardly allowed them to pause for breath. With the captured supplies of water, fuel and provisions from the Tmimi camp they were despatched to Tobruk. Tobruk was the objective. Tobruk, the Pearl of North Africa, the harbour, the supply base, the key to Egypt. On the 7th April Churchill had telegraphed to General Wavell: "You should surely be able to hold Tobruk, with its permanent Italian defences, at least until or unless the enemy brings up strong artillery forces. It seems difficult to believe that he can do this for some weeks. He would run great risks in masking

Pak 88

Tobruk and advancing upon Egypt, observing that we can reinforce from the sea and would menace his communications. Tobruk, therefore, seems to be a place to be held to the death without thought of retirement. I should be glad to hear of your intentions."

General Wavell replied on the following day: "Tobruk is not a good defence position. The long line of communication is to all intents and purposes unprotected and lacks the necessary installations." His growing pessimism was evident.

Churchill thought—quite rightly—that General Wavell intended to abandon Tobruk. The old war horse in London was angry. An order was sent to Wavell to hold Tobruk. It was an historic order.

On account of it, Rommel, in an attempt to take Tobruk by assault, ran up against insuperable resistance. On the 10th April, before Tobruk—near kilometre stone 16—the Commander of the 15th Panzer Division, General von Prittwitz, was killed. On Good Friday, the 11th, and also on Easter Saturday, the 12th, Rommel with part of the 5th Panzer Regiment reinforced by Nos. 1 and 2 Companies of the 605th Panzerjaeger Unit, tried to break through the defence girdle of Tobruk. But the attack was repulsed by artillery fire from the 20th Australian Infantry Brigade.

Bad luck, thought Rommel, and ordered a further attack on the 13th and 14th. The 8th Machine-gun Battalion under Lieutenant-Colonel Ponath penetrated the fortress. The 5th Panzer Regiment also negotiated the tank traps but then came under strong fire from Fort Pilastrino, and could advance no further. The 8th Company was badly shot up and the rest of the force had to retire. The Italian armoured Ariete Division, which usually fought so bravely, showed no stomach for the business. Ponath and his men were mown down in murderous hand-to-hand fighting by the Australians. The plan for taking Tobruk in a swift raid had come to grief.

But Rommel was not the man to be discouraged so quickly. He did not believe that the British, who had seemed so weak and confused, could suddenly become hard as steel, and he refused to let Tobruk stand in the way of his advance. Two speedy combat groups were ordered to advance eastwards, by-passing Tobruk: The 3rd Reconnaissance Unit, under Freiherr von Wechmar, and the 15th Motorised Infantry Battalion—incidentally, without the two heavy companies which were still in Italy on the way to Africa—reinforced by the 33rd Anti-tank Company with a battery of 88 mm. guns commanded by Lieutenant-Colonel Knabe.

Sergeant Krügel of No. 1 Company of the 15th Motorised Infantry Battalion spat in the sand of Benghazi. Sergeant Wolff followed suit. This accursed sand. Nevertheless, it was preferable to the dangerous Mediterranean which they had crossed a few days before from Naples to Tripoli in the old tub *Alicante*.

What a journey!

It had not been a joke. In fact, it was appalling. They suffered badly from seasickness. Unfortunately, Regimental Sergeant-Major Ebel did not suffer from seasickness at all. He swept across the decks and on catching sight of his two best sergeants green in the face felt at once that such men must immediately be given a job of work to do. "Both of you won the Iron Cross 1st-Class and you look as scared as any raw recruit. Get forward there to the bows and keep your eyes skinned for submarines and mines. If this tub sinks it will be your fault." He turned on his heel but called over his shoulder: "And if you've still got an offering in your bellies for Neptune, get rid of it now."

They came through safely, despite the *Alicante* and their seasickness. But there was no anticipated eight days' rest in Tripoli. The Quartermaster, Captain Otto, was already on the quayside and ordered: "March off immediately. Direction Benghazi."

The three artillery companies of the 15th Motorised Infantry Battalion travelled along the Via Balbo. Each company with 66 motor-cycles and sidecars, 25 light and heavy trucks and a complement of 210 men. They reached Benghazi, where they heard that Tobruk had been by-passed. They also heard that their battalion, together with the 33rd Panzerjaeger Unit Company as Combat Group Knabe, was to take Fort Capuzzo and the harbour city of Sollum.

Bardia fell on the 11th April. On to Capuzzo and Sollum!

Capuzzo and Sollum—the names had a sinister ring! Where were these places? They were only names, but soon they would become part of history. History and ruins... and graveyards. It was the 12th April, 1941.

The column arduously made its way along the dusty track. Five miles and then a halt to let the engine cool off.

Those were the regulations and they were obeyed strictly. It was soon evident that these motor-cycles which had been so invaluable in Europe were completely useless here. Too much had been expected of them. A crew of three with machine-guns, boxes of ammunition, three packs, reserve petrol can, water can and three rifles. To drive in the shifting sand at 120 degrees in the shade. The idea of recording temperature in the shade was somewhat of a joke because there was absolutely no shade. The motor-cycle had not been built to function at such a temperature. They struck.

It was a most unpleasant trip. Camel thorn, stones, dust, heat and flies . . . "Ideal country for a war," said Schriefer, the No. 1 company runner. "Here at least nothing can be destroyed." "Except ourselves," replied the other runner, Disque.

Night fell at last. Capuzzo must lie some 35 miles ahead. Two reconnaissance officers with radio equipment went to find out . . . They returned home in 1947 from a prisoner-of-war camp.

When the rest of the company woke the following morning a few imperturbables cried: "Happy Easter!" Yes, they had almost forgotten that it was Easter. Easter in the desert. "Where shall we hide our eggs here?" asked someone. He received no applause for this sally because Tommy suddenly flung his Easter eggs at their heads.

The shells burst in the middle of the column. Three motor-cycles were put out of action. "Flak ahead!" Forward to Capuzzo. The former Italian frontier barracks was now a pile of rubble. It had been an attractive fort with modern quarters for men and officers. Now the bare concrete gleamed in the sun. The defence fire of the British made the first holes in the company. "If we don't get on they'll shoot us to pieces," Lieutenant Steidle cried to his section. Together with Löffelbein of No. 2 Section they continued to advance. If they wanted to survive they had to press on, to make for the ruins where they would find some cover.

But now scout cars and self-propelled guns, firing point blank at the attackers, made a sortie from Capuzzo. The 5 cm. Pak anti-tank guns went into action. Fire! The first "recce" car came to a standstill, then the second and the third rolled over on its side. The others fled. They were hotly pursued.

Towards midday, Capuzzo fell—"*E ridotta Capuzzo.*" This pathetic heap of ruins was no longer even a village.

They had dreamed of an Arab bar and real coffee and at least a cistern. But what were dreams? Outside on the sand lay those whose dreams were over for ever. Major Ehle from Uelzen, commanding the company at the time, told me this story. "Yes, it was like that," he said with a nod.

The survivors tore open their collars and laughed as Corporal Eimecke ran up, out of breath. Under the columns of smoke and ruins he had discovered a provision dump. He had brought tins of peaches, apricots and ham. They celebrated Easter. On this 13th April, 1941, they did not suspect that the ruined hulk of Capuzzo would be lost and won again four times; that soon a graveyard would stand here with wooden crosses bearing the names and numbers of German, Italian and British soldiers.

Sollum also fell. It was No. 3 Company of the 15th Motorised Infantry Battalion together with No. 1 Company of the 33rd Panzerjaegers which stormed the heights and harbour of Sollum. The men advanced in rushes through the old abandoned Italian positions, from pillbox to pillbox, up the slopes of the wadis and over the plateau. Ahead lay the brilliant blue Mediterranean.

They clung fast to the burning slope which led down to Sollum. They could see the broad bay, the broad white beach. Far behind them in the haze towered the Jebel. A British destroyer in the harbour, firing with all its guns, raked the slope, but Lieutenant Krauss silenced it with his 88mm. flak gun, the miracle of the Second World War. What would the African campaign have been without the "88"? It had originally been designed as an anti-aircraft weapon but was used in Africa as the most effective field gun against tanks and artillery. In all the British reports from the Africa theatre of war the German 88 mm. was spoken of with respect and fear.

There was another feature in the battle for Sollum—the old Italian gun emplacements. They had been built with great care and cunning by Italians sappers in 1940. The Italians have a genius for earthworks, but unfortunately they could not hold these redoubts. Well, they have other engaging characteristics. Naturally, the German soldiers swore when the Italians "took a powder," but one should never tip the baby out with the bathwater. When the Italians were led well they fought bravely.

Before Sollum and Capuzzo, at Halfaya Pass and before

Tobruk, iron toughness was needed rather than swift Roman bravado. For the opponents were New Zealanders, Australians and British of the 22nd Guards Brigade and hard as steel. When they attacked or crept by night in crêpe-soled shoes to raid the anti-tank and gun positions, then God help everyone. Hell broke loose. Wearing long trousers, pullovers and Basque berets, with hand grenades in their broad trouser pockets and carrying Tommy guns, they came on. At night they suddenly appeared inside a stronghold, threw their grenades, emptied the magazines of their sub-machine-guns and left as swiftly as they had come. If one of them were captured no one could get a word out of him. He merely grinned and shrugged his shoulders. "I'm saying nothing." And he stuck to his principle.

The Sollum area was stoutly defended by the British. They retired step by step and took up more favourable positions behind the town on the high ground. They lay there with their "recce" cars in the gorges of the Jebel on the alert, firing at anything that moved. It was advisable to remain quietly by day in the slit trenches. But the heat was almost worse than the war. And then the flies, a greater enemy than all the armies in the world! They crawled between a man's lips and crept up his nostrils. Even the friendly "gendarmes," as the water wagtails are called in Germany because of their light-coloured breasts, did not help very much although they were so bold that they picked the flies off your cheeks. But against this inexhaustible army not even the hunger of the wagtails was of avail.

As a result of the British resistance in Tobruk, far behind the Sollum-Capuzzo line, Rommel's forces were split between two fronts. This taxed his strength, and it was the reason why Rommel was determined to take Tobruk in order to free the investing troops for his further advance. The British, however, intended to hold Tobruk at all costs with the Australian garrison. "It must be held to the death" was Churchill's order.

On the 10th April, 1941, the day Rommel launched his first attack on Tobruk, the two heavy companies of the 15th Motorised Infantry Battalion had landed in Tripoli. They were immediately despatched to Tobruk. Captain Busch in command of No. 5 Company, who had driven on ahead, had seen Rommel in person at Acroma and received his orders to prepare for the attack. "You must make the British think that you are at least in battalion strength." Deception was Rommel's great trick during those weeks. Between Tobruk and Sollum his "dust makers" were constantly driving round to disguise troop movements from the English reconnaisance. This stratagem caused the British to take many a wrong decision.

On the 19th April these two companies, led by Major Schraepler, Rommel's adjutant, attacked. Rommel himself watched the attack from his command tank. All the heavy weapons of the motorised infantry and anti-tank units were put out of action by enemy artillery fire. Penetration was impossible and the attack cost more than fifty men.

Finally, on the 30th April, detachments of the 115th Artillery Regiment and the 33rd Engineer Battalion succeeded in penetrating in depth. The strongly fortified Ras el Madauer was taken by No. 3 Company of the 2nd Machine-gun Battalion under the resolute leadership of Gottfried Muntau. The German assault troops forced their way into the first tank traps and held them; but their losses were heavy. Lieutenant Cirener, Knight's Cross and company commander of the 33rd Engineer Battalion who had led his troops to capture several of the perimeter strongholds, was killed. Lieutenant Friedl Schmidt, commanding the sapper section of the 104th Artillery Regiment was sent on the evening of the 30th April to reinforce the Müller Combat Group of the 115th.

On the 1st May the 15th Motorised Infantry Battlion and the 104th Artillery Regiment attacked to broaden the gap which had already been pierced by the 115th Regiment. The 140th Artillery Regiment, the first Battalion and its staff had been sent to Africa in April. They left the Baumholder barracks in a raging snowstorm. The orderly officer of the Regiment, Lieutenant Gröger, had his newspaper on his lap and commented: "Incredible what the 5th Light Division is doing over there: Agheila, Mersa el Brega, Agedabia, Benghazi, Mechili, Derna and now they're at the gates of Tobruk." The M.O. poured cold water on his enthusiasm. This experienced man smiled superciliously and filled his pipe. "Things can't go as fast as all that. You'll be there in time, believe me," he said.

Later they often thought of his words.

After leaving Rome they no longer spoke of war. They played cards instead, 18, 20 and Ace; 24, 40, 48 Grand Slam.

Skat was the main interest of the day. They saw Naples but had no time to enjoy the city. The Ju 52s were already revved up on the airfield. Everything which could be taken aboard in two jerry cans was stuffed in the machines. The thermometer registered 104 degrees. A few days before they had shivered with cold at home. Thousands of men experienced the flight over the Mediterranean. The fully laden machine usually took 16. Below them the water gleamed. Would they meet the British fighters? Would they get away with it? On the horizon they could see a thin white line—Africa. The desert... Benghazi...

The sun was blazing hot and the fine russet sand stung their eyes. The light trucks were ready and waiting to take them into unknown country. None of them knew their destination. They knew but one thing: time pressed. There were rumours that the fall of Tobruk was imminent and that they would be in at the kill of this important stronghold. Rumours... rumours...

They came to a halt by a pile of rubble called Acroma. This was the assembly place, the approaches to Tobruk. They fell asleep to the thunder of the guns. Captain Distel came back from the briefing and told them that the sappers were to prepare for action. They set off with machine-guns and hand grenades. The stony desert here is as flat as a plate. No trace of cover as far as the eye could see. No house, no bush, nothing. . . . Nothing but stones and sand.

They passed the first smashed barbed wire entanglements and saw the first traces of tank tracks. The noise of the battle grew louder. Ahead of them clouds of dust thrown up by the shell bursts. A wall of dust marked the front line and they had to enter that front line. This was the first experience of the 104th in Africa. They saw the first dead British soldiers in this theatre of war; their faces had been swollen out of all recognition by the heat. The corpses were in such an advanced state of decomposition that the uniforms had burst. Three or four Australians lay close together. They must have been killed by a machine-gun burst.

Soon they met the first German soldiers returning from the front line, covered with filth and mud. A sergeant-major staggered past. He was bleeding from the shoulder. The first shells fell close to them. Take cover! Nose in the muck and spread out in open formation. Things were growing serious.

In short, sharp rushes they made their way forward. The battlefield was covered with dead. They could not have been lying there very long for the bodies had not yet begun to swell. The grenadiers quickly averted their eyes. Were there any trenches? Where were the bunkers? Bunkers—like those on the West Wall or those they knew from the Maginot line? Obviously there was nothing like this here.

But there were bunkers. Very dangerous things, and the worst of it was that you could not see them.

Night took them by surprise. It was the night of the 1st May, 1941. They had reached their action stations. The units of the 104th, together with the decimated companies of the 115th Artillery Regiment, were to widen the bridgehead at Fort Pilastrino. At dawn they received orders to attack.

The first surprise was that the German gunners fired on their own troops. "Cease fire—we're Germans!" the cry rang out. But it was useless. An anti-tank gun was shot up together with a number of stretcher-bearers. Now the artillery began to fire into a massed Italian company to the right of the road. The men screamed for help. At last the German armour arrived on the left flank. The companies advanced with them, delighted to get out of this disastrous situation. The Italians, too, leapt from their trenches. It had grown light. In sharp rushes the company gained ground but their ranks had thinned out. Mines exploded and the tanks lay there with broken tracks. The crews jumped out and ran towards the rear. The artillery lashed the terrain; machine-guns and mortars barked. The country was entirely without cover. And there was no soil in which to dig a foxhole. It was like concrete. 09.00 hours, and they had launched their attack four hours before. The thirst was hellish. But even worse was the dysentery to which half the men had succumbed. Some way away beside the motor-cycles Lieutenant Bucher and his runner, Wievelhofe—both of them teachers in civilian life—were suffering from a severe attack. They had taken off their trousers and washed them with their last mouthful of coffee. They would soon dry in the burning sun on the edge of the trench. But, crump! A mortar shell destroyed their trousers, and for two days both the lieutenant and his runner had to wage their war in their pants. Rommel continued his attempts to break into Tobruk until the 4th May, but his forces were too weak. The defence—in particular the artillery—was

far too strong. The motorised units fought like the devil; they
fetched their provisions from the British positions. Sergeant-
Major Noack carried wounded men out of the firing line, but
none of this heroism was of avail. On the night of 4th May the
motorised units were taken out of the line and sent back to
the Capuzzo front. The 104th, too, retired to a more favourable line. Only at night and during sandstorms did they dare
to crawl out of their holes. Then the German positions came
to life. Stones were collected and piled up as protection
against infantry fire round the shallow gun emplacements.

Lieutenant Friedl Schmidt reported to the Combat Group
commander, Major Müller, of the 115th Artillery Regiment.
His headquarters were in R6. The bunkers were numbered
R6, R5, etc. You could not see them until you fell into them.
They were level with the ground. They were merely trenches
dynamited in the rocky soil, lined with concrete and joined to
a bunker-like room.

This skilful art of entrenchment cost the lives of many
German soldiers. They ran over the bunkers because they
could not see them and were then subjected to a murderous
fire from the rear. That was the hell of Tobruk. Two of these
accursed bunkers—R5 and R4—separated the Engineer Section from the 104th. They must be neutralised, was the order.

How simple it sounded! They must be neutralised. You
can switch off a light, turn off a machine, but you can't put two
fire-spitting bunkers out of action. The two Engineer Sections
of the Regiment were to carry out this task. The attack was to
be at dawn.

Shortly before midnight the cookhouse orderlies arrived.
The soup was swallowed avidly more because it was warm
than for its content. In addition there were processed cheese
and sardines with black bread. That was the standard diet in
Africa. Sometimes the cooks sent up *Alter Mann*, otherwise
known as "Poor old Musso"—bully beef with the letters A.M.
on the tin which the German soldiers called *Alter Mann* or
Armer Mussolini, and the Italians referred to as *Asino Morte*—
dead donkey.

For the attack on R5 and R4 the heavies were engaged as
support: 88 mm. flak, French field guns and—the star turn of
all—a 21 cm. mortar. A mortar! That was something quite
new. Now nothing could go wrong, the howitzer type weapons could smash the bunkers in the fortress perimeter.

Under cover of night the two Engineer Sections assembled near R6. At the first streaks of dawn the assault troops crawled forward. At hand-grenade distance from the enemy position white flares were to be fired. This was the signal for the heavies to start their barrage. The mortar was to concentrate on the bunkers. Then the fire was to be lifted. Gunpowder charges in the trenches, the bunkers stormed and held until the following night. Then the relief. A splendid plan!

In silence the assault troops crawled over the stony ground. Their elbows bled, but what did that matter? They must make no sound. They had reached their goal . . . flare pistols raised and the white flares hissed through the darkness, lighting up the landscape eerily with their magnesium reflection. Now the firework display must begin.

Must!

But nothing happened. A deathly silence . . . Not a shell fired.

On the Tommies' side, however, things sprang to life. The attackers were cut to pieces. There were cries of: "Kamerad. Hilf mir!" Agonising screams and an occasional death rattle.

"I've been hit," moaned little Sigrist. He was the baby of the section and very popular. No one would abandon him. Lieutenant Friedl Schmidt pulled him to his feet. "Come on," and the youngster staggered to the rear after him.

Sigrist was back in the line a week later. The shot had gone clean through his open mouth and come out close to the top of his spinal column. As if directed by a magician's hand it had missed every vital spot—not a vein, not an artery, not a sinew and not a bone touched but a very minor flesh wound. The doctor said to him: "In future I should go through life with your mouth open, if I were you. You've obviously lucky." The 18-year old gunner, Sigrist, related this when he returned to his unit. And he was lucky. He got through the war and today he is flourishing.

The assaults continued unabated. No one could discover why the heavy artillery had not been engaged. Rommel snarled at his Engineers: "What the British risk in broad daylight you can't even manage in the dark!" The casualty figures rose alarmingly. Day after day the 104th lay in their foxholes. They dared not move. The Australians were crack shots. Their sniping was superb.

It is no joke lying for twelve hours motionless under the African sun in a hole in the ground, particularly when for several days there were no rations. They had to eat when and where it was possible. The men could not always hold out until nightfall. Even the most trivial movement could result in a hero's death. Rump too high in the air—ping!—and you'd had it.

Fortunately sandstorms were frequent. Then shapes rose out of the ground like ghosts, ran a few steps to have a chat with their comrades in the neighbouring foxholes. That was possible in a sandstorm. None of the guns could fire for there were many examples of premature bursts. The British went completely to ground. The Germans, on the contrary, when the sandstorm raged, began to live. That was the paradox of war at Tobruk.

By day it was dangerous to show your nose outside. The British were so well supplied with ammunition from the sea that they could even fire their mortars at a single German soldier. When Friedl Schmidt visited Lieutenant Wettengel in the next section, they spotted him and fired. Schmidt had to advance in a series of rushes. He knew from the whine of the shells when he had to do a bellyflop. But once he found he could not get into a slit trench. It was occupied. He was half in the trench and half out. The stench was appalling. Was that a German uniform? Those shoulder straps? He looked at them. Two stars and between them the staff of Aesculapius ... The missing doctor. How long had he been there with those wide open, staring eyes?

Until the middle of May the Engineers of the 104th Artillery Regiment lay in the fiery furnace before Tobruk. Then at last came the longed-for relief. They were delighted to have survived once more. The stronghold had not devoured them but an even worse tragedy lay ahead. Both they and the 115th were transferred to the second bloody North African scene—the Sollum–Capuzzo–Halfaya Pass sector. Here, too, the battle was raging.

2

THE HERFF COMBAT GROUP STORMS HALFAYA PASS

During April, 1941, the advanced units of the 5th Light Division thinly occupied the strategically important Halfaya Pass. In this way a covering outpost position had been secured before the Sollum front. If the British tried to relieve they would first have to capture Halfaya Pass. In the middle of May—to be precise between the 15th and 17th—General Wavell attacked with units of the 22nd Guards Brigade and ejected the companies of the 15th Motorised Infantry and an Italian battery from the pass position. The whole German garrison with the exception of twelve men was captured. None of the other objectives was reached. Temporarily occupied Capuzzo and Sollum were retaken in bloody counter-attacks by the Herff Combat Group.

Halfaya Pass in British hands would have been a standing threat to the weak German defence front in the Capuzzo Bardia area. Rommel, therefore, decided to recapture the pass from the British. The attack was scheduled for the 26th and 27th May. The eastern theatre of war round Halfaya Pass was 65 miles from the invested fortress of Tobruk. It comprised the sandy desert of Sidi Omar and Capuzzo with the broad, smashed barbed-wire entanglement which had once marked the frontier between Libya and Egypt. A barbed-wire fence, 85 miles long in the middle of the desert! The Italians had constructed it in the old days as a protection against the raids by the Senussi on the Italian colonies. In the early summer of 1941 it was no longer an obstacle. The triple line of wire had been shot to pieces in many places and trampled down as the tanks rolled through it. The iron supports hung limply among the broken wire. Rusty petrol cans, empty canisters, pieces of uniform and old newspapers gleamed eerily in the entanglement. Many of these objects had once served as markers for patrols and "recce" troops. Others were merely the jetsam of war.

Here in the Sollum–Capuzzo area of the desert leaned a high plateau that fell 600 feet sheer to the sea and also to the coastal strip from Sollum to the south-east, forming a 23-mile long escarpment. The road from the coastal strip to the plateau was the Halfaya Pass. The approaches were cleft with deep gorges, the wadis—age-old, dried-up river beds full of scree and boulders.

Here in the wadis raged the war of the grenadiers—a bitter war. They had nested like birds in the slopes of these primitive valleys; on the plateau above them the Tommies were entrenched.

On the 26th May the order was given: "Herff Combat Group is to take Halfaya Pass." How simple such an order sounds. On the map, too, it looks quite simple. The 8th Panzer Regiment under Lieutenant-Colonel Cramer advanced from Sollum south into the desert, then veered northwards and attacked the British defenders of the Pass from the rear. The heavy artillery of the 33rd Panzer Artillery Regiment, flak, the 15th Motorised Infantry Battalion and the experienced No. 1 Company of the 33rd Reconnaissance Unit supported the armour of the Panzer Regiment. The first battalion of the 104th Artillery Regiment made a frontal attack on the Pass on foot. From the area west of Capuzzo the 5th Panzer Regiment advanced with an artillery battery and five 88 mm. guns together with units of an Italian artillery section in a feint attack to the south-south-east in order to divert the Tommies' attention from the Pass. These were the orders and the way it looked on the map.

But how did it look through the eyes of the simple soldier who had fought his way from Sollum to the heights of the Pass?

The first battalion of the 104th Artillery Regiment had lost its commander on the second day of its African service in the battle for Tobruk. Former Company Commander Captain Wilhelm Bach had been sent to replace him. "A devil dodger," grinned the private soldiers. "A pastor in this mess-up. Cheers!" growled the N.C.Os.

A pastor! This was not a nickname, for their new C.O. was a reserve officer and in civilian life a pastor of the Evangelical Church in Mannheim. When Lieutenant Friedl

Schmidt reported to him he was surprised at the genial atmosphere. Schmidt had already introduced himself to the adjutant and the orderly officer when the old military blanket which divided the crates and cases into two huts was drawn aside. The man who appeared did not look in the least like what one pictures an officer to be. A friendly, amiable gentleman of about 50, over six feet tall, with a moustache. He nodded to the lieutenant. He was holding a cigar in his left hand. He wore long trousers, no jacket and his broad braces hung comfortable over his shoulders. "Well, my friend, so you got here safely," was his first remark to Lieutenant Schmidt before the latter could report his arrival at battalion H.Q. in the correct military manner. "Could you do with a good cigar?" "Thank you, Captain. I only smoke cigarettes. Cigars make me feel sick." "It's healthier to smoke cigars, but have a cigarette if you prefer it."

He spoke in a broad Baden dialect and smoked his cigar with devotion. At each puff he put his head a little to one side with the air of a gourmet. On first impression he appeared to be a contented, self-possessed family man.

"Well, my friend, I hope that you'll enjoy it here with us." Never in his whole military career had Lieutenant Schmidt ever heard a superior officer express the wish that he would enjoy himself. In wartime to boot! And moreover in Halfaya Pass. That was Pastor Bach.

This pastor enriched the annals of the African campaign as a shining example of military virtue. He never gave an order which he was not prepared to carry out himself. The soldiers loved him as soldiers rarely love their commanding officer. After he was captured the British continued to sing his praises. The newspapers called him "The Hero of Halfaya Pass," or "The Pastor of Hell-fire." But of that, more later.

The company were firmly entrenched in the Qualala Wadi. It was 130 degrees in the shade. They did not dare to take the leap over the edge of the wadi. As soon as anyone raised his head there was a hail of bullets flying over his steel helmet. The "ratsch-bum," the dangerous British 75, fired at intervals. No one knew from where the British gun was firing. Corporal Jung of the wireless section could not discover its position. The C.O., Captain Bach, called to him: "Jung, go back and fetch the 3.7 anti-tank gun. It must be brought up on our flank to paste those fellows over there." With oaths, sweat and tears, the gun was brought into the required position. Just imagine what it was like to bring up a gun in that heat!

But the German anti-tank gun did not disturb the British. Its fire was obviously inaccurate. The gunners had no wish to pop their heads out and risk observing their fire. "Pack it up. You're wasting ammunition," said Captain Bach. He stumbled out of the wadi and took up his position on the edge with his field-glasses to his eyes. At the right moment he took cover and the bursts of fire whistled way overhead. But he had spotted the position of the 75. Jung was sent over to the battery to give them the information. A quarter of an hour later they were dumbfounded. "Did you see the 'old man'?" they called to each other. They nodded and when the "old man" raised his arm they went into the attack.

They were faced by the 3rd Coldstream Guards. One of the crack British regiments, it held out throughout the night. At dawn as the sun rose red as blood, the attack of the 104th began very much in the ancient manner with fixed bayonets, wild cries and a nagging fear in the stomach. When the 3rd Company of the 15th Motorised Infantry attacked from the other flank the tanks, artillery and flak from the steep slopes laid their fire beyond the Pass and plastered the coastal road, the Guards broke and the Pass was once more in German hands.

The German infantrymen flung themselves in the sand panting heavily. They slept. But there was no respite. The cries of their comrades who had been left behind woke them. Everyone helped the stretcher-bearers and carried back the wounded. The dead were buried. It all sounds so simple but this last service lay heavy on their hearts. It was hours before they could dig a hole in the rocky soil. Then stones were collected and each man had his own little fortress to protect him against the jackals.

The survivors, too, now began to go underground. They built nests of stones and foxholes for the next episode. This had already begun five weeks before in London.

3

OPERATION "TIGER" AND THE BATTLE OF SOLLUM

It was past midnight. Outside Chequers the rain poured down. Welcome rain. Welcome filthy weather because in such weather the "damned Jerries" could not drop their bombs. Between Dover and Edinburgh people had drawn aside their black-out curtains for a brief instant, looked out into the darkness and then retired to bed with a sense of relief.

Winston Churchill, the Prime Minister, was also in bed that inclement night of April, 1941. To be accurate he was sitting up in bed propped up by pillows, reading the late telegrams from Cairo. He did not underline the passages viciously as he usually did, but sat there and pondered. For him one of his worst nights was when he learned of General Wavell's defeat in Cyrenaica. How much this disaster preoccupied him can be read in a passage from his memoirs: "My supreme object continued to be a victory in the Western Desert, to destroy Rommel's army before he became too strong and before the dreaded new armoured division reached him in full strength." The 15th Panzer Division which the British agents in Germany had reported as on its way to Africa.

Now everything depended upon who would win the race of bringing up supplies; if the British lagged behind the German 15th Division then all possibility of a surprise offensive was out of the question. The British supplies would undoubtedly arrive later because, for fear of German U-boats and the Luftwaffe squadrons in the Mediterranean, the British sent them all the way round the Cape, through the Red Sea and the Suez Canal, to reach Alexandria.

On 20th April Churchill received news from Wavell that the advance units of the 15th Panzer Division had landed in

Tripoli. In actual fact these units were the 33rd Reconnaissance Unit, the 33rd Panzerjaeger Unit and the 15th Motorised Infantry Battalion which had already landed in March and April and had long since been in action. Wavell did not know this and feared that the whole division with 400 tanks would be in the front line by the end of the month. It was "panic stations." This could mean the end of Great Britain's position in Egypt unless help was speedily forthcoming. At this juncture Churchill decided to pull off a fast coup. On 21st April he compelled the Admiralty to send a convoy laden with a huge cargo of new tanks through the Mediterranean instead of on the long journey round the cape.

Five large merchant ships, protected by naval units of Admiral Somerville's Fleet, with 295 tanks and about 50 fighter aircraft aboard were despatched to Alexandria via the Straits of Gibraltar.

This undertaking naturally needed a code name so that telegrams should be able to refer to the operation. But it must not be a simple code word. It must have punch and a tonic effect on the pessimists. It had the requisite punch: it was christened: "Operation Tiger." This name suited the new death-dealing cargo of tanks to perfection. Churchill leaned back contentedly on his pillows. The next day he sent a

Matilda

telegram to Wavell demonstrating his confidence in victory: "If 'Tiger' comes through it will be a moment to do and dare. I am asking for a rapid transfer from Malta of Hurricanes to your command once the 'Tigers' tail is clear. Those Hun people are far less dangerous once they lose the initiative. All our thoughts are with you."

London's thoughts that week were indeed focused on Egypt. There was the greatest danger that Great Britain would lose her old stronghold, the Suez Canal. Churchill breathed a sigh of relief when he learned that "Tiger" had reached Alexandria safely on May 12th.

The "Tiger" had swum the Mediterranean. The German and Italian U-boats had missed a splendid opportunity. A single ship, the *Empire Song*, sank with 57 tanks and 10 aircraft aboard after hitting a mine. The remainder arrived safe and sound in Alexandria. They had brought 135 of the latest heavy infantry tanks, Matilda II's, weighing 26½ tons with 3½-inch armour-plating, and in addition to this 82 brand new Mark IIs. These speedy 14-ton cruiser tanks with ½-inch armour and a 4-cm. gun were the hope of the British War Cabinet. They were to turn the tables in the desert. Finally there were 21 Mark IVs, a light 5½-ton tank with ¾-inch armour and a speed of 40 m.p.h.

"The Tiger now only needs to grow claws," Wavell telegraphed to London on 25th May, meaning that they merely had to be assembled and the new crews trained to handle them. Three days later he informed the Prime Minister that he was ready to attack Rommel with his new forces, to throw the Afrika Korps back to Tobruk to relieve the fortress. Churchill had also invented a code word for this undertaking: Operation Battleaxe. It was to be a tank battle on a scale which had not so far been seen in the desert. Five hundred tanks were to clash and Churchill was convinced that the British tanks were superior and that they would win the battle.

In the early hours of June 15th, 1941, the telephones rang shrilly in all the British Staff H.Qs., the morse apparatus ticked, and orderlies hurried to and fro. The whole procedure prior to a well-organised and well-prepared major offensive was set in motion. Operation Battleaxe was launched. D-Day, June 15th, Zero Hour 04.00 hours, General Creagh led the British 7th Armoured Division, which included the powerful

infantry tanks of the 4th Armoured Brigade. General Messervy
commanded the 4th Indian Division and the 22nd Guards
Brigade. General Beresford-Peirse was commanding the operation. He went into battle with 200 tanks and 25,000 men.
The objective: to engage Rommel's forces and destroy his
armour in the Sollum-Bardia area; to occupy Halfaya Pass and
to restore land communications with Tobruk.

At 04.00 hours precisely the British tank motors roared—
the new Mark II's which had been brought up to the front on
special carriers and the stocky infantry tanks, Matilda II's.
Lieutenant Clark and his friend Miller were pleased to see
them. These two were "Nobby" and "Dusty," the two officers
who had been the first to spot the German armour before El
Agheila when Rommel's offensive began—a thrust which took
him past Tobruk and beyond Halfaya Pass. Of the four men
who two and a half months before had fled in their green and
brown camouflaged scout car and alerted the 2nd Armoured
Division only Nobby and Dusty had survived. Driver Felton
fell at Bardia and wireless operator Farquhar lay buried near
Tobruk by kilometre stone 31. He was buried by the Germans. Nobby and Dusty were back with the 7th. They had
joined the 11th Hussars. It was a different matter this time.
They had better tanks. They were standing in the turret of
their brand new Mark II. The battalion commander raised his
arm and waved three times. Forward! The force got under
way.

At Halfaya Pass the German engineers had been consolidating the hardly won position for fourteen days. A gun
emplacement was now ready. They were delighted with the
results of their labour. It is strange what things give pleasure
in a war. God knows that the 88mm. was' no toy gun that
could easily be disguised. Lieutenant Richter walked 150
yards ahead of it and lay flat on his belly to test the camouflage. Not a trace of the emplacement was visible. The secret
of this lay in the perpetual desert haze. Anything up to a
height of three feet above the ground was to all intents and
purposes invisible. On the other hand anything above this
height was greatly enlarged.

The flak pom-pom battery was equally well placed. It
had an ideal field of fire. The desert makes an admirable
artillery range. Wars should always be fought in deserts.

Behind the flak lay Lieutenant Ermel's battery of four 15.5 em. French field guns. They were as weighty as their battery commander. The Würzburg Technical School teacher had disposed his heavy charges in magnificently concealed positions. Close to Ermel's battery were the emplacements of the Italian Major Pardi's battery. This was a crack Italian battery as it was soon to demonstrate.

The calendar in the sapper commander's dugout showed 12th June, 1941. A light truck was loaded with "T" mines and sent down into the coastal plain. Minelaying is a highly dangerous job. Holes were made first in chessboard pattern six to nine feet apart so that they lay in depressions. This can be done with a yardstick, but experienced sappers are good judges of distance. In the centre of each hole was fixed a small stake with a second crosswise in the wall. To these stakes were attached a thin wire with detonators secured to the ground and to the side of the mine. The art consisted in tautening the wire so that on the least movement to right or left or at the slightest rise the mine would explode. On the lid of the "T" mine was a third detonator which acted on pressure. Anyone who inadvertently stepped on a mine set it off. Anyone who tried to raise it from its hole would also find that it exploded immediately. A crafty fellow who spotted the mine, cleared the sand away and unscrewed the detonator on the lid must not on any account try to detach the detonators on the side. If he turned the infernal egg a fraction or by some ill-chance touched the thin wire the eighteen pounds of high explosive in its container went up with a roar of thunder. As soon as the laying was completed the mines were made active. The field was carefully camouflaged.

During the work a squadron of Hurricanes sped over the Pass on a reconnaissance flight. Something was cooking. For days the R.A.F. fighters had been strafing the position. Surely the 10th Fliegerkorps must have noticed them. Just as the sappers were about to grouse, a Messerschmitt dived out of the sun on the tail of the last Hurricane and immediately its guns went into action. A black trail of smoke; a white parachute opened and the Hurricane crashed between Halfaya Pass and Capuzzo. A mighty column of dust and flame marked the spot. The Me zoomed.

It was a treat to see the "air chauffeurs" in action. Now a second machine-gun burst raked a second fighter and the machine crashed in flames. The pilot, hanging on his liftwebs, was driven out to sea. They could clearly see the white dot descending slowly on the water. Would the German Air Sea Rescue go to his aid? There was no need, for a British boat soon fished the pilot out of the "drink." The air battle had lasted barely a minute. The German machine returned, lost altitude, shook its wings in sign of victory and flew off over the Pass. The men below waved. That evening they learned that the successful pilot had been Captain Müncheberg.

Had there been no sub-machine guns by their bedsides and no calls to action stations they might have thought they were at peace—or at least that there was a long pause in the drama of Halfaya Pass.

A German "recce" truck drove up from "Ave Maria," the wayside Shrine to the Virgin in the Pass. It was Sergeant-Major Barlesius of No. 1 Company of the 33rd Reconnaissance Unit. "Something's up," he said. "They're massing at Sidi Omar." They spoke like peasants discussing a thunderstorm. Names were mentioned which none of them had ever heard before. But now these places had a definite significance. When for example "something was up" at Sidi Omar, in the desert flanking Halfaya, it was quite different from Benghazi being bombarded from the sea or the start of a duel at Tobruk. Sidi Omar was a focal point, a pivotal point in the Sollum–Capuzzo–Halfaya–Tobruk area.

The night drew to a close and nothing happened. They could resume their work. A second night . . . . Their clothes stuck to their bodies and their automatic weapons with reserve magazines lay next to their bunks. The machine-gunner had his weapon to hand and the belts in readiness. No. 2 gunner had meticulously cleaned the reserve barrel and stowed it carefully protected from dust and sand. The munition boxes were also full. Everything was prepared, for Papa Bach had seen to everything. He never groused or swore, but when he said: "Boys, I want . . ." his wishes were expressed lucidly and with intelligence. He never asked for anything absurd, but his orders had to be obeyed. Everyone knew that. Papa Bach, in command at Halfaya Pass, was the right man in the right place. That, too, was one of the arts of Rommel's leadership and one of the secrets of his victories.

No one sleeps well with clothes on. The mood was one of irritation. A curse came from a neighbouring foxhole. "God

Almighty, if they had heads like oxen we could bludgeon them to death." Yes, if they had heads like oxen! The Bavarian Sergeant-Major Fleischmann was referring to the sand fleas. They really could drive a man crazy. God help the man they attacked when they began sucking his blood. The creatures were so small that they could practically only be seen through a magnifying glass. The female jumped on a man, bored his skin until only her rump was protruding. Then she began to suck his blood. She went on sucking until she became a round, thick ball. Sergeant Ehrhardt was tattooed with them from top to toe. Many of the men had to be sent home because the sand fleas had sent them half out of their minds. Even a man like Sergeant-Major Fleischmann could be driven mad in his impotence. "What can you do to these bastard creatures?" Unfortunately they did not have heads like oxen. Many of the infantrymen had discarded their camp-beds and lay down in hammocks. This was all right at Halfaya Pass but try it out in the Libyan Desert. If such a thing existed it had no long pole unless it had been brought from Europe, and even if it did have a pole it was almost impossible to erect. Moreover, it was not worth while. The fleas could jump from the ground into the hammock.

It was not the sand fleas alone that irritated the men. There were also rumours, the "buzzes", that ran the rounds. Sergeant Brindel brought a brand new one into the wadi. "The Tommies have a new tank off which the anti-tank shells ricochet like peas. It's called the Mark II." No one had yet seen one, nevertheless miracles were recounted of this British tank. Gradually a "Mark II panic" took hold. They had been on the alert too long and waiting always gets on the nerves.

On the evening of 14th June the field telephone rang. "Something's in the air. Tonight, or early tomorrow morning," Captain Bach informed them calmly. "You're an old shock trooper and have a capable sapper section," he said to Lieutenant Schmidt. "I have a particular mission for you. You are to be the sapper reserve, and if the Tommy actually breaks through somewhere it's up to you to throw him out again." *"Jawohl, Herr Hauptmann."* A simple enough mission: if Tommy breaks through somewhere then simply chuck him out again. A clear and obvious mission. Nothing could be clearer. Sounds like a recipe in a cookery book. Take such and such. . . . and the cake is ready. *"Jawohl, Herr Hauptmann."*

Sergeant Major Fleischmann, Becker, Brindel, Gerhard and Habel were notified. Then they had to wait.

Towards evening the sappers swiftly closed the mine lane between No. 3 Company and the flak section. A double guard was posted and patrols were sent out. Every man was on the alert in his foxhole. A deathly silence lay over the Pass, but the darkness seemed to teem with ears. No sound of tank tracks. . . . The stars shone brightly in the African sky and a full moon lit up the harsh desert landscape. It was light enough to read the newspaper, but who had a newspaper and who was in the mood for reading?

21.57 hours. The quiet voice of the announcer was heard on the wireless set: the German military broadcasting station in Belgrade. Then a gramophone record of Lili Marlene was played. How many soldiers in their lorries, on the wireless or the receiving sets in their tanks were now listening to this syrupy tune? It had travelled round the world.

> *Underneath the lamplight*
> *By the barrack gate*
> *Darling I remember*
> *The way you used to wait . . .*
> *'Twas there that you whispered tenderly*
> *That you loved me, you'd always be*
> *My Lili of the lamplight*
> *My own Lili Marlene.*

The troops listened in France, in Poland, in Norway, in submarines and in the desert. They sat in barracks, in cafés, messes and in shell-holes and dreamed to the voice of a young woman. Simple, naïve, alluring voice singing a naïve simple song. The soldiers' favourite. People today are inclined to criticise this song and call it claptrap, but that would be unjust to millions of soldiers who listened to the melody and the words because they embodied their homeland and a touching sentimentality, an antithesis to the appalling reality of war and death.

This song conjured up thoughts of home, of peace, of wives, cities and villages. It could even bring tears to the eyes of the hard-bitten Desert Foxes. But not to the German soldiers alone. Alan Moorehead in his *African Trilogy* writes: "Not only the Germans, but the British soldiers tuned in their radio sets and listened to it every evening. All over the desert British soldiers could be heard whistling the melody." This popular hit went beyond front lines. "Lili Marlene" was so powerful that British generals ordered their officers to forbid the men to sing and whistle it or to listen to the German broadcasts.

This popular song was resurrected when war broke out and its success was only thinkable in wartime. In 1938 Willi Schäffers had persuaded the comedienne, Lale Andersen, to sing it in a cabaret show. It was a flop. "Twaddle" was the verdict of the audience. Nor did the gramophone record have any great success. A few days later, however, in Crefeld it won its own particular audience. Here in the spring of 1940, before the French campaign, was stationed No. 2 Recce Company of the 3rd Reconnaissance Unit. The N.C.O.s foregathered every evening in the park cafés where they heard the record for the first time. They liked it and it became the favourite request during their beer-drinking sessions. A member of the company was the Reservist, Sergeant-Major Karl Heinz Reintgen who had been with the Berlin Broadcasting Station in peacetime; he in particular appreciated "Lili Marlene." When No. 2 Company was transferred to Africa in the spring of 1941 and Reintgen, who in the meantime had been promoted to Lieutenant and was now Chief Broadcaster in Belgrade, the fate of "Lili Marlene" was decided. Reintgen had taken the record with him and played it as a compliment to his old company which he occasionally greeted with a few friendly words. A few days later there were reverberations. The record was repeated and from then on it was played every evening, at twenty-one fifty-seven hours CET. Not only at the front but also at home conversation ceased a few minutes before eleven o'clock. "Get on to Belgrade," people would say. Everyone knew that the troops were listening and thinking of their homes, and everyone listened to this ridiculous tune which was powerful enough to bring tears of longing to many an eye.

That was "Lili Marlene" and it is also a fragment of war history.

The barking of the jackals interrupted the tune in Halfaya Pass and reminded them of reality. The men were not at home; they were in Africa. From the boundless desert the carrion eater had sent them a reminder. Filthy dirty beasts of prey with raised hackles and the spittle dripping eternally from their chops... They slunk round soldiers' graves and pushed the stones aside. For this reason the dead were given solid graves like miniature forts. By their watches it was already 04.00 hours and dawn would soon break. Dawn and dusk are nearly non-existent in Africa. The transition takes place in a matter of a few minutes.

Now they could hear the sound of motors quite clearly. Sergeant-Major Fleischmann shouted the news into the dugout. The telephone rang. Alert! The cry: "Tank motors, tank motors!" ran through all the positions. The tension caused by the night of waiting eased. Now they knew something definite. Thank God for that! This thought was not inspired by a spirit of aggression or heroism. It was merely the end of waiting. The feeling of fear had acquired a tangible enemy. Now they could see him and fight.

Slowly the drone of the motors increased, and in the distance they could now see black dots in their field glasses, and in the direction of these black dots a gigantic cloud of dust on the horizon. They were coming.

It was the 4th Indian Division supported by the 4th Armoured Brigade.

Captain Bach took up his position with the flak. The miracle weapon, the 88mm., was to hold the stage in the next few hours. "What do you think, Richter? How far away are the tanks?" "I estimate 3,500 yards, Herr Hauptmann." Bach, leaning on his walking stick, puffed at his cigar and said calmly: "Well, we still have time, Richter."

"Under no circumstances fire. Let them come on," was the order. It was an easy order to give—and the correct one. But they lay there in the desert in a slit trench and the steel monsters slowly approached. Hands began to tremble. The sun was burning hot; it blinded them and reduced the visibility, for the enemy tanks came from the east out of the sun. Their hearts pounded. A deathly silence as the tanks sped on... Heavy black monsters. Powerful monsters. So this was the dreaded Mark II? More and more appeared, and far behind them the thick infantry tanks. Slowly, too slowly in fact for the infantry. In several places this would prove fatal. The steel giants had not yet passed Halfaya village. "Take cover!" The enemy artillery had opened fire and the battle of Sollum began. Salvo after salvo was sent over. The whistle of the shells and the explosions were simultaneous. The earth was ploughed up and pitted with shell craters. Lumps of rock flew through the air and all around rose columns of smoke. The shells continued to fall in the empty wadi between No. 3 Company and the flak positions. Not a man, not a vehicle was there. The weight of the bombardment fell for some minutes on this position. "You can carry on like that as long as you like," cried Hohmann, and his mate Mees retorted: "Anything that falls there won't fall on our heads." The main thing was not to let them know that they were on the wrong target. To behave as though the attackers had half won the battle. Tank after tank rumbled towards No. 3 Company—all of them Mark IIs—followed by the light armoured trucks. The infantrymen of the 11th Indian Brigade detrucked, formed up into companies and marched behind the tanks. Quite unperturbed as if on the parade ground... Not a shot was fired at their tanks. "They must have been wiped out," the Indians said to each other. "It must be a Jerry graveyard." Prisoners repeated this later as an explanation for their carefree advance.

On the German side nothing stirred. Why at least did the guns not fire? More British trucks arrived. They halted by the ruins of Halfaya village and put down their infantry. They obviously had no idea how close they were to the barrels of the German guns.

And then a deafening explosion tore the air. It was clearly distinguishable from the British artillery fire. The 88 mm. had spoken. The order was: "Open sights!" Now a hail of death spat from the German positions. Rapid fire from all batteries. Direct hits, columns of flame, more direct hits... the heavy turrets of reinforced steel were torn from the under-hulls of the Mark IIs and flew several yards into the sand. "That's the 88. Did you see? What a gun!" shouted the German infantrymen. Their fears had vanished. The Mark II could not stand up to the 88. But the British did not retire. They were determined to take the Pass and the coastal road in order to have the harbour of Sollum as a supply base.

Pardi's Italian battery was now under fire from the British artillery. But Pardi's men continued to shoot. Here the battle was even noisier. The sound of the reports and the explosives merged into one. Lanky Major Pardi gave his firing orders as if on a practice shoot. The Italian gunners were magnificent. The 2 cm. flak barked between the heavy explosions. Officer-Cadet Gentzler singled out a Mark II and fired until his barrel grew hot. He was furious to observe that the shells ricocheted off the monster. But when he registered a direct hit on the side of a tank as it turned—on the tail where the engine was only covered with corrugated plates— his 2 cm. flak gun was also successful. Gentzler now aimed as if on safari. He observed, gave his orders and fired until a direct hit silenced his gun. When the stretcher bearers arrived only the 19-year-old cadet was alive. Although badly wounded, he survived.

Hell broke loose. That is modern warfare—technical murder, scientifically accurate destruction. A dozen burning tanks lay helpless in front of the German positions. The 88 mm. fired into the close-formation infantry columns. The effect was murderous. From this moment Halfaya was known as "Hellfire" Pass.

But what had happened below in the coastal plain where No. 1 Company was trying to prevent the British reaching Sollum? From the plateau the British tanks, as they rolled towards No. 1 Company's positions, looked like toys. Supply trucks and tankers followed behind. The Germans lurked in their positions and did not interfere with them. Exactly the same procedure was followed as on the top of the Pass. But now all eyes were focused on the minefield. Excitement was at its peak. Five Mark IIs advanced. When only a few yards from the minefield a gigantic cloud of black smoke enveloped one of them. Then they heard the dull thud of an explosion. The second, third, fourth and fifth Mark II continued to advance. They had not been warned by the explosion. The second was blown sky high. The third and fourth also touched off mines, and now four tanks lay there out of action. The turret of the fourth tank opened and a Tommy leapt to the ground. An explosion, a mushroom of smoke and the man was blown to pieces. "Good God, how could the man . . ." growled Corporal Folz. There was no note of exultation in his voice. It was compassion for the man over there who had foolishly and for no good reason jumped from his damaged tank. That is what annoyed Folz. It was simply not done. He felt no antagonism but a kind of dull rage that the enemy had not observed the rules which every soldier in Africa obeyed.

When you entered a minefield you had to crawl inch by inch, feeling your way with your foot. Get through the field with your hands raised. No one would shoot at you. And this Tommy simply jumped to his death.

Now only one of the five Mark IIs remained. It would soon be blown up, too. But now they were due for a surprise. It had gone through the minefield. It had crossed the six rows of mines without the slightest damage. The men in their slit trenches were frozen to stone. Now they were in a serious position. One of the Mark IIs had reached its objective after negotiating the minefield. It could now overrun the infantry positions, and the road was free for the steel monster as far as lower Sollum. But suddenly it stopped. What was the trouble? Fear, because it was alone? That was possible. It turned round and made its way back through the minefield. A violent explosion and No. 5 had ceased to be a fighting unit. The crew had at last realised what was the matter. With hands above their heads they crawled out of the minefield, following the tracks of their tank.

The sun began to descend slowly towards the horizon but the shells continued to rain down on the positions at Halfaya Pass. Most of them were still falling in the false wadi where there were no German infantry. Pardi's battery alone lay in the hurricane of fire. Pardi himself manned the gun since his layer had been wounded. His crew glanced from time to time at their officer. "Look at Ricardo—" "The *Tedeschi* should see him now!" Rommel did arrive later and congratulated Major Pardi, but at that moment there was no time for handshakes.

The British infantry now launched a second attack. In waves they broke out of the ruins of Halfaya village.

They came out swinging their arms, their flat steel helmets cocked to one side. The men of the 11th Indian Brigade and the 22nd Guards Brigade. . . . Strapping fellows. They had to advance across the level plain to the German positions where death waited with finger on the trigger. The 11th Hussars and Indian Colonial troops were with them. They had mothers, wives and sweethearts and they loved life. But all of them had one idea—they must fling the Jerries out of their miserable foxholes on Halfaya Pass. They were shot to pieces. But the British mortar fire made great holes in the

German positions. There, too, many sons and fathers were killed. The night of the 15th/16th June laid its merciful mantle over the battlefield.

The following morning the sun rose fiery red and the Battle of Sollum entered upon its second day. At midday the temperature registered between 130 and 140 degrees. No water except a few mouthfuls in their water bottles mixed with aniseed. It tasted filthy but it burned the throat and was a good remedy against thirst. It was a recipe they had learned from the Italians.

While at Halfaya Pass the Indian troops and the men of the 4th Armoured Brigade in a savage tank and infantry attack tried to storm the heights, General Beresford-Peirse's two combat groups by-passed Halfaya Pass.

One of these advanced parallel to the coast towards Capuzzo and Musaid, against Rommel's 15th Panzer Division in the Bardia zone. The second made a wide sweep to the south into the desert and tried to bring off a bold outflanking movement. The idea was to force the 5th Light Division northwards, and after encirclement together with the 15th Panzer Division cause it to be beaten in open battle by the aggressive 7th Armoured Division. The British breakthrough in the centre was successful. Capuzzo and Musaid fell. The 7th Armoured Division came up against the 15th Panzer Division which did not succeed in halting their advance.

The first phase of the British plan had succeeded. Now everything hinged upon two things. The German Halfaya Pass position must fall and the outflanking movement through the desert must succeed, so that the 15th Panzer and the 5th Light Divisions could be taken in the rear.

The southernmost German stronghold of the Sollum front, which the 7th Armoured Brigade had to by-pass, bore the name Hill 208 and lay deep in the desert. Strongpoint is a euphemism. In actual fact, nothing distinguished it from the sparse desert except that an Arab graveyard stood there as a geographical feature. Italian infantry and sapper units, together with men of a German Oasis Company, had built 208. These Oasis Companies—five in number—were ordered by Rommel to capture and occupy the desert oases of Giarabub, Siwa and Kufra. For this task, picked men had been engaged. With the exception of the officers none of them must be over thirty. The Oasis Companies left their mark not only at stronghold 208 but also at Halfaya Pass and particularly at Sollum. Later they were amalgamated into the 300th Oasis Battalion for special purposes.

"What a fine oasis," said the men when they saw stronghold 208. Five hundred yards wide and six hundred yards long, it lay about twenty miles south-east of Capuzzo in the heart of the desert. In the appalling heat the Italians had bored out slit trenches with drills and carried up the camouflage for the heavy armament. They had done a magnificent job. Not a gun emplacement could be seen from twenty yards away. The garrison commander was Lieutenant Paulewicz. His "fortress troops" consisted of No. 1 Oasis Company, a battery of 3.7 cm. anti-tank guns, a machine-gun section and an 88 mm. flak battery commanded by Lieutenant Ziemer. Stronghold 208 was the southernmost point of the German front. If the British were to succeed in their outflanking movement against Rommel's 5th Light they had to crack this nut. Nothing happened on the 15th June. The British were still fully occupied with the first phase—the Battle for Halfaya and the advance to Bardia. That evening radio communication between 208 and the 15th Motorised Infantry Battalion was interrupted. The stronghold was left to its own devices. A tiny island in the desert ocean . . . a mere dot on the vast chessboard of the battle.

Early on the morning of the 16th, while it was still dark, the 7th Armoured Brigade rolled towards it. At the first reported sound of tank tracks Lieutenant Paulewicz was on his feet. He broke off shaving, rushed out and warned his men: "No one must fire too soon. Hold your fire until the infantry attack and the tanks are almost on top of us."

It was soon light. The tanks were outlined against the sky and the desert, raising a mighty cloud of dust. Paulewicz joined the 88. Through their field-glasses the gunners had already counted thirty tanks. "When do we start?" asked Lieutenant Ziemer. "I suggest we let the first ones come in," replied Paulewicz. "But hold it or else they'll turn away and we shall be shelled at long range." Paulewicz finished shaving. He felt a trifle nervous. How would his men stand up to this? He had only known them for ten days. Perhaps one of them would poop off too early and give the game away as a result of nerves.

The tanks drew nearer. Ziemer calmly counted seventy of them—all Mark IIs.

"Don't get nervous, boys," he said, to encourage his gunners. The leading tank crossed the perimeter. "Fire!" The 88 roared and the tank turret with its gun flew into the air. Now it was blow for blow. The second and third tanks received hits and were out of action. The anti-tank guns barked and the machine-guns hammered against the approaching British carriers. Their crews could not be detrucked. Eleven Mark II tanks already lay burning and smoking close to the stronghold. The others broke off the action, followed by the lorried infantry. A captain was captured when the wounded and prisoners were taken from the shot-up tanks. He wished to see the 88. When he was shown it he shook his head. "It doesn't look so hot but nothing can be done against it. It will prove the undoing of the Mark II." He was right.

In the early afternoon the second British attack was launched. In this engagement they lost seventeen Mark IIs. The hulks of twenty-eight of Churchill's magnificent new tanks lay off stronghold 208. The attack of an entire tank brigade had been repulsed. This was too much for the British. What was the meaning of this? Once more they attacked, flung their infantry against 208 but this assault was halted three-hundred yards from the stronghold by machine-gun fire. The battlefield was a tank graveyard, full of burning and smoking monsters. The losses of the garrison were two men slightly wounded and one anti-tank gun put out of action. But what would happen next day? The 88 mm. battery was running short of ammunition. Water supplies were running low. The anti-tank gunners had to economise their ammunition. Where was the enemy and where were their own troops in the German front line? That evening the wireless operator managed to get into contact once more with division. They were delighted to hear that the southern outpost in the desert had held. Water and shells were sent to 208 and the men of the Oasis Company waited for a resumption of hostilities. But the British did not reappear. The great tank battle of Sollum had passed its peak. General Beresford-Peirse's calculations had been wrong in two instances—Halfaya Pass and stronghold 208. In one position a bare battalion and in the other slightly more than a company had upset all the plans, thanks to the 88 mm. all-purpose gun.

The official history of the African war which was published by Her Majesty's Stationery Office in 1956 after a careful study of the sources stated: "Operation Battleaxe which had begun so hopefully failed because Halfaya Pass could not be taken or Point 208 by-passed. The determination and fire-power of the defence were too strong. The 88 mm. guns, well concealed, proved deadly to any British tank. The surprise element also played an important rôle in the British defeat."

The final summing-up of the Battle of Sollum may be described as follows. On the first day the spearhead of the 7th Armoured Division advanced through Capuzzo and Musaid and threatened Bardia. Capuzzo, Musaid and Upper Sollum fell. At Capuzzo it was chaos. Fifty British tanks suddenly appeared before the position. Quite correctly orders were given to the motorised infantry to retire. All they could do was run as fast as their legs could carry them. But the tanks were faster. More and more soldiers were wounded and had to abandon the race.

An 88 mm. proved their salvation. Lieutenant Tocki of the 33rd Panzerjaegers had brought it from Bardia. Three shots and three tanks were out of action. Forty tanks halted their attack and put up a smoke screen. A brilliant action by Captain Kümmel and men of the 8th Panzer Regiment who, with the 7.5 cm. guns of their two heavy tanks, destroyed half a dozen Mark IIs and discouraged a further British advance. Kümmel, who was awarded the Oak Leaves, was later known by the nicknname: "The Lion of Capuzzo."

Lieutenant-Colonel Knabe lay with his aide, Lieutenant Kuhnow, and Sergeant-Majors Mankiewicz and Goltz with runners and signallers in a drain beneath the road during the fluctuating battle. Forty yards away lay Knabe's destroyed car. They watched a British tank crew search the kit for loot and laughingly appropriate Knabe's uniform, and later, under cover of night, they made their way in ones and twos back to the German lines. Knabe and Kuhnow were picked up by the 8th Panzer Regiment which was holding the road to Capuzzo.

Bach's Combat Group, with men of the 1st Battalion of the 104th Panzer Grenadier Regiment, flak and anti-tank guns, continued to hold Halfaya Pass on the British flank. As already mentioned, this position was of vital importance because the supplies for the great tank battle in the Bardia-

Mk IV

Tobruk area were to have been brought up to Sollum Harbour and along the coastal road. Everything depended upon Halfaya Pass being held. "The Pass must be held under all circumstances," Rommel had telegraphed to Bach. The Pastor understood. The British attacked five times. Time after time British and Indian units stormed the German positions. Hour after hour the artillery thundered and the shell bursts echoed eerily in the wadis. But Bach held on. Here, too, ammunition supplies ran low. Pardi collected old Italian artillery shells which had been dumped in the wadi, had them polished, greased and fired them. Bach not only held the position, he even launched counter-attacks and threw the British infantry out of Halfaya village.

In the centre of the battle the position had at one moment been extremely critical for Rommel. His attempt to recapture Capuzzo failed. The 8th Panzer Regiment lost most of its motorised vehicles. The 5th Panzer Regiment was chased across the battlefield. Upon this Rommel embarked upon a decisive stroke. The crux was that strongpoint 208 held out. This enabled him to despatch the 5th Light Division to 208 in order to attack from there the enemy's flank. It was a masterly yet at the same time simple coup. The British had wanted to outflank him, now he would turn the tables on them. The turning point was 208. The 5th Light Division fought its way South to Sidi Suleiman and on the evening of the 16th reached the zone to the east of Sidi Omar. Now Rommel carried out an even bolder stroke. He withdrew the troops before Capuzzo under the very noses of the British and sent them to join the 5th Light attacking Sidi Suleiman and at the same time against the flank of the British operating at Bardia and Halfaya Pass. This caused the British front to collapse. General Beresford-Peirse gave the signal to retire and the retreat became a rout.

It was the 17th June, the day of which Churchill writes in his diaries: "On the 17th everything went wrong." It went wrong because a few officers and a few hundred soldiers of the Afrika Korps held out at Halfaya Pass and at stronghold 208. A mighty battle had been won by the courage of the troops and Rommel's bold decisions.

But we must be honest. It was not courage alone. It was also a question of weapons and, in particular, of the superiority of the 88 mm. gun.

The battle raged for seventy-two hours. In British records it is known as "Operation Battleaxe." For seventy-two hours the British Commander-in-Chief in Cairo, General Wavell, with Churchill's "Tiger" tried to change the fortunes of war in Africa. But the German weapons and cunning were still superior—not only the 88s but also the German Mark III and Mark IV tanks. The 15th Panzer Division suffered heavy losses in motorised vehicles. But the Germans, with their well-organised recovery forces, hauled the damaged tanks with tractors out of the battlefield and had them repaired in travelling workshops. This was an achievement which amazed the British and for which Churchill expressed admiration in his memoirs. "Battleaxe" was over. The greatest battle of armour yet witnessed by the desert had resulted in a German victory.

The British losses totalled 122 killed, 259 missing, and 599 wounded. Over 100 British tanks were destroyed. Countless others, heavily damaged, could only be withdrawn. Wavell's armour had been destroyed.

The German losses totalled 93 killed, 235 missing and 350 wounded. The total loss in tanks amounted to 12, while 50 were damaged.

Superior leadership and better weapons had conquered. But the war was not yet over. The British were determined to learn from their defeat. Would Rommel allow them time to do this? That was the burning question in the summer of 1941. But the answer did not depend solely on Rommel.

4

A BRITISH COMMANDO ATTEMPT TO CAPTURE ROMMEL

Rommel's men considered him to be invulnerable. "No bullet has ever been forged for the Old Man," they used to say in amazement, or with a shake of the head, when he had once more sensed the danger and moved off in his armoured car just before a shell had burst. They lay in the desert muck under a hail of enemy machine-gun fire—could not even put their noses out of their slit trenches without the risk of having their heads blown off. The attack was halted, Rommel came rushing up and stood upright in the trench, shielding his eyes with his hands against the sun. "What the hell's the matter with you fellows? When things get a bit hot over there you don't have to do a belly-flop every time!" Hardly had he gone than there were casualties once more. It was always the same story. Many of the old desert foxes have told me similar stories—men who returned home with the Iron Cross and the Knight's Cross and who certainly were not scared of a bombardment. Yes, no bullet had ever been forged for Erwin Rommel.

Naturally the legend of Rommel's invulnerability ran the rounds of the front lines; prisoners carried it across to No Man's Land and the German general was soon considered invincible by the Tommies, also. Bewildered British officers took note of this mystique and reported: "Rommel's very name and legend are in the process of becoming a psychological danger to the British Army."

On the 18th June, 1941, among the routed members of

the 7th Armoured Division, were our friends, Clark and Miller. How confident of victory they had been when they set out on the 15th in their Mark II. Now it was all over. In the nick of time they had slipped out of Rommel's great "bag" between Sidi Omar, Halfaya Pass and Capuzzo. It was a dispiriting retreat.

Were these Germans really invincible? Could nothing be done to defeat them? These were the thoughts that ran through the heads of the two men. And many others thought the same. Our morale is bad, was the verdict of the Staffs.

Winston Churchill reluctantly relieved Sir Archibald Wavell of his desert command. He was appointed Commander-in-Chief in India. A new man took the helm in Africa, a man with a reputation for drive and stubbornness—Sir Claude Auchinleck. Would he defeat Rommel?

That damned Rommel!

Bold strokes were at that time the order of the day. It was not surprising, therefore, that the thought of taking Rommel prisoner should have blossomed in high places.

Erwin Rommel had no idea of the dark thought harboured by his adversaries. At this particular time he was neither as invulnerable nor as self-assured as legend maintained. He was worried. How would the Africa campaign develop? On the 18th June, the day after his victory, he knew that the German attack on Russia was imminent and that this banished all hopes of his receiving generous reinforcements of armour, aircraft and fighting men.

He knew only too well that Hitler and the German General Staff persisted in thinking on European lines and had little sympathy for the African theatre of war with its great strategical possibilities. The Chief of General Staff, General Halder, held the view that it was impossible to defeat the British in North Africa. For him the North African war was merely a diversionary measure to gain time.

It has often been maintained that Rommel was a magnificent tactician, a brilliant leader of men, but no far-seeing strategist. History, however, has shown that Rommel's strategic plans were by no means fantastic—in fact they were more realistic than those of the Führer, who in the summer of 1941 in the Wolf's Lair at Rastenburg, East Prussia, directed the battles in far-off Russia like some woodland ghost.

Rommel had conceived a bold idea which he duly proposed to Hitler and the General Staff—to take Tobruk and to press on to the Suez Canal. But this was not his final objective. He would continue his advance beyond Basra to the Persian Gulf, using Syria as an occupied base and a main supply centre. Was this fantasy? Was it any more fantastic than Hitler's plan to cross the Caucasus and capture the oilfields of Baku? His plan came to grief; Rommel's plan had a much sounder basis. One need only read General Auchinleck's report, No. 38177, on the African position between November 1941 and August 1942. In this one learns the interesting fact that the British C-in-C in the Middle East actually feared the plan which was in Rommel's mind. There were no strong British forces available to defend Syria. In Iraq and Persia, on the route to the Persian Gulf, he had very weak forces at his disposal. According to Auchinleck, Cyprus could easily be taken by German paratroops. Auchinleck feared for his north flank and prayed that the German leaders would not embark upon the undertaking that Rommel desired.

But in the summer of 1941 Rommel was not only faced with the problem of grand strategy; he also had tactical difficulties. What would happen if the British attacked again? It was obvious that they would try to force a decision. They brought up everything that their ships could carry and British superiority increased day by day.

Tobruk must fall whether Hitler and the German High Command wished it or not. This was Rommel's obsession.

At this moment he received support from an unexpected quarter. It came from the head of the German Secret Service, the Abwehr: Admiral Canaris, the man who vacillated between "resistance" and duty. Although found guilty of acts of sabotage he rendered great service to the German war leaders.

In Jerusalem Canaris had a very brilliant agent in the person of a British hospital nurse. She learned all manner of important information from wounded British soldiers. She was struck by the remarks of a trusting Englishman who was holding forth about an approaching offensive in North Africa. The sister encouraged other soldiers to discuss the matter and found reasonable confirmation of this information. Her report so impressed the Admiral that he forwarded it to Hitler and Jodl.

Rommel was also informed. His view was as follows: it was most important to take Tobruk with the greatest possible speed. After urgent telephone messages and a long telephone conversation from Rome with General Jodl, he overcame the opposition of the German High Command. As soon as permission had been given Rommel made preparations for the attack. It was to take place, if possible, at the end of October.

Thus a hospital nurse—a German agent in Jerusalem—for a brief moment directed the course of the war.

The British were actually feverishly preparing their offensive. They were dominated by the thought that Rommel must be put out of action. The brain of the German campaign in North Africa must be paralysed and Rommel must be killed or taken prisoner.

The Long Range Desert Group was a special unit created for acts of sabotage and intelligence in the desert.* Its counterpart was the Brandenburgers, the German organisation to fight behind the enemy lines.

This Long Range Desert Group was composed of Commando volunteers. Its headquarters were in the caves of the Siwa Oasis and later at Kufra. From there they carried out audacious raids, several hundred miles behind the enemy lines. Outstanding actions were the attacks on German airfields which lay 350 miles behind the front. The Commandos were away for weeks on end in a few trucks, as in canoes on the high seas. They reached their objectives and destroyed nearly every bomber and fighter on the field. They blew up the petrol dumps, caused heavy casualties among the airfield staff and even took half a dozen prisoners on their long journey back to the caves of Siwa.

Suppose such fellows were used against Rommel! They could perhaps shoot the much-feared opponent in his headquarters or take him prisoner; it was merely a question of discovering Rommel's habits.

This was done in due course.

That the British Secret Service made a terrible blunder led to one of the greatest cloak-and-dagger episodes of the African war.

The Quartermaster-General of Panzer Gruppe Afrika, Major Schleusener, had made his headquarters during the German offensive preparations far behind the front in the

---

*For the full story of this fantastic unit read STIRLING'S DESERT RAIDERS by Virginia Cowles. Another volume in the Bantam War Book Series.

Cyrene area. It was a historical zone. In antiquity magnificent buildings stood here, for Cyrene was once a charming Grecian settlement. Columns and temples survived until a disastrous earthquake on the Cyrenaican coast destroyed everything. In 1913, after a cloudburst, Italian soldiers found one of the most beautiful works of art in the world in a wadi—the Venus of Cyrene.

Cloudbursts gave no particular cause for surprise, for sudden heavy rainstorms are quite frequent in this region. The ruins of Cyrene stretch almost to the little Italian settlement, Beda Littoria. On a slope stood a gloomy cypress grove with a two-storied house which had served as a prefecture. Round it copses, ravines, caves and rocks... The Quartermaster-General took up his quarters here in late August 1941.

On the 17th November an autumn gale, which had been raging for several days in the Beda Littoria area, brought a heavy downpour of rain.

The Quartermaster-General Schleusener was not at his headquarters at the time. Like his able deputy, Captain Otto, he lay in hospital at Apollonia. Schleusener had gone down with dysentery and Otto with inflammation of the lungs. Otto's adjutant, Litchwald, was also in hospital with dysentery. Acting Quartermaster-General was therefore Captain G. Weitz. Major Poeschel was acting second-in-command. A couple of dozen officers, orderlies, runners, drivers and the usual personnel to be found on a Quartermaster's staff were sitting in the gloomy building of the old prefecture listening to the rain pouring down.

Shortly before midnight they retired to the various rooms on the ground and first floors where they slept on camp beds.

There were no sentries. What was the use of posting sentries so far behind the front? An M.P. kept watch in the corridor below. His sole weapon was a bayonet. He was less a guard than a distributor of late-arriving mail. A private soldier, Matthe Boxhammer, of the Quartermaster's motorised section was on late duty in the guard tent, where he was allowed to lie down on his camp bed after midnight.

Beda Littoria, situated well behind the lines, was asleep. But in the undergrowth on the heights ghostly figures lurked. They had black-painted faces and wore British battledress. From time to time a shadow moved in the harsh light of a lightning flash. And then it was gone. The thunder growled dully and the last light of Beda Littoria went out. It was ten minutes to midnight.

The ghosts in the cypress grove had come a long journey. Two British submarines, *Torbay* and *Talisman,* had landed them on the night of 15th November in a small deserted creek on the Cyrenaican coast. These were the men who were to kill or capture Erwin Rommel twelve hours before the great offensive was launched.

To quote Winston Churchill: "In order to strike at the brain and nerve-centre of the enemy's army at the critical moment, fifty men of the Scottish Commando, under Colonel Laycock, were carried by submarine to a point on the coast two hundred miles behind the enemy's line. The thirty who could be landed in the rough sea were formed into two parties, one to cut telephone and telegraph communications, and the other, under Lieutenant-Colonel Keyes, son of Admiral Keyes, to attack Rommel's house."

Everything had been planned in the office of Admiral of the Fleet Sir Roger Keyes. The Admiral was head of all Special Commandos and raiding parties on the British side. He was the man who in 1918 had led the bold attack by a British naval flotilla against the German U-Boat base at Ostend. In those days he blocked the entrance to the harbour with cement ships and inflicted a grievous blow on the German navy. He was eager to repeat his success in 1941.

Of the hundred officers and men who had undergone several weeks' intensive training in London, fifty-three were finally chosen. Geoffrey Keyes, Sir Roger's elder son, at that time a Major, had chosen the toughest youths he could find. His second-in-command was Captain Campbell who spoke fluent German and Arabic.

On the 15th November they landed in a storm on the coast of Cyrenaica. Huge breakers foamed over the *Torbay,* and the submarine was flung about like a box of matches. The rubber dinghy capsized several times and each time the crew had to be fished out of the sea. Keyes then ordered the men to hold fast to the dinghy line and fight their way ashore. The manoeuvre was successful. Keyes, Campbell and twenty-two men at last had firm ground underfoot. Things went worse for Colonel Laycock's Commando in the submarine *Talisman.* Two men were drowned. A greater part of the contingent had to abandon their struggle with the waves from exhaustion and be taken on board again. Only seven men reached the shore, thus reducing the strength of the Commando by half. Keyes then decided to concentrate solely on the main action against Rommel.

Colonel Laycock remained behind at the landing place with three men to cover the re-embarkment after the action. The remaining three officers and twenty-five men, shivering with cold, marched for a quarter of an hour inland where a mysterious Arab awaited them. This was Lieutenant-Colonel John Haselden, a senior officer of the Long Range Desert Group, who had lived behind the German lines for some time disguised as an Arab and was one of the key figures of the British Secret Service behind Rommel's front. Haselden acted as a guide. He explained the exact position, which Keyes recorded in his notebook, and gave the latter three Arab guides. The mysterious agent had now completed his job. M15 did not wish to endanger Haselden's life by letting him take part in the action. He disappeared as silently as he had come. Keyes and his men went on their way.

On the night of 17th November, 1941, then, Keyes stood with his Commandos on a sand dune close to Beda Littoria. They took their bearings. Ahead lay the huts, and a little farther away the cypress grove. In the centre were the huge stone buildings. That was the objective. It was where Rommel slept or worked—according to the British Secret Service, and this information had been confirmed by John Haselden from Arab agents' reports. Keyes and his men fully believed this, but all of them were victims of a grotesque error. The reason is not too difficult to discover. At the end of July 1941 General Rommel had been given command of the newly formed Panzer Gruppe Afrika. GHQ was stationed in Beda Littoria. Chief of Staff was Major-General Gause, while General Westphal was G.S.O.1 (Operations). The offices were in the prefecture building and several houses in the neighbourhood had been requisitioned. The offices were in individual buildings and could be recognised by the plates on the doors—Adjutant, C-in-C, G.S.O.1, 2, 3, etc.

These interesting plates were known to the British Secret Service. Presumably agents had photographed both the layout and the nameplates.

At the end of August, however, Rommel left Cyrenaica with his staff for Cantoniera Ain El Gazala, 40 miles west of

Tobruk, and later moved to the Cantoniera Gambut between Tobruk and Bardia. The Q.M.G. and his staff took up their quarters at Beda Littoria.

This the British Secret Service did not discover. Did the Arab agents deliberately deceive the British? Was greed on the part of the spies the cause? Whatever the reason, in September, both in Cairo and London, it was believed that Rommel's headquarters were in the prefecture at Beda Littoria. A grave error! But Major Keyes was blissfully unaware of this error and thought he had now reached his goal.

In his farewell letter to his father before leaving he had written: "If the raid succeeds, England will have advanced a step further and that is worth a great deal, even if I fall into the bag." Keyes was not entirely wrong. Even if Beda Littoria was not Rommel's headquarters it was the headquarters of the Q.M.G., the nodal point of all reinforcements and supplies. It was the nerve centre of the German-Italian Panzer Gruppe. Great havoc could have been wrought there.

The rain poured down. Thunder and lightning—as though ordered—were the accompanying music to this adventure. It was 23.59 hours when Keyes gave his men the final details of the plan. He himself, Campbell, Sergeant Terry and six men crept towards the entrance of the prefecture. Three others made their way round to the back door. The German sentry stood in the open front door. Sergeant Terry was to kill him with a dagger. Who knows? Possibly the soldier made an unexpected movement. The blade missed its mark and in a flash there was a tussle in the corridor.

The German called loudly for help, but the thunder and the noise of the storm drowned his cries. The storm also drowned the sound of the demolition of an electricity power house thirty paces from the house; it was blown sky high by men of the Commando.

During the struggle in the dark corridor the raiders could not use their tommy guns. They tried to grab the sentry and silence him. But the German soldier was a strong man and defended himself bravely. Finally he fell against the first door of the corridor. This proved fatal for Geoffrey Keyes.

There are several British versions of what ensued at Beda Littoria.

Churchill writes rather vaguely of it in his Memoirs.

Desmond Young, Rommel's British biographer, gives a detailed description in his book of the raid on the German General's Headquarters. But accurate information about the raid is missing and he does not mention why Rommel was not there. So far the most detailed account of this raid is to be found in the January 1957 issue of the magazine "*Men Only*." According to this the German-speaking Campbell called the sentry out of the entrance and Keyes shot him. Then Keyes, Campbell and Terry jumped over the dead man and wrenched open the door of the first room.

"They were faced by a blinding light. The German officers seated round the table, stared motionless at the intruders. Without a word, Keyes mowed down the best men of the German Supply Corps with his tommy gun."

Then, according to *Men Only*: "They went into the next room and once more tore open the door. But here the light had already been switched off and they were met by concentrated revolver fire. Keyes was hit by five bullets but Terry jumped forward and fired a few bursts into the room."

Outside on the dunes Campbell, according to the British official account, realised that Keyes was mortally wounded and that he himself had been hit in the leg. He handed over to Lieutenant Cook who was to take the party back to the beach. Nothing is mentioned about the absence of the Commando troop. To make the account more dramatic four General Staff Officers were presumed to have been killed, but unfortunately Rommel had not been caught for he had left his headquarters at 20.30 hours to attend the marriage of a sheikh and had only returned at 00.40 hours. In other words, thirty minutes after the raid. Pure bad luck!

There are many similar versions and they are all very dramatic. The British are always depicted as bold and contemptuous of death and the German officers as paralysed with terror. . . .

What is the true story?

I think I have found the true answer. I have questioned all the surviving German eye-witnesses and their reports give an unequivocal picture.

The Assistant Quartermaster, Major Poeschel, remembers the turbulent events of that night extremely well and has given me an impressive account of his experiences and the results of his enquiries. I have been able to augment them

P-08 Luger

with the original report which Sergeant Alfons Hirsch and Corporal Otto Barth compiled the day after the raid. Sergeant-Major Lentzen, the M.O., Doctor Junge, the driver Friedrich Honold and the Wireless Operator Erwin Schauer have furnished important details which throw some light on the event. It seems to me that there is no possible doubt that the raid progressed after the attack on the sentry in the corridor in the following manner:

When the powerfully built sentry fell to the ground with the British soldier in their wrestling match, he hit against the door of the munitions office. Sergeant-Major Lentzen and Sergeant Kovacic, who were sleeping in the room, woke up, jumped from their beds and grabbed their P-08s. Lentzen leaped to the door and pulled it open. He sought for a target, raised his Luger and fired. At the same moment Major Keyes hurled two hand grenades which flew past Lentzen's head and exploded in the middle of the room. The blast knocked the Sergeant-Major over but he was unhurt. Kovacic, who was on his way to the door, received the full benefit of the blast and lay dead on the tiles. A third N.C.O., Sergeant Bartel, who was about to jump out of bed, was able to fall back and remained unscathed. Things went at lightning speed. The sequence of the account cannot disturb the unity of the event. Had Sergeant-Major Lentzen's bullets found their mark? We shall see this at once for at that moment the fate of the carefully organised raid was decided. Upstairs on the first floor the Orderly Officer, Lieutenant Kaufholz, had not yet fallen asleep when the cries of the sentry rang out. He was the first person in the house to hear them. He leapt out of bed but had to fetch his revolver from a chest. Then he ran into the corridor and down the stairs. At this moment the hand grenades exploded in the munitions office. By the light of the explosion Kaufholz caught sight of the British soldiers. But Captain Campbell had also spotted the German Lieutenant. Kaufholz was the first to fire and the British Commando leader, Major Keyes, slumped to the ground with a little cry of pain. At the same moment Campbell's tommy-gun barked. The bannisters were splintered but the burst had hit Kaufholz. While the Lieutenant writhed in his death agony and fell to the ground, he fired and hit Campbell in the shin. The British officer collapsed.

Thus the two leaders of the raid were out of action. In the dark corridor remained only Sergeant Terry and two privates. Voices rang out from the first floor and the German officers rushed from their rooms. The surprise is now over, thought Terry. But where are the others who should have entered the house by the back door? Yes, where on earth are the others?

At this moment there was wild machine-gun fire outside. Are the Germans counter-attacking, Terry wondered. Once more it was one of those tragic errors, for there was no question of any German counter-attack. Something rather eerie had happened. Lieutenant Jaeger, in the next room to the munitions office, had been virtually flung out of bed by the explosion of the hand grenades. His room was separated from this office by a partition of three-ply wood. It was smashed to pieces. Jaeger in his pyjamas jumped out of the window—which had been blown in by the explosion. This was his undoing. Outside, in his light pyjamas, in the pouring rain and lit up by a lightning flash he ran straight into a British sentry's tommy-gun. The Tommy did not hesitate or call for surrender. What could they have done with prisoners? Firing from the hip he shot the unfortunate Lieutenant to pieces from a distance of ten feet. He was riddled with bullets.

But these shots were soon avenged. These were the

shots which Sergeant Terry and his men in the dark corridor had heard and had caused the Sergeant to surmise that fighting had broken out outside. Deprived of their leader, they rushed into the open air.

The shots which had killed Lieutenant Jaeger had the same effect on the second Commando which was still outside the back door, unable to enter the house. Actually these men had the best prospect, if not of capturing Rommel, of putting the Q.M.G.'s headquarters completely out of action five hours before the British offensive. A can of water was the fly in the ointment and Major Keyes could not possibly have taken this can of water into account.

The back door led into a small office that had formerly served as a kitchen. It was crammed full of files and office tables. A small hatch at the back of the room led via a spiral staircase to a cellar. Here Sergeant-Major Alfons Hirsch and Corporal Barth had their sleeping quarters. The corporal was an elderly man who hated to have open doors at night. Since the back door had no lock he placed a full can of water before the door every evening and barricaded it from behind with a filing cabinet. This was a lock that no skeleton key could open. Although the raiders tried to force it the door refused to yield. They remained outside and held a conference while their leaders, Campbell and Terry, had already been discovered in the house corridor and the fighting had started. When the tommy-gun fire which mowed down Lieutenant Jaeger was heard coming from the garden the troops at the back door suspected a trap, and took to their heels.

"Lower your torches," Major Poeschel shouted to the German officers as they rushed out of their rooms on the first floor. But the nightmare was over. From outside came one more burst of machine-gun fire. A long scream rent the night, then everything was silent.

On the stairs they found the dead Lieutenant Kaufholz and in the corridor lay a British officer with a blackened face: the courageous Major Keyes. He had been killed by a shot through the chest which broke his sternum and had entered his heart and lungs. He had a second light wound in the thigh. This shot had obviously been fired by Sergeant-Major Lentzen. The shot that killed him must have been fired by Kaufholz, for Keyes, according to Campbell's later report, after throwing his grenade and after Lentzen's firing had cried to Campbell: "Damn it, I've been hit!" At the same moment in the glare of the grenade explosion he had seen Kaufholz on the stairs and called to Campbell: "Look out! Let him have it!" Then he collapsed after Kaufholz had fired. Almost simultaneously Campbell's machine-gun rang out and in the exchange of shots that followed Kaufholz's gun spat and smashed Campbell's shin bone. The Captain crawled as far as the door. There he stumbled over the legs of the sentry who lay with the upper part of his body in the office, his back riddled with hand grenade splinters, but by some miracle, not mortally wounded.

The whole operation came to grief because of this sentry. He is the only man whose name, despite all my efforts, I have been unable to discover. This is because he belonged to an M.P. unit, and the Q.M.G.'s staff kept no record of the personnel of this unit. An unknown soldier.

Outside after a search the German patrols came across the body of Lieutenant Jaeger. But towards the end a tommy-gun had spoken again and a man had uttered his death cry. They sought for a long while and then in the light of their torches they discovered the fourth dead German. This was Gunner Boxhammer of the Q.M.G.'s Motorised Detachment. Matthe Boxhammer, a 20-year old youth from Malling in Bavaria, had been on duty to receive later incoming mail and to show the couriers to their quarters which lay some way off on the Via Balbo. Boxhammer in his small tent had obviously heard the sentry's cries for help, had jumped up without a thought and run to the prefecture entrance to help his comrade. He ran straight into the retreating Sergeant Terry and his men who mowed him down with a burst of tommy-gun fire in his belly. Matthe Boxhammer's death notice was worded quite correctly: "The fatal bullet hit him as he was trying to come to the aid of a stricken comrade."

The nightmare was over. The great adventure had failed. It failed as a result of a few unforeseen circumstances and the work of a few men. It is unthinkable what would have happened had they managed to enter the prefecture without making a sound and destroyed the whole of the Q.M.G.'s apparatus five hours before the British offensive started, or for a few hours had been in a position to give confusing orders to the Panzer Gruppe.

There remains only to add a little human story told to me by the surgeon, Doctor Werner Junge:

Captain Campbell had received a shot from a tommy-gun or a revolver at close quarters which had completely smashed his shinbone in the centre. He had no other wounds. By rights the leg should have been amputated, since the prospect of healing was very small and the danger of infection very great. At his request, Doctor Junge did not amputate and tried to save the leg. Since Junge spoke fluent English he was given orders to question Campbell. The latter did not betray the fact that he knew German. Junge could discover nothing of any importance. On the contrary, Campbell saw at once through the Doctor's game and said at last in German: "You needn't bother—you won't get anything out of me."

Doctor Junge kept Campbell in plaster for fourteen days in hospital until Derna had to be evacuated and the patient was sent by air to an Italian hospital. "Campbell was a charming man," said Junge. "As a doctor I should be very interested to learn whether I had saved his leg. I wore his 'sandcreepers,' as we called the British crêpe-soled shoes in the desert, for the rest of the war. They brought me more luck than they brought him, but I didn't get up to such escapades as he did."

And what was the fate of the rest of the members of the Commando?

The fleeing soldiers had not dared to return immediately to the waiting submarine. Fearing that a large search party would be sent out they hid with the Arabs. Not until next morning was a thorough combined German-Italian search made! For days on end the countryside was combed. Arab huts were ransacked and the Military Police searched every corner. They looked intently at the Arabs, but nothing could be got out of these alternately passive or wildly gesticulating fellows. Not a British soldier, not a piece of uniform.

Then an Italian Carabiniere arrived who had lived for many years in the region and knew it like the palm of his hand. "I'll show you how you should act," he said proudly. He fetched an Arab girl from the village and had a long gesticulating palaver with her. The sense of it was as follows:

"You and your family will be given eighty pounds of corn

and twenty pounds of sugar for each Britisher that you betray to us."

Eighty pounds of flour and twenty pounds of sugar—they represented a real treasure for the Arabs at that period. Their greed for this treasure was stronger than the British pound notes or the Senussi Chief's talisman which each one carried representing a kind of passport. The lady left and soon the first British were taken from the very huts which the German Military Police had searched so thoroughly. They were clothed in Arab rags. Eventually the entire Commando fell into German hands. Only the crafty Sergeant Terry managed to escape with two men and found his way through to the British lines. The prisoners were not treated according to Hitler's orders as partisans, which would have meant that they would have been shot: Rommel ordered them to be treated as prisoners-of-war. The fallen British leader of the raid was buried in the cemetery of Beda Littoria with full military honours next to the four dead Germans.

5

THE BETRAYED OFFENSIVE PLAN

What would wars be without traitors? They would be mathematical formulae according to which the best strategists and the bravest soldiers with the most powerful weapons would invariably win. But this is never the case. Treachery is the evil genius of war. Treachery throws a spanner in the works and sweeps plans of genius off the campaigning table. It turns heroism and the art of warfare, the supremacy of weapons and the courage of soldiers in the face of death into a farce.

How many battles have been decided as the result of iniquitous treachery? Certainly just as many as have been won through bravery.

This has been the case down the ages. But there is one consolation in the story of the most flagrant pieces of treachery: they often failed to bear fruit because they were not believed. When the German master spy, Cicero, the Armenian valet of the British Ambassador in Turkey, sold to Adolph Hitler the top secret telegrams from London on the Allied war plans, the German High Command did not believe that they were genuine. Hitler suspected a clever trick on the part of the British Secret Service. He realised his mistake too late.

Similarly, when a German courier plane with the plans for the offensive against France in 1940 landed by mistake on Belgian soil, and the crew had no time to burn these documents, the generals at Allied headquarters thought that Hitler was trying to encourage them to make wrong decisions by some infernal trick. They laughed. They did not do what they should have done according to the plans which had fallen into their hands. Hitler's offensive, carried out with unaltered plans, became the foundation stone of a victory in the west. In history there are many such examples of treachery which have not been exploited. It is a chapter where the traitors worked in vain, lost a golden opportunity or made it a source of their own destruction.

War in the desert also had its traitors. One particularly tragic case, still wreathed in mystery, occurred during the bloody battles for the vital fortress, Tobruk. In the autumn of 1941 this cunningly fortified town, once the main fortress of the Italian colonial possessions in North Africa, still held out against Rommel's attacks. As we have seen, Churchill himself had ordered it to be held to the last man. The "Rats of Tobruk" held it. Thus it remained a constant threat to Rommel's flanks and rear. He had to halt his advance on Alexandria, Cairo and the Suez Canal. If he wanted to reach the Nile, Tobruk must fall. "It must be taken," said Rommel. "It must be taken," repeated his generals and his troops. But all their assaults failed.

This was the position in November 1941. The preparations for the great offensive had been completed; supplies had arrived at last even though they had been decimated by the Royal Navy in the Mediterranean.

At the beginning of November 1941, Rommel drove in his Mercedes staff car to inspect the front. He bobbed up everywhere, and at night he pondered in the omnibus which served him as living quarters. Once more he checked his plan—the plan which he had sketched with his own hand. He had taken into account the experience of all previous attacks on the fortress. His map, with the units and the zero hours of the different actions marked in, was the key to the great offensive. It was intended not only to bring about the fall of Tobruk, but, as I have already indicated, it was to be the beginning of his advance to the Nile and the Suez Canal from where he dreamed of pushing on further into Syria, perhaps to the Persian Gulf to attack Great Britain's oil resources in the Near East and open up the route to India.

But first and foremost Tobruk. Based on Rommel's plan, the details were recorded on the secret map by his staff. The commanders of various units were given their objectives verbally and everything was practised down to the last detail. This time it must succeed.

The commander of the 15th Panzer Division, General Neumann-Silkow, had formed a special unit which was to serve as a kind of "travel service" for the attack on the fortress. This formation was to direct the various units to the particular sectors which would take them across the tank ditches and allow them to force their way in depth through the fortifications. This formation knew every bunker, every ditch, every battery. The attack had been planned more meticulously than any previous operation.

Everything was ready. The "travel service" unit had prepared signposts and ground lights. They were waiting for orders to attack. These could be given any day and at any hour. No one knew the date and it was not to be found on any document—not even on the map that Rommel himself had drawn. No one, apart from Rommel and a few of the initiated, knew that after several postponements D-Day had been fixed for the 23rd November. Since it was known that the British were also preparing for an offensive, eventual enemy attacks were given the code name "High Water" for a normal attack and "Deluge" for a full-scale attack. When choosing these code names no one had foreseen that a real flood might take place. It started on the 17th November—not the attack but the rain.

"Rain," cried the delighted troops. "Rain!" They thrust their hands outside their tents and washed their faces in the rain. On the 17th November this downpour was universally acclaimed. Rain in the desert—how remarkable! In the Jebel area of Halfaya Pass it had not rained like this for sixty years. But soon it gave cause for anxiety. The special unit of the 15th Panzer Division lay in their tents on the edge of the Jebel east of Gambut listening to the downpour. They felt protected. They even laughed when the water entered the tents and drew up their knees. "Good God," they shouted to each other above the thunder, "this is something quite new—to drown in the desert!" But a moment later the mockery died on their lips. A mighty roar could be heard as the water from the plateau streamed down on them. It had become a vast flood which coursed headlong down the edge of the Jebel like an avalanche, tearing up rocks and masses of sand in its progress. In a matter of minutes the tents had been washed away. Trucks were swept aside as if by a giant's fist and smashed to pieces on the rocks. The men's cries for help were drowned—actually drowned in the middle of the desert. Others were buried, knocked unconscious by rocks and suffocated in the shifting sand. It was a gruesome night. Moreover, it was so dark that no one could see his hand before his face.

The same tragedy was being enacted at Halfaya Pass. The lightning revealed a ghostly scene. "It's like the opera *Freischütz*," Wireless Operator Jung remarked sarcastically to his friend, Degen. But this was no theatrical performance. Tents, light trucks, weapons and guns were swept away by the storm flood. Jung and Degen had difficulty in saving their own lives. The tent, the wireless set, spades, even their mess tins and iron rations had gone. They climbed a rocky escarpment and rescued an Italian who was being whirled away by the waters. "*Madonna, Madonna mia,*" he moaned and groaned. They could see nothing, but from scraps of conversation they could guess that others were also fighting for their lives in their holes. "We must get help," said Degen. They felt their way forward, fell into water holes, stumbled into fast-flowing brooks and over filled-in trenches. Where once the No. 1 Company had lain was a shambles.

Now they heard sharp, ear-splitting explosions which they soon recognised as the detonations of the T-mines in the minefield. The German mines had been exploded by the pressure of the shifting sand after the waters had exposed them. The crash and glare of the exploding mines vied with the thunder and lightning.

God be praised that at least the British had not attacked. Jung and Degen hurried on up the Pass to battalion head-quarters. The two men were stared at as though they were Job's messengers. "Have the British already overrun No. 1 Company?" the two drenched wireless operators were asked. "The British?" they echoed in astonishment. "It's high water—not the British." The officers were at a loss. They exchanged glances.

Had they received the code word "High Water"? Was this merely the warning of a natural catastrophe or was it the genuine alert for a British offensive? What a crazy situation. At last the solution came when the code word "Deluge" was received. Now everything was clear. But it seemed sardonic: a natural flood and a full-scale offensive by the British. What would be the result? Many of the positions had been engulfed and the weapons washed away. Like ants, the men rushed back to Halfaya Pass and began to work. Like amphibian creatures the troops at Gambut tried to salvage their trucks.

General Neumann-Silkow's special unit went into action. But not for the storming of Tobruk. The British had forestalled them. Had the German reconnaissance failed? Had the Ger-man attack been betrayed? There was no time to give such matters a thought. So far in the history of the war the British offensive on the 18th November, 1941—five days before Rommel himself proposed to launch a full-scale attack—has been considered one of those remarkable coincidences, a stroke of luck for Sir Claude Auchinleck which was to ensure him victory. This is not strictly true. British Intelligence also played an active part in the drama.

Officers of the Long Range Desert Group under Lieu-tenant-Colonel Haselden, disguised as Arabs, were despatched behind the German lines. But the news which reached G.H.Q. in Cairo was sparse. Arab girls brought the British a certain amount of information. Camel drivers reported Ger-man and Italian troop concentrations. But this was very little. British spies at that time were active not only in Africa. They also worked on the mainland, in Sicily and, above all, in Rome. Here the Secret Service had a number of good contacts. According to well-informed Italian sources the Italian Admiral Maugeri was a British agent who divulged details of the supplies for Rommel despatched from Italian harbours. Is it any wonder that seventy-five per cent was sunk? The full extent of the treachery has never been revealed, but one thing is certain—British agents received a wealth of information which led to many of the German defeats in Africa.

Admiral Maugeri, however, could not have been the only British source of information in the African theatre of war. From high places in Berlin, important information reached the British Secret Service via Rome. This is a chapter of war history which is both obscure and delicate, for the leakage of military information was partly coupled with political resistance against Hitler. This political struggle against German and Italian fascism, skilfully exploited by the British and American Secret Services, often became military treachery without the informant ever being aware of the fact.

One of the most profitable sources for the British espionage in Italy was the discontent of many high-ranking Italian officers with Rommel's command and his successes in Africa. The German general's victories so overshadowed the Italian defeats that wounded pride, injured vanity, together with the knowledge that the war could not be won, allowed the British spies to get a foothold in the Italian staffs. To this must be added the passionate hatred of fascism felt by most of the Royalist officer corps, a hatred which was transferred to Hitler's General—Erwin Rommel. Naturally the British knew of this rift in the Italian command. British agents sat in Rome, had their friends on the General Staff and exploited the discontent in influential circles of Royalist society.

It would be quite wrong to maintain that the officer corps in Africa was a source of treachery. This was not so. Had it been, how could Rommel have achieved his great successes? As a general rule the Italian officers were brave, decent and courageous. The Italian soldiers did their best. Their military leadership was, to a great extent, lamentable. The General Staff carried out Mussolini's orders half-heartedly, and even more grudgingly did it follow Rommel's proposals. The Italian front-line troops did their duty as soldiers. Their tragedy was that they had very poor commanders and very poor weapons. Their tanks were, to all intents and purposes, traveling coffins. Their ammunition was faulty. Here, too, it was not only the technical bankruptcy of the talented Italians that was to blame. A great part of it can be attributed to sabotage. Sabotage assumed proportions hitherto unknown in the history of the campaign.

Enthusiastic and, at the same time, skeptical, General Auchinleck examined a sheet of paper lying on his desk. His G.S.O.3, the Intelligence Officer, was excited too.

What had caused the two men to get so enthusiastic? Before them lay a sketch in Rommel's own hand showing his plans for attacking Tobruk. Nothing was missing—the points of attack, the units engaged, the position of the reserves and the weak spots in the line, and the zero hours of the individual attacks. Everything was there. Everything save one detail: there was no date. The sketch was marked D-Day. But what did that matter? They were in possession of the enemy's plans, the dream of all generals.

There were long debates. Was the plan genuine or was it a trick of the old Desert Fox? Could not this master schemer, who had so often deceived the best British strategists in Africa, have conceived such a stratagem? Why should not the man who worked with recovery units, with aircraft engines fitted to trucks to throw up dust pretending to be tanks while he attacked elsewhere, have let a false plan of attack fall into the hands of the Secret Service in order to deceive the British command? The Intelligence Service insisted that the photographed sketch and the notes on it were definitely in Rommel's handwriting, having compared it with the handwriting on other captured documents. Auchinleck immediately recognised that the details entered, the units and the whole concept of the attack bore the stamp of Rommel's genius. The crux of the matter was: "Is the source reliable?"

But what is reliable in such cases? The greatest pieces of treachery invariably bear the mark of uncertainty. After long discussions it was decided at Auchinleck's staff headquarters that there was no doubt as to the genuineness and the source of the planned attack. What a crazy business! So they had caught the Fox in his own trap. It was like a bridge player who had been given a view of his opponent's hand. In this way even the best player could lose.

Once Auchinleck had decided to accept as genuine Rommel's plan of attack, a few decisive questions remained. Firstly, the date? Rommel's attack was obviously imminent and could be launched any day. Secondly, how could this piece of luck be exploited? The sketch showed that Rommel proposed to attack the fortress from south and east. The attack could be launched tomorrow or the day after. There

was only one solution—to speed up their own preparations
and launch a counter offensive.

There was the possibility of making dispositions in besieged Tobruk to counter Rommel's plan so that the German
attack must result in a defeat. But Auchinleck decided that
this was too little. No, the whole British offensive now in
preparation must be geared to Rommel's plans. He must be
allowed to attack, and while he was in action they must fall on
his unprotected right flank and bring about the destruction of
the whole Panzer Gruppe Afrika. To Auchinleck this seemed
the only possible method of exploiting this unique chance. It
naturally meant that no changes must be made in Tobruk
itself to arouse the suspicion of Rommel's reconnaissance.
What did the defence position of Tobruk matter? It was no
longer a question of this town but of victory in Africa.

Nevertheless some steps had to be taken. The British
moves in Egypt must be swift but, above all, they must not
be spotted by the German reconnaissance. Lightning speed
was the essential. Auchinleck's staff officers put up a magnificent show. Troop movements were disguised as camel caravans. The positions were brilliantly concealed. German and
Italian reconnaissance aircraft fell down badly in the face of
these precautions. Not a single report that might have aroused
suspicion reached Rommel's headquarters.

On the 14th November Auchinleck, thanks to the almost
super-human achievements of his staff and troops, was fully
prepared. The jumping off positions were reached. "Now let
Rommel start," said Auchinleck's officers with a smile. But he
did not start.

Field Marshal Auchinleck revealed the sensational betrayal of Tobruk for the first time in the magazine *Picture Post*
of the 25th April, 1953: "In every war plan there is always a
but. In the case of Tobruk the but was the fact that we did not
know the date which Rommel had chosen for his attack. We
knew that the attack was imminent and it was possibly a mere
matter of days. But it still remained an unknown quantity."

The 14th November passed and the 15th. In Cairo and
London Rommel's offensive was feverishly awaited. But nothing happened on the 16th either.

On the 16th November London began to grow nervous.
The assault troops had been for three days in their jumping
off positions, some of them in the middle of the desert. With

each day the danger increased that the German reconnaissance would discover them. Moreover, jumping off positions for an offensive in the desert had time limitations. When nothing happened on the 17th November London lost its nerve. It is understandable when one thinks that the British had gambled everything on one card—in this instance a map. Now the doubters began to cavil. Suppose it had all been a great big swindle? Would not all their preparations come to grief? Would not they themselves perhaps be surprised? Messages sped between London and Cairo. Auchinleck wanted to wait a little longer. Churchill and the War Cabinet were opposed to this. Churchill believed from his knowledge of the German offensive position, of his own dispositions and the strength of the 8th Army as well as the surprise element, that with or without the start of Rommel's attack victory was in the bag. In his opinion to wait any longer was to ruin everything.

On the 17th November Churchill placed his commander, Auchinleck, in a cleft stick by setting the final date for the attack as the 18th November, in an order of the day to the Desert Army.

How certain Churchill was that victory was in sight can be seen in this message he sent to Auchinleck, in the name of His Majesty the King: "For the first time the troops of Great Britain and the Empire are meeting the Germans with a profusion of weapons of all types. The result of the battle will influence the whole course of the war. It will be necessary to deal the heaviest blow for final victory, for our homeland and for freedom. The Desert Army will write a new page in history, comparable with Blenheim and Waterloo. The eyes of the world are upon you. All our hearts are with you. May God uphold the right."

Churchill recalled Blenheim. This was the English name for the Battle of Hochstedt in 1704 when the Duke of Marlborough—one of his ancestors—together with Prince Eugen, in the War of the Spanish Succession, won a decisive victory over the allied French-Bavarian Army. At Waterloo, Wellington and the Prussian Marshal Blücher destroyed Napoleon's army. Rommel was to be destroyed in the same way.

Auchinleck had no alternative but to launch Operation "Crusader." This was the British code word for the attack which, in the early hours of the 18th November at Halfaya

Pass, Gambut and along the whole African front had called forth the alert signals "High Water" and "Deluge" while the skies opened their sluices.

The storm, however, was not a tragedy for the German–Italian forces alone. It also prevented Auchinleck's carefully planned use of Bomber Command which, in the opening stages of the offensive, in a mighty surprise raid was to paste the lines of communication, supply bases, harbours and staff headquarters. The R.A.F. could not take off on the 17th and 18th. In this way the bad weather was an equal handicap to both sides. While the Germans fought at Halfaya Pass and at Gambut against mud and water, while the minefields were flooded by minor avalanches causing the mines to explode and heavy weapons were washed away, while Rommel was on a visit to Rome and at Beda Littoria the casualties of Churchill's picaresque Commando raid were carried into the tents, the British spearheads broke out of their muddy holes and the British tanks skidded forward along the flooded desert tracks.

The battle began.

Who was the traitor who had delivered Rommel's plan into the hands of the British?

Field-Marshal Sir Claude Auchinleck is the only man who could give the true answer. But the British War Office evidently do not consider the time yet ripe for releasing the details of this intriguing story of betrayal.

Field-Marshall Kesselring, at that period C-in-C South in Rome, wrote to me: "At the end of November, 1941 I took over command of the German Luftwaffe forces in the Mediterranean as C-in-C South. I never heard either from Rommel or from his general staff anything about the betrayal of the German plan of attack on Tobruk in 1941. This, of course, does not mean to say that there was no treachery.

"The striking security which Rommel observed and ordered later with regard to his counter-offensive from the El Agheila position to recapture Cyrenaica can presumably be attributed to unpleasant past experiences.

"I myself mentioned to the Italian Chief of General Staff, Marshal Count Cavallero, with whom I worked on the best of terms, the probability of the betrayal of the convoys from Italy to North Africa but I could not tear down the veil which protected this treachery. Nor did the usually highly efficient listening-post service produce a satisfactory explanation.

"And yet there were irrefutable proofs that the Allies were well informed of the place, time and course of the Axis convoy sailings. Countless convoys were undiscovered and unattacked when ordered by us to alter their sailing plans. The same statements hold good when fast German ships left port. What was the source from which this information flowed into the enemy camp? The composition, loading, port and times of departure of these ships and convoys were decided by a handful of the highest-ranking Italian and German Luftwaffe officers. But would it not be a paradox to accuse any of these Italian or German leaders of treachery? Did not all these men know that the result would not only be the loss of ships and supplies but that many brave Italians and Germans would drown in the Mediterranean or be blown up with their ships? Could any man of conscience justify himself before his soldiers, his countrymen and the Good Lord?

"We are faced with a riddle. As a result of the introduction of German naval and Luftwaffe officers into the Italian supply staff mutual inspection and at the same time the greatest possible security was given against treacherous behaviour on the part of the individual.

"The losses decreased and eventually ceased when the Allied air and naval forces were employed elsewhere—for example, protecting a convoy—or were pinned down by German bombing attacks and the U-boat blockade. They increased alarmingly when large Axis convoys put to sea with the most important reinforcements and supplies. As C-in-C South I had to provide more and more air cover in order to get at least the most important reinforcements and supplies to Africa. The pilots became exhausted by their trips over the open sea by day and night, rarely being able to be in overwhelming strength at the right spot at the right time. In this way the treachery had a twofold and threefold effect on the African battle.

"The post-war years revealed a partial solution. The American, Ellis M. Zacharias, who as auxiliary officer and later head of the Office of Naval Intelligence in Italy, relates in his book *Secret Mission* that he learned everything that was planned at the Alto Commando Navale. All the important military dispositions discussed there came to his ears. He learned the secret figures of the Axis fighting forces from the

Servizio Informazione Navale. His key contact was the Italian Admiral Maugeri whose services were subsequently rewarded by the Allies."

So much for Kesselring.

Lieutenant-General Fritz Bayerlein, one of Rommel's closest, most trusted collaborators replied to my questions as follows:

"At the time of the British winter offensive of 1941 I was a lieutenant-colonel serving as Chief of Staff to the Afrika Korps, which consisted of one German and three Italian corps. At the start of the battle my headquarters were at Bardia but later I was constantly on the move.

"During the course of the offensive I learned that Rommel's plan of attack against Tobruk had been betrayed to the British. This was corroborated by statements from British prisoners. It was impossible to ascertain the name of the traitor. High-ranking Italian officers were present at many of the staff conferences of the Afrika Korps before the offensive, and also at the practice exercises which were carried out in sand boxes. I should not, however, like to tax the Italians with treachery in the case of Tobruk simply because treacherous behaviour on the part of our Allies has been proved in other instances."

General Siegfried Westphal, in November 1941 a Lieutenant-Colonel and G.S.O.1 of Rommel's Panzergruppe, told me the following:

"Since the end of September 1941 Rommel had planned to take Tobruk in a large-scale attack. He gambled upon a renewed British offensive which, in his opinion, after the replacement of General Wavell by General Auchinleck, was merely a matter of time. Rommel wanted to forestall this offensive. For him, therefore, it was a race with time and he was constantly forced to postpone his plans because supplies did not arrive. In order to learn the intentions of his adversary a reconnaissance sortie was made by the 21st Panzer Division on the 14th September, 1941, to Bir Habata. It discovered no signs of an imminent British offensive. In the following weeks the British managed by brilliant camouflage and defence to deny any view behind the lines to the Luftwaffe. Nor did any agents' reports come through to us. Thus on the 18th November, 1941, Rommel was surprised by the British offensive, not operationally but tactically. I did not know that Rommel's operational plan of the attack on Tobruk had fallen into the hands of Auchinleck."

General Westphal considered that the grouping of the defence forces in Tobruk did not suggest that the British had any knowledge of Rommel's attack tactics from the East.

Lieutenant-Colonel von Mellenthin, at the time G.S.O.3 of the Panzergruppe is of the same opinion.

I also got in touch with the man who was Rommel's clerk and secretary for many years, Sergeant-Major Böttcher; he served with the Field-Marshal from the summer of 1941 to October 1944. He was in charge of the files and had access to all personal and Secret Service documents.

Albert Böttcher wrote to me: "Field-Marshal Rommel always insisted upon the strictest security precautions to the point of pedantry. The relative importance of all documents were differentiated by the designation 'Top Secret,' 'Secret Commando matters' (Gkdo) and 'Confidential.' Top secrets were worked out exclusively with General Staff officers and transmitted by special officer messengers. Secret Commando orders could also only be taken to the units by courier. Everything else was carried by motor-cyclists or runners. The orderly room clerks were carefully chosen and had to swear a particularly heavy oath of secrecy. While top secrets had to be kept under lock and key the secret Commando documents were entrusted to the adjutants of the individual units. No one was allowed a glimpse of them unless he were personally involved. Communications to the Italian units and the Italian High Command, which had to be kept informed of all important operational decisions, took place through the Italian liaison officers.

"As a result of the fluid war and the Field-Marshal's habit of going up to the front line with his staff, there was often a danger that all the material would fall into the hands of the enemy. Many a time we stood ready with petrol to burn everything. The sketch made by Field-Marshal Rommel was returned as usual to the filing cabinet in headquarters office among his private papers so that he could elaborate on it when the time came. His correspondence was voluminous and the making of copies caused us a great deal of trouble.

"For communicating secret matters on the tele-autograph a code was used. The apparatus was not kept at tactical H.Q.

but far back behind the lines. The messages had only to be decoded and the code was changed at regular intervals. If Intelligence reported that the enemy listened in or had broken the code it was immediately changed. The head of Army Intelligence was responsible for the whole of the Information Service.

"The Intelligence in the operational zone was the province of Lieutenant-Colonel von Mellenthin, the G.S.O.3. It was his job to get information about the enemy and to furnish the G.H.Q. Staff with material for working out their plans. Of particular interest naturally were the formations, armament, land of origin and positions of the troops in the front line or in the back areas. Interrogation of prisoners, tuning in to the enemy radio, the use of interpreters, listening posts, wire-tapping and special missions into enemy territory were all part and parcel of the G.S.O.3's work. In addition he dealt with the information furnished by our own troops. The Intelligence in North Africa behind the lines was the responsibility of the Italian H.Q. staff. Since Rommel's staff was always near the front line the work often got behind-hand because we were harassed by bombers or low-flying fighters. The clerical work was not always easy, particularly at night when the light failed and we had to work in a tent or in the truck by the light of candles." This is Albert Böttcher's version.

There is an old saying—all roads lead to Rome. In our case it has a special significance. The reports of the experts on Rommel's staff show that an intelligent enemy Secret Service had plenty of opportunity to acquire valuable information via Rome. One man in the chain along which Rommel's plan passed was in the pay of the enemy. Who was it? This last question still remains to be answered.

6

AUCHINLECK ATTACKS

The "Rats of Tobruk," as the Australians in the fortress proudly called themselves, had no sleep on the night of the 17/18th November, 1941. They lay among the ruins listening to the rain, the marvellous, interminable rain which the desert could not absorb because the downpour was so heavy. The British garrison had been besieged since the summer in this seaside fortress. Admittedly they were masters of the sea. In spite of heavy losses British naval units crept secretly into the harbour at night bringing vital supplies and even reinforcements. For seven months, therefore, the defenders could thwart all Rommel's attempts to reduce the town. When the rumours started that the Germans were preparing to launch a new attack they laughed in their slit trenches. On the night of the 18th they listened to Churchill's words broadcast from London: "The Desert Army will write a new page in history comparable with Blenheim and Waterloo."

They continued to listen to the rain. Although they could not hear them they knew that British tanks, trucks and artillery were already forcing their way through the wet sticky sand. Columns several miles long were marching westward towards Tobruk—against Rommel.

A powerful armada of nearly a thousand tanks and armoured trucks was approaching to challenge some five hundred German and Italian tanks. The 30th Corps, comprising the 7th Armoured Division, the 1st South African Division and the 22nd Armoured Brigade left its assembly area at Maddelena and pressed onwards to Tobruk. The 13th Corps with the 4th Indian Division, the 2nd New Zealand Division and the 1st Army Tank Brigade came from the east to attack along the Sollum front. Fast motorised troops advanced from Jarabub, piercing deep into the lines in Rommel's rear to block his lines of communication.

The Germans had not spotted any of the dangerous British preparations. The Luftwaffe's reconnaissance had failed. Not even the British supply dumps in the southern desert on the left flank had been discovered. No agents' reports had come through. No radio messages had been intercepted, for Auchinleck had imposed the strictest radio silence.

Thus the gigantic armoured column wended their way unnoticed that night towards Tobruk. Their aim was to relieve the fortress garrison and to destroy the German army, unit by unit, as outlined in Rommel's sketch which lay on Auchinleck's desk in Cairo.

We have many accounts of the battle from the German side which started on 18th November and reached its peak on Sunday, five days later.

No one, however, has ever really assessed the achievements of the German troops between "Deluge" and Sunday, 23rd November, or the brilliant leadership of Rommel and his officers.

Just north of Gambut Sergeant Hubbuch of No. 8 Company, 8th Panzer Regiment, jumped into Lieutenant Wuth's commander tank and gave the alert. Were they about to attack Tobruk? They had practised for weeks on end with sand box models and received instruction. But for Sergeant Hubbuch it was not a question of Tobruk but of saving his own skin. The British had arrived and an ordeal lay ahead. The M.O., Doctor Estor, would have his hands full. Many of his patients would be beyond aid: Lieutenant Wuth, Lieutenant Liestmann, Gunner Packeisen, Loader Ohr and many, many others. They would all be killed. At Halfaya Pass on the morning of the 18th they were still at work repairing the heavy damage to the positions caused by the cloudburst. The commander of No. 1 Company, 104th Artillery Regiment, Lieutenant Gehrig was only saved with difficulty from drowning. Sergeant-Major Ziegler rounded up the men and weapons of the company like a mother hen safeguarding her chicks.

On my desk as I write lie accounts from men of various units, grenadiers, tank drivers of the 5th and 8th Panzer Regiments, from men of Major Bach's company at Halfaya Pass; men from the 33rd Reconnaissance Unit, motor-cyclists, men from the 82nd Magdeburg Panzer Intelligence Unit which had absorbed the survivors of the 33rd, from pioneers, flak and anti-tank gun sections and from men in isolated posts—the legendary 361st, the Legionaries of the Afrika Korps. This unit was composed of the German nationals of the old French Foreign Legion. Originally considered "unworthy to bear arms" they fought bravely and accomplished astonishing feats. All the reports and verbal accounts of this winter battle are in accord that it was the bloodiest that had so far been seen in the desert war.

On midday of the 18th November a German reconnaissance unit near Sidi Suleiman surprised a staff car of the 4th Indian Division which had lost its way and captured the crew, including a staff-sergeant. Bayerlein had this man taken to Bardia for interrogation. What came to light took his breath away. The staff-sergeant was in possession of a map which he maintained was Auchinleck's plan of attack. He also declared that the British G.H.Q. was in possession of Rommel's plan of attack for Tobruk.

"The Tobruk betrayal," therefore, had its British counterpart, with the sole difference that Rommel could only decide at a later date that his booty was genuine. His G.S.O.3 and his staff pounced upon the document eagerly, and there is no doubt that the staff-sergeant of the 4th Indian Division rendered great service to the German defence in the ensuing battle. Fritz Bayerlein, the Chief of Staff at the time, told me how the battle developed.

Units of the 7th Armoured Division, in particular the famous 11th Hussars, broke through the German–Italian positions on 20th November and reached Sidi Rezegh on the fringe of the Jebel at Tobruk. The Afrika Korps operated with success against these troops, destroying a number of tanks and winning a favourable position to attack this enemy spearhead from the rear. Enemy superiority forced Rommel to attack the enemy formations in succession in order to destroy the whole British offensive force approaching Tobruk from the south. But would General Cunningham, the Army commander, oblige and throw his armour piecemeal into the battle? He duly obliged and failed to concentrate his strength.

On the morning of 21st November the Afrika Korps attacked the 7th Armoured Brigade in the rear from the area west of Sidi Omar. In this first duel the British had two hundred tanks, a host of anti-tank guns and artillery superiority. But the British were driven back; they consolidated on the heights of the Trigh Capuzzo and organised themselves for a fluid defence.

A sortie by the Tobruk garrison during the night of 20/21st November was repulsed. The subsequent attempt to break out by fifty Infantry tanks was more successful. Units of the 70th Division attacked the positions of the Bologna Division, broke through their front, over-ran the Italian artillery and destroyed two battalions and 35 guns. The 3rd Reconnaissance Unit closed the gap but the threat to this sector of the front remained.

Rommel had ordered "fluid action" for 22nd November. Unobserved, General Crüwell had deployed the 15th Panzer Division during the night and grouped it on the enemy's flank. The 21st Panzer Division, formerly the 5th Light Division, attacked Sidi Rezegh airfield and flung the enemy back to the south. Major-General Neumann-Silkow with the 15th Panzer Division attacked the enemy on the flank and in his rear, encircling him. The 8th Panzer Regiment wiped out the 4th Armoured Brigade, one of the crack shock detachments of the British offensive. The British official history of the war emphasises that the defeat of the 4th Armoured Brigade decided the battle. Naturally the sober statement that "an Armoured Brigade was destroyed and the survivors taken prisoner" is one of those historical comments that give no hint of the audacity and cold-bloodedness behind the action.

During the evening of the 22nd, Lieutenant-Colonel Cramer's 8th Panzer Regiment lost contact with the retreating enemy. Completely unexpectedly No. 1 Section, in the pitch-black night, ran into a concentration of tanks. Not until they approached to within ten yards could they be distinguished as British. Friend and foe alike were so taken by surprise that not a shot was fired. In a flash Major Fenski, the commander of No. 1 Section, took the initiative. He drove his commander tank straight through the British hedgehog position. He radioed his orders: No. 1 Company... right hand column... and then he directed his columns and company round the enemy concentration of armour. The adjutant, Lieutenant Beck, continued to fire white flares to illuminate the scene. The enemy concentration was now brightly lit. The British were dumbfounded. In the meantime, despatch riders, under Sergeant Sauter, had forced their way into the ranks of the astonished British. "Hands up!" they ordered at the point of their sub-machine-guns. A tank crew tried to drive off. Sauter leaped on it and forced open the half-closed hatch. A burst of fire from his automatic weapon. A few of the tanks in the northern part of the hedgehog also tried to break out. "Open fire on fleeing enemy tanks!" rang out in their headphones. Explosions... Now the ring round the enemy position was complete. To avoid any panic the detachment was given repeated orders to fire only on tanks which tried to break away. Then came Fenski's order: "Commanders dismount with automatics and take prisoners. Gunlayers and loaders mount guard on the tanks." In the harsh light of the tank searchlights the British were disarmed. A few crews put up resistance. Three of Fenski's sergeants were killed. An English captain managed to set fire to three tanks before Fenski captured him.

This was the end of the 4th Armoured Brigade. Among the prisoners were 1 Brigadier, 17 officers and 150 N.C.Os; 35 tanks and countless motorised vehicles were captured. It was one of the craziest tank encounters of the war.

Major Fenski was killed on the following day.

Sorties from Tobruk did not occur that day. But now the British brought up their 13th Corps and launched an attack on a broad front against the rear of the Sollum front and Halfaya Pass. The strongpoints held with the exception of Fort Capuzzo, which was taken by the New Zealanders.

Rommel then devised the following plan: firstly the destruction of the main enemy forces operating at Tobruk by a concentrated attack of all available German–Italian forces, then a swift thrust eastwards to relieve the Sollum front.

D-Day for the first operation was Sunday, 23rd November. Rommel was a long way from the Afrika Korps and could not give his commanders orders by word of mouth. He proceeded to do something rather unusual. He sent a long telegraph message. General Crüwell in command of the Afrika Korps saw at once that the decoding of the six pages of text would take most of the morning. Should he wait? Should he lose those decisive hours during the decoding?

"Since we had a magnificent overall picture of the enemy position we did not wait for the message to be decoded but left Afrika Korps H.Q. at 05.30 hours to join the 15th Panzer

Division," Bayerlein told me. "We took only the Mammoth, "Moritz" and two staff cars, leaving all the rest behind. This was unfortunate because half an hour later the entire staff together with the G.S.O.3, Count Baudissin, were overpowered by a troop of New Zealanders who approached unobserved from the rear, and after a brisk encounter taken prisoner. General Crüwell and I escaped the same fate by a mere hairsbreadth."

A staff officer gave me the following account of the episode: "When the Korps Staff prepared to drive down from the Jebel to the Trigh Capuzzo it was already light. To our half-right we could see field guns and at the same time vehicles approaching from all directions. Were the rear units of the 15th and 21st Panzer Divisions still here? While we discussed this the first shots began to whistle. Our column immediately broke formation. The "recce" trucks and light flak went into action and fired with all they had got. Then came a lull in the firing. We took advantage of this to leap into our trucks and drove off in all directions at full speed. But we did not get very far. Beneath the combined fire of British tanks, anti-tank guns and infantry one truck after the other was put out of action. We had casualties, wounded and dead. The "recce" trucks were on fire. Exploding ammunition flew round our heads. The most important documents were quickly destroyed just before the British tanks reached us. It was General Freyberg's 2nd New Zealand Division. We were taken prisoner."

This was a common occurrence in the desert war: generals without staffs, all the experts captured together with their maps, intelligence apparatus destroyed. But Crüwell continued to lead his men toward their objective.

On the morning of the 23rd November the German–Italian forces stood south of Tobruk ready for battle. In the Sidi Rezegh area the 21st Panzer Division was in readiness for the defence. The Italian Ariete and Trieste Divisions were massed in the Bir el Gobi sector. General Crüwell intended to attack the enemy from the rear after joining forces with the Ariete advancing from Bir el Gobi in order to make full use of his armour. Towards 07.30 hours the 15th Panzer Division arrived from the south-west. All companies received the radio message: "The enemy must today be decisively beaten." Strong forces of enemy armour were recognised round Sidi

Muftah and immediately engaged. Bitter fighting ensued. Further enemy forces with huge transport columns, many tanks and guns were observed. General Crüwell, therefore, embarked upon a far wider encircling movement.

The 21st Panzer Division was still waging a heavy defensive battle against fresh enemy forces storming Rezegh—the 7th Armoured Division. Around midday the Tobruk garrison attempted a sortie with sixty tanks and strong infantry support in order to join up with the advancing armour. But the investing Italian forces put up a stout defence and the Pavia Division held its ground. Nevertheless the enemy captured several strongholds on the perimeter. The spearhead of the Ariete Division arrived with a hundred and twenty tanks. General Crüwell now flung in his combined German and Italian forces in an attack on the enemy's rear. The attack was pressed home—8th Panzer Regiment in the centre, 5th Panzer Regiment on the right and the Italians on the left. These troops, however, soon ran up against a broad field gun and anti-tank barrage which had been formed surprisingly swiftly by the South Africans. Guns of all types and calibres put down a barrage ahead of the attacking Axis battle wagons and it was impossible to penetrate this wall of fire. Tank after tank exploded in this hail of shells.

No. 8 Company of the 8th Panzer Division suffered particularly heavy losses. The company commander, Lieutenant Wuth, resolutely reached the enemy positions in his commander tank. He fell dead, shot through the head, into the arms of his gunlayer, Sergeant Hubbuch. When Lieutenant Liestmann, the leader of No. 2 column, tried to take over command there was no reply from the former leader's tank. A self-propelled 4 cm. gun had put it out of action. Liestmann was able to rescue the crew with the exception of the dead commander and the loader, but then he succumbed to an enemy bullet. The gunlayer, Packeisen, at his side was also killed. This was the fate of only one tank commander and his men. But there were many similar incidents that grim Sunday. In the second detachment of 8th Panzer Regiment alone, in addition to Wuth and Liestmann, three more tank commanders fell—Lieutenants Koser, Adam, Pisat and their crews.

The massed artillery had to be employed to silence the guns one by one. Not until late afternoon were the Germans able to breach the line in several places. The armour then rolled forward.

By the use of every trick in the art of "battle in movement" the enemy was finally compressed into a narrow sector. Since the sortie from Tobruk had brought him no relief he saw that the only choice was retreat or capitulation. Over a thousand prisoners were taken.

At that moment the Mammoth Moritz in which Crüwell and Bayerlein were sitting was suddenly surrounded by British tanks. The German cross was barely distinguishable on this captured vehicle. The British were bewildered. "The visors of our armoured car were closed," said Bayerlein. "The British tank gunners did now know with whom they were dealing." Some of them left their Mark VIs, approached the Mammoth and banged on the armoured plates. Crüwell opened the hatch and stared into the face of a British soldier who was astonished at meeting a German general in this unusual manner. "Our fate seemed to be sealed, but at that moment there were bursts of fire from somewhere near by. We flung ourselves on the floor. A German 2 cm. flak gun was firing at the roaming British tank crews. They leapt back into their battle wagons and disappeared at full speed to the south. Once more the Afrika Korps operational staff had got out of a dangerous situation."

The wide area south of Sidi Rezegh had, in the meantime, been transformed into a sea of dust and smoke. Visibility was limited, with the result that many of the British tanks and guns could slip out of the cauldron to the south and east without being captured. But a great part of the enemy remained encircled. When dusk fell the battle was still not ended. Hundreds of burning trucks, tanks and guns lit up the battlefield. Not until long after midnight would an overall picture of the event be obtained. The contingents were mustered, losses and successes recorded and the general position reviewed. The result of this battle was the removal of the immediate danger for the German troops encircling Tobruk, the destruction of a great part of the enemy's armour and the moral effect on the enemy whose finely laid plans had been so completely upset by Crüwell.

On the morning of November 24th General Crüwell reported to General Rommel on the Axis Road that the

enemy at Sidi Rezegh had been destroyed and that very few
had escaped. Victory! An incredible victory in view of the
chances possessed by the enemy and the numerical inferiority of the German defence troops. History has so far refused to
acknowledge the victory of General Crüwell and his contingents of the Afrika Korps.

Rommel would not have been Rommel if this victory had
not inspired some bold idea. He immediately conceived a
plan for attacking the enemy on the eastern front to destroy
the New Zealanders and Indians before they could join up
again with the rest of the British main forces. At the same
time he wanted to capture Habata and Maddalena, far to the
rear in the desert, in order to cut off the enemy's supplies.
"We must exploit the shock effect of the defeat and advance
in strength to Sidi Omar." That was Rommel. His Chief of
Staff, Lieutenant-Colonel Westphal, warned him, but Rommel
would not be side-tracked. He saw his great opportunity of
destroying the enemy and hammering on the gates of Egypt.

All his mobile troops took part in this operation. A weak
fighting force was left behind south of Tobruk under the
Afrika Korps Artillery Commander, Major-General Böttcher.
The ring round Tobruk was held with non-motorised forces.
"This was one of the rashest decisions ever made by Rommel.
While the tanks were still locked in this bloodiest of all
battles in the desert, he had decided upon a gamble that had
the element of genius and the wildest possible folly," writes
Alan Moorehead.

But this bold plan was based on the premise that the
main body of the British in front of Tobruk had already been
defeated and was in full flight. Had the British leaders
already thrown in the sponge?

Weary and full of bitterness, General Cunningham faced
his staff officers. He was almost in despair at the failure of the
great British plan. With a mighty offensive built up on the
knowledge of the betrayed Rommel offensive plan, Cunningham
was to have relieved Tobruk and caught the Axis forces in a
pincer movement between Sollum, Sidi Omar and Tobruk
where they were to be destroyed. And he thought it best to
break off the battle, to return to Egypt and to save what was
to be saved and try to erect a last line of defence before the
Nile.

His staff officers looked rather sceptically at their gener-

al. The younger officers had long since begun to criticise the
inflexible British leadership. Bitter remarks were to be heard.
"The R.A.F. is at its peak and the Navy rules the coast. We're
superior to them in manpower and yet we lose. Why do we
lose? Because we fight in driblets. Because we take no
gambles whereas Rommel always takes one. When the battle
began against the 7th Armoured Division and the South
Africans, the Guards Brigade and New Zealanders did not
come to their aid. When the New Zealanders were involved
in the fighting the Indians did not arrive. It's always the
same. It's like this since El Agheila." It was easy to understand the despair felt by the British officers. A few hours after
Cunningham had announced his intention of retreating, General Auchinleck arrived by air from Cairo.

There was a stormy scene between the two generals.
Auchinleck dismissed all Cunningham's protests and declared
that this battle must not end in a defeat, for that would be the
end in North Africa and would mean a British defeat on the
Nile. Auchinleck, normally the dry, raw-boned Britisher, was
inspired by that fire which so often reveals itself in British
history in moments of crisis. He threw all caution to the
winds. At this critical moment he was prepared to sacrifice
the last man and the last gun in order to avoid defeat. The
8th Army must come through or never return.

Auchinleck dismissed General Cunningham on the
battlefield—a disturbing measure. He replaced him by General Ritchie, a man who had also grown up in the old school
of British strategy. But in face of Auchinleck's firm order he
had no other alternative than to gamble everything on one
card. He stopped the retreat of the 7th Armoured Division.
He resorted to the most audacious action to restore the
fighting spirit of the troops so that they would hold against
the determined German attacks until the British forces were
reorganised. Ritchie and Auchinleck stopped at nothing to
achieve their object. There were for example the "Jock
Columns", Brigadier Jock Campbell's storm troops. The British
war reporter, Alan Moorehead, writes concerning these special units:

"Each commander's orders were simply these—'Get out
and behind the enemy. Attack anything you see. . . .' So the
partisans of the desert were born. As fast as they could be
put together Auchinleck rushed them out into the desert.

Within a few days he had twenty or more groups behind the enemy lines, burning, shooting, cutting in and running away, laying ambushes in the wadis, diverting enemy tanks, breaking signal wires, laying false trails, breaking up convoys, raiding airfields, getting information. It was a makeshift while the 8th Army worked desperately to reorganise itself, but it began taking immediate and heavy effect."

This admission of the use of these British partisans must be considered in order to see in the right perspective the employment of the Brandenburgers, so harshly criticised by the British after the war. These German counterparts of Campbell's "Jock Columns" and the Long Range Desert Group repaid an eye for an eye. On their daring and adventurous missions they penetrated almost to Cairo, operating behind the enemy H.Q.s, blowing up bridges, installing listening posts and inflicting heavy losses behind the lines.

The "Jock Columns" caused great havoc among the Italian units, far to the rear. The Italians were therefore particularly ruthless in their clashes with these partisans.

Corporal Gerhard Freydank was collecting water supplies one day at the fresh water spring in Derns. A young Arab of about twenty asked for a lift in his Volkswagen. Freydank refused—it was forbidden. At this the boy, who by his looks must have been of novel origin, proudly and mysteriously brought out a pass signed by Rommel asking that all help and support should be given to the holder of this document since he was in the pay of the Germans. Naturally Corporal Freydank took the man along with him. On the road to Sollum they were stopped by a squad of Italian Military Police. The Italians looked suspiciously at the Arab and hauled him out of the car. The brown-skinned youth protested vigourously and called upon the German to protect him. But the Italians refused. They stripped him and found what they were looking for. Between his thighs he carried a special bag of Morocco leather full of Egyptian notes, Italian lire and the British special identity pass issued to the "Jock Columns" operating behind the Axis Lines. Corporal Freydank, greatly shaken, climbed back into his Volkswagen. He had given a lift to a fine guest. He turned his head away as the Arab fell on his knees and begged the Italians for mercy. He put his foot hard down on the accelerator, and above the sound of his engine he heard the reports of three revolver shots. A little tragedy by the roadside and the great trek continued, the tanks rattled and the motor-cycles spluttered. The desert could absorb a great quantity of blood.

In the meantime the battle was still raging round Tobruk. Rommel, believing that he had defeated the British assault troops, had started on his bold raid. On the morning of 24th November, after General Crüwell had reported his success in the Sunday battle, Rommel had jumped into his staff car and called out to his G.S.O.1, Lieutenant-Colonel Westphal: "I'm driving to Sidi Omar. I shall lead the 21st Panzer Division against Halfaya Pass." Westphal tried to remonstrate with him. He had received the first reports from the Luftwaffe Reconnaissance which showed that the British had already taken up their positions at Bir el Gobi. But Rommel would not listen. He pulled his Chief of Staff, Major-General Gause, into the car and drove off at full speed. He continued to drive at full speed through the routed enemy troops towards the Egyptian frontier. He wanted to make a surprise attack on the 2nd New Zealand and the 4th Indian Divisions operating in the Sollum area before they could rejoin the retreating units. Furthermore, he wanted to cross the Egyptian frontier zone and attack Habata and Maddalena and, at the same time, destroy the British G.H.Q. and the great British supply bases. In this surprise attack he intended to cut off the whole British army from its source of supplies and then destroy it. Rommel sped like a maniac ahead of the 15th and 21st Panzer Divisions to Sidi Omar. The mirage of a ravished Egypt lay before his eyes, the Suez Canal, the Nile and a great victory. He did not know that Auchinleck had stopped the rout before Tobruk.

Rommel sped on at fifty miles an hour, followed by his signallers. But the radio trucks soon lagged behind and Rommel went on without them. That evening he reached Sidi Omar. The British leaders were flabbergasted. Where on earth had the Germans come from? What was their destination? Rommel immediately despatched the 21st Panzer Division against Sidi Suleiman in order to seal off the Halfaya Front from the east. He led the division in person through the broad barbed wire at Gasr el Abid on the Egyptian frontier—through the actual breach that the British had made in it for their offensive. The 15th Panzer Division was given orders to attack the enemy at Sidi Omar. For this attack

Rommel had detailed the 5th Panzer Regiment to join the 15th Panzer Division.

But the battle did not go according to plan. There seemed to be a jinx on it. The reinforced 4th Indian Division had dug in round Sidi Omar just before Rommel's attack. His forces were too weak. Once more his plan had been too bold. The German attack failed and the 5th Panzer Regiment suffered heavy losses. Its brilliant commander, Lieutenant-Colonel Stephan, was killed. Night fell over the desert. The burning wrecks of tanks glowed eerily in the darkness. Corpses lay all around, friend and foe side by side.

In the meantime Rommel had accompanied the 21st Panzer Division further north and despatched them to attack the New Zealanders who were storming the Sollum front. Major-General von Ravenstein was to penetrate deep into Egypt with the 21st Panzer Division after the defeat of the New Zealanders.

On his way back to Sidi Omar to rejoin the 15th, Rommel's car broke down. The German C-in-C remained all night alone with Gause in the desert, in the centre of a giant battlefield. No one knew the whereabouts of his own troops or those of the enemy. By a remarkable coincidence General Crüwell's Mammoth Moritz suddenly arrived in this desert ocean with Bayerlein. They spotted the German car and stopped, "My God—Rommel!" "Give us a lift," laughed the general, although he was shivering with cold.

Anyone who thinks that everything now went well is mistaken. Crüwell and Bayerlein were also without escort. They had fled in their Mammoth and Rommel had only this circumstance to thank for his rescue. The leaders of the Axis troops in Africa were now in a single vehicle, the wooden floor of which would not even have kept out a single mine of the thousands which lay in the desert. Then suddenly they spotted the tanks. They were not German but tanks of the 4th Indian Division. It was a stroke of luck that the German leaders were in a captured Mammoth which did not arouse the curiosity of the Indians. To right and left the tanks rattled past only a few yards away, followed by Indian motor-cyclists. Finally they reached the barbed wire entanglement. But there was no gap to slip through—impossible to cross this obstacle.

Rommel was furious. "I'll take over," he said. He pushed

Frazier-Storch

the aide-de-camp aside and directed the driver. "Right—left."
But this time Rommel's legendary sense of direction failed
him. Once more the Mammoth met a group of British trucks.
They were heavy Dodges. What irony? The German C-in-C
within a stone's throw away! That was the war in Africa!

While Rommel on his desert trip was cut off from his
staff, things occurred in Tobruk as Westphal had feared. The
British forces in the Sidi Rezegh area, thanks to Auchinleck's
initiative, had pulled themselves together and now attacked
the front abandoned by the Africa Korps. The garrison at
Tobruk at the same time resumed its sorties. The German
ring round Tobruk was pierced and Böttcher's troops were
subjected to a devastating bombardment. In vain Westphal
tried to reach his commander, Rommel, to inform him of the
position. Five Storchs were lost in the attempt. The wireless
operators sent SOS after SOS over the air. No reply!

Then Westphal decided to take matters into his own hands. He called the Afrika Korps back into the crisis zone—back to Tobruk.

Wireless operator Carl Dorn rushed with the message received to the Chief of Staff of the 21st Panzer Division, Major Freiherr von Susskind. The latter was standing with von Ravenstein who looked tired and depressed. The runner handed him the paper and asked for a receipt. Von Ravenstein signed it, read and obeyed. With his few remaining tanks he fought his way back through the New Zealanders to Tobruk. Rommel's prophesy, "You could end the campaign today," had proved wrong.

When Rommel, on his return, learned of von Ravenstein's order to the 21st to retire, he flew into a rage, for he believed it was an enemy trick and a faked message. However, after examining the strategical map in his headquarters he did not utter another word but retired to bed. The following day he applauded Westphal's order. He realised that his Chief of Staff had had to take a bold decision; developments had dictated this decision to break off the rash adventures ordered by the C-in-C. Rommel himself would probably never have given the order—he would have reacted in a different way to the position at Tobruk. This is pure theory, for he himself never made a comment on this subject.

He jumped once more into his car and drove from unit to unit in order to master the difficulties which were becoming ever more serious. He drove through the enemy lines, crossed an airfield occupied by the British, was chased and shot at but what Frederick the Great once said held good for this man: "A successful General does not only need to be capable, he must also have luck." And Rommel was lucky.

At full speed he crossed a small sand dune and came upon a New Zealand field hospital. He could not afford to show the slightest sign of nervousness. He got out of the car, ordered his driver and his aide to drive round the tent and wait for him at the other end. He himself marched boldly inside, played the conqueror and behaved as though the hospital and the surrounding territory were still in German hands. He greeted the officers of the guard and the doctors jovially, asked them if they were lacking in anything and promised an immediately despatch of medical supplies. As he took his leave the British doctors saluted. And he was gone.

Ten minutes later the New Zealanders, on the arrival of a British transport, realised the trick Rommel had played on them. The story ran like wildfire through North Africa. But of what use was all the bravado of generals, officers and soldiers? An unlucky star stood over the November campaign.

Many people believe that Major-General von Ravenstein, at the moment he gave the order to retire, was close to a huge British supplies dump. Another quarter of an hour's march and the destruction of these vital supply dumps could have brought Auchinleck into a disastrous position.

Rommel continued to rebel against the knowledge that Sunday's victory had turned out to be a defeat. He would not accept that the retreat of the Afrika Korps from the Tobruk front had given Auchinleck an unexpected opportunity. Both sides fought with the courage of despair. The British because they knew that their defeat would mean a German victory in North Africa, the Germans because they knew that a defeat would cancel out all the blood and sweat of a whole year. There were no longer any fronts. Rommel now recalled all the forces he had sent to the Sollum front for the struggle for Tobruk. Bach's men on Halfaya Pass defended doomed positions, but they fought like tigers.

In the meantime General Freyberg and his New Zealanders fought their way through at the point of the bayonet from the east to Tobruk. Freyberg's troops had held out against two mighty tank and artillery attacks and now went over to the attack themselves. During this they made a valuable capture. They caught the general commanding the 21st Panzer Division, von Ravenstein. Much "fiction" has been written about this episode, and I therefore asked the general to give me his version of the story.

During the night of the 28th November von Ravenstein had met General Crüwell's staff car and had reported the arrival of the 21st Panzer Division. Once more Crüwell had two armoured divisions at his disposal and decided immediately to exploit the favourable position. He ordered both divisions to attack the British forces at Sidi Rezegh on the following day. This thrust was to change the situation in the sector south-east of Tobruk. Before General von Ravenstein drove back to his division that night it was agreed that on the following day at 07.00 hours the same order should be given to No. 15 Panzer Division. Von Ravenstein drove off at full speed. On his lap lay the map on which Bayerlein had marked with a cross the position of the 15th. They had a drive of ten miles ahead of them. Corporal Hans Kranzke from Berlin-Oberschoeneweide drove in the old-fashioned way by compass and Tacho, aided by Gunner Peltel, an eighteen-year old baker from Berlin, who had the reputation in the division of being one of the best and most cautious pathfinders. In Africa they were called "Franzers." At times, however, even the best of them were caught.

In the grey light of dawn they saw vehicles on the horizon. According to the map it was the sector which Bayerlein had marked with a cross. That's the 15th, thought von Ravenstein. Suddenly they were fired on by heavy machines at a distance of twenty yards. The car came to a standstill and caught fire. The driver, Kranzke, was wounded. They all got out and took cover but it was too late. They had stumbled into a well-camouflaged New Zealand position. They were called to surrender. General Freyberg learned at breakfast that the famous von Ravenstein of 21st Panzer Division was his prisoner.

General von Ravenstein's capture had an exciting aftermath a few months later on the 30,000 ton troop transport *Pasteur*. Eleven hundred German P-O-Ws were being taken in this former luxury liner from Cairo to Canada. On board were also British service personnel, and wives and children of the former garrison troops in the Near East. The German prisoners, divided into officers and other ranks, were berthed in the middle and boat decks. The two generals, Schmidt and von Ravenstein, had cabin 269 on D Deck. In the neighbouring cabin were the M.O., Dr. Werlemann, an assistant M.O., Wingender, and the Catholic chaplain, Frense, from Hamm. They were all keen skat players. Instead of playing skat they worked out plans for escape. Things looked quite promising. The *Pasteur* sailed through the Red Sea. If the British crew were overpowered it would not be very difficult, with the aid of the German mercantile marine officers among the prisoners, to steer the ship to Singapore. All the preparations were made with the greatest care. Knives were procured and hidden, bludgeons were made. The men were formed into Commandos and rehearsed in their tasks. Naturally, a large number of the prisoners below decks had to be initiated. The doctor and the chaplain saw to this on their visits. They

cautioned the men to be discreet but there was far too much
gossip. The British guards got wind of the affair and noticed
the nervousness and zeal of the German infantrymen. They
placed a German-speaking stooge among the prisoners and
then the Tommies went into action.

On the 11th March at 23.00 hours a detachment of sailors
burst into cabin 269. The generals were placed in solitary
confinement. In three other separate cells sat Major Bach,
Pastor Frense and the M.O. The British sailors wanted to
fling the generals and suspected ringleaders of the conspiracy
into the sea, for the rumour had spread through the ship that
in the event of the success of their plan the Germans intended to lower the women and children in boats and cast them
adrift. Naturally this was nonsense and the crew of the
Pasteur eventually came to their senses.

Later, in Canada, the Afrika Korps boys worked out
many plans for escape. Wherever they cropped up these
planners of escapes found boon companions among the submarine men and the airmen. The desert warriors, even as
P-O-Ws, brought a spirit of adventure into the prison camps.

7

WHERE IS GAMBARA?

They sat in the shade of their light truck and discussed
God and the Universe. Moreover, in spite of the heat and the
flies they discussed these subjects with enthusiasm. "No one
relishes dying and it is ridiculous to expect him to," said
Dreyer, in reply to a sceptical corporal. "Naturally no one
wants to die. Even Christ on the cross rebelled against
death." They all knew that their lieutenant in civilian life was
a pastor in Hitzacker, a popular pastor with a charming wife
and four delightful children all of whom they knew from
photographs. But Dreyer was also a very well loved and
capable officer. Everyone in the detachment found it odd that
such a serious man of God could also be a very capable

lieutenant who understood his machine-gun to perfection and had a great reputation among the motorised troops. One of the young soldiers asked: "And can a pastor be an officer and kill?"

"Naturally," replied the lieutenant. "You've only got to look at me."

"But what about the bible?" was the curt reply.

"Mm," said Dreyer. He wanted to talk about the translation of "to kill" and "to murder" in the holy script, but this reply remained unspoken in the burning African desert. It was never given... neither that day nor in Africa—in any case not by Lieutenant Dreyer—for there was a sudden alert.

A despatch rider drove up at full speed. The order was: an immediate assault on Sidi Azeiz. There was no further time for discussion. The order was there, vivid and urgent.

It was one of those complicated situations which so often occurred in the Tobruk-Sollum area between June and November 1941. The British spearhead had advanced and captured Sollum and Sidi Omar. Enemy armour had been reported north and west of Capuzzo and Sidi Azeiz. The 15th Panzer Division waited off Bardia on Rommel's orders. The reinforced 33rd Engineers Battalion was ordered to attack Sidi Azeiz.

It was a battle full of surprises. Reconnaissance units had reported that Sidi Azeiz was only weakly held, but at the end of the conflict the battalion brought in two generals and seven hundred prisoners; sixty guns and one hundred trucks were captured. One of the British generals captured was Brigadier Hargest who had made his name in Greece and Crete. He was disgusted and depressed at being taken prisoner and stood by his car as Rommel drove up. Hargest raised his hand to his cap. Rommel returned his salute and said consolingly: "There's no reason to be depressed. You and your men fought very gallantly."

Lieutenant Dreyer was ordered to take the two generals back to Bardia. When he had not returned that night his C.O. began to get worried. He was even more worried when Corporal Willy Voigt reported that Lieutenant Dreyer had driven off in the general's car following the British driver and a few soldiers. "Well, you can say goodbye to him," said Major Ehle. "Dreyer was always an optimist who believed in human nature. The British naturally turned off somewhere after Sollum and Dreyer is a P-O-W." Corporal Voigt's face was a study. He was as offended as though he had been accused of cheating at cards. "That doesn't go for Lieutenant Dreyer, Herr Major. He'll get them to Bardia—I'll bet my life on it."

Voigt paused for a long while and looked serious—"He knows every inch of the route, every track. He never lost his way in France and could find every foxhole in Capuzzo blindfolded. No, Herr Major, with Arnold—I beg your pardon—with Lieutenant Dreyer—nothing doing! He'll take the Tommies where he was told to take them or else I'll eat that camelthorn bush." Voigt was proud of his long speech and his C.O. was almost convinced. "All right," he said, "I'll make you eat that bush if you're wrong, even if I have to stand over you for eight hours." Corporal Willy Voigt did not have to fulfil his bet because half an hour later they received marching orders for Bardia. Excitement was at its peak. Voigt's conversation with Major Ehle had been repeated throughout the battalion. Only in Dreyer's company did calm reign. "Arnold? If he's not already in Bardia and the British generals with him, I'll eat my . . ." Heaven knows what they would all have been prepared to eat.

But there was no need to worry. The generals were there with the pastor, although he was not found immediately. He was sitting with an Italian chaplain having a long conversation about God and the Universe and had completely forgotten the war. He had had a few glasses of chianti which the Italian had provided. Dreyer poured out the last contents of the bottle.

The men of his company were sad when Dreyer became aide to the 15th Panzer Division. This Hitzacker pastor was a very versatile man. He could roast a gazelle in the middle of the desert and make your mouth water. He could lead a patrol without getting it fired on. He never ordered one of his men to fetch a wounded comrade out of the line, but always jumped to it himself and was fully prepared at any moment to perform a service over a man when he had to be buried. Even the most cynical youngster refrained from mocking when he said the Lord's Prayer and almost believed, because the man who prayed in front of him was so sincere.

In this faith, too, he died in September 1942 in the thick of the fighting at El Alamein. In a loud voice he said the

Lord's Prayer as he had so often said it before his men... "And forgive us our trespasses...." Lieutenant Dreyer, the pastor from Hitzacker. Why did I tell this story—a minor episode in the history of the war? Not to palliate the horrors of war, nor to divert the reader's attention from its grim fury by a sentimental tale. I have told it merely to show that in the war in North Africa, in spite of everything, a vestige of humanity remained. Friend and foe alike were in the thrall of the desert. Here the war was still to a certain extent a military adventure. It was the burning, menacing wilderness of sand that laid down the rules, but it was the spirit of the soldiers who fought there which insisted that these rules were kept. Usually, but of course not always.

On the 2nd December, 1941, Rommel sent the following telegram to the Führer's headquarters at Rastenburg. "In the uninterrupted heavy fighting of the 18th November to the 1st December, 814 enemy tanks and scout cars were destroyed and 127 aircraft shot down. The amount of booty taken in weapons, ammunition and trucks is considerable. The number of prisoners exceeds 9,000, including three generals." These figures give a sober report of what happened in the grim days of the 18th November to the beginning of December in North Africa.

But the drama was still not over. Face to face like gladiators Rommel and Auchinleck wrestled for Tobruk, the cornerstone of Egypt. Rommel's reconnaissance had reported that the British were constantly bringing up new troops. Around Bir el Gobi, Auchinleck was massing strong forces which were intended finally to wrest Tobruk from the German clutches.

Rommel's reply was to attack. The eastern part of the Tobruk perimeter was abandoned in order to free troops. On the night of the 4th/5th December the Afrika Korps advanced westwards through the 3,000-yard wide corridor between El Duda and Sidi Rezegh. The blow was to be delivered with the support of an Italian Corps approaching from the northeast. But since the Italians neither massed nor were ready for battle the Afrika Korps had to "go it alone" on the midday of 5th December. The stalwart Young Fascist Division alone joined the Afrika Korps north-west of El Gobi. The first assault ran up against the Guards Brigade and a little later against the reformed 7th Armoured Division. These units which Rommel had believed to be defeated appeared once more on the battlefield in strength. Now the miracle of the British reinforcements and supplies was revealed. While the Afrika Korps was heavily engaged at Bir el Gobi the 70th Infantry Division made a sortie from Tobruk, attacking the weakened German–Italian perimeter defences in the rear. The vital heights of Duda—Belhamed were taken. Rommel's forces were hard pressed. Nevertheless he tried to stage a diversion. He demanded a superhuman effort from his officers and men.

On 6th December the Afrika Korps was in action again. Unless it succeeded in repulsing the enemy a major defeat was unavoidable. General Crüwell with his 15th and 21st Panzer Divisions pressed home his attack and once more the Ariete and Trieste Divisions did not take part. The Italian commanders reported that their men were exhausted and no longer capable of fighting a battle. Italian aid might easily have turned the scales in this battle. The British had already retreated at Bir el Gobi before the desperate blows of the Afrika Korps, in order to avoid encirclement, but the Germans were short of troops. The Italians should have been there. They need not even have fought, but merely ensured the flanks and closed the rim of the cauldron.

Crüwell saw his opportunity, the last great opportunity. He kept sending signals to Rommel and to the Italian Corps Commander, Gambara. He begged, he implored, he ordered. "Where is Gambara?" was sent time after time "in clear" to Rommel. "Where is Gambara?" The slogan became monotonous. Neither Gambara nor his divisions appeared on the battlefield. The faces of the German officers grew hard and embittered, and in those days it was not wise for Italian officers to approach them.

On 7th December the battle was still raging. Rommel was now in danger of being outflanked by superior British forces and encircled. One by one the German tanks were put out of action, either shot to pieces, set on fire or left without fuel. One of the most brilliant commanders in Africa, General Neumann-Silkow, commanding the 15th Panzer Division, was killed standing up in the turret of his command tank. He was a popular general, very much respected by his men. They all knew of the incident which took place a few days before his death.

A British supply dump was to be captured and the 15th had fought their way to within two hundred yards of it. Motorised infantry dismounted and attacked. Close behind the tanks, which were under heavy artillery and anti-tank fire, the men leapt from their motor-cycles and attacked. General Neumann-Silkow, as usual, was in the front line in his command tank observing from his open turret. One of the infantrymen called to him: "For God's sake close the lid, man!" In the firework display he had neither recognised the command tank nor the general. Some slap-happy sergeant-major, he thought. When the infantryman once more had to take cover from the heavy bombardment near the general's tank he shouted again: "For Christ's sake close the lid or you will have had it!" As though to stress his words a shell burst close ahead of the tank, making the worried infantryman press his face in the mud. At this moment the figure standing in the tank turret roared: "Get cracking out of this barrage!"

"Good idea," replied the infantryman. "You can report to me later and share my loot."

The stronghold was captured. Corporal Potas was an expert "organiser." One of the first men inside the captured position, he was interested only in the booty. Moreover, this was his job, for each company had its own special loot section and Potas of the motorised infantry was almost a genius. He had a sixth sense for brand new trucks, fuel, water and delicacies. Obviously Potas had tanked up the best British light truck and taken on a full cargo by the time the "fall-in" was sounded. At this moment General Neumann-Silkow drove up. He called to No. 1 Company commander: "I have to report to one of your men who is collecting the booty," he said with a laugh.

"That must be Potas," replied Lieutenant Buhr. "Potas, report to the company commander."

Potas appeared. He was a trifle suspicious. What soldier is not suspicious when he is ordered to report to the company commander? Neumann-Silkow recognised him at once and said: "Where's the booty you promised, Corporal?"

Potas apologised profusely and was about to make the excuse that he did not recognise the general when Neumann-Silkow cut him short. "It's not a question of that, Corporal, but I want the booty you promised me."

"At once, Herr General." Potas rushed off and returned

with three of his mates carrying a load of chocolates, cigarettes and tinned meat. "Have you enough for yourselves?" asked the general. No senior officer could ever have seen such a look of surprise on an infantryman's face. The look seemed to say: "No private in the world could be so dumb as to give a general so much booty that he deprived himself." Neumann-Silkow understood and made off with his treasure trove, a broad grin on his face. He did not live long enough to enjoy all the chocolate and the tinned meat. Corporal Potas also fell in action six months later while driving one of Lieutenant Servas' self-propelled guns on the 1st June, 1942, before Got el Ualeb.

On the 15th December Rommel reported to the German High Command: "After four weeks of continuous battle with heavy casualties, despite brilliant individual achievements, the fighting power of the troops has been impaired because we have received no supplies of weapons and ammunition. I intend to hold the Gazala sector, but a retreat vis El Mechili-Derna will be unavoidable at the latest on the night of the

Kubelwagon

16/17th December in order to avoid being encircled and destroyed by a superior enemy."

This retreat from Cyrenaica, the possession of which had been disputed in eight months of bloody fighting, cannot be recorded as a mere event of military history. Only the strategists can do this. Those dramatic days at the end of 1941 must be reported by the men who were actually harried along the dusty tracks—fighting day after day, making forced marches by night, a prey to the heat, sandstorms and the icy cold at night, constantly in battle, often several days without food and with rationed fuel, and even worse: without water. No wonder that various units had to amalgamate.

"How strong is the Motorised Infantry Battalion?" asked Major Kriebel, the G.S.O.1 (Ops) of the 15th Panzer Division.

"Five officers, fourteen N.C.O.s, fifty-eight men, three self-propelled guns, ten Volkswagens, five heavy trucks and six motor-cycles," reported the adjutant, Lieutenant Kordel.

"Is that all?"

"Yes, Major, that's all."

A few weeks before this battalion had a complement of four hundred and eighty men. The missing lay in their graves before Sidi Rezegh, before Sollum or far in the desert between Tobruk and Sidi Omar, or had been taken prisoner.

Major Kriebel turned to Lieutenant-Colonel Ballerstedt: "The divisional commander does not wish the motorised infantry to be engaged any more as rearguard troops. The survivors must be reorganised."

"But they must continue today," replied Ballerstedt. "Just once more."

"Sollum must be held until dawn," was the order. Once more they had to act as rearguard, cover the retreat, beat off the enemy as long as they could . . . and then get away if they could.

Sollum lies to the east of Benghazi. When these motorised troops forming the rear unit drove through it at midday, the British were already on their heels. They hardly had time to take on the free provisions, ammunition and fuel before the dumps were blown up. Mighty columns of flame and smoke rose into the air. Material worth millions of pounds was destroyed.

Lieutenant Kordel, who had done two years philosophy at college before becoming a soldier, stood with Lieutenant

Dreyer, the aide, and Lieutenant Servas by the road on the
Via Balbo with the pathetic remains of the battalion.

"About turn to Sollum. Same drill as yesterday. Hold out
until dawn tomorrow."

"Provided the Tommies are not already there," grumbled Kordel.

Servas led the column, consisting of captured self-propelled
guns which he made famous throughout the Afrika Korps, a
heavy truck with machine-gun crew and two cyclist despatch
riders.

"Sollum free of the enemy and occupied by one company," reported Corporal Raug on his return from a reconnaissance. Actually No. 11 Company of the 361st Infantry Regiment had already taken up defence positions in Sollum while
a Mark IV tank with broken tracks provided the artillery. "It
smells like a barber's shop back there," said Raug. This was
not surprising. In Benghazi they had discovered an undestroyed
German dump full of soap and other toilet articles. They had
filled their packs and each man possessed at least ten tooth
brushes and enough soap to last him a lifetime, besides toilet
water which the Germans had appropriated from the British
loot. Now they sat in their positions delighted with their
haul.

"Motorised Infantry Battalion to secure the Jebel descent south-west of Sollum," ran the next radio order.

"God be with you," said the C.O., as he took leave of
the company commander whose prospects of avoiding captivity were very slight. "We'll come and fetch you if we possibly
can."

At Solluch the Jebel extends a good ten miles into the
desert. According to the map, two tracks led over the steep
escarpment. When the battalion entered the village shortly
before dusk they found a company of the 361st Infantry
Regiment covering the plain in front of the Jebel. Since they
had no mode of transport they had become rearguard troops.

"The Jebel is free of the enemy. British scout cars, trucks
and tanks on the other side," reported the company commander.

On exploring the second track Lieutenant Servas, just as
he reached the top of the Jebel, ran into an English scout car
coming from the other side. A surprise encounter. It was a
question of who fired first. Servas was the winner and barred
the way back to the next two scout cars. Then he had to beat

a swift retreat, for an entire British reconnaissance unit was making its way up the Jebel.

"Things look grim for tomorrow morning. We shall be a sitting target for those fellows up there," commented Sergeant-Major Friedrich. He himself still had a heavy machine-gun. The trucks were hidden as well as possible in a depression and an outpost placed on the edge of the Jebel. The remainder of the little troop spread out into a semi-circle.

No. 10 Company received orders to retire. "Travel north-west, and when you reach the Via Balbo you will have made it." Lieutenant Kordel drove to Solluch to see whether the battalion had occupied the position. He returned after three hours carrying a lamb only two hours old. On the way back in the pitch darkness he had lost his way and met an Arab shepherd who had given him the lamb as a present. "I couldn't refuse it," said Kordel. Corporal Siegfried Behrens shook his head. As a peasant from the Altmark his heart was touched. "You must take the little fellow back, *Herr Leutnant*. It's not worth slaughtering, and we've got no milk so it will die on us."

"Good God, Behrens, you'd better start thinking how we're going to get out of here tomorrow morning. If you have any bright ideas I promise you we'll bring back the lamb alive."

They sensed that the night was drawing to a close, and in a flash it was daylight. The outpost reported: "Tommies are getting ready. Their engines are already revving up."

They took their bearings, for the first light of dawn had to be exploited. Tommy must be made to think that the front line was there . . . and then—up and away!

Now the Jebel and the descent were lit up by the dawn. Night was over and the first British scout cars drove slowly down the slope. Couldn't Servas see them? He and his self-propelled guns were hidden in a depression. Now he must fire at any moment. Almost at once he scored three direct hits.

The Tommies on the slope jumped out of their cars to be met with a hail of machine-gun fire. They had not yet spotted the German positions and they fired their two-pounders into the open terrain. But soon the shells were falling among the battalion half circle. More and more often Sergeant-Major

Schulze heard the familiar cry: "Stretcher bearer! Stretcher bearer!"

Once more all weapons fired with everything they had, trying to fox the Tommy that they were in strength. Then cease-fire, and to the trucks. Leap back, flat on their faces, about turn and fire. Then the next man jumped as though playing leap frog... but this time they must make it snappier. Lieutenant Servas was firing madly, but not at the Jebel. He was firing to the right where Tommies had appeared in carriers and scout cars.

In the meantime the others leapt into their vehicles and drove off at full speed in a north-westerly direction. Corporal Voigt had to wait until he had got his staff into the truck. Then he, too, sped off in order to reach the head of the column. One of the Volkswagens had stopped. Bad luck! That was the fate of rearguard troops. Nothing remained for them except captivity.

Servas as usual was magnificent and roared up to the lead of the column with his guns. Halt... Fire... And off again. What a bit of luck that they had these superb British self-propelled guns.

Suddenly they saw tents. It was an Arab group and they were firing from a kneeling position as in the time of the Boer War. They fired at anything that barred their passage. Weren't those aircraft? "Italians!" Behrens suddenly shouted. It was true. The Arabs were firing at Italian aircraft on a desert airfield. Now the spearhead of the battalion had reached them. The Arabs flung themselves on their faces in the sand. But Lieutenant Kordel and his men had neither the time nor the inclination to bother with them. They forced their way through to the Italian airfield and there they were due for an even greater surprise. The Italians stood there with their hands above their heads. They had mistaken the approaching Germans for the British.

Servas with his three anti-tank guns was already firing at the attacking British scout cars. This restored the morale of the Italians. They rushed over to their three ack-ack guns and four tanks. And suddenly two Italian companies appeared from nowhere. They were inspired by the German example and fired as best they could. Two hours before, British scout cars had appeared on the airfield and been repulsed by the

Italians, but when they saw the motorised infantry bearing down they thought they must be British and had lost their nerve. Now they were in good fettle once more and as happy as children. "Avanti! Avanti!" They were delighted that someone was there to give them orders. They leapt into their trucks. The three aircraft took off and the ground staff drove away.

Major Ehle's men could not shake off the Italian airmen and invited them to a party. When the battalion commander reported to Lieutenant-Colonel Bayerlein he nodded his head. "You've been lucky again."

The motorised infantry had been lucky, but the 11th Company of the Panzerhagen Regiment had been taken prisoner. "Now we have only nine trucks. Nine little nigger boys . . . ." quoted Servas.

"But we have three anti-tank guns," broke in Kordel.

"All of them will go in the bag," said Dreyer with a grin.

Dreyer, Servas, Kordel! None of them ever returned home. Dreyer and Servas were buried nine months later before El Alamein and Kordel met his death in Russia.

8

"THE SKY PILOT OF HELLFIRE"

From the 21st November, 1941, the positions around Sollum were held by the 10th Oasis Company, with the remains of the 12th and the staff of 300th Oasis Reserve Battalion commanded by Captain Ennecerus. On the 11th January, 1942, a complement of only seventy remained holding this outpost. In the near-by Halfaya Pass, Major Bach with his men barred the coastal road to the British advanced front. Night after night the enemy tried to break through the Sollum position. Hand to hand fighting was the order of the day.

On the 10th January, 1942, Ennecerus ordered the last rations to be issued: 20 grammes of bread, a handful of rice and a spoonful of currants per man. Morale sank to zero. "This must be the end," said the men. On the following morning the British attacked and the troops who, the day before, had muttered "this must be the end," fired like demons. They fired until their barrels were hot. An enemy break-through in strength between the pillbox and the battalion "casemate" was repulsed by the signallers. Prisoners were taken. The positions remained in German hands.

A report from Ennecerus' battalion reads as follows: "On the morning of the 12th January the British put up a heavy barrage, training all their batteries and mortars on our position. Houses which had previously been only badly damaged were now razed to the ground." The first attack was repelled; a second attack followed. All that remained in the battalion "casemate" were tracers. After the last of these had been fired, Captain Ennecerus sent a prisoner forward with a white flag. Capitulation. The captain gave orders to his three strong points: "Destroy your weapons! Prepare to surrender!"

Black with filth, lousy and in rags, half-starved and exhausted after fifty-six days of continuous fighting, the men fell in.

"Comrades," the captain began, "comrades. . . ." Then he shook his head and turned abruptly on his heel. He did not want them to see the tears in his eyes. He thought of the dead. Sollum had fallen.

And what happened at the famous "Hellfire Pass"? At the old, strongly contested keypoint on the route to Egypt?

I listened to two men's accounts of this tragedy which earned for Major Bach his British nickname: "The Sky Pilot of Hellfire!"

I do not propose to alter a single word of this account and so I have preserved its own personal dramatic form:

"We were running short of water. Once lower Sollum fell the British occupied our waterhole. Our lips began to crack, our throats were dry. Something had to be done. Papa Bach ordered a storm troop to recapture the waterhole for a short time so that we could replenish our supplies. The battle for water! Lieutenant Eichholz of No. 2 Company was given orders: 'Take the waterhole with your Commando. Hold the position until the water truck is filled up and then retire!' Eichholz and his men were successful. The British were taken by surprise, but in the chaos and darkness the two

German detachments with which Eichholz attacked the waterhole from both flanks fired on each other. A corporal was killed and a cry from one of the wounded men for a stretcher-bearer revealed the tragedy. The expedition returned with one dead, one wounded man and a full water truck. Corporal Jung nearly lost his life during this foray. In order to obtain an extra can of water for himself and his comrades he entered the fray, overlooked the time, was forgotten in the excitement and only after a long foot slog was picked up shortly before daybreak by his comrade, Braun, on his motor-cycle. Jung managed to salvage the canful of water. He had clung to it like a treasure throughout the night. A can of water was indeed a treasure at Halfaya Pass around Christmas 1941. No Christmas greetings were sent home that year nor was there a Christmas tree. Only the words read to us from the Bible by Father Bach, our major and chaplain. But there was a special issue of water. The Christmas bells were replaced by the British 25-pounder shells which thundered down on our foxholes in the rocks. What a Christmas Eve!

"In vain Rommel tried to organise supplies of food and water by aircraft from Crete. On the second flight the British night-fighters were waiting for them. The Ju's were brought down in the sea, and after this, no more got through.

"In the wadis among the rocks the men waited for the stand-to call at sunset. From their trenches, dug-outs and gun positions, from the transport and the field cookers, in musty uniforms and with grimy skins emerged small grey figures. They looked like ghosts—like men from another world. They raised their heads, limbered up their stiff limbs and breathed the cool night air."

"By night we came to life again," another combatant told me. "At night the rations were distributed—two cupfuls of watery soup and a tin of corned beef. A jug of coffee made with salt water—intended for three men per day; too little for dying, too little for living, let alone for fighting. 'On this diet life can only be borne lying down,' was the current joke in No. 3 Company."

The British naturally knew exactly what it was like in the positions on Halfaya Pass. After their bloody experiences in trying to capture it they relied on starving out the garrison.

One evening in the middle of January a few hundred Italians from the Savona Division, commanded by General Di

Giorgis, arrived at the pass. With Rommel's consent they had fought their way from their strongpoint west of Halfaya Pass to Bach's position and provided a courageous body of reinforcements, but also an additional burden on the meagre rations. After a week the end came.

Captain Voigt, the senior company commander, was sent to parley with the South Africans. After his preliminary negotiations for capitulation, Major Bach and Lieutenant Schmidt from the Engineer Corps drove to arrange the surrender terms. The South Africans were very fair and the parleys went smoothly and rapidly. When Bach had signed the document and left the tent, Lieutenant Schmidt beckoned to the driver of his car. The man understood without a word and exchanged the white flag from the right to the left hand mudguard. Why? This was the last military gesture of the Mannheim pastor's officers, and men. After signing the capitulation terms Bach was pledged to give no more military commands to destroy weapons and equipment. His officers had therefore devised a trick. Before the pastor drove to the parley he had given orders: "The first German sentry who sights the returning car with the white flag on the left side is to report to battalion headquarters: 'White flag on the left mudguard.'" This was the prearranged signal for all positions to blow up guns, trucks and equipment. Had the parleys for an honourable capitulation come to naught the white flag was to remain on the right wing of the car, which meant that all weapons were to be kept loaded and in readiness for firing.

The trick succeeded. The South African general's wish to capture an 88 undamaged was never gratified.

On the 17th January, 1942, the sun shone brightly over Halfaya Pass. Fiery red, purple and violet, its rays lit up the mountains in the early morning light. Not a shot was fired. Haggard figures staggered from their foxholes and stumbled towards the assembly place. It was weeks since the battalion had fallen in during the day. There was an exchange of greetings. Hunger, thirst and filth had altered the men's faces. They looked old—old and tired. The South Africans arrived and issued water and provisions. The badly wounded were given medical attention. Then the company commander announced: "Prepare to march off!" At this moment took place the shabby deed at Halfaya Pass which is a blot on the history of the North African campaign. Suddenly firing broke out. A heavy battery from the direction of the Salt Lake fired on the troops as they formed up. The target was No. 1 Company, commanded by Lieutenant Dr. Gehring. It was appalling. At first the men were dumbfounded. Then they scattered according to the text book. "The dirty swine!" they shouted. "The filthy swine!" The major stood there as white as a sheet before the South African officer, who was just as amazed. At last the firing ceased. The South Africans, too, were lying flat on the ground. A few minutes later a British runner arrived and whispered in the ear of the South African officer. The latter went over to Bach and informed him through the interpreter: "Free French Forces. General de Gaulle's troops have disobeyed orders, ignored the capitulation and fired at the German soldiers as they fell in." Major Bach did not say a word.

Then they drove away. The German High Command announced in a communique that they had fought to the last bullet. It sounded magnificent but the reality was very different. War is never magnificent. They still had plenty of bullets left. Hunger and thirst brought them to their knees. Father Bach, the Chaplain Major from Mannheim, one of the most courageous soldiers in Africa, also knew the old motto: "He who fights and runs away, lives to fight another day!"

9

MALTA EATS UP THE SUPPLIES

The sinister background to Rommel's war in Africa was supplies. Never mentioned in the Wehrmacht reports, haunted by the tragedy of a futile race with death, officers and men of the Merchant Navy sailed their ships to Africa. A large proportion of them sailed to their death.

Behind each soldier who fired a bullet, drove a tank or who took off on a bomber mission stood a chain of invisible helpers without whom no bullets could have been fired and no victories could have been won: the long columns of men behind the line who brought up weapons, ammunition, fuel supplies and reinforcements for the front. In the Second World War more victories were won by properly functioning supplies and more defeats suffered from lack of material and fuel than could ever have been believed. This also applied to North Africa. No one, therefore, should speak of the Desert Foxes and their achievements without also mentioning the merchant ships of the Africa convoys, the transport pilots and the battalions who brought up the supplies. This war in Africa was lost because the German High Command did not understand how to master the problem of bringing supplies across an ocean which they did not command and across the endless waste of the desert.

Three hundred and fifty miles of Mediterranean separate Sicily from Tripoli. On the bottom of this stretch of sea lie as many soldiers as lie buried in the African sand, and more war material than the Germans and the Italians ever used in North Africa. For the British ruled the Mediterranean and to conquer in Africa the British Naval forces had to be destroyed. Malta, the base for air and sea attacks on the German-Italian supplies, had to be reduced.

This was the major problem in the African war. Rommel's first swift victories obscured this problem, but it soon appeared in all its urgency.

Most of the 250,000 German soldiers who fought in Africa made the crossing from Naples or Taranto. A very small proportion of the Desert Foxes and, later, the Tunisian detachments were flown across. This was no joke, but at least the trip lasted only a few hours. The journey in overloaded cargo vessels, on the contrary, often took eighty-four hours under the constant fear: Would they get through? Would they meet the Tommies? When the ship's sirens wailed, when the engines of the British torpedo-carrying aircraft droned, the troops crouched helplessly on the deck, tucking their heads into their shoulders. Against the aircraft at least there was the flak.

But when in the middle of a game of cards, or while they were taking a nap, there was a violent explosion and the cry ran through the ship: "Direct torpedo hit!" and when the boat began to sink and the rush to save their lives began...then things were terrible. Could they get into the water or were they to drown among the crates and weapons? That was the question which tortured them.

Long before German soldiers were fighting on the North African front the first merchant seamen met their death in the Mediterranean. Between January and May 1941 eleven German supply ships amounting to forty-two thousand British Registered Tonnage were lost. On the 16th April a whole convoy of German transports were painfully aware of this. The Royal Navy attacked at 02.20 hours and the action lasted half an hour. The *Arta, Aegina* and *Iserlohn* were sunk before dawn. The *Adana,* burning furiously, floated until 16.00 hours. The following day the *Samos* went to the bottom. On the 1st May, 1941, there were three naval actions between Naples and Tripoli. The *Larissa* was sunk by a mine. British M.T.Bs sunk the *Arcturus* of the Argo Shipping Line. A few hours later Hapag's *Leverkusen,* a proud vessel of 7386 B.R.T. suffered the same fate. And so it continued. The German Mercantile Marine defended itself bravely.

During the second morning watch Captain Morisse went on to the bridge and checked the course; he scanned the horizon and had a little chat with the Italian liaison officer. An enormous shudder ran through the ship. A torpedo hit! The flak gun emplacement was blown away but the ship did not sink immediately. There was plenty of time to take to the boats. Other vessels in the convoy picked up the crew and the troops. Now the *Arcturus,* which had made so many trips between Naples and Tripoli, had also gone. She was one of the medium-sized vessels which sailed from Naples. Half the ship was reserved for Italians and the other half for the Afrika Korps Germans. The same distribution applied to the Italian ships. This arrangement was at first an equitable one, but as a result of the great losses suffered by the Italians in the first half of 1941 and with the increase of German troops sent to the North African theatre of war this fifty-fifty arrangement was an unequal reinforcement condition of which Rommel often complained.

On the previous trip the *Arcturus* had got away with it. The convoy was attacked for six hours by British bombers. Many of the soldiers on board held their breath when the bombs crashed down a few yards away from the ship. On the quayside in Naples everything had sounded so simple. The captain had stood on a crate and addressed the men: "No smoking at night on the upper deck. No lights must be shown at any porthole. The ship will sail completely blacked out. No one must leave the ship of his own accord or jump overboard, whatever happens. The order to abandon ship can only be given from the captain's bridge."

Many of the soldiers had never seen the sea or a big ship before. For them it was an adventure, but when things grew serious this adventure turned to Dead Sea apples. "Don't start worrying," the captain said in Naples. "On board our ships you will be properly looked after. There are enough lifeboats and rafts aboard. Lifeboat stations have already been allocated. Whatever happens there will always be a sailor at hand to give orders. If the captain is killed the first, second or third officers will take over command should the occasion arise. You will never be left in the lurch." This is what the captain had said and he kept his word. The soldiers brought out their spirit lamps and prepared their meal. The galleys of these small cargo boats could not provide food for six hundred men.

Submarine alert! The first aircraft appeared. In white trousers, khaki shirt and life jacket, wearing a steel helmet, the captain stood on the wireless deck from where he could see everything. The eyes of all the soldiers were on him. "Aircraft approaching on the starboard beam. Aircraft approaching astern." He had got away with it several times, until the 1st May.

The Chief of the Naval Transport Command in Tripoli, corvette Captain Meixner, arrived this time at the quayside to receive the captain of the *Leverkusen* and Captain Morisse of the *Arcturus* as shipwrecked mariners. After his ship had gone down Captain Morisse had taken his shoes off in the water in order to swim better. He could not find a pair of shoes to fit him in Tripoli and for a few days was seen walking about barefoot in the Uaddan, the smart Tripoli hotel.

The huge Italian liner *Birmania* lay in Tripoli harbour with a cargo of ammunition at the time. Captain Morisse's former First Lieutenant, Hoppe, was responsible for the unloading of the German part of the cargo. On the 4th May Captain Morisse paid him a visit and took his leave after drinking a glass of gin. He was not two hundred yards away from the vessel when there was a thunderous explosion.

Morisse took cover in the military headquarters. A second explosion followed and black clouds of smoke rose above the harbour. What had happened?

The *Birmania* had blown up. The *Citta di Bari*, an Italian auxiliary cruiser lying alongside loaded with petrol, had also exploded. Since the *Birmania* was being unloaded many Arabs and German soldiers were in the ship and on the quay. The casualties were appalling. On the German side 28 dead and 38 wounded. The Italians had 42 dead and 50 wounded, and the Arab helpers 150 dead and a number of wounded.

The quayside looked as though it had just been subjected to a heavy bombing attack. The stern of the 10,000-ton *Birmania* was flung by the force of the explosion on to the quayside. Captain Hailer of the unloading staff had a remarkable escape from death. The stern thundered down on top of him. Was it to prove his coffin or a shelter? Hailer came to his senses beneath a strange roof which protected him like a huge sheet of armour plate from a rain of shrapnel. His three colleagues who had been standing a few paces away were all killed.

Experts soon arrived at the scene of the tragedy and confirmed that the German cargo had consisted of small twenty-pound anti-personnel bombs. They were held together in tens by a strip of tin to which a single explosive charge was fastened. The charge was set to become live as soon as the stick of bombs was dropped. After a fixed time, usually two to three seconds, the lead was melted by the explosion of the charge and each bomb continued to fall independently. The detonator was so sensitive that the slightest touch would make the bomb explode immediately. This was the secret of this devilish weapon, designed to deal with columns of men on the march and other targets in the open.

These small anti-personnel bombs had been sent for the first time to Africa. Great attention had been paid to the packing, but the authorities had omitted to build the right crates for their transportation. The bombs were packed in ordinary crates where they lay too loosely. When they were hoisted aboard, the bundles of bombs came loose in their holders. Several of them turned over inside the crate. As a result the detonator, which was secured with a simple pin, became live. At the least shake the bomb would now explode. Since the *Birmania* also carried heavy bombs, it is easy to imagine what would happen if only one of these little "devil's eggs" exploded. It was impossible to reconstruct the cause of the tragedy, but obviously on lowering one of the crates one of the small live bombs had exploded and caused the catastrophe. Rommel's right hand man in all questions of supply, Captain Otto, subsequently Quartermaster-General, had left the ship only a few minutes before the explosion.

Otto and the man responsible for Naval Transport, Captain Meixner, were still busy investigating the cause of the disaster when a further piece of disquieting news arrived. Two more Italian ships loaded with these small bombs were already approaching.

Meixner directed them to the wharf with instructions for the anchors to be lowered very carefully. But Meixner was now faced with a great problem. At the news of the *Birmania* tragedy Berlin lost its head. Goering, anxious about the packing of his bombs, telegraphed: "Order the ships to put to sea and have them sunk. In no circumstances must men's lives be endangered." It was easy for him to give this order to scuttle them, but each ship and each cargo had a direct effect on the fate of Rommel's army in North Africa.

Meixner was in a desperate dilemma. Hardly a soldier who fought in Africa did not know him by sight. He was certainly not the man to obey an order blindly. In the First World War he had rammed and sunk an Italian destroyer. He had escaped five times from Italian prison camps only to be recaptured as many times. Between the two wars Meixner had studied law. As a Lieutenant-Commander on the reserve he had been called back to the Navy in 1940. He was an instructor for Operation Sea Lion, the planned invasion of England. Later he was sent to Tripoli and became more than merely one of Rommel's closest collaborators. He was a friend, although their friendship had begun with a dispute. Meixner made it quite clear that he had an enormous respect for Rommel's capacities as a soldier, but he must ask him not to interfere in naval questions of which he knew absolutely nothing.

Meixner now had to find a solution somewhere between Goering's order and his own desire to unload the ships without loss of life. One thing was certain—if there was an accident he would be court-martialled. He sent for a man whom he knew to be an experienced and courageous seaman, Captain Reinen, skipper of the *Menes*. He was in Tripoli because his ship had been torpedoed. "Do you think we can unload the ships?" Meixner asked. "And would you undertake to unload one?" "I'll do it," said Reinen. Meixner's adjutant, Lieutenant Krüger, supported him. Each of them sought ten German volunteers. The Italian crews left the ships and the highly dangerous operation began.

As in the *Birmania*, in addition to the small bombs there was a cargo of heavy bombs. The first crate was raised and opened to see if the safety pins were still in the right position. They were. It was hoisted ashore and the same procedure followed, crate after crate. But they could not take things for granted. The fourth case revealed a bomb with a missing safety pin. It was live. Now things were serious. Captain Reinen and a fireman cautiously moved the infernal machine to one side. Reinen held the stick of bombs and the fireman prized off the tin band. He took the live bomb out, placed it carefully in a corner and removed the detonator. Captain Reinen stood at his side to see how he worked, for this fireman had only been borrowed for one day and had to return to the ammunition depot where important preparations were under way for the next offensive. Should the same thing recur, Reinen and Krüger would have to fend for themselves. They paid great attention. On the first day they discovered six live bombs, on the second day nine and on the third day four. The unloading of this cargo took five days. Twenty-two bombs had become live as a result of the badly constructed crates. Sixteen times after the fireman had left, Reinen and Krüger sat on a crate and rendered the bombs harmless. Sixteen times they were faced with death. Each time they sent their ten men ashore and each operation took five minutes. The sweat poured down their cheeks. The silence in the hold was heaven and hell alike. Each turn of the screw was a stride through the universe. Both ships and the entire cargo were salvaged. The merchant ship captain, Reinen, was the first "civilian" to be awarded the Iron Cross 1st Class. Lieutenant Krüger received the same award.

This is only one of the calm acts of courage which Rommel's forwarding agents performed. The public never learned anything of their activities during the war. Their work, their achievements and their deaths had to remain secret. The enemy must not know how vital was the transport and supply position, how many ships arrived at Tripoli, Tobruk and Benghazi from Naples or Taranto, how many set sail and how many were sunk. The balance sheet in the secret records of the Naval High Command was appalling.

The layman can hardly realise the significance of the report that such and such a ship was sunk in the Mediterranean by British naval craft or by a Bristol Blenheim. Let us take, for example, the *Preussen,* which was sunk by a direct bomb hit on the 22nd July, 1941, off Pantellaria. On board were 600 soldiers, a crew of 64, about 6,000 tons of ammunition of all types, 1,000 tons of petrol, 1,000 tons of food supplies, 3,000 sacks of mail and 300 vehicles, ranging from tanks to omnibuses, from Volkswagens to motor-cycles. Particularly valuable items of the cargo were the first 4,000-lb. bombs for the Luftwaffe and the first battery of 21 cm. guns. The whole cargo was lost. Two hundred soldiers and sailors were lost. The *Preussen* is only one example of the many sinkings on the route from Italy to Africa. Were there tombstones for ships, the route from Sicily to the North African harbours would be paved with them.

The reason for all this destruction was of course Malta. The rocky island, the main stronghold of British naval forces, submarines and aircraft in the Mediterranean was an important factor in the British victory in North Africa. The cliffs of Malta cancelled out all the boldness and courage of the German troops in Africa. However paradoxical it may sound, the desert war in North Africa was decided at sea. Malta spelt Rommel's defeat. This is obvious to anyone who studies the campaign.

A visitor to Malta before the war found an island with sunburnt meadows and waving fields of corn, fishing nets hanging from the rocks and age-old stone houses. The Maltese earned a living on their thickly populated island as farmers, tradesmen, fishermen and mariners. Malta is the home of a favourite European delicacy, tunny fish.

From the harbour a lift led to the town of Valetta, which received its name from the first Grand Master of the Knights of Malta. The history of this order is bound up with the old fortress which, for a long time, was the seat of the British Governor. In the sixteenth century the Emperor, Charles V, leased the island to the Knights of St. John. It was inevitable that the island should have an adventurous history since it was a natural pirates' eyrie, lying on the direct route between the Western and Eastern Mediterranean.

Malta has always played a part in history. From here the Phoenicians controlled the trade between the East, Europe and Africa, around 400 B.C. it was occupied by the Carthaginians and in 218 B.C. by the Romans. Ostrogoths, Vandals and Byzantines fought for this keypoint, from which Mediterranean trade could be controlled. The Arabs conquered Malta in A.D. 870, and 200 years later the Normans captured it. In 1798 Napoleon took the main island and a little neighbouring island of Gozo. The British occupied both in 1800 and built Malta up as one of the strongest naval and air bases of the Empire.

Naval and Royal Air Force officers dominated the life on land and British warships the picture of the harbour. Great docks and repair sheds were built into this natural harbour. Malta was beautiful, proud and mighty. Fifty miles from Sicily as the crow flies this fortress flouted Mussolini's claim that the Mediterranean was *Mare Nostrum*. No, the Mediterranean was Great Britain's sea, and any power who transported soldiers across this sea had to defeat Malta, or pay heavy tribute.

"Had the Italians been Japanese they would have opened their war on the 10th June, 1940, by doing a Pearl Harbour on Malta, which at that time was merely a defence base. For Malta was for the Italians what victory at Pearl Harbour would have been for the Japanese." That is the considered opinion of one of the greatest naval experts of the Second World War, the German Vice-Admiral Assmann.

But the Italians were no Japanese. After they entered the war on Germany's side in the summer of 1940 they were content with trying to subdue the British fortress in the Mediterranean by air attacks. "Air attacks" is a euphemism, for in reality they were only pin pricks. No furious hail of fire or carpet bombing, rather sharpshooting by Knights of the air—a kind of aerial joust. A German Admiral, Chief of the Naval Liaison Staff in Rome, Weichold, was the first to propose on the 9th August, 1940, that Malta should be captured. But the Italians refused and even the German leaders did not, at first, see the overwhelming importance of this island for the African war. It was very different with the

British. Although they may have felt a trifle nervous at home when they learned of Hitler's "Operation Sea Lion", the invasion of England, they sent considerable reinforcements to Malta. Thus it became ever more difficult for the Italians to try to take the island. It is extremely doubtful whether they could ever have taken it, for the Italians entered the war in a pitiable state of preparation.

Nothing was ready. Marshal Badoglio himself explained the facts to me in rather cautious words. An overall picture can be obtained today by an examination of the war records. Mussolini in 1939 watched the German victories in Poland with stupefaction. Spellbound, he saw General Dietl's Alpine troops take Narvik. With a shake of the head he realised that Denmark and Oslo had fallen into German hands without a shot being fired. With growing concern, the Duce saw how Hitler's armies had swept away their French adversaries like chaff before the wind. Hitler, who considered Mussolini as his pupil, stormed as a victor through Europe. He had even planned the invasion of England. Did it not look as though the war would be over in three months and result in an unqualified victory for the Hun? Then the Führer would dictate the peace terms and what would happen to Italy? "If Italy wants to sit at the Peace Conference table when the world is to be apportioned, she must enter the war and enter it fast," Mussolini said to his Marshals Balbo and Badoglio on the 26th May, 1940. They stood as though frozen to stone in the huge hall of the Palazzo Venezia. Enter the war?

Mussolini noticed their negative attitude. Balbo, the C-in-C Italian forces in North Africa, exchanged glances with Badoglio, the army Chief of Staff. Then the Duce raised his hand and said very pompously: "I have to inform you that yesterday I sent a message to Hitler assuring him that I did not intend to stand and look on with my hands in my pockets, and that from the 5th June I am ready to declare war on France."

Badoglio stepped forward. "Are you aware, Duce, that Italy is completely unprepared from a military point of view? You have read the routine reports. Only twenty per cent of our divisions are up to war strength. Over seventy per cent of our armoured division have not a single tank. We haven't even enough shirts for our soldiers. How are we expected to wage war? In our colonies there is no real military prepared-

ness. Our merchant fleet is scattered over the high seas."
Badoglio tried to continue but Mussolini waved him aside:
"History cannot be reckoned by the number of shirts," he
said.

And so Italy entered the war. Badoglio did not resign.
Nor did the generals revolt. How could they have done?
They would have had to admit that with ten years of bravado
and words they had disguised the fact that the Italian army
was a useless tool.

Admittedly things looked better in the Navy and, according to Mussolini, everything rested with the Navy. In
this he was not far wrong. Where could the Italian army
fight? But the Navy—6 battle cruisers, 29 cruisers, 59 destroyers, 69 torpedo boats and 115 submarines stood in the
lists. Was that nothing? Italy had the largest submarine fleet
in the world. What could Great Britain put up against them
in the Mediterranean? What had the harassed British in the
way of troops in Egypt? Thirty-five thousand men, no heavy
armour. As opposed to this Marshal Balbo in Libya had 14
divisions, totalling 220,000 men. Admittedly they had no
heavy and not enough light armour. Only four divisions were
more or less on a war footing and only two were motorised.
But, all the same, 220,000 men against 35,000! They would
quickly steamroller the British.

We know the result of this steamroller process. We know
how Hitler in Berlin suddenly, to his chagrin, recognised the
danger that Mussolini could be chased out of Africa. What
would the result be when the soft underbelly of Europe was
laid wide open to the attack of the British? This was the
reason why Hitler sent the rapidly mustered Afrika Korps
under Rommel to stop the rot in Africa. Had these German
divisions been sent to Africa six months earlier, as General
Guderian had proposed at the end of June 1940, they might
have decided the war the same autumn. Then probably
Alexandria, the Suez Canal and Cairo would have fallen into
the hands of the Axis.

Before the first German ship with the advance detachments of the Afrika Korps sailed for Tripoli, the German High
Command despatched the 10th Flieger Korps, under General
Geissler, with about 200 planes which were soon increased to
500, to Sicily. The task of the Stuka fighters and fighter
bombers was to wage war against the British Naval Forces in

the Mediterranean and to safeguard supplies for Africa. The
first trial of strength soon took place.

On the 7th January, 1941, British Naval Forces were
reported both in the Eastern and Western Mediterranean
sailing towards Malta. Four cargoes had sailed from Gibraltar
with a valuable consignment for Malta and Greece aboard.
The British convoy was heavily protected and as a result of
their experience with the "fine weather Navy", as Churchill
dubbed the Italian fleet, the British were not unduly worried. In the afternoon of the 9th, for the first time, a number
of Italian torpedo-carrying aircraft attacked the convoy south
of Sardinia. The presence of the Luftwaffe worked wonders
on the Italian morale. Two Italian E-boats also attacked the
convoy. The enemy units were caught up in the newly laid
German minefields and two ships were blown sky high.
Shortly before midday on the 10th January the king pin of the
convoy escort, the British aircraft-carrier *Illustrious*, was
some hundred sea miles west of Malta. She was carrying
urgently awaited aircraft for the island.

Ju 88

On the deck of the carrier the Fleet Air Arm planes were
ready to take off when German Stukas, Ju 87s and 88s,
launched a surprise attack. Their bombs ripped open the
flying deck and large fires broke out. The rudder was damaged and the carrier sailed round in circles. Again and again
the Italian torpedo-carriers and German Stukas rained down
their bombs on the damaged carrier's deck. According to the
official British naval history of this battle only the German
attacks were successful. Within ten minutes six 1,000-lb.
German bombs exploded on the decks of the carrier.

"First encounter of the British Naval Forces in Mediter-

ranean with the German Luftwaffe." The British admiral
radioed to Cairo and London. This report was read with some
consternation.

But where was the Italian Fleet? Where was Mussolini's
armada? It did not appear. With superb seamanship the
captain of the *Illustrious,* steering with the screw, brought his
damaged ship to Malta. But the day was not yet at an end.
The cruiser *Southampton* struck a mine and was hit by
several bombs. One British cruiser less in the Mediterranean.

The German pilots gave the *Illustrious,* which now lay in
Malta harbour, no peace. They continued to attack her and
the British had to use all their aircraft in her defence and no
action was taken against Axis convoys. The German transports to Tripoli got through unharmed. This was one of the
most important factors in Rommel's first victorious advance.
Protected by fighters, the German bombers flew day and
night from Sicily to Malta. Bombs crashed down on the small
island, on quays, repair workshops and supply dumps, on
ships and airfields. On 7th March, 1941, Air Vice-Marshal
Maynard in Malta informed Cairo that he could no longer
protect his Sunderlands and Wellingtons against the German
fighters. They were therefore transferred to Egypt. On the
same day the Governor of Malta, General Sir William Dobbie,
sent an SOS to the War Cabinet. "The enemy air attacks are
so heavy that Malta is in danger of losing its importance as an
air and naval stronghold." Cairo despatched Hurricanes to
Malta, but the Germans continued to attack the island. In the
period between January and June 1941 the British lost 78
aircraft.

Whereas the Italian attacks from June 1940 to January
1941 had caused no significant damage to this rocky island,
after five months of German air attacks the picture looked
very different. Despite the natural caves which were used as
shelters, the number of dead and wounded exceeded four
hundred. The Maltese began to murmur and to refuse to join
in the clearance of rubble. In March the island was short of
food. Severe rationing was ordered and the time was almost
ripe for invasion. The British High Command sent infantry
reinforcements from Egypt, for every day they expected the
event which seemed inevitable should the Axis continue the
battle in North Africa—the invasion. The British had eight
battalions and an artillery regiment for the island's defence.

In addition to this a few batteries of 3.7 inch and 6 inch guns and a few 18-pounders. As regards armour, a special group of the Royal Tank Regiment was available but this was armed only with two light and four infantry tanks. Things looked grim for Malta. At this point the Axis powers had the chance of forcing a decision against Great Britain in the Mediterranean. Grand Admiral Raeder's plan was obviously the correct one: to take Malta in order to be able to send mass supplies unhindered to Africa. Rommel would then have been in the position to crown his victory in Cyrenaica with the conquest of Egypt. Churchill would clearly not have survived such a political development.

But what did Hitler do? On 22nd June, 1941, he opened the Eastern Front. He attacked Russia which delivered some of his corn and oil; she was unreliable of course but had no immediate designs on Germany.

As a result of the Russian war, units of the 10th Flieger Korps were transferred from Sicily to the Eastern Front. Fewer bombs fell on Malta and Churchill strengthened his island fortress. Once more British naval and air forces wreaked havoc on Rommel's supplies. And Rommel stood before the gates of Tobruk in desperate conflict because he could not get enough supplies.

But could Malta have been taken? That is a question which is constantly asked today by German war historians. In my opinion, it could have been conquered. The successful German operation against Crete proved that a 33-times larger and better defended island could be taken from the air. This was the first capture of an island by airborne troops in history. It was successful. Here in Crete the legendary Icarus, a few centuries ago, had tried to realise the ancient dream of man—to fly. He stuck wings on to his body with wax but he crashed into the sea.

The German Major Koch, on the other hand, who on the 20th May, 1941, at 07.30 hours hovered in the haze above Crete in his transport glider and landed on the island at the head of No. 1 Battalion of the Paratroop Regiment, did not crash into the sea. The powerful air fleet of Ju 52s, ready to drop their paratroops, followed him. Thousands of modern descendants of Icarus, heavily armed with weapons and ammunition, fell like white clouds out of a steel-blue sky. They jumped on to the rocky island below from which death and destruction rained up at them. What did Churchill say later of these troops? "These brave and reliable parachutists were the flower of German youth." This was the truth. Staff Bugler Ernst Springer, a huntsman from Upper Silesia, who was with the first battalion to jump, took out his trumpet while in the air and blew the old signal for the attack. It echoed like an eerie victory fanfare out of the sky in the ears of the bewildered men of the 5th New Zealand Brigade.

Crete was taken. The first airborne landing in history was successful. But the success was very expensive. The paratroops suffered appalling losses. While in the air they were easy targets for the machine gunners below. Dead or wounded, many of them hung on their white parachutes. On landing, they were dragged along the ground until some bush or a stone stopped their progress and the white silk subsided like a huge shroud over its tragic load. The German élite arm, the parachutists, in the first major action were sacrificed in the truest meaning of the word. But Crete, the powerful island between Greece and Tobruk, was in German hands. Churchill sent a desperate appeal to Roosevelt. Great Britain would lose the war unless the United States quadrupled her aid.

There were several German military leaders who wanted to make this dearly bought victory the jumping-off point for further decisive operations against the Allies in the Mediterranean and Africa. Raeder was the protagonist. In those weeks Churchill feared nothing so much as a German landing on Malta. On the 28th May, 1941, he sent a telegram to General Wavell in Cairo in which he intimated his fears that Malta would be lost and the Mediterranean line of communication with Cairo destroyed.

But Hitler did not seize this heaven-sent opportunity. He also rejected the plan of the Luftwaffe General Student who wanted to take Cyprus and from there carry out air-sea operations against the Suez Canal. The heavy losses suffered in Crete had impressed him. Moreover, Mussolini had the ambition of staging an attack on Malta himself. The result of this was quite obvious to Hitler but he had not the heart to offend Mussolini. The start of the Russian campaign relegated all plans for taking Malta into the second line. The bill had to be paid by the Afrika Korps.

From June to October 1941 forty ships carrying supplies

for North Africa were sunk, totalling 179,000 B.R.T. In September nearly forty per cent of all ships which sailed were sent to the bottom. To add to the appalling sacrifice of soldiers and war material, the shortage of shipping began to be felt. As a result the tonnage available for Rommel's supplies in October fell to 50,000 B.R.T. of which sixty-three per cent was sunk. In November only 37,000 B.R.T. were despatched for Rommel and seventy-seven per cent was sunk by the Royal Navy and the R.A.F.

It now became obvious that Rommel's campaign in North Africa would come to grief as a result of the blockade of his supplies. Hitler at last realised this. Now there was a general alert at headquarters. A radio message recalled a man from the Eastern Front who was to change everything—Kesselring.

The soldier in Africa suffered most from this grim tragedy of supplies. He was not conscious of the strategic problem, knew nothing of the tonnage sunk, but he observed that his company was not brought up to full complement, that no tanks arrived, no fuel and no beer, and none of those small comforts which might have made his life in the desert a little more tolerable.

Sometimes heaven or rather the sea produced some fabulous treasure. The men of the 33rd Reconnaissance Unit still lick their lips today at the memory of such a coincidence.

The patrols of the 33rd had to report by radio when they returned to the German lines. The divisional commander was struck by a strange code word added to this report: "Tiger." He made some enquiries and was surprised to find that it meant nothing more than the report of the company leader that his men had gone bathing.

One day Captain Héraucourt of No. 1 Company grew anxious when his "recce" leader, Lieutenant Englehart, after giving the code word "Tiger" did not turn up for some hours. When at last he appeared he behaved in rather a mysterious manner. He had found something with which his company commander had certainly not reckoned, he said with a smile. At this he took a bottle of real Scotch whisky from his trouser pocket. His story of the find was most exciting. Captain Héraucourt would not believe it. "Come and see for yourself," Englehart said excitedly. They drove to the escarpment at Bardia and there was the secret. A wreck had been washed up in the little bay. To be more accurate half a small ship—its

bows were missing—had been driven ashore. On the stern
stood the name *Hekla*. The two officers swam over to it. The
contents of this half ship were most appetising. The forward
hold was full of crates—excellent tinned vegetables, fruit and
fat, chocolates, cigarettes and whisky. The gymshoes and
other comforts of the British troops were ignored. The two
German officers swam back and the company was mobilised
to unload the booty. That was the first job. It took five days.
But seldom in Africa in the glaring sun did men sweat
cheerfully as they did in that little rocky cove near Bardia.
The crates were lowered into the water, loaded on rubber
dinghies and then rowed to a little beach; this took three
quarters of an hour. From there they were carried down the
steep slopes of the Jebel and put on trucks. Four hundred
bottles of whisky! Those were happy days for the 33rd. There
was no soda water in the *Hekla's* cargo, but the Scotch tasted
better straight, and a drop of salty drinking water made it
taste even better. Although many units profited by this find
the provisions lasted for quite a time. It was only half a small
ship, one of those many British and German ships which
were sunk in the Mediterranean in the war. Idiocy when one
comes to think of it!

10

A WEDDING IN THE WADI EL FAREGH

"When were we here before—yes, when was it? About
nine months ago. But then we were advancing towards
Tobruk. Our objective was Cairo and the Suez Canal."

Good heavens!

Now they were on the way back and there are no songs
to celebrate a retreat. Retreats are twice as long and twice as
difficult.

"Was the road as bad during the advance?"

It was, but they had not noticed it. Victories lighten the
burden or make one forget the load.

How long was it since that November Sunday, 1941, when they had fought in front of Tobruk?

Only a few weeks but they seemed like months. Each day had been an action, each day a battle against the aggressive, victory-conscious and superior 8th Army. No one knew the precise whereabouts of friend or foe. Positions were captured and abandoned. Many a prisoner was back in the line again after a few hours marching. Field dressing stations sometimes changed hands three and four times a day. The German and British doctors no longer bothered about it; they remained in their operating tents and went on working side by side. This continued for three weeks from the beginning to the end of December 1941.

Then came the winter rains and it was cold in Africa.

Rommel knew that in this modern war it was not a matter of possessing a strip of desert, either Marmarica or Cyrenaica. The North African campaign could be decided only by the complete destruction of the enemy. Winning of territory was no victory and loss of territory no disaster. Both Rommel and the British had experienced this. Nevertheless the British commander, Auchinleck, made the same mistake as his predecessor Wavell. Again he confused the issues.

On Boxing Day, 1941, Reuter from Cairo reported to its newspaper readers in London: "The remains of the German Afrika Korps and the Italian Army are retreating along the coastal road of the Bay of Sirte to Tripoli. The main objective, the destruction of enemy forces in the Western Desert, has been achieved. The German armour has been defeated. Only a handful of German tanks have survived and they are fleeing in panic to Tripoli."

The history of World War II is rich in such fatal errors. Hitler succumbed to them and, as we have seen, Churchill also made mistakes.

In London towards the end of the year there was triumph in the air: "Rommel has been defeated. Rommel has been destroyed!"

The British public should have been more cautious; they should not have believed everything they were told. But they were a long way from Africa and people very much closer made the same mistake. They did not know Rommel nor did they know the German infantrymen. Rommel had a will of iron, and a plan. Admittedly he had difficulties with the

Italian C-in-C who feared the political effect of a retreat. "I'm retiring because I must do so, or else I shall lose not only a battle but my whole army," Rommel growled to General Bastico. The Axis divisions, therefore, had been on the run since the beginning of December 1941 and abandoned the Tobruk sector for the west. But it was not a rout as it had been in the case of the Italians the previous winter. The Afrika Korps retired in good order. Picked troops led by brave officers covered the strategic withdrawal—motorised units, armoured reconnaissance and flak units, and the Oasis companies.

On the 16th December Marshal Count Cavallero visited Rommel from Rome and implored him not to give up Cyrenaica. "An obvious defeat would be dangerous for Mussolini's prestige," he said.

"And what about total defeat with the loss of the whole army and North Africa?" Rommel retorted acidly.

Still, Cavallero demanded the cancellation of the German order to retire. He forgot what had happened ten days ago when General Crüwell kept sending his messages of despair into the desert. When the 15th and 21st Panzer Divisions at Bir el Gobi had victory within their reach. "Where is Gambara?" Crüwell kept asking. But Gambara did not turn up. "My troops are exhausted," was the reply. As though the soldiers of the two German armoured divisions had not fought themselves to a standstill.

Rommel refused to be influenced. His order was: "Fight your way back to a good defence position." But according to all experiences, no such position existed in Cyrenaica, for it had already been proved that in a case of need there was nothing to defend. The only chance lay in a favourable area where the British had once before been halted—in the winter of 1940, when Wavell had chased the Italians from the Egyptian frontier across the Via Balbo to the bend in the Great Sirte—the actual spot from which Rommel had launched his first offensive nine months before.

Yes, in war there is ebb and flow, and now for Rommel it was ebb tide. On the night of the 20th December, 1941, Major Ehle's motorised troops, reinforced by a battery of armoured artillery and a company of the 33rd Panzerjaegers, were already southeast of Agedabia. Once more they were fighting a rearguard action. They put up the necessary de-

fence while the Afrika Korps consolidated in the desert.
Those were decisive days for Rommel. Could he reach the
favourable Brega position and stop the victorious advance of
the British? The British naturally tried to scotch Rommel's
plan but all their bravery was of no avail. Their long lines of
communication robbed them of their fighting impetus. Rommel's
rearguard troops, such as the men of the Ballerstedt Combat
Group, kept repulsing the British spearheads. They smashed
into their opponents, leaped into their vehicles and continued to retreat. Naturally among the German contingents,
too, vehicles were gradually lost. Rommel's theory, however,
was that vehicles must be supplied by the British.

From the 27th to 29th December the Afrika Korps
inflicted heavy losses on the British in the defensive battle for
Agedabia. The British armoured strength was virtually
destroyed.

New Year's Eve, 1941, lay cold and dark over the desert.
The flares of the "recce" units illuminated the night. Signposts for stragglers who had lost their way. By means of flares
the troops in Africa fought their way back to their units. And
then someone looked at his watch. New Year's Eve! "It's still
the old year but in ten minutes we can date our orders 1942."

Adjutant Marwan-Schlosser of the 135th Flak Regiment
wanted to empty his mess tin of champagne at midnight
precisely. He had captured a bottle and placed it to cool in a
sandhole. Major Hecht had brilliantly distributed his defence
force, strong in fire-cover, at Agedabia. The 114th non-
motorised Reserve Flak Unit defended the northern sector
with thirteen 88mm. guns and nine 3.7 cm. and 2 cm. flak
guns per battery. The Italians with seven 88s held the eastern
sector. The motorised remains of the 18th, 33rd and 35th
Flak Regiments had remained with the Afrika Korps and
were detailed for fluid battle. Rommel had cunningly ordered
whole batteries of dummy guns to be placed in position. The
114th Reserve Flak Unit achieved the miracle of collecting
the necessary material in the desert. The gunners laughed to
themselves as the Tommies rained shells down on these
dummy guns.

Captain Marwan-Schlosser had taken out his last letter
from home and almost missed the imaginary twelve strokes of
the clock, heralding the New Year. But in the nick of time he
drew the cork of his bottle of Veuve Cliquot, thinking of old

Wilhelm Busch's judgement: "How sweet and mild the bubbles of champagne rise like pearls in the glass." The cork popped. But what was that? At that moment a mighty cannonade broke out along the whole front. That could only be a full-scale attack! The adjutant rushed out of his tent. Major Hecht also rushed from his. Green, red, yellow and white flares hissed into the sky. The artillery, machine guns and rifles all started to fire. Thousands of flares sped like comets across the sky.

But it was no battle. Rommel's army was greeting the New Year in its own particular fashion. The troops were delighted with this firework display. Who could have had the heart to restrain them? The Italians protested on the telephone, but the imperturbable Bayerlein replied: "Calm yourselves, it's still dark over your line so what can happen to you?"

It was a fantastic sight. The flares formed a bright corridor and in the harsh light, without a thought and full of gaiety, the men emerged from their foxholes. And then an incredible thing happened. Had it not been true, had it not been engraved a thousand times on their memories, who would have dared to relate it? It was a manifestation of defiance. They were clinging on to an idea—for without an idea they could not have borne this tragedy, this fighting and dying—and they still believed in their idea. Even though it had long been exploited, misused and betrayed, the soldiers still believed. One man began and the others joined in.

On New Year's Eve, 1941, in the desert by Agedabia, they sang *Deutschland, Deutschland über Alles*. Harried, exhausted and filthy, legs stiff as though encased in concrete, in sweaty socks full of sand and torn shoes, their companies reduced in strength to a handful of men, but they sang. Next day the 22nd Armoured Brigade sent a signal to Cairo: "Maybe Rommel's troops have no tanks left, but it would be premature to speak of a defeated army. In their front line positions last night the men of the Afrika Korps sang the German National Anthem. We should not deceive ourselves that these soldiers commanded by a resolute officer are prepared to give up the battle." Had the British general accompanied the commander of the 15th Panzer Division, General von Vaerst, on New Year's morning as he visited the foxholes he would perhaps have sent a very different message. From each slit trench the soldiers reported in the prescribed manner. Only one sentry had his field glasses to his eyes and did not report. "You must improve in the New Year," said the General to encourage him, "I hope Herr General will do the same," was the reply. Old Vaerst laughed.

The Afrika Korps reached the Mersa el Brega position on the 4th January, 1942. In a violent rainstorm the decimated units prepared for defensive action. The 1st Battalion of the 115th Panzer Grenadier Regiment with the survivors of the Motorised Infantry Unit including some men of the Machine-gun Battalion—making three full companies—took up their positions south of Wadi el Faregh. Tractors drove back to fetch the derelict light trucks. The battlion settled down and the winter rain came as a blessing to wash away the filth from their clothes and bodies. The vehicles were waterlogged. The men sat in their foxholes, freezing, waiting. Armourer Sergeant Dierichsweiler took out a keen party of reconnaissance troops to salvage British trucks and to capture new ones. Lieutenant Ruf soon had collected with his tractors three battleworthy anti-tank guns. The war began to breathe slowly once more in the Wadi el Faregh and everywhere between Mersa el Brega and Marada.

On the 6th January the storm was still raging. The rain poured down and the wind chased rustling sand clouds over vehicles and tents. It was the Ghibli, the desert wind which blows all the year round. In the summer it had powdered sweating faces with reddish yellow dust. Now, in the winter, it covered men and beasts with sand like small shell splinters, tearing tents and overcoats. It was part and parcel of the African war, like the flies, the salt water and the "Alte Mann"—the inevitable bully beef. For the attacker it was the bitterest foe, but a benevolent friend for the defender. This time it was on the side of the Afrika Korps.

Finally the weather cleared and there were calm, sunny days. Now for the first time the positions they had taken up on the 5th January could be seen to the south the mighty Wadi el Faregh, the largest dry valley of the Sirte area. The ancient river bed was covered with thick vegetation, and from the top of the Jebel they had a view of the bare, lifeless waste of the Libyan Desert. Here and there, like islands, were a few occupied oases in the south Marada, the most advanced strongpoint of the German–Italian front, the right

flank of the Brega line, and a hundred and twenty miles
farther east, the oasis of Gialo, an ancient caravan centre on
the road to Kufra. Gialo had been in British hands since
November 1941 and served as the most advanced post of the
much-feared Long Range Desert Group. Their commandos
travelled far into Libya and across the desert to carry out
their rash acts of sabotage. In December 1941 they had even
appeared on the coastal road. Colonel Haselden's privateers
had shot up Italian tankers and trucks and, shortly before
Christmas, had destroyed a dozen German bombers on Agedabia
airfield. What were their present plans? Patience! They would
soon show themselves. Their opposite numbers on the German side, the Brandenburgers, would become active in March.
There would be dangerous developments.

The first old friend to reappear was the heavy 902nd
Battery. The gunners had enjoyed a few days' rest among the
dunes to the west of El Agheila. The dreary weeks of Sidi
Rezegh and El Adem were forgotten—perhaps not completely
forgotten, for who could forget the shells that fell that Sunday
among the British tanks, blowing them away as though a
giant's fist had struck them. But ultimately the crews of the
902nd Battery also had to retire. In the pouring rain they
made their way back through Cyrenaica. It was there that the
orphaned battery received a new leader: Captain Grimm.
Despite his name he was an amiable man, a courageous
soldier and a magnificent gunner. The German soldier was
devoted to this calm type of man, and they needed him in
those hectic days of the rearguard action. For the British
troops advanced within sight of the Germans. They could be
seen, and the pessimists wagered that the Tommies would be
lurking "in the famous corner near Agedabia to put them in
the bag." This is what happened to the Italians in February
1941 when 20,000 fell into the trap. Now, ten months later,
the British obviously intended to repeat the manoeuvre. It
was high time to travel light. Nothing counted except fuel,
ammunition and food supplies. Everything else was jettisoned.
On the C.O.'s orders the battery tailor had to open his crate of
clothes which so far he had managed to salvage. Gnashing his
teeth he looked on while the carefully folded cellulose shirts,
trousers and jackboots found a customer in the flash of an
eye. But it was an even greater joke when the paymaster,
Haare, had to open his cash box. The contents were distribut-

ed equally. "We'll march through Cairo in our Sunday best and with gold in our pockets if the blighters catch us," was Captain Grimm's comment on this rare occasion.

But the British did not catch the men of the 902nd Battery. They slipped skilfully out of Cyrenaica, drove through Benghazi where they found a bag of mail awaiting them, bought themselves a few tins of sardines and bottles of schnapps from the quartermaster's stores and then relaxed in the dunes between the Via Balbo and the beach. They had made it. They reached Rommel's position; they turned about, which meant that they were now facing east.

Now they lay on the steep cliff of the Wadi looking out into no-man's land. From time to time a few British scout cars approached. Then the two guns spat. A few heavy shells were lobbed among the intruders. Tall columns of smoke rose into the pale blue winter sky. The British did not like this. Finally reinforcements arrived. Kesselring's 2nd Air Fleet had been transferred from the Eastern Front to Sicily to escort the transports across the Mediterranean, enabling most of them to arrive without loss. If only things had been like this a few months before! Italian tanks, anti-tank guns and infantry arrived and then the star turn: Burckhardt's paratroops, a hot-headed bunch of youngsters under an even more crazy leader. They brought their own fighting methods with them— small motorised commandos, a couple of Volkswagens, escorted by paratroopers armed to the teeth riding motor-cycles and sidecars. They penetrated far to the south. They looked formidable. When one of their patrols arrived at an Italian post in front of Marada the sight of these wild fellows shocked their allies so much that they asked: "British or Germans?"

They always brought something back with them—prisoners, vehicles, food or cigarettes. At the worst a few sheep. One day they appeared with drums and some odd-looking trumpets, the band instruments captured from an Indian unit.

Now night after night the drums rolled and the trumpets blared. Some bright lad had constructed a kind of devilish violin which whined and screeched in time with the rest. Burckhardt and his men soon became a nightmare to the Tommies in Cyrenaica. When their leader was captured the British communiqué reported proudly: "We have captured Major Burckhardt, the commander of Rommel's paratroops."

While the 902nd Battery was enjoying this idyll in the

B.M.W. Model R 75

Wadi el Faregh a big yellow envelope arrived from Germany. It looked very official. The letter had not lain for half an hour in the commander's tent before the voice of the orderly room clerk rang out through the positions: "Corporal Raskowski report to the C.O.!" Paul Raskowski, a veteran who had survived the Polish and French campaigns, hurried over to the C.O.'s tent and disappeared inside. He reappeared after a considerable time carrying the yellow envelope. He was very excited and sat down rather weak in the knees by a radio set. Anton, his best friend, who could never curb his tongue, came over and asked inquisitively: "Well, what's up, Paulchen? What is it? A legacy or the Knight's Cross?" The mocker was greeted by a look of embarrassment. It is strange how embarrassed even old soldiers can be at certain moments. "I am getting married the day after tomorrow," Paul admitted at last. Anton stared at him. "Getting married the day after tomorrow? Are you sick?" But now Paul replied proudly: "Long distance marriage," he said. "Good God!" replied Anton, and rushed off to tell the rest of the troop. "Paul's having a long-distance marriage." Now events moved swiftly. What the men learned from the prospective bridegroom amazed them.

Paul had met his bride before the battery had been transferred from Germany to Naples. It was love at first sight and Paul had promised to marry the girl on his next leave. But the bride did not want to wait any longer. She had written to him, but the mail had been lost somewhere in the Mediterranean. In all the excitement of the past months Paul had found no time to write. So the girl took matters into her own hands. An official letter had been sent to the C.O. requesting compassionate leave for the purpose of marriage. Should Corporal Paul Raskowski be indispensable for military reasons then he could agree to a long-distance marriage. The necessary papers had been enclosed and now that the demands of military bureaucracy had been satisfied the day of the wedding had been fixed for the 11th January. A written acknowledgment would suffice. The reply agreeing to the ceremony was despatched. Paul was flabbergasted by this officialdom. On the 11th January! The calendar showed the 9th January and the unit became feverishly active. A stage was built—a piece of beautiful desert—in the centre of which was placed a huge crate covered with bunting to serve as a lectern for the C.O. To the left and right piled rifles, but after examining the setting carefully the C.O. decided that the setting was too austere. "Rifles and a flag are not enough," he said. "We must have some palms." A few motor-cyclists streaked off along the Maradi road to the south to fetch the greenery. Two Volkswagens were despatched along the wadi carrying two broad-shouldered men who in civilian life were slaughterers. They were given orders not to return without three or perhaps four sheep.

On the morning of the 11th January, 1942, the sun shone out of a cloudless sky. The battery fell in and Paul took up his position in front of the beflagged crate. In place of the absent bride his friend Anton and the orderly room clerk, who were to act as witnesses, stood at his side. "Battery attention! Eyes Left!" "All present and correct, sir! Stand at ease!" The "old man" made a magnificent speech which warmed the hearts of the toughest members of the battery. He conjured up their homeland, now so far away, where at this very moment a girl stood at the altar thinking of the desert or at least of Paul; across the sea and across half Europe she would reply: "I will" to the corporal in the Wadi el Faregh. The amused grins disappeared from the men's faces. When they were dismissed they all shook Paul by the hand, but the serious mood did not last very long. The newlywed himself gave the signal for the start of an unofficial part of the ceremony. The C.O. had given him a couple of bottles of brandy as a wedding present. The Italian anti-tank boys who had heard the news brought a large can of red wine. A paratroop sergeant-major produced three bottles of "firewater" from the sidecar of his machine. Everyone was eager to bring something for an occasion in this war where there were real grounds to celebrate life instead of death. The high spot, however, was the four sheep. Hannes and Wilhelm bartered with an Arab for the beasts. With the help of a generous dose of looted curry and a sack of onions Jupp prepared a delicious couscous.

As night fell icy cold and the stars appeared Paul got ready for his wedding night. He retired with a few good friends and a full bottle to his tent. Outside the paratroopers were bashing their Indian drums. To the north over El Agheila the intermittent flashes of exploding shells lit up the sky. A salute for Corporal Raskowski and Wadi el Faregh, a quiet spot in Rommel's broad new front between Mersa el Brega and the Marada oasis.

A few miles away Captain Marwan-Schlosser of the 135th Flak Regiment pulled the blanket over his head. "That bloody creature!" he growled. Night after night it was the same thing. A hyena slunk up to the position and began to howl in the night. Yesterday it had broken into the mess tent and torn its nose on empty tins, but undaunted continued to come and could not be caught. Only once had a sentry caught sight of it beyond the dune in the early morning light. Night after night the beast howled its hunger to the stars. The German infantry heard it and so did the Tommies who lay in their cold sandholes in the advanced posts or pulled their blankets over their heads in their tents. "Why doesn't it move on?" they asked the following morning. "Why don't we finish the Jerries? They're on the run. Have we chased them five hundred miles to let them settle down here in peace? What the hell are they up to in Cairo?"

11

IN BENGHAZI SEVEN MILLION CIGARETTES GO UP IN FLAMES

The Christmas victory race of the 8th Army caused great enthusiasm in Cairo. Here, where the winter sun still gave its warmth things looked rosy. In the city the bars and clubs were filled to overflowing with men on leave. New night clubs sprang up like mushrooms. One of them was in a luxurious houseboat on the Nile.

Nothing was in short supply in Cairo. Naturally the prices rose, but the British soldiers had plenty of money and where could they spend it except in Cairo? The Egyptian Capital laughed and enjoyed its security. At the end of January the news came through that Rommel's combat groups at Halfaya Pass and Sollum had surrendered; when the pictures appeared in the papers showing Major Bach, the famous Pastor of Hellfire, as a prisoner-of-war the hopes of the Cairo Staff knew no bounds. Soon hundreds of tanks would roll forward for a new attack. The 8th Army would set out once more and no one would be able to halt it. It would reach Tripoli and then those bloody Germans and their Rommel would give them some peace. There were plenty of men and now all they needed were a few hundred machines, tanks, aircraft and the guns—according to Cairo.

And the machines arrived: American aircraft and American tanks. General Auchinleck walked in the rose garden of Cairo headquarters and developed plans for the destruction of Rommel. From time to time he would stop and be photographed. The victor of tomorrow! But in the rose garden of Cairo the calculations had been made without the landlord.

Erwin Rommel sat in El Agheila and there was no rose

garden. On the 10th January he visited his new headquarters and inspected the positions with Lieutenant-Colonel Westphal, his Chief of Staff. Westphal still remembers clearly his drives through the desert with Rommel. In the front line now were the pathetic remains of the 10th, 20th and 21st Italian Corps. The Afrika Korps units were reinforced, for supplies had finally arrived. Kesselring's 2nd Air Fleet provided cover for the transports. But would Rommel's forces suffice to repel a serious British attack? Admittedly the British were gravely hampered by their long lines of communication but they were growing stronger every day.

Westphal suggested an immediate counter-offensive. His argument was that they must forestall the enemy before he was ready to attack. Rommel stayed up all night in the caravan which served as his headquarters. Maps, Luftwaffe pilots' observations, reports of conversations intercepted from the enemy wireless during the past few days, lay on the table and chairs.

"The old man's on to something," said Sergeant-Major Böttcher, Rommel's private secretary. Orderlies were summoned, and time after time Böttcher had to produce from his countless chests and briefcases sketches of the terrain, old plans of attack and reports. "Something's cooking," said the orderlies.

They were right!

At last, at about half past five, Rommel switched off his reading lamp and flung himself down on his camp-bed. "Wake me in an hour," he ordered. The morning of the 13th January, 1942 dawned. When the General appeared at the normal morning briefing his officers could see by his face that he had something up his sleeve. He was radiant, and his Swabian accent was more than usually pronounced.

He did not keep them on tenterhooks for long. "We're going to attack," he said.

Going to attack? We, who at great pains saved our skins and have taken up a safe position. Some of our companies are only thirty men strong, our vehicles and ammunition park decimated during the rearguard action, and we're going to attack! They were flabbergasted. They all knew that the 8th Army was preparing for the final battle. Every morning they remarked that a new day without a British attack would be a godsend. They could improve their defences and build the Tripolitanian East Wall into an impregnable position.

Westphal alone evinced no surprise at Rommel's words. He merely smiled. During the past few days he had never left the general. Rommel insisted: "If we give the Tommies a break until February they'll chase us out of here. Nothing could stop the 8th Army in that event. Even if our supplies arrive faster, even if Kesselring's 2nd Air Fleet has pinned down Malta and the Royal Navy we can't get enough strength together fast enough and above all not enough heavy material."

But this time he added, after a slight pause as though speaking to himself: "So we must not wait. We must throw a monkey wrench into Tommy's plans." It was a bitter pill.

He revealed that morning to his staff everything that he had discussed in the past few days with his chief of staff, and had pondered over during the night of the 13th January. His plan was daring in the extreme.

The actual aim of his offensive was to hamper the enemy advance and delay the awaited British offensive. Should the affair go well there was always a chance of enlarging his plan. It was a desperate coup. But he saw no other possibility: to avoid certain defeat he must wrest the initiative from the British. As his first step Rommel, the cunning fox, pretended that he intended to abandon the Brega position. Like wildfire the rumour spread through the staffs and reached the Italians. "Rommel proposes to retire again." The Italian staff officers were filled with terror. They immediately alerted Rome. "Rommel proposes to retire again." In Rome it was impossible to guard even a top secret.

It traveled from the staffs to the bedrooms of beautiful women, to the barbers, sped from flower stall to flower stall, through the bars and hotel lounges. "Rommel can't hold the line and will retire to Tripoli." The Italian High Command discussed whether it should question Rommel, but decided against this.

As a result, in Cairo on the 18th January, agents' reports from Rome, Naples and from behind the German lines lay on the C-in-C's table. They all read: "Rommel is planning a further retreat." Auchinleck was not convinced. He ordered reconnaissances in strength.

The results seemed to corroborate the reports. No movements were observed on the Axis side of the front. Although the British reconnaissance air crews kept their eyes open, they could see nothing. Naturally they could not reconnoitre at night. They saw nothing of what happened during the hours of darkness. But there remained the British agents behind the German lines. They too reported: "Rommel is planning a further retreat." If a British offensive were launched to attack him in the rear it could result in final victory. So . . . further details please!

"What does Berlin know?" asked Auchinleck.

"In Berlin we have no information as to Rommel's deci-sive plan. He certainly isn't planning an attack," was the reply from the fifth column.

"What does the Italian Supreme command know?"

"It knows nothing, but is afraid that Rommel is going to retreat."

"What does the Bastico Army Group know?"

"The Bastico Army Group has only heard rumours of Rommel's proposed retreat. An offensive is out of the ques-tion. That is quite certain."

On 19th January there was an appalling sandstorm which made all reconnaissance impossible.

On the following day houses began to burn in Mersa el Brega; ships exploded in the harbour. They were empty houses and hulks that Rommel in his cunning had ordered to be blown up. Naturally the British agents and reconnaissance planes were unaware of this. The Secret Service contact men simply repeated to their masters what the German officers were saying. The British agents signalled to Cairo: "The Germans are setting fire to their supplies in Mersa el Brega. All unseaworthy ships are being blown up in the harbour." The reconnaissance troops of the British advanced units confirmed the fires and explosions. Cairo, therefore, conclud-ed that Rommel was making his final preparations for a retreat. He was pulling out. The mood in Cairo was one of exaltation. They toasted each other. "Rommel is burning his boats. Rommel is pulling out! Cheers!"

This was the position in Cairo on the night of 21st January, 1942. Many of the staff officers and men on leave did not cross the Schradi Kamel on the way home to their quarters until the early hours of the morning, and on the

Nile, in the smart houseboat of the dancer, Hekmat Fahmi, gramophone music was still being played at eight o'clock. "Rommel is pulling out. Cheers!" The beautiful Hekmat Fahmi flung a champagne glass against the mahogany pan- elled wall. "To victory!" she cried. But to whose victory? There seemed to be no doubt about this in the minds of her British officer guests.

At the very moment that Hekmat smashed her cham- pagne glass, far behind the lines in Tripolitania, a man in a tattered Arab burnous—he was known as Mohammed Ali, but was in fact a spy for Haselden's Long Range Desert Group—opened his eyes and pricked up his ears. A German M.P. had nailed a sheet of paper on the door of the house. German and Italian soldiers of the supply unit crowded round. The men in the back ranks cried: "Read it out." And then Mohammed Ali heard something incredible, something which he simply could not accept. The evening before he had sent a radio message to Cairo reporting the conversation of private soldiers who had spoken quite openly in his presence. As an Arab they imagined that he could not understand a word of German, although in actual fact he could speak Berlinese as well as any cabby on the Potsdamer Platz. He had reported to Cairo the conversations he had overheard: "Rommel is planning a retreat. Rearguard positions are being prepared." But what did this German N.C.O. read out to his comrades?

From the Supreme Commander   H.Q.
    of   21 . 1 . 42
   Panzer Group Africa.
   Army Order of the Day

German and Italian Soldiers!
  Behind you lie heavy battles with a vastly supe- rior enemy. Your morale remains unimpaired.
  At this moment we are considerably stronger than the enemy facing us in the front line. There- fore we shall proceed today to attack and destroy the enemy.
  I expect every man to give of his utmost in these decisive days.

> Long live Italy! Long live the Great German
> Reich! Long live the Führer!
>
> The Supreme Commander.
> ROMMEL
>
> *Copies to all Divisions.*   G.O.C. Panzer troops.

Like Mohammed Ali in Tripolitania the British outposts
at Mersa el Brega stood open mouthed when at 08.30 hours
on 21st January they saw the German tanks speeding towards
them. "Alert! German attack! Rommel is here!"

The surprise was complete. Rommel's trick had been
successful. Warned by the experience of treachery, he had
thought out a clever plan to deceive the enemy. He had
caused the reports of his intended retreat to be circulated
according to plan by certain staff officers. All traffic up to the
front line took place at night. The final preparations for the
offensive had been superbly camouflaged by nature on the
19th January in the shape of a violent sandstorm. The commanders of various units were given the plan of attack at the
last moment. Rommel had failed to consult the Italian and
German High Commands and the Führer's headquarters at
Rastenburg. He knew the leakages that could occur. He had
personally informed the Chief of Staff of the Italian High
Command in North Africa, General Gambara. "A small foray,"
he said, "a mere skirmish—you might call it a commando
raid—is to be carried out." Gambara placed fuel and column
space at his disposal and did not bother his head very much.
He did not even mention the matter to his own commanders.
A small raid. Why cause needless anxiety? But the small
"foray" was a drum-beat which echoed not only through
North Africa to Cairo but thundered throughout the whole
world: "Rommel has gone over to the attack."

On the German side a new division appeared in the
ensuing battles—the 90th Light. It had been formed from
the support division Afrika which had fought successfully
on the Tobruk front. Its commanding officer, Major-General
Summermann, was killed during the retreat to El Agheila.
Now it had been taken over my Major-General Veith who
came from Russia.

By and large Rommel's plan was as follows: A combat
group, led by Lieutenant-Colonel Werner Marcks, with units
of the 21st Panzer and the 90th Light Divisions were to attack

the positions held by the Guards Brigade along the Via Balbo, pierce the enemy lines and then push on to Agedabia. The 20th Italian Corps with the main body of the as yet unmotorised 90th Light Division was to follow. This was the northern arm of the pincer. The Afrika Korps formed the southern pincer arm and was to advance through the desert along the Wadi el Faregh to the north-east, and after making contact with the northern combat group attack the British units and destroy them. Rommel would decide the further progress of the offensive according to the outcome of the battle.

It was a cold sunny winter morning when Rommel left his headquarters at 0.600 hours to visit the Marcks Combat Group. Before he left, two messages arrived from the Führer's headquarters; the first announced that the Panzer Group was now to be known as the Panzer Army Afrika and the second that Rommel had been awarded the Swords and Oakleaves to his Knight's Cross.

By 11.00 hours the Marcks Combat Group had pierced the enemy defence position. The Italian Corps, under its new commander, General Zinghales, known as the Italian Guderian, could be relieved. The Marcks group pushed on to Agedabia, which was taken by surprise the following day. The British Mark VI tanks were never in action because they had run short of petrol on the way up the line. The petrol and munitions dumps had been overrun by the German combat group.

How surprised the British were by this attack is described by Alan Moorehead in his *African Trilogy*: "Communications seem to have failed badly almost from the first moment. Hard-pressed infantry could not get support and reinforcements either lay idle, or when they attempted to reach the threatened quarter found their path blocked by the enemy. In three strong columns the Axis forces streamed straight into the British lines. They fanned out and it was the same old story—isolated British groups being mopped up one after another. In two days the British cutting edge was gone. In three days the British advance had definitely turned into a retreat."

This is a correct report. It reads so simply, but in actual fact things were not nearly so simple.

Let us follow the battle with the adjutant of the 135th

Flak Regiment, a unit which played an outstanding part in these battles. Not until the 19th January had Rommel sent for Major Hecht, the commander, and said to him abruptly: "I propose to take the advancing enemy by surprise. Zero hour is early on the 21st. Your Flak regiment is to give support to the attack in the greatest strength possible."

The detachments of the regiment were divided between the northern and southern arms of the pincer. After the capture of Agedabia the northern flak sections were ordered to reinforce the motorised forces for a further advance. Everything was moved forward. The 114th Reserve Flak Unit became temporarily a heavy motorised battery. The remaining batteries of the 114th remained in support to give air cover to Agedabia. In the meantime the Afrika Korps had pushed forward in the Antelat-Saunu sector and encircled the 1st Armoured Division. On the 24th January Rommel intended to destroy this British Armoured Division which was now pinned down. With several columns he set out to effect this. Rommel himself led his combat staff which consisted of the temporarily motorised 114th Battery and the regimental headquarters staff of the 135th Flak Regiment. "We had put about forty miles behind us," related Captain Marwan-Schlosser, "when the ruins of Giof el Matar appeared on the horizon. Rommel suddenly shouted: 'Flak ahead. Fire!' We flak gunners exchanged glances and asked: 'Where is the target, Herr General?' 'Can't you see those enemy massed trucks ahead?' Major Hartmann, the C.O. of the 114th, looked for a target for his 88 mm. He shook his head. Rommel called for a white flag. 'We must send someone over to parley.' A man appeared with a sheet. 'Go on wagging that white sheet and the Tommies will surrender. Then go over and tell them they're surrounded. In the meantime we'll stir up a bit of dust!'"

"Raise the dust!" ran the order, and soon everything that had wheels was raising dust in the neighbourhood. At this moment a Fieseler Storch landed near by. Rommel made up his mind in a flash. "The envoy is to fly over." Major Hartmann scanned the horizon with his field glasses once more and shook his head. But it was of no avail. The Storch took off and the envoy waved his white flag from the cockpit. The pilot landed, but since nothing stirred he returned. The terrain was completely free of the enemy. In the haze Rommel had mistaken some tall camelthorn bushes for trucks. This often happened in the African war. It would not be worth while recording except to show the optimism that radiated from Rommel in every situation.

Ahead of the 8th Panzer Regiment they were not camelthorn bushes which loomed on the horizon. Lieutenant-Colonel Cramer let the regiment go on marching. Far on the flank were the four tanks of the left column of No. 4 Company. "Attention! Orange 2. Attack enemy tanks on the left!" echoed in the leader's headphones. Orange was the code word for the two flank tanks of the column, and the commander of Orange 2 understood. "Eleven o'clock, engage enemy armour," he called into his intercom. Inside the tank the driver, gunner, leader and wireless operator heard the order. Eleven o'clock meant of course a slight turn to the left. "Eight-hundred yards, armour-piercing shells fire!" Inside the stifling metal box in a temperature of 120 degrees the leader and gunner worked like clockwork. The turret and gun was aimed, the driver had stopped, for firing could only take place when the tank was stationary. Now the gunner pressed the electric firing button. "Up fifty!" came the commander's order. The shot had been fifty yards short. "Reload. New range. Aim. Fire! On the target!" cried the commander.

Now the British despatched an Indian contingent from Benghazi to attack the German flank. This could have been dangerous but Rommel's listening service was on the alert. It had picked up a British message according to which this detachment was fifteen miles north of Agedabia serving to a certain extent as an outpost. The British commander, General Ritchie, did not want to involve the whole division in the dogfight. He tried to bluff the Germans, but now that Rommel knew his intentions his plan was pointless. Rommel decided to ignore the Indian division and to fling all his strength against the 1st Armoured Division.

He was justified as the results show. Twelve aircraft, ninety-six armoured vehicles and thirty-eight guns were captured. Over a thousand prisoners were taken, including the staff of a British tank division. A huge supply centre with enormous quantities of material fell into German hands. The soldiers were amazed when they saw this wealth. God, what material these British had and what treasures. Pity that pockets were so small and that weapons were more important than Players' cigarettes, orange marmalade, whisky and biscuits. The sappers had a particularly good haul when in an enemy tank repair shop they found thirty battleworthy British Valentines.

When Rommel accompanied by Westphal flew over the battlefield to get a picture of the position they had a narrow escape. It was one of those episodes which show how the fortunes of war commanders in battle hang by a thread.

The two men were in their Fieseler Storch flying at low altitude towards a concentration of vehicles where they presumed they would find General Crüwell. They suddenly came under anti-aircraft fire. British! The Storch was riddled like a colander. Splinters and pieces of metal flew in the air. But Rommel did not lose his head. He directed the pilot. "To starboard . . . now to port, gain height, dive . . ." While the aircraft was being flung about the sky Westphal suddenly spotted twelve Hurricanes above the Storch. This is the end, he thought. But fortunately the British aircraft did not spot the little fly below them. They were lucky to get out of this spot. There seemed to be a jinx on them that day. On the return flight they came once more under fire from an enemy ack-ack unit. The Storch was again peppered. Rommel got back to his headquarters unwounded. With a little more luck on the part of the gunners Rommel and his Chief of Staff would have fallen, dead or alive, into enemy hands.

With the Battle of Msus Rommel's plan for disrupting the British offensive preparations and winning time had been successful. But Rommel was not the man to be content with a surprise and a brilliant four days' success. Marshal Count Cavallero visited the battlefield to implore Rommel not to proceed with his offensive. Kesselring flew with his Italian colleague to Rommel's headquarters. The reason for the Italian's apprehension was not hurt pride at Rommel's secret and single-handed offensive but fear of a military defeat. As Fritz Bayerlein told me, Rommel recorded his dramatic conflict with the Italian High Command in his diary:

"23rd January. Marshal Cavallero arrived today from Rome with Mussolini's directives for the pursuance of the campaign. . . . Rome does not agree with my attack and wants me to conclude it. Cavallero said: 'Disengage and retire to the Brega position.' I opposed him resolutely and informed him that as long as my troops and supplies allowed I was determined to harass the enemy. Now at last the Panzer

Army is once more on the move and the initial blows have been successful.... More will follow. Marshal Cavallero implored me not to do this..."

Rommel did not give way. Cavallero withdrew in anger. His reply was to withdraw the Italian Corps from Rommel's command, and to refuse to let it leave the Agedabia–Mersa el Brega sector. If Rommel wanted to continue to fight he could do so with German units. And this is precisely what he did.

Why were the Italian staff so cautious? We Germans are inclined to judge them rather contemptuously. But things are not as simple as all that. The Italian High Command was not given to making bold decisions. The Italian soldier, on the contrary, fought bravely: it was not his courage that was in question but the quality of his weapons. Nor did the Italian nation understand why Mussolini wanted to wage another colonial campaign with blood and tears. The Italian Colonial empire was already quite large enough. The military saw things from this angle and failed to appreciate how this German, Rommel, after a 500-mile rearguard action could start once more thinking of victory and be sure that his exhausted troops would still follow him with full confidence. The Italians considered this pure madness. The Italian army was incapable of embarking upon such adventures. It was outdated and its appearance betrayed the fact. The officer corps went to war with a vast baggage train. Waiters from the best Italian hotels were engaged as orderlies, and even in the desert waited on the generals in white gloves. In addition to the officers' mess there were messes for senior N.C.O.s, junior N.C.O.s and private soldiers. While three courses were served in the officers' mess the rank and file had to be content with a tin of "Alte Mann". The Italian soldiers stared in amazement at the Germans whose generals and privates enjoyed the same rations at the front.

When Rommel attacked from the Mersa el Brega line on 21st January only an armed reconnaissance in strength had been envisaged. The attack took the British completely off their guard. Rommel now planned to attack Benghazi.

It was spring in the desert. The calendar registered the end of January but North Africa is different from Europe. In the newly-conquered positions at Msus the German soldiers were surprised at the unusual vernal beauty on the fringe of the Cyrenaica desert. Fragrant crocuses were in bloom. They were larger than those at home in the Altmark, in Swabia, East Prussia or the Rhineland—yellow, red and blue exotic blossoms. A riot of colour, this marvellous though short-lived spring seemed to be a protest on the part of nature against the stupidity of warring mankind. The sun beat down and there was an atmosphere of peace.... No long drawn out wail for stretcher-bearers. No stench of oil fumes and corpses. Sweet smelling flowers.... How enchanting was this spring in the shadow of death. With what joy man smelled flowers when the odour of death was not far away.

The men had built cages outside their foxholes and slit trenches for tortoises. Others enjoyed the antics of chameleons and the skill with which they caught the flies with their long tongues. The soldiers placed these delicate creatures alternately on the white sand, green camelthorn and then swiftly on a red handkerchief. "Just look, just look..." they cried when the chameleon changed its colour.

And then the tortoise races! All that was needed was an old table or even a table top to prevent the runners from scuttling away off the course. The veterans of the 115th invariably won with their favourite. They made high wagers and always won. The 115th was a proud regiment from Hesse which carried on the traditions of the Hessian Grand-ducal Body-guard.

"Ten Gold Flake on Napoleon." "Fifteen Players on Auchinleck." "Twenty Senior Service on Wilhelm." These English cigarettes were considered the best loot of all, and this last bet was invariably a winner. Wilhelm always won. He gave them a golden opportunity to increase their supplies. Who would have not preferred them to the dry, crumbling cigarettes which for lack of tropical packing became as dry as straw? Wilhelm was a land tortoise, and these species are far more cunning than their brothers from the marshes. This was the old soldiers' trick: they never employed a marsh tortoise although at first sight it looked faster. Wilhelm was a sprinter. Despite all the coaxing of the cooks he ignored the proffered plate of soup. In gratitude he was given his freedom as soon as their dream of peace was rudely shattered. Their three days release from hell was over. They were back at war!

Through reports from his listening posts Rommel learned that the British staff were in two minds whether Benghazi and Mechili could be defended. This was all grist to Rommel's mill. He decided to wrest the decision from the British and attack Benghazi. The harbour would be very useful for his supplies. Once more he favoured surprise tactics. In the spring of 1941 he had taken Benghazi from the south. "The British will obviously think we shall repeat the experiment," he said to Westphal. He, therefore, decided to approach from Msus and take the harbour by surprise from inland. With this trick he proposed to cut off the British garrison in the city. Admittedly the difficult terrain and lack of fuel restricted the number of troops he could employ.

Rommel drove with his fighting staff to pay a visit to the Marcks combat group. This doughty commando reinforced by the 2nd Machine-gun Battalion and Major Hecht's flak combat group was to cross the mountainous region of Cyrenaica and press on to Benghazi. Colonel Geissler's Combat Group was ordered to by-pass Mechili and capture Maraua, thus securing the Benghazi operation to the east. This group consisted of sections of the 115th Panzer Regiment, two companies of Panzerjaegers and an armoured artillery battery.

The combat group worked its way painfully across the difficult going. Then darkness fell. A reconnaissance patrol returned and reported that a strong enemy detachment of about twenty guns and a hundred trucks lay in the valley. The British were happy-go-lucky. From the valley they could be heard preparing their supper. "Quiet! Quiet!" ordered Geissler, and then in the pitch darkness the anti-tank guns were brought into position. The attack was fixed for dawn. The night was so dark that the machine-gun had to be posted by instinct. The heavy battery could not select a suitable gun position. It remained in readiness to fire on the approach route.

The British were never particularly early risers. This was a well-known (and human) weakness and Geissler had based his plan on it. At 03.00 hours he issued his orders. "Fire when you see the white flare." Lieutenant Ruf with his three anti-tank guns found the period of waiting intolerable. The outlines of the British guns and trucks gradually emerged in the first grey light. Not a movement on the other side. The Germans were already at their action stations.

At last! A white flare! The three anti-tank guns fired and the artillery went into action. Below it was hell let loose.

Caught completely off their guard the British manned their trucks and fired into the blue as they drove off. Men ran behind them shouting at the tops of their voices. Columns of flame. The Horsemen of the Apocalypse were riding. They were riding to their death.

Now the German motorised troops poured down the valley. The route had to be cleared of damaged vehicles. Commandos were detailed to collect the corpses and attend to the wounded.

A lanky major stood there by his truck, his hands folded in prayer, staring down at his friend, a lieutenant who lay dead at his feet. An English M.O. was kneeling by the body. Doctor Godde of the 115th leaped from his armoured car, but no help was needed here. He and the British M.O. began to attend to the wounded. The major continued to stand like a statue beside the corpse. A lieutenant approached him and said quietly: "Come along, Major." The senior officer gave a start, nodded and walked away to the prisoners' assembly point. Captain Schuster, Geissler's adjutant, a veteran campaigner and very popular with the 115th, shook his head. "It gets you down," he said, and added as though for his own ears: "Starts praying and forgets the war. That's a bad show for a major, but you can't help liking the fellow for it."

The advanced sections of Geissler's Combat Group pushed on well towards Maraua. 28th January. Was this really Africa? What a country! Green bushes, meadows, cypresses, birches, pines and flowers everywhere. This fertile area had been the granary of Ancient Rome before the desert encroached to the north. Now they came to a brook with a wooden bridge. They might have been in Lower Saxony. But war has no respect for the idyllic charms of nature.

Next morning enemy fighter-bombers flew over the Geissler group. They were mistaken for British troops and no bombs fell. Suddenly, however, there was a huge explosion and the right wheel of the leading command truck flew into the air. Mines had been laid in front of the bridge. The driver, Herringer, was about to jump out but Lieutenant Moritz restrained him. "Stay where you are man or else you'll be blown sky high." Cautiously they climbed out of the truck and followed its tracks back to the rear. "Sappers forward!" The mines were soon swept, but the rest of the battalion drove through the brook to avoid the barrage which had been laid on the bridge. A "recce" troop returned and reported the heights before Maraua free of enemy troops. Toni Streit, orderly officer of the 115th, nodded: "Then we shall soon have a brand new commander truck 'Made in England.'"

The company commanders were detailed to their sectors. Two reconnaissance sections were despatched in the direction of Benghazi and Mechili respectively. "Battalion ready for action," reported the C.O. of the 115th.

But what had happened in the meantime to Rommel's attack on Benghazi?

Rommel had set out with his combat group at 17.00 hours on January 28th. But the operation seemed to be ill-fated from the start. A sandstorm with torrential rain broke over them. The storm lasted for two hours. One column which the weather had overtaken while crossing a wadi was pinned down. Frozen and hungry they had to stay there until the following morning. The morass made any advance impossible. This can't be Africa, they thought. Beneath the burning rays of the morning sun the ground soon dried and their nightmare was over. The heavy trucks of course had to be left behind. What matter, they could advance all the quicker! The old Turkish fortress, Er Regima, was occupied. Press on! Rommel at their head! On to Benina! At the last moment a flight of Ju 52s which the British had captured took off. What a pity!

To offset this, fabulous supply dumps flanked the road. They were the new dumps which the British had assembled for their projected offensive to Tripoli. Moreover, the old German dumps abandoned in the retreat had been untouched. War knows no economy and is extravagance personified. There were treasures to be had. Whole cities could be supplied with the contents.

The British garrison in Benghazi was doomed. The commander of the Indian Division in the town sent his demolition squads into action. Against a background of the great white cathedral the dumps began to burn. Seven million cigarettes went up in flames. Countless barrels of rum were destroyed. A hundred thousand tons of bully beef smouldered in the burning dumps. Nevertheless there was plenty left.

The Marcks Combat Group brought in the first columns of prisoners and reported the capture of many trucks which had tried to break out of Benghazi. But Rommel hardly listened to them. He wanted to enter the city. There followed an interlude of light relief which the staff thoroughly enjoyed. The wireless operator of a "recce" unit picked up a message from Mussolini. The Duce suggested that Rommel "on this favourable occasion should take Benghazi but that the Italians should remain where they were at Agedabia and Mersa el Brega." Rommel's reply was curt: "Benghazi already taken."

At 12.00 hours on 30th January Rommel at the head of his staff group re-entered the Cyrenaican capital. The Arabs gave him a noisy welcome and waved the green flag of the prophet. He drove through a city of ruins. But the Arabs rejoiced as they had rejoiced some weeks before when they had welcomed the British armour.

Although Rommel often took risks he could on occasions display great caution. When he heard Geissler's report that his combat group was ready to storm Maraua, he cancelled the operation. This was at the very moment that Major Ehle had sent his message: "1st Battalion ready to attack." "Wait for the arrival of the Machine-gun Battalion. Benghazi already captured," was Rommel's reply to Geissler. He would take no risks of being contained in Benghazi. The sun stood low on the horizon when the 2nd MG Battalion joined forces with Geissler's troops. The operation was then neatly rounded off. As usual Sergeant-Major Mankiewicz produced a few bottles of "firewater" to celebrate the occasion—a tot for all commanders and company commanders. Captain Mitros, as usual, was the only one to drink two doubles. He was from East Prussia.

At nightfall Maraua was in German hands. Auchinleck stood grimly in front of his map at Cairo headquarters. He sent his staff officers one after the other by air to the front to restore some order in the British retreat. But where could the British make a stand? How much strength had Rommel still left? The first reports of Rommel's advance on Derna soon came through.

Was there no halting the wily fox?

Yes! Rommel, too, was subject to the law of reinforcements and supplies, and the British were therefore able to consolidate on the Gazala line. This defensive position held the same significance for the British as the Mersa el Brega line had held for the Germans.

In seventeen days Rommel had won back nearly every-

thing he lost, but his forces were inadequate to take Tobruk.
It remained in British hands, and once more all the British
hopes rested on this "fortress in the sand." Would it once
more prove a thorn in Rommel's side as it had done in 1941?
The unassailable gateway to Egypt, the downfall of the Afrika
Korps?

12

BOMBS ON FORT LAMY

Sergeant Hein carefully twiddled the knobs of his Storch
receiving set "Caesar." He held his breath and listened.
Da-da-da-da. No, that was not it. Once more nothing on the
air. For two days they had sat in Agedabia each morning
between 08.00 and 09.00 hours and in the evening between
20.00 and 21.00 hours in the radio truck of Luftwaffe Command Afrika exploring the ether. They could hear the spluttering
of interference and other stations but the message they
wanted did not come through. "Still nothing," sighed Hein,
removing his headphones. The time was 20.10 hours, Friday,
23rd January, 1942. "Go on trying until 20.30 hours," said
Hein, handing the headphones to Wachsmuth. His subordinate sat down, started to twiddle the dials and to listen.
Sergeant Hein put on his cap and went off to eat. He was
already at the door when Wachsmuth called out: "I've got it!"
There was silence in the truck. No one stirred. Hein stood as
though frozen to stone by the door while all the others turned
their eyes on Wachsmuth. The operator listened intently and
his pencil flew over the paper. Hein tiptoed across and looked
over his shoulder. "VQBJ, VQBJ, VQBJ." The signal was
repeated. Wachsmuth exchanged glances with the N.C.O.
They smiled. "That's them. Send a reply." And the corporal
in the pause between the call sign sent his reply over the air.

At the same moment seven hundred and fifty miles from
Agedabia, in the tropical African desert, for thousands of
years the domain of the wind and the sun, came a shout:

He 111

"We've made contact!" A captain of the German Luftwaffe jumped to his feet and rushed over to the operator who was squatting in the sand beside his little three-watt agent's transmitter. The other men surged forward—bearded, thirsty men. Lieutenant Franz Bohnsack, the Italian Major Count Vimercati-San Severino, Lieutenant Fritz Dettmann and Sergeant-Major Heinrich Geissler. They stared at the operator, Wichmann, who, with head bent forward, was listening by candlelight to the signals. Their faces lit up. For the first time for two days they were able to laugh in this forlorn spot hundreds of miles south of Agedabia.

Back there in Agedabia they listened to the faint tones coming from the remote African desert. Painstakingly and with many demands for a repeat they deciphered the message: Special Commando Blaich reports successful mission with direct hits on the fuel dump and hangers of Fort Lamy on Lake Chad. Forced landing on return two days ago from lack of fuel in unknown territory. Location of forced landing approximately in the map sector Tuommo. Water almost exhausted.

"Over," transmitted the Agedabia operator. "Over," repeated Wichmann far away in the desert as he wrote down the end of the message. Then he jumped to his feet and, contravening all military discipline, the crew began to dance in the sand in front of their He 111 which stood there in this God-forsaken desert like some strange fairy-tale bird. To give them shade their tents hung like fantastic bunting over the wings. Their flea bags lay in the sand. Heinrich Geissler, the engineer, approached Captain Blaich. "What about a few drops of water to celebrate this news, Captain? Only a few drops?" They all looked at the pilot but he shook his head. The smile died on their faces. They realised that it had only been a contact made seven hundred and fifty miles away. They were still prisoners in the endless Sahara, and in the five-gallon tank which they had tapped only two days before little more than two gallons remained. They retired to their sleeping-bags in silence. A silence as profound as the desert which held them in thrall.

Would they ever break their bonds or would the desert be their grave? Geissler got up once more and went over to the aircraft to fetch a stone he had been examining carefully that morning. Next morning he would begin to carve his name on it, so that later people would know to whom the white bones belonged and the fate of the men who, in the spring of 1942, had carried out such a fantastic mission. This is their story:

Almost in the centre of the giant continent of Africa on the latitude which denotes its broadest part, lies a huge lake 120 miles long—Lake Chad. It is fed by two rivers, the Logone—the poisonous river—and the Chari. Seen from the north this watershed with the mighty Lake Chad is the frontier of the Sahara. Observed from the south the lake is the last bastion of the Central African primeval jungle against the perpetually encroaching desert. It is the north wall of the jungle, a giant dam of vegetation against the majesty of the void. Here desert and jungle wage a bitter conflict, but the desert is winning. The north wind drives the sand constantly and tirelessly towards the south. Already parts of the lake are silted up, and in the east it is already reduced to a small pond. And the sand continues to trickle, fighting against water and forest. A silent, unobtrusive, relentless battle waged without a sound as is the nature of a desert.

But Lake Chad is not merely a geographical feature. It is also a focal point in African traffic, strategy and world politics in the Dark Continent. Here at the edge of the tropical jungle meet the frontiers of the former German colonies, the Cameroons, Nigeria, Equatorial Africa and French West Africa.

Since nature had created a natural bastion, the conquerors and pioneers of the colonial epoch built a fort at this spot—Fort Lamy. It lies almost in the centre of Africa. A modern citadel of the rulers of a continent at the junction of the most important traffic routes, from the Atlantic coast and the harbour of Duala, Lamy is at the crossroads to the Belgian Congo and Algiers. Thus it was a flank protection and flank threat to Libya and, in the year 1942, a key point in the overland route from the Atlantic Ocean across which the Americans supplies arrived for Egypt.

To understand against what enemy strength Rommel and his Afrika Korps fought with the most modest of means, it must be realised that this campaign was fought not only in the north but in the coastal region but in effect deep into the heart of Africa. In Fort Lamy, too, the battle was waged against Rommel with supplies—and on the plane of grand strategy. Here was situated the supply junction for Egypt, beyond the reach of Rommel's operations. For De Gaulle's troops, which had occupied the Tibesti Mountains and threatened Rommel's flank from Southern Libya, it was the great assembly point, the point of departure for long-distance targets.

Berlin knew little of these African secrets. The continental strategy of the Western Powers was unknown, and Berlin had no idea that the Allies had laid their supply routes straight across Africa to Egypt. They were quite unaware of what was happening at Lagos where the Standard Oil and Shell companies had their large refineries. Nor had they any knowledge of events at Duala and Brazzaville in the Belgian Congo from where oil and petrol were transported to Fort Lamy.

But one man knew it all. One of those great lone wolves who pulled no political or strategical wires, a pioneer and a passionate explorer, an owner of plantations and an adventurer in the truest sense of the word, an old colonial and the only soldier in the German Army in 1939 to report for service in the Luftwaffe with an aircraft—Theo Blaich. He flew—if one can call it flying—his "Typhoon" for Rommel. A secret report which he compiled in January 1942 before Rommel's offensive reads as follows: "Fort Lamy is the assembly point for enemy operations. This focal point is the junction of several lines of communication, including the route to the east which can be used throughout the year and which extends as far as the Nile. The Allies swiftly recognized the advantages of this line of communication beyond enemy range which stretched form the west coast of Africa to the Nile, and built it up to the dimensions required.

"Tibesti, the advanced post in the north, which serves as a bridgehead between Libya and the Lake Chad region, is in the hands of De Gaulle; it represents a threat to the Libyan Desert and therefore to our Tripoli-Benghazi lines of communication. The South Libyan border must therefore be safeguarded to counter a possible enemy attack from central Africa. The alternative is a military operation with the object of harassing or capturing the Fort Lamy–Nile supplies route."

The general staff in Berlin read this report in amazement. Capture the Fort Lamy–Nile line? The man is crazy! But Theo Blaich gave them no peace. He insisted that bomber formations at least should be sent to destroy the important centre of Fort Lamy.

An air offensive against a place separated from the Luftwaffe airfields in North Africa by 1250 miles of Sahara! Rommel read Blaich's report with interest. He was always in favour of boldness and imagination. He scrutinised his maps and nodded his head, appended a green "R" to the report and sent it to the Luftwaffe Commander Africa. Blaich's report bore many signatures but they were all overshadowed by the green "R". As a result, on the day that Rommel opened his new offensive that historic Wednesday, 21st January, 1942, six airmen took off on a raid which deserves to be classed as one of the great adventures of the modern age, and to be incorporated in the history of the war. The Blaich Special Commando flew to Fort Lamy.

Campo Uno was a natural airfield with a firm shale surface. The natural runways were obstacle free on all sides. Wind-breaking crests framed the loneliest airfield in the world. Taking off from Hun Oasis airfield they landed here on the 20th January. They were the only guests on this strange desert strip of sand and shale which did not possess a single shed or hangar. "They" signifies Captain Theo Blaich and his "Typhoon," Lieutenant Franz Bohnsack, the pilot of an He 111, Sergeant-Major Geissler, the engineer, Sergeant Wichmann, the wireless operator, and Lieutenant Dettmann, the war reporter. Dettmann, who lent that touch of brilliance that never verged on the "corny" to all his reports of land and air battles, was popular with the airmen on account of his courage and chivalry. He was, I believe, the only war reporter to be awarded the German Cross in gold.

One other man took off with them from Campo Uno to raid Fort Lamy, a figure straight from the days of the Caesars: Major Roberto Count Vimercati-San Severino. He was the desert expert of the Italian Army in Africa. He, too, had discovered Campo Uno in 1935. When on one of his safaris he had landed on the resilient carpet of sand and shale. He patrolled the heights and marked the ideal airfield in unexplored territory on the edge of the South Libyan Sahara with white stone. Since then there had been a Campo Uno.

Vimercati was a much travelled man, and his great love was the Sahara, the realm of the wind, the sand and the stars. He had served as an officer in Libya for sixteen years. His comrades called him the Prince of Gialo after the old oasis to which he was so attached.

Vimercati landed at Campo Uno on the 20th January in a large Savoia. It served as the mother ship, with fuel supplies for the raid on Fort Lamy and for the return flight. It was to wait at Campo Uno. The crew and their comrades at Hun Oasis would count the hours until the German He 111 returned from its bold raid. The Italians were touchingly anxious: Scorzone the agile little wireless operator whose shorts were far too long and made him look like a gnome; Sergeants D'Agata, Zaratini and Tulliani; the engineer, Masuade, and the man with the provocative name which did not suit him in the least, Alfredo Scandalo.

It was wonderful in Campo Uno, an ideal spot for a man who loved the desert and who had water and a tent to protect him against the pitiless sun. Vimercati checked his "one-man house", a contraption consisting of a tent and the sleeping bag which experienced Saharans carry as Europeans carry a cigarette lighter. Franz Bohnsack, the pilot of the He 111, a born airman, always calm and with a huge appetite, was busy with his saucepan, boiling water over a spirit lamp. Geissler, the engineer, was tightening screws and checking the rigging. Dettmann was dreaming in the sunset. Night fell. As usual it fell within a matter of seconds and they crawled into their sleeping bags.

"In bocca al lupo," the Italians shouted to the crew about to take off at 08.00 hours on Wednesday, the 21st January. This was the equivalent of "Happy Landings." The He 111 taxied across the sand with one thousand gallons of petrol on board—a flying tank.

The engines roared. Bohnsack sat calmly at his control column. Blaich, as leader of the raid and observer, had the seven-foot-long rolled map on his lap. Vimercati kept a sharp look-out for landmarks. The Tibesti Mountains, with their nine-thousand-foot peaks, loomed ahead in the morning haze. Vimercati and Blaich made hasty entries on the map of this area which was still terra incognita, unexplored territory. Sand and dunes without a trace of water and vegetation. This is the abode of the wind, where no beast and no plants thrive. No human foot has ever trod this soil.

The weather was bad and a storm was brewing. "We shall need more juice than we reckoned," grumbled Bohnsack. Every gallon had been carefully calculated, with only a narrow margin of reserve, for at Hun they had forecast calm, fine weather. A Luftwaffe meteorologist had turned up at the Italian strongpoint. His white cap worn rakishly over one ear, he had announced quite cheerfully: "I'm the 'weather frog', to give you the benefit of my experience for your special mission." Fine experience his turned out to be!

"That bloody fool," grumbled Bohnsack. No one had a good word to say for the met. expert from Saxony. They did not know that the man had done a good job, but not for the crew of the He 111 now on its way to Fort Lamy. The "weather frog" who had appeared out of the blue was one of Jock Campbell's British agents, a member of his sabotage group. When he tried to slip away after the He 111 had taken off a captain spotted him as a result of a peculiar coincidence with which even the most intelligent spy could not reckon.

When the men of Blaich's special commando returned, all they would find of the meteorologist was a wooden cross on a mound. It bore no name, for the "Jock Column" agent refused to give it, "Just write an Anglo-Saxon," he said with a smile, speaking in the broad Saxon accent he had picked up whilst studying in Dresden.

But Bohnsack and Blaich, Vimercati and the others in the He 111 that day knew nothing of this as they sped towards Lake Chad and grumbled at the wind and the failing visibility.

Towards midday the eastern arm of Lake Chad came into view. The water glittered in the sunshine. Now they could no longer lose their way. Visibility deteriorated and a greyish-yellow veil hung in the air. It was the Harmattan, the dry dust storm of Equatorial Africa. The thermometer on the instrument panel at 7,500 ft. registered 78 degrees Fahrenheit. They suspected that below in the tropical midday heat the temperature would be somewhere between 104 and 120 degrees Fahrenheit.

Bohnsack made a wide sweep to the south in order to reconnoitre the roads and river traffic of the strategic centre, Lamy. At about 14.30 hours he changed on to a northerly course.

"Action stations," Blaich ordered calmly.

The outlines of the town were now visible and soon the picture grew clearer. They could see the broad, straight avenues, the dilapidated native quarter and the airfield. The shutters of their cameras clicked.

Lamy airfield possessed two large hangars, surrounded by workshops. Huge white patches with semi-buried oil storage tanks. They looked like sandcastles. No ack-ack? Were they asleep?

"Sticks or single bombs?" Bohnsack asked Blaich.

"Sticks," replied the captain.

Bohnsack nodded and adjusted his bomb aimer. They carried sixteen bombs—5,000 lbs. of death and destruction. "On the target, ready to release."

Blaich nodded and Bohnsack pressed the button.

In the aircraft they did not hear the detonation but they saw the results of the explosion. Columns of flame and black smoke rose in the air. The sea of flames and smoke spread out and the sheds were pulverised. The fuel storage tanks caught fire. In the aircraft they were roaring with delight. They were crazy with excitement and had to give vent to their feelings. "What a blaze! It's well alight!" Not a single shot was fired by the defence. Sixty miles from the target on the way back they could still see the pall of smoke. The war had left its mark on Lake Chad deep in Central Africa. A daring coup had been successful.

Six weeks later the German High Command learned from a captured French corporal how surprised they had been on Lake Chad when a German bomber appeared. In their bewilderment they forgot to give the ack-ack orders to fire. Eighty thousand gallons of octane and the entire oil supply went up in flames. Ten aircraft were destroyed on the ground and all the airfield buildings heavily damaged. Fort Lamy was out of action for weeks.

They had taken off at 08.00 hours from Campo Uno and had bombed Fort Lamy at 14.30 hours. Now they flew for four hours on a northerly course. In the west they could see the unmistakable signs of the end of the day. The sun descended rapidly, painting gigantic shadows on the dunes and rocks. "Are we on course?" asked Bohnsack. But he received no reply. No man could take his bearings in this shadow show. They still had petrol for another half hour's flying. Would they ever find Campo Uno, a tiny dot in this bizarre evening desert sea? Vimercati's eyes scanned the desert. From time to time he shook his head. Time was running out. And so was their petrol. Finally they all knew that they would not make it. They would never be able to find Campo Uno before night-fall. In a quarter of an hour their petrol would be exhausted and by the last light of day they would have to find a place to land. They must go down into the desert. "Pay out the aerial," ordered Bohnsack. The antenna of the powerful seven-watt transmitter was a hundred yards long.

"Wichmann," called Blaich. The latter bent over to the leader, and then sent out his S.O.S. But he received no reply.

"Fasten your belts and hold tight," Bohnsack said calmly.

Throttle reduced. . . . Silence. . . .

Then the engines roared again. Franz had to switch them on again to avoid a wadi.

Within a few seconds it would be dusk and then a moment or two later the desert night would engulf them.

Once more throttle back. They held their breath. Would the crate crash about their ears? No, everything was all right and after a few gentle bounces the He 111 came to a standstill.

There was a silence and everyone looked at Vimercati, the man of the desert. He felt in his pocket and brought out a gold cigarette case. In it were three cigarettes, for he never smoked. He took them out and broke each of them in two, so that now there were six. Six cigarettes... six days.... Did the old desert fox Vimercati think they would be there six days? Wichmann, the enthusiastic wireless operator, immediately thought of the little set which Blaich had procured for him. It was a three-watt agent's transmitter, a little box run off a battery, for the aircraft transmitter could only be used when the engines were running. Wichmann swiftly put up his aerial. It was just before 20.00 hours, the appointed time for making contact with the Luftwaffe headquarters station at Agedabia. By the light of a flickering candle he sat in the sand and tapped the key. VQBJ, VQBJ—the commando's call sign. He kept repeating it, then paused and listened. Nothing. And once more VQBJ VQBJ. After half an hour Wichmann gave it up. He had to spare his batteries.

"Let's pitch our camp," said Bohnsack, with forced gaiety. The emergency rations were fetched from the machine: four canvas tents contained sleeping bags, mosquito nets and rubber mattresses. Plates, mugs compass, rifles, clasp knives, hurricane matches, cigarettes and spades.... Nothing had been forgotten. Their food was stored in six large containers. "One man for six days" was stencilled on the tin. Another coincidence: six days. They had plenty of provisions for that time—bully beef, port, ham, biscuits, spicy delicacies provided there was plenty to drink with them. In addition there were tins of condensed milk, vitamin tablets, tinned fruit, rusks, tea tablets, salt, sugar and Ryvita. To think that a large tin could contain all that! They admired this treasure but where was the water? The water to wash down all that heavily spiced food. Then Geissler unloaded a single five-gallon canister. Blaich said immediately: "Drinking water will be rationed. Half a pint per man at eight o'clock in the morning and half a pint at five in the evening. Water for cooking will be issued separately." Water for cooking? They would not do very much cooking. Perhaps a few peas to eat with the pork and the corned beef. Thanks very much! To cheer them up Blaich added: "This evening there will be a large pot of tea with three pints of water." Bohnsack brewed it over the spirit lamp. The water sang, the tea tablets were put in. One more. How good it smelt. Now for the sugar. Franz took the packet marked: Sugar. "I like mine very sweet," said Vimercati. Bohnsack plunged in his spoon. The tea was served. "Good health!" said Wichmann, but spat the tea out in the sand.

They all tasted it. My God, it was salty! Bohnsack looked like
a whipped cur. He held the package he had opened to the
candle. It was marked quite clearly in large letters: Sugar.
Then he tried the other packets, tasting them carefully with a
moist finger. Salt! But in the salt packet they found sugar.
Two pints of water had been wasted. It could have meant
death. The language they used was appalling.

The spot where they had landed was in a gigantic
depression. To the east two mountain chains and to the south
a high, rocky escarpment. To the north two curiously shaped
hummocks.

Next morning, as soon as he had finished his morning
drink Wichmann hurried to his "keyboard" and began to
hammer once more. But there was no reply. Vimercati sat
under the wing of the machine poring over his map. His
finger finally came to rest at a certain spot but he made no
comment.

Wichmann and Geissler set off to reconnoitre. They
wanted to climb the plateau to see whether they could spot
some landmark. The mountain seemed quite close. But although the two men kept on walking it never seemed to get
any nearer. After two hours they realised that the dry air
made any estimate of distance impossible. The plateau was
several miles away. With parched throats they returned to
camp after four hours. The thermometer registered 100 degrees in the shade of the He 111's wing. The air was as dry as
a bone. It was no wonder, for they were in one of the driest
latitudes on earth: average moisture 18 per cent per annum
as opposed to 65 per cent in Berlin.

They were tortured with thirst. Bohnsack calculated
from his map and decided that they could not be more than a
hundred and twenty miles from Campo Uno. But what did
that mean? They were a mere dot in the desert ocean. "We
must get into contact by radio." This became the *idée fixe*.
They discussed the matter and night came round again. The
thermometer sank from 100 degrees to 8 degrees below.

Wichmann sat down once more at his set, tapping and
listening, tapping and listening. But the vast outside world
did not reply.

The second morning and still no reply. Wichmann had
made a second aerial out of tent poles so that one prong could
be directed towards Agedabia. Everyone waited eagerly for

the appointed hour. Wichmann sat down punctually and hammered away for ten minutes giving his call signal. Ten minutes was like an eternity. Then he gave a start, "Reception," he shouted. "I can hear them. They are calling us." His pencil flew over his pad. "VQBJ, VQBJ Come in," and then again: "Come in." There was a pause and now Wichmann tapped out his reply. "VQBJ, here, VQBJ here. Can you hear me?" They could see by the expression on his face that he was in radio contact. Soon the signal came through once more from Agedabia. "The book," he cried. Bohnsack jumped into the aircraft to fetch it. The book in question was *Abel with the Mouth Organ* by Manfred Hausmann. This was the agreed key code. "Page 63, starting from the top," Wichmann deciphered. "Getting your signals but very weak. Go ahead." Wichmann reported that they had succeeded in their raid and had forced landed without water in the Sahara.

He sat for two hours at his set, his fingers were trembling. Agedabia kept signalling: "Not getting you. Repeat." And Wichmann repeated until finally they knew everything back there. No one thought of sleep that night. The question that occupied their minds was: Will the Italians ever find us?

On the third day, Saturday the 24th, there was a sandstorm. A thick yellow brown veil lay over the depression. A south-westerly wind lashed the aircraft. "No one could take off in this weather. Even the birds are grounded," Bohnsack said resignedly. They retired into the fuselage of the He. That evening Wichmann again made radio contact. The Italian search had begun but so far it had had no success.

Sunday dawned—their fourth day in the desert. Their limbs ached and their lips had cracked. Their tongues were coated and their metabolism had been upset. A single thought in their heads: water. They lived for eight o'clock in the morning and five in the evening. How marvelous when that first drop of water passed their lips. Dettman managed to make his mug last for an hour. Blaich issued an extra pint that day since it was Sunday. They lay there and dozed, musing bitter thoughts. Blaich began to relate his dream of the previous night: "I met Bohnsack in a smart wine bar in Rome. We ordered two large light ales. The waiter was disgusted and fetched the manager, who offered us the finest wine. No, we wanted beer. Light ale. The proprietor arrived with the wine list. 'Look, gentlemen, I have the finest Rhine and Moselle wines, vintage Burgundies and Bordeaux,' No, no, we want beer. Light ale. The proprietor shook his head. He shook it faster and faster like a spinning top. Then I woke up... with a terrible thirst." They all laughed grimly.

During the transmission period they learned that the Italians were still looking for them.... Still looking but without success. If they had not been discovered by Monday or Tuesday between 16.00 and 16.20 hours signals would be given from an aircraft with a powerful set to facilitate the search. The searching aircraft would have to be within fifty miles of the transmitter, otherwise they would not be heard. Fortunately there was enough petrol left in their tanks to allow one engine to run so that the message could be picked up on the long-wave transmitter.

The fifth morning arrived and brought a surprise. They woke to see the leafless thornbush near the aircraft covered with small blue blossoms. The bush had appeared to be dead for its branches were as brittle as glass. If someone banged against them they broke off. Geissler looked at this miracle and leapt to his feet. He fetched a spade and began digging a hole in the sand. "If that bush has blossomed there must be water," was his theory and he refused to be denied. He dug and dug but the sand continued to fall back into the hole. The sweat poured down his face. Then he slumped under the wing of the aircraft muttering: "Water, water!"

The day drew to a close and still the Italians had not found them. Tuesday, 27th January: the sixth day. Shortly before 16.00 hours Geissler started up the port engine with the remaining fuel. The great transmitter was working, sending out its invisible rays. If the rescuers were within fifty miles they must arrive immediately. They stood there, ready with their flare pistols. They waited five, ten, twenty minutes. "Switch her off, man!" Blaich said to Geissler, but the engineer begged him: "Let's run her another five minutes." "Switch her off, man!" Geissler was obdurate. "It's our last chance, captain. Let the engine go on running until it peters out."

Blaich went over to Geissler and spoke to him as to a child. "We must keep a few drops even if only to light a fire."

Geissler lowered his head as though he were listening, then he went and switched off the engine. Fear took hold of them.

Morale was at its lowest ebb. At 17.00 hours Blaich issued the last half a cup of water. They could see that his hand was trembling. Yes, this old colonial's hand was trembling. "Without water I've no more orders to give," he said calmly. "Now we shall have to decide what is the best thing to do tomorrow morning." They squatted on their sleeping bags under the wing.

Each man was to make up his mind what he intended to do.

"You have your own choice of death," muttered Franz Bohnsack. Geissler went on carving his name on the flat stone. Bohnsack looked at him and then leapt to his feet. "No," he said, as though in conjuration. "They must come. They can't let us rot here."

And as though he had uttered the words of a magic spell the cry went up: "An aircraft!" They rushed for the flare pistols.

It was an Italian reconnaissance plane—a Ghibli. Like maniacs they fired their flares: white, red and green.

"He's coming this way," shouted Geissler.

The Prince of Gialo had stood there like a graven image clutching his glasses to his chest. "A Ghibli, S.1. Lieutenant Duarte," he said professionally. He knew his men, but this remark was made to hide the excitement that could be read in his eyes. Wireless Operator Scorzone was the first to leap out of the little Ghibli. He was waving two Italian water bottles. He laughed as he sped towards them on his short legs. They crowded round him. Then the others appeared: Duarte, D'Agata and Tulliani. They knew what was wanted. Each was carrying a flask or a whole can in his hand, and there were greetings and embraces and the tears must wait until they drunk their fill.

It was like a magnificent feast. Each man had a bottle to his lips. Vimercati and Blaich had even attacked a full can; the man in charge of water who had counted every drop for six days let the liquid run down his shirt and his chest, and merely said: "Ah!" as he put it down.

The Italians left them melons and water—vast supplies of water. Then they took off again for Campo Uno which was only half an hour away by air. The following morning they would bring petrol.

Radio location had saved them. The Italians, however,

had not caught the signals in the air but had landed. They had set up their poles in order to calculate the position correctly. That is why they had been so long in coming. It had really been their last chance, for the batteries of the three-watt set were dry. The desert night that descended upon them seemed enchanting. They cooked a meal of spaghetti and pork. They drank tea and plenty of water. Then they rolled themselves up in their sleeping bags.

It was still dark when they heard the drone of engines overhead. They sprang to their feet and fired their flares. Were the Italians back already? Bohnsack stood there with his ears cocked: "No," he said at last, "that's a Ju52." The machine circled above them and landed in the first light of dawn. It really was a Ju52, and from it sprang Lieutenant Becker of the Desert Rescue Squadron. There were warm greetings and laughter which ended with a breakfast of coffee and the sausage Becker had brought with him.

The Ju52 had taken off from Agedabia at midnight "without permission," as Becker said with a laugh. "You've been the sole subject of conversation for a whole week on every airfield and when we had no news of you I said to myself I must have a try. My crew felt the same." They had set out on their crazy adventure disobeying orders. Providence must have guided them.

Becker had brought three cans of petrol which they immediately pumped into the belly of the He111. When the message reached Agedabia from the Italians that the Blaich commando had been found and was to be fetched next morning, the He 111 with the call sign VQBJ was already on its way to Campo Uno and the north.

On the ninth day after they had set out they were circling once more over the Hun Oasis. On the track below a camel caravan was progressing discreetly, slow as the footsteps of eternity.

13

PRELUDE TO THE 1942 SUMMER BATTLE

Corporal Gustav Grossman from Bochum-Langendreer stood sweating at his stove in the Umm er Rzem Oasis near Derna in the middle of the gruelling hot desert. The trucks of the Cookhouse Company bore a green heart—the symbol of Thuringia, for most of the company bakers came from that province and baked devotedly not only black bread but rolls and cakes. In the early morning hours of 20th March, 1942, Gustav Grossman wanted to show the corps what a real baker could achieve in the desert. With his friend, Rudi Funke, from Heiligenstadt, he had made a "cream and chocolate tart". His comrades stood round to see how it would turn out.

Two huge odorous masterpieces stood on the table outside the oven. The decoration had been carried out in the most tasteful manner. There were cries of admiration. "Good heavens, such a thing has never been seen in the desert!"

This, too, was the opinion of General Crüwell who that afternoon was presented with the tart on his fiftieth birthday under the palms of Umm er Rzem. He had driven over from Army Headquarters to drink with the officers of the Afrika Korps, for he had been deputising since the beginning of March for the C-in-C Panzer Army, General Rommel. The Afrika Korps during this period had been under the command of General Walter Nehring.

The bakers had placed their tarts with a bottle of looted French champagne on a draped table near the palms and giant cactuses.

How very bourgeois soldiers are at heart. In fact, the men from Heiligenstadt and the Wuppertal, the men from Sondershausen and Dortmund, like so many others, infinitely preferred baking cakes to killing their fellow men. Fundamentally they would all have preferred to drink coffee with the soldiers from Wales and London, Manchester and Edinburgh, rather than slaughter them.

For General Crüwell it was to be his last celebration for several years. The Germans were enjoying a well-earned rest—after the great effort of throwing back the British to Gazala at the end of January and reoccupying most of Cyrenaica. Both sides were exhausted. They had fought to a standstill: now there was a pause while they re-armed for a new round in the great gamble—for Egypt, Suez, Africa and the Near East.

The troops were "freshened up," as they say in the army. N.C.Os and men came back from hospital and from leave. The 15th Motorised Infantry Battalion, for example, was once more a real fighting unit, four companies strong. On the 15th March it formed up in a square for church parade. The 4th April was its anniversary in Africa. It was celebrated with the 21st Panzer Division, for the motorised infantry had joined this division as the 3rd Battalion of the 104th Regiment under General von Bismarck. With field cookers and quartermaster stores, including two oxen, five barrels of red wine and a Volkswagen loaded with "Löwenbräu Export", this veteran, war-scarred battalion joined the division. The 104th Regiment, after the bloody battle of Halfaya Pass, had been completely formed. The rest of the proud old regiment from the Pfalz made up the complement of the 2nd Battalion, while the 1st Battalion was formed from the former 8th Machine-gun Battalion.

The 115th was in the same straits as the 104th, and the same applied to the 200th and the 55th Regiments of the 90th Light Division. The artillery and the flak, the Luftwaffe squadrons, the sappers and the Oasis Companies, after the murderous winter battles and the January offensive, had to be reformed, not to mention the decimated 5th and 8th Panzer Divisions.

With the new soldiers and new weapons a most civilised innovation arrived in Africa, for Rommel's Staff Combat Group received a transportable field closet. It was the only one of its kind on the North African front, and with its little heart-shaped hole in the door it aroused the envy of all the troops who had to continue with the old-fashioned latrine fatigue.

The British, too, were arming for new deeds. The German reconnaissance reported huge earth-works in the Gazala position. British supplies travelled from Egypt along the coastal roads to Tobruk. The German intelligence reported strange field fortifications which suggested a new tactic on the part of Auchinleck and Ritchie.

Rommel, who had spent a whole year in the desert and during this time had had no time to have a verbal exchange with the German High Command, had left in February 1942 for a conference at the Führer's headquarters. He had announced his visit for February. The reply was a rather curiously worded telegram. "Rommel can report if the situation is so secure that his temporary absence from his theatre of war can be risked." Rommel wired laconically that only because of the secure situation did he propose to fly to Europe. But the German High Command was still not satisfied. It sent a second telegram: "Please report your arrival in Rome. Instructions will await you as to your further flight to East Prussia." This was the treatment they meted out from the green baize table in Rastenburg to the man who, against all expectations and premises, had restored the position in North Africa. No, this thick-headed Swabian go-getter who won victories where the High Command had envisaged defeat was not popular.

On the 15th February, 1942, at 04.00 hours, Rommel and Westphal took off from Misurata in Tripolitania for Rome. This was their first flight in the New He111, Type 6. Rommel's pilot, Lieutenant Hermann Giesen, still remembers that day quite well. Hitler had given orders that army commanders were only to fly in aircraft equipped with at least three engines; but the three-engined Ju52 was too slow for Africa. The Condor or the Ju90, as four-engined machines, would have been suitable, but the enemy intelligence service would presumably have been quick to recognize the use of these striking machines for special missions. Rommel therefore had special permission to use the less obtrusive He111. It was equipped with three comfortable seats, a map table and a cupboard for refreshments, but carried only the normal armament. General Westphal described this trip to me. Mussolini's reception in the Palazzo Venezia was as usual friendly and amiable. Military matters, however, were not discussed. The Duce had long since refrained from interfering in the conduct of the war, although he was nominally the Supreme Commander Mediterranean.

On the 16th Rommel flew on to Wiener Neustadt to visit his family. The following day he landed on the Rastenburg field close to Hitler's headquarters, the "Wolf's lair." Both Rommel and his Chief of Staff had expected the Führer to show a particular interest in the events of North Africa, but they were very much mistaken. He was preoccupied with the Russian campaign and his setbacks before Moscow. He listened almost with indifference to Rommel's long account of the British winter offensive, the German counter-attack in January and the present situation in Africa.

When Rommel finally asked: "*Mein Führer,* what are the High Command's plans for the future conduct of the war in North Africa and the Mediterranean for 1942?" Hitler evaded the issue. He ignored Rommel's suggestion to take Malta, and confined himself to the following words: "If we decide to wage a further offensive in the Mediterranean zone then no expense must be spared to put it on a sound basis." Nothing more could be got out of him. Nor was the position clarified when Westphal, on the evening of the 17th and the morning of the 18th, had a long conversation with Jodl. The German High Command was under the spell of the Eastern front, considered Africa as a secondary theatre of war and had no appreciation of the struggle against Britain in North Africa. They did not realize that Great Britain could be defeated in Egypt, the most vulnerable point of her Empire. In Africa Churchill staked everything on a single card. He saw that Britain's decisive front was there, but Hitler and the German High Command either failed or refused to see this. Rommel and his Chief of Staff left East Prussia in very low spirits.

That Hitler at this conference was beset by the difficulties of the winter campaign in Russia, and as a result was moody and disinclined to bother about Africa, is proved by the fact that twelve days earlier, actually on the 5th February, in a conversation with General Nehring he had been much more open-minded on the Africa problem. Nehring was received by Hitler on his way to Africa from the Eastern Front, and had a fifty-minute conversation with the Führer in the presence of Jodl and General Bühle. On the subject of Africa Hitler insisted that it was important to advance as far as possible and pin down British forces there. It would be a good thing if Tobruk could be taken. He flirted with the idea of laying a mine barrage straight across the Mediterranean at its narrowest point in order to protect his supplies. The Navy objected to this plan as posing too many difficulties. Hitler praised the achievements of the Panzer Army and said: "Tell Colonel-General Rommel that I am filled with admiration for him."

Fourteen days later Rommel did not notice much of this admiration.

On the return flight to Africa Rommel had a further conversation with the Duce and tried to win him over to his plans. He expressed his ideas most eloquently—firstly the capture of Malta in order to eliminate this constant threat to his African lines of communication and, secondly, a new offensive designed to capture Tobruk.

Since preparations for the taking of Malta would have demanded considerable time, Rommel suggested changing the order of his objectives. But Mussolini was "cagey", and not until the end of April did Rommel win over the Führer's headquarters and the Supreme Commander for his plans. His main argument was that the British were already arming for a summer offensive and that it was imperative to forestall Auchinleck. Rommel worked feverishly on his plans for an offensive. "Supplies," was his constant cry. "More supplies!" But at the beginning of April things looked very grim. Malta, like a giant spider, devoured ships, men and weapons. In March only 18,000 of the required 60,000 tons of supplies reached African soil.

But now Kesselring began to bomb the George Cross Island with his 2nd Air Fleet. It was to be softened up for the assault, and captured by airborne troops if possible before Rommel's offensive. To this end the 2nd Parachute Division was despatched to Italy. It was soon apparent, however, that the Italians would not be ready for their invasion of Malta before the end of June. Rommel, therefore, altered his timetable: he would launch an offensive to capture Tobruk and the invasion of Malta would follow.

This change of schedule brought about a decisive development, but no one yet suspected that it would end in tragedy.

Kesselring's Stukas pounded the island, bombed the harbour, reduced the quays and the fortifications to dust until Admiral Cunningham's ships fled from this hail of bombs. The R.A.F. planes could not take off. Rommel's supplies got

Stuka Ju 87

through. Hardly an Axis ship was sunk from April until the middle of May 1942. Had any proof been needed that it was essential to put Malta out of action, here it was. But as time showed, neither Hitler nor Mussolini followed this obvious indication. The British were aware that Malta in the long run could not hold out. The British knew that without Malta they could not hold Egypt. But in Rastenburg they could not—or would not—see it.

The Stuka and bomber pilots of the 2nd Air Fleet in Sicily were ignorant of the errors made by the German General Staff. They bombed Malta. They made Rommel's offensive possible. For two months the Luftwaffe enjoyed complete air supremacy in the Mediterranean. The days were over when out of thirteen Ju 52s taking off from Crete eight or nine fell a prey to the Malta fighters. The Italian convoys arrived in Benghazi. Heavy tanks, 88 mm. guns and shells were unloaded on the quays of Tripoli. Supplies!

Summer arrived and the desert was like a furnace. Until late into the night the stones and sand were as hot as the malt coffee in the mess tins. The thermometer showed temperatures of up to 120 degrees. The text books maintained that in such conditions the white man could not work, let alone wage war. To sit in a tank? Impossible! But nothing was impossible.

British, Germans and Italians sat in their broiling tanks, which were massed in their hundreds. Infantry and flak soldiers built positions, sappers laid their mines in the torrid heat. The men were tanned black, lean and sinewy and their skin grew leathery. The flies tortured them. The sand trickled into their socks and underclothes. The sand fleas bit them viciously and dysentery was rife, but they were all preparing for a new battle. Ten Suez Canals could have been built with this manpower, energy and self-sacrifice... and the intent was merely to capture one Suez Canal.

Rommel knew that the British were preparing an offensive: the British knew that Rommel had the same idea. Who would win this race with time? "Will the Tommies forestall us this time?" the German soldiers asked.

"Will Rommel beat us again?" questioned the Tommies. They said "Rommel", because he was the personification of the bold ruse, the lightning attack, the wild chase across the desert. This mystique of a brilliant, courageous, legendary German general was bad for the morale of the British troops. "Rommel is coming," rang like an evil spell. The British High Command knew the effect of such psychological factors. General Auchinleck, therefore, issued an interesting order of the day: it is a very curious war document:

> To all Senior Officers and Departmental Heads at G.H.Q. and with the Middle East troops.
>
> There is a very real danger that our friend Rommel will become a "bogy man" for our troops in view of the fact that he is so much discussed. However energetic and capable he may be he is no superman. Even were he a superman it would be undesirable that our troops should endow him with supernatural attributes. I must beg you to make every effort to destroy the concept that Rommel is anything more than an ordinary German general. Firstly we must stop speaking of Rommel when referring to the enemy in Libya. We must speak of the Germans, the Axis troops or the enemy but never, in this particular context, of Rommel. I

must ask you to see that this order is carried
out and that all our junior commanders be
instructed that the matter is of great psychological significance.

Signed: C. J. AUCHINLECK.
C-in-C Middle East Forces.
P.S. I do not envy Rommel.

The postscript "I do not envy Rommel" displayed that
personal touch which is so often to be found in orders of the
day issued by British commanders. It is a custom which
would have been unthinkable in the German army.

14

FLAK SAVES THE AFRIKA KORPS

Auchinleck's original intention was to begin his offensive
in the middle of May, but then came the reports of Rommel's
strong armoured reinforcements and the British C-in-C considered that his superiority was not great enough. The War
Cabinet in London, therefore, postponed the offensive until
the middle of June. It was a fatal decision.

On the other hand Rommel had planned since April to
start his attack on the 26th May. Once more he set the ball
rolling with a ruse, dictated by the peculiar nature of the
British defence positions. The Gazala front, where the Tommies
had dug in, was a technical marvel. It reached from the coast
to Bir Hacheim deep in the desert, and was forty miles
long—a brilliant defence system consisting of isolated mined
strongpoints called "boxes" about two miles in diameter.
These boxes were arranged as follows: first came a circular
barbed wire entanglement, then a minefield in depth with
listening posts, machine-gun nests and gaps covered by artillery. The garrison was usually in the strength of a brigade. It
was supplied with everything necessary for a long-term de-

fence. To the rear of the boxes were the operational reserves, the armour and the motorised units.

The garrison's task was to observe the minefield so that the enemy—as they had done in the past—could not clear a path through the field. Moreover, these boxes were hedge-hogs of resistance which an enemy, who had broken through the front, had to eliminate to avoid the danger of being constantly attacked in the rear, on his flanks and on his lines of communication. Should the attacker concentrate on the boxes then the armour, deployed far outside these nests, could be directed against him.

Rommel had only two possibilities in his offensive against Tobruk—either a frontal attack on the strongholds, a break-through and the destruction of the enemy armour, or to outflank the Gazala position to the south: a thrust through the back door of the open desert into the heart of the defence positions, cutting off the British forces in the boxes from their armour in the rear and the piecemeal destruction of the enemy's striking power.

Rommel would not have been acting in character had he not chosen the second alternative. Naturally he deceived the enemy by making a feint frontal attack.

He had two German and one Italian armoured divisions, to each of which was attached a German and an Italian motorised division and four Italian infantry divisions. General Ritchie's 8th Army consisted of two motorised and one infan-try division in the Gazala position. Two further reinforced divisions were in readiness to strike a hammer blow. The Guards Brigade, a brigade of the Free French and the Indian brigades held the boxes. All in all each army had about ten divisions, totalling 100,000 men. On Rommel's side stood 320 German and 240 light Italian tanks and 90 motorised guns. Ritchie had 631 tanks but later received a further 250.

This was the most powerful tank armada that had ever been seen on a battlefield.

"Attack at 14.00 hours in broad daylight? I don't like it. The whole thing stinks, boys," growled Corporal Bruno Preuss of No. 2 Company of the 361st. Bruno always called his men boys and was notorious for this among the lads of the 361st of the 90th Light Division. They were ex-Legionaries, the back-bone of the foot soldiers in Africa, a hot-headed bunch and splendid fighters. When Rommel approached their regimen-

tal positions he always used to say to his driver, Huber:
"Padlock the spare tyres. We're coming to the 361st."

On the 26th May, at the unusual zero of 14.00 hours, the
361st was the mainstay of General Crüwell's frontal attack on
the Gazala position. On the left and right flanks were Italian
infantry from two corps. Behind them came motorised units
of the Afrika Korps with a host of recovery vehicles and
"dust-makers"—aircraft engines on trucks which threw up so
much sand with their propellers that the enemy reconnaissance suspected the presence of a whole Panzer army.

That was the ruse. The British were to believe that
Rommel was making a frontal attack with all his forces against
the northern and central sectors of the Gazala position.

The whole show was a magnificent piece of stagecraft. To
the minute the artillery thundered on a broad front. The
machine-guns rattled and the desert shook as in the throes of
an earthquake. Stukas roared over the boxes. Lieutenant
Pfirmann, the nineteen-year-old No. 2 Company commander
of the 361st, raised his arm. Bent double, the veterans of the
Foreign Legion rushed towards the minefield. Bruno Preuss
and his friend Erich were the first to reach the British
advanced posts, the boxes of the 50th Division. "Hands up!"
The reply was a burst at their feet from a well-camouflaged
South African machine-gun post. The sand spurted about
their ears. Flinging himself to the ground Preuss emptied the
magazine of his sub-machine-gun. Then they halted. Between the boxes along the whole front were small barbed
wire lanes. Wire and a million mines lay ahead of the
attackers from the coast to Bir Hacheim, a distance of forty
miles.

Among the British staff confusion reigned, as was often
the case during large-scale attacks in those days. What were
the intentions of the enemy? Where was the weight of his
attack? The R.A.F. reconnaissance planes could not give very
much information, but confirmed a mass advance of motorised
units, following up the infantry employed in the frontal
attack. So Rommel intended to break through? But General
Ritchie was cautious with his forecast. He knew that old fox,
Rommel.

Flares lit up the battlefield. The stretcher-bearers leapt
through the torn, barbed-wire entanglement. The artillery
still growled, machine-guns rattled, and behind the German

lines there was great activity. But this was not for a new
attack. Everything the British evening reconnaissance had
confirmed—advancing motorised units and armour—suddenly
changed in a flash. They withdrew in a wide sweep to the
south towards the concentration of armour which was to
deliver the actual blow through the desert, by-passing Bir
Hacheim to the rear of the enemy defence. Punctually at
20.30 hours Rommel gave his code word: "Venezia."

Like a gigantic column in the bright moonlit night ten
thousand vehicles of the offensive forces got under way. Five
divisions advanced by compass and speedometer through the
desert.

At the wheels of their captured light and heavy trucks sat
the veterans of Rommel's motorised division. The "lords of
the road," the supply drivers, were in the three-tonners.
These men were never mentioned in the Wehrmacht
communiqués or in the histories of the war. They drove
across burning tracks, through the cold night and lashing
sandstorm 100, 150—sometimes 300—miles. They repaired
their trucks and mended punctures in the burning heat.
Eight or ten burst tyres a day was a common occurrence. The
tyres exploded like air balloons and the axles sank deep into
the sand. There was no one at hand to help, no one to give
them orders. But they repaired the damage, sweated, returned
to the wheel and drove on. Utterly exhausted they were
constantly threatened by fighter bombers and enemy scout
cars. The troops were devoted to these brilliant drivers and
pathfinders.

The leading man had to be in the van where the dust
was thickest. "Press on, close up and keep contact!" The
"lookouts" lay on the front mudguards clinging to the radia-
tor. Visibility was about one yard. "Step on it! Step on it!"
they would cry to their drivers, or suddenly call a halt in
order to avoid a collision.

But the worst sufferers were the motor-cyclists. The
muck was flung up into their faces, their machines got stuck
and they had to jump off and push them.

"Despatch rider to the front!"—they had to be Jacks of
all trades: fetch ammunition, direct the anti-tank guns and
take the wounded back to the dressing stations. In No. 9
Company of the 104th Grenadier Regiment was a certain
Corporal Borstel from Stendal, a painter's apprentice by

profession. He had already seen active service in the Polish campaign. When his company lost fifty-two men in the forest battle of Odrzywol he drove his motor-cycle and sidecar through the pines, without heed for Polish snipers, bringing up munitions and taking back the wounded. He had also fought in France and driven reconnaissance troops on the Rhône and in the Savoy Alps.

Since the beginning of April 1941 he had been in Africa and had taken part in all the battles. He had gone down with dysentery but now, as thin as a rake, he was back on his machine once more. One of a hundred thousand who had to bear the burden of war. Why did they not pull out? Why did they go on driving, sweating, fighting and dying? If this question had been put to the corporal he would have been unable to find a reply. He would probably have shrugged his shoulders and said: "Anyone who gets scared is a lost man."

They looked greyish black, like Negroes. They pressed on and the objective was the coastal road to the west of Tobruk. For the infantry that meant filth and heat somewhere in the desert. For Rommel, however, it meant cutting the 8th Army's approaches behind the Gazala positions in two, with the possibility of attacking piecemeal the two enemy forces which had been separated from each other. It was the ancient tactic according to which Napoleon marched, Frederick the Great fought and the Greeks waged war. Would the coup be successful? It looked hopeful.

The morning of the 27th May dawned. The wide sweep round the British southern flank at Bir Hacheim had been successful. The advance continued north. An Italian Panzer Division on the left wing; the 90th Light Division and the combined reconnaissance units on the right; in the centre the two Afrika Korps Panzer divisions, the 15th on the right, the 22nd on the left. Their objective: the coastal road between Tobruk and the front line.

In spearhead formation the 8th Panzer Regiment, under Lieutenant-Colonel Teege, led the 15th Panzer Division. Ahead the light companies and the heavy to the rear. The regiment had one hundred and eighty tanks. The first section pressed forward on a broad front of one and a half miles and about a mile deep, closely followed by the second section. There had been no early morning reports from the Luftwaffe. Land reconnaissance was impossible because the 33rd Reconnaissance Unit had been taken out of the division and sent on a special mission against Tobruk. Somewhere the enemy must be lurking with his armour.

There was a click in the headphones of Captain Kümmel, better known as the "Lion of Capuzzo."

"Enemy armour, twelve o'clock!"

The Tommies had spotted the oncoming tanks. "It looks as if Jerry's come with a Panzer brigade," a lieutenant of the 8th Hussars in his "recce" tank reported to regimental H.Q. A moment later he corrected his message. "There's more than a brigade, it's the .whole bloody Afrika Korps. Alert! Alert!"

The battle had begun.

For the 8th Panzer Regiment the show developed in the following way: "Enemy armour, twelve o'clock! Attack! Attack!" droned in the headphones. At first all they could see were a few black dots on the horizon. The main body of the enemy armour was skilfully concealed behind a small hillock. Captain Kümmel advanced at full speed. The first shots were exchanged. Forward! Halt! Fire! And again—Forward! Halt! Fire! One of the tanks became a casualty and then another. What was the matter? How could the Tommies fire at a greater distance than themselves? Crump! Another direct hit on a German Mark III. This was some devil's work. The Panzer commanders raised their field glasses. Those silhouettes ahead were something new. One of them shed its camouflage to reveal a completely new type of tank.

That was the big surprise. American Grants had arrived. With its 7.7 cm. this tank was far superior to the German Mark III with its 5 cm. gun. The Mark IV alone could master it, but it went into battle with a short barrel and therefore had a shorter range than the Grant. There were only a few of the Mark IVs with long barrels, and unfortunately these were not equipped with armour-piercing shells.

It was a grim battle. When the men of the 8th Panzer Regiment picked up the first wounded they discovered that their adversaries were the reformed 4th British Armoured Brigade. So they were here again, the boys of the 4th, and today they were taking their revenge for the 23rd November when Major Fenski captured the entire brigade with No. I Section of the 8th Panzer Regiment.

Their revenge was crowned with luck in every respect.

Not only did the surprise armament have its effect but German artillery support for the 8th was long-delayed. The batteries of the 33rd Panzer Artillery Regiment were dispersed as a result of the great fire-power of the new enemy tanks. Moreover, the batteries had not been able to keep up with the advancing Panzers and had been left far behind. In addition, the battery leaders of No. I Section were driving Mark II tanks which had been placed at their disposal by the Panzer regiment. This proved to be a mistake. In these tanks the battery leaders were not sufficiently mobile and were soon more or less out of the action. The 8th Panzer Regiment fought practically without artillery support. Their casualties were very heavy. To their left the 5th Panzer Regiment of the 21st Division under Colonel Gerhard Müller fought in similar difficult conditions. In the van the section commander, Martin, was killed by a direct hit.

Teege's Panzers tried desperately to approach the Grants with their longer range of fire. A well-planned attack by the 2nd Section on the British flank finally brought a decision. The tactics of the German commanders were a triumph. The men from the Pfalz managed to rout the British. The 8th Hussars were almost wiped out. The 3rd Royal Tanks lost sixteen Grants.

General von Vaerst, G.O.C. 15th Panzer Division, to which the 8th Panzer Regiment belonged, raced forward in his armoured car. When he passed the head of the leading Panzer company the company commander called out: "What is our direction?" Before Vaerst could reply his adjutant shouted to the man: "Over there! That's where Rommel is." It sounded like a fairy tale, but it was the truth. The C-in-C was leading them as he so often did.

The 4th Armoured Brigade should have been the bastion guarding the approaches of Auchinleck's 8th Army. Rommel's armour had broken the line and the way was open through the back door. The 90th Light, under Major-General Kleemann, three reconnaissance units and the 20th Italian Motorised Corps were in this way able to sweep round to El Adem, pin down the Tobruk garrison and come between the British and their eastern supply dump. This part of the plan succeeded.

The 21st and 15th Panzer Divisions under Nehring continued to advance north, parallel to the Gazala position. The British armour, cut off from its supply bases, was to be

British 6 Pounder

engaged and destroyed piecemeal. This part of the plan did not succeed. The men in the tanks, trucks and cars on the 21st May did not know this. The 21st fought its way to Acroma. The infantry and Panzer troops could see the Via Balbo ahead. Behind it lay their objective, the sea.

Was the enemy already beaten? Nobody really believed it, but they continued to advance and because of this the mood was high. But storming ahead did not always mean victory.

Lieutenant Paulewiecz, company commander of the 2nd Battalion, 104th Panzer Grenadier Regiment, kept his special jokes for critical days. This time he did not need them. It was his birthday. Two hours before dark he spotted a British light truck which he engaged. It was loaded with tinned beer and whisky—naturally in bottles. There was enough for the whole company. The necks of the bottles were broken off against the side of the vehicle. In Africa, too, alcohol was an effective stimulant. The regimental commanders, however, were not happy. They knew that the day's objective of the Afrika Korps had not been reached. The enemy forces between the Gazala position and Tobruk could not be destroyed. General Ritchie did not live up to Rommel's hopes. He did not join battle. He retired with his armour eastwards and raked the long flank of the advancing army, consisting of over ten thousand vehicles. His nine Grant tanks wreaked havoc on the German armour.

The R.A.F. continued to paste the supply columns. Attacks from the boxes of the encircled Gazala position—above all Bir Hacheim—inflicted heavy losses.

This time luck did not seem to be on Rommel's side. Not only were the new Grant tanks an unpleasant surprise, which had remained completely hidden from the German intelligence, but the Tommies also produced a new anti-tank gun. The six-pounder, almost equivalent to a 7.5 cm., tore holes in the German tanks. The British had learned by experience and now American aid began to be felt.

The advance was halted. Rommel's plan to drive from the south to the coast through Ritchie's rear and divide the British forces was unsuccessful. Nevertheless, the "recce" trucks of the 90th Light advanced to El Adem, and the main body of the Afrika Korps pushed on far to the north, its spearheads actually reaching the coastal road. But then another misfortune occurred. The entire transport of the Afrika Korps was cut off.

It was suddenly apparent that Rommel and not Ritchie had been caught in the trap. The lines of communication of the 90th Light, which had advanced to the north-east to join the Afrika Korps, had been cut. At the same time Ritchie's armour had separated the Panzer divisions fighting in the north from their transport and supplies. The German reconnaissance had been gravely at fault. Rommel had not been informed of the presence of strong British armoured forces. Not only had he learnt nothing of the Grant tanks and the new six-pounder, but he was insufficiently informed of the defences of the Gazala strongpoint and the strength of the Knightsbridge box. Late in the afternoon of the 27th the situation was becoming critical. In the north the armour was immobilised; in the east the 90th Light was encircled. The troops were exhausted, without supplies and water. The wounded could not be tended or taken back to the rear. They lay there in the desert. What was to be done? Since Westphal, the G.S.O.1, could not contact Rommel, who was far ahead with the fighting units, he drove with his radio unit to join Nehring. Together they tried to master the situation.

General Nehring gave me the following picture of the situation on the afternoon of the 25th: "At 16.00 hours an attack was launched by about sixty-five tanks on the flank of the 15th Panzer Division advancing in the north. The battalion detailed to cover our left flank was wiped out. The transport and supply trucks fled south and west. The situation for this division, whose armour was far ahead, as well as for the whole Afrika Korps would in a short time have become critical."

It was one of those situations in which catastrophe overtakes an entire army. Alternately they can be moments when a single bold decision can turn defeat into a victory. The man who conceived such a bold idea and enriched military strategy with a new tactic was General Walther K. Nehring. The man who executed the idea was Colonel Alwin Wolz.

General Nehring and the commander of the 135th Flak Regiment on a reconnaissance suddenly found themselves surrounded by transport, supply columns and staffs which were fleeing before the British armour. Colonel Wolz told me the story: "After driving around for a long time we ran into fleeing trucks of the corps staff, which in turn was being overrun by the fleeing divisional H.Q. transport. We lost our entire regimental H.Q. staff until at one time our group had been reduced to four men. In this chaos I spotted a few 88 mm. guns. We rushed in among the troops and suddenly came face to face with Rommel, who was completely hemmed in by the fugitives. He gave me a "rocket" and said that the flak had been entirely responsible for the mess-up because it had not fired. I pulled myself together and ran over to the guns, halted them and collected three 88 mms. ... Within a few moments I had rounded up the other half of the heavy flak battery of the Corps operational staff. The enemy armour suddenly appeared at a range of fifteen hundred yards—a tank fleet of between twenty and forty tanks. They were pursuing the fleeing transport of the Afrika Korps which had no artillery protection and was helpless in face of an armoured attack. In the centre of the chaos were Rommel, the staff of the Afrika Korps, regimental staffs, intelligence trucks—in short the nerve centre of the advanced fighting units.

"The great decision lay in the air—in other words, a catastrophe for us. Our guns were dragged into position in record time. Just as I was about to give the order to fire I gave a start. Through my glasses I could see that the enemy tanks were about to attack the infantry battalion on the right flank. If they reached their objective I could no longer shoot

without endangering the lives of my own troops. We must
fire quickly and with great accuracy. Fire! The shells sped
towards their targets. The first direct hits! The British halted.
The tanks which had advanced upon us, surprised at this
unexpected resistance, also turned back. But they reformed
for a new attack. 'A flak front!' shouted General Nehring.
'Wolz, you've got to build up a flak front to act as a flank
defence with all available guns.' It was an inspiration. Fortunately
Major Gürke appeared with a second heavy battery. After half
an hour the Army adjutant arrived with the heavy batteries
belonging to the Army operational unit, directed personally
by Rommel. In feverish haste a flak front of nearly two miles
was built up against the British armour."

Hardly had Wolz erected his powerful wall of guns than
the attack was renewed. Bright yellow turrets. . . . The commander tanks sported flags on the aerial. "Twelve hundred
yards, fire!" Sixteen 88 mm. anti-aircraft guns poured their
shells into the approaching British tanks. The gun, Dora,
fired a salvo of three shells from sixteen hundred yards and
registered a direct hit on an approaching Grant. The new
American tanks were not up to this treatment. They fired
with everything they had got. With grim resolution they
returned to the attack. The British had seen their opportunity
and wanted to exploit it. But when night fell the columns of
smoke from twenty-four enemy tanks rose to the sky in front
of the flak. This was the first time in the history of the war
that a flak artillery commander had fought with his heavy
units against armour at close range. But the battle was not yet
over. The British brought up artillery and pasted the flak
position. At all costs they were determined to neutralise this
wall of steel. But on this very wall the fate of the Afrika Korps
depended.

General Nehring had his tactical headquarters about half
a mile behind the flak front and stressed the decisive importance of this sector. The enemy artillery subjected the batteries to a rain of steel. Entire crews were wiped out. Major
Gürke and Colonel Wolz drove tirelessly up and down the
front encouraging the crews, for the collapse of this defence
line would have meant a disaster for the whole Afrika Korps.
As though heaven-sent the ghibli sprang up, covering everything in its mantle of dust. The danger was temporarily over
but the great crisis was ever present. The situation of the

Panzers continued to deteriorate as the result of lack of supplies.

"What's happened to Crüwell's frontal attack?" Rommel asked his Chief of Staff, Gause, on the evening of May 28th, and without a pause he ordered: "He must break through the minefield from the west to disengage the rear." Crüwell was informed by radio.

Let General Crüwell tell in his own language what happened:

"During the night of the 28/29th May a radio message was received from General Rommel ordering an immediate attack by my Italian Corps. I sent the artillery commander, Colonel Krause, to Italian H.Q. He was to see that from 08.30 onwards a sentry was posted with a flare pistol to indicate the Italian front. I took off at 08.30 in my Fieseler Storch. My pilot did not have the right map ready. The O.C. Luftwaffe Afrika, General von Waldau, gave him precise direction: make for Segnali and then turn due east. It was soon clear to me that we were still flying directly into the sun. The pilot reassured me and said that we could not possibly miss the flares. But then the worst happened and we were over the British lines. We were flying at about five hundred feet and came under machine-gun fire. The first burst hit us in the tail, the second riddled the engine and the third killed the pilot. He slumped back dead in his seat. As though by a miracle the machine did not crash but flattened out and made a perfect crash landing, smashing the undercarriage to pieces. The fuselage cracked and splintered around me but to my good fortune the door did not jam. I was in the foremost line of the box held by the 150th Brigade. The British soldiers rushed up and took me prisoner. After a year I learned from General Krause, who was a prisoner-of-war in Tunis, that the flares were never fired because the officer in charge had been called to the telephone in his dugout just as I flew over."

This was the situation then on the 29th May, 1942. Naturally the frontal attack by the Italian Corps was delayed. Kesselring, however, leaped into the breach and took over Crüwell's command on the Gazala front. He even offered to act as second-in-command to Rommel—a field-marshal subordinate to a Colonel-General!

Rommel held a council of war. Nehring, Gause, Westphal

and Bayerlein all agreed that in their opinion the position was
very serious. They ordered a break-out from the pincers.
Since Crüwell's advance had been held up the only alternative was to penetrate the Gazala position to the west in order
to regain contact with the supply bases. Rommel hesitated
but finally agreed. The battle was lost but perhaps a bold
decision could avert a real disaster.

On the 30th May, shortly after midnight, the plan was
put into operation. Towards morning the dense enemy minefield of the Gazala main line was reached from the east. Now
it was a question of opening a lane through the minefield to
create the necessary escape route to the supplies. Rommel
left the battle honours to the enemy. His motto was never to
fight a hopeless battle.

But the boldly conceived operation had not yet succeeded,
although a lane through the mines was quickly opened. The
Italian Trieste Division had done preliminary work from the
west, but now the efficient disposition of the boxes became
unpleasantly apparent. The German command did not know
of the existence of the Got el Ualeb box. There in the centre
of a mine belt was ensconced the 150th Brigade, two thousand men and eighty heavy Mark II tanks strong. The lanes
through the mines were covered by artillery fire. Thus a
passage through them by day was impossible and at night a
dangerous and risky business. Moreover, General Ritchie, no
longer undecided, grouped his tanks and attacked. The Guards
held Knightsbridge against the 90th Light and the 3rd and
33rd Reconnaissance Units, breaking through from the east
together with the 580th Reconnaissance Unit under Captain
von Homeyer. The contingents of the 21st and 15th Panzer
Divisions were in danger of being overrun. The relief break-
through to the west, however, was still thwarted by the
British strongpoint, Got el Ualeb.

General Ritchie judged Rommel's strategic withdrawal as
a defeat. "Rommel is on the run," he radioed to Cairo.

"Bravo, 8th Army! Give him the coup de grâce," replied
Auchinleck. But he was premature.

"Got el Ualeb must fall. The 150th Armoured Brigade
must be evicted," was Rommel's strict order. This was the
last chance. If it did not succeed it presumably meant the end
of Rommel and his army. The German C-in-C knew it. His
commanders knew it, and the soldiers sensed it. Thus the

fate of a campaign, as so often happens in military history, depended upon the fighting strength of a brigade and upon the question whether the order to destroy it was capable of being carried out.

It was the 1st June, 1942. No one who took part in the African campaign will ever forget it. Everything was at stake.

Rommel despatched the 5th Panzer Regiment to storm Got el Ualeb. In vain! Twelve Panzers were wrecked in the minefield. The Kichl Combat Group attacked, but the British massed machine-gun and artillery fire also repelled this assault.

So it was impossible! The commanders looked through their range-finders and field-glasses. Where were those accursed machine-gun nests? Where did the minefield end? Nehring and Bayerlein recorded their observations on their maps. Then a decision was taken. The well-proved motorised 3rd Battalion of the 104th must pull the chestnuts out of the fire.

Its battalion headquarters was in a deep sandpit six feet below the ground. Next to it an 88 mm. was in position.

At that moment the German Stuka formation flew in. Nerves keyed to breaking point the men watched to see whether they would bomb the tanks drawn up in the front line. Suddenly Lieutenant Kordel shouted: "Good God, they are dropping their load."

They pressed their faces into the sand just before the bombs exploded. The 88 mm. gun and its tractor were hit: exploding ammunition made help impossible. Wounded everywhere...burning Volkswagens all round them. The British immediately exploited the position and attacked. Only with difficulty could they be repulsed. The oaths were unprintable. During a lull in the fighting came the call: "Commander and Adjutant to Divisional H.Q."

General von Bismarck, commander of the 21st Panzer Division, sat in his omnibus and pointed to a burnt-out tank on the horizon. "Do you see that tank, Ehle?"

"Yes, Herr General."

"Over there is the British box, Got el Ualeb. Your battalion has to take that strongpoint. It's a difficult job, Ehle. So far all attacks have failed. Work out your plan of attack and tell me how you propose to do it. It's pressing, Ehle." Bismarck added: "The attack will be supported by a detachment of artillery under Major Beil."

On the way to the briefing Ehle met Major Beil, who was standing with General Nehring and Colonel Bayerlein beside an 88 mm. gun. Bayerlein explained the position to Kordel on the map. Suddenly someone shouted: "Take cover, low-flying aircraft!" They had already fired and wounded Ehle. He would not take Got el Ualeb. Captain Reissmann took charge of the battalion and the attack. Lieutenant Wolff gave me the following account of the action: "Everything depended upon a good take-off position and a quick break-through at the greatest possible speed. At the first light of dawn a salvo from the artillery gave the signal for attack.

"On the left, 9th company, 10th company on the right, battalion staff in the centre... in this order we advanced at 40 m.p.h. across the mile and a half stretch to the British positions. Each company was accompanied by a sapper section to deal with the wire and the mines. The 10th Company succeeded in breaking through the minefield in the first rush, but No. 9 was caught up in the middle of it. The massed fire from the box was concentrated on the men and their vehicles. Captain Reissmann roared to me, his aide: 'Wolff, hurry over to the 9th and tell the men they must get out of the mines. To lie there is worse than to attack.'"

"No zigzagging! Straight at the enemy," was the drill. This of course was the right idea. But were they to retire for a mile and then make a second assault? It may sound all right in theory but who would do it in practice? In a series of quick rushes Wolff joined the 9th. The text book was right. The Tommies were entrenched in solid, well-camouflaged positions. They only had to sit put, and that is precisely what they did. Lieutenant Wolff was hit. A shrapnel splinter pierced his shoulder. But Wolff went on running. He staggered on to the 9th and Sergeant-Major Friedrich caught him as he fell. On Wolff's orders a section of sappers and volunteers were mustered; a small lane was cleared through the mine-field and the company was through.

Now they could advance. Three rushes, flat on their faces and three more rushes. That accursed Tommy machine-gun over there! But now it was silent. Had it jammed? Faster. ... Who was winning? The Tommies were still tugging at the belt. "Hands up!" called Sergeant-Major Friedrich. The gunners obeyed and the first British positions had been captured. Hand-to-hand fighting followed, with grenades and machine-guns. Beil's artillery hammered the camouflaged positions, Stukas roared into action and dropped their bombs— this time on the target.

At the height of the battle Rommel suddenly appeared at Reissmann's side. To right and left the machine-gunners were emptying their belts. "The enemy's weakening," said Rommel, in broad Swabian as usual when he got excited. "Wave a white flag and he'll surrender." Wave at this moment? thought Reissmann. The old man's got a bee in his bonnet. What's the point of waving? They're still fighting like hell. When the general began to wave his white flag the enemy did likewise. Very few of them had white handkerchiefs, so they waved their scarves. One man had removed his shirt and was waving it wildly. Then something astonishing happened. The Tommies came out of their positions with their hands above their heads. Two thousand men surrendered to the three hundred men of the 3rd Battalion of the 104th. The 150th Brigade capitulated. Auchinleck's chance of giving Rommel the coup de grâce had vanished. Rommel hoped that General Crüwell, who had been shot down and taken a prisoner on the 29th over Got el Ualeb, would still be in the box, but the British had sent him off in a scout car a few hours before the German attack. The British mess cook who was captured told them that Crüwell had been given a delicious rump steak but that he had had no appetite.

The losses suffered by the 3rd Battalion were very heavy. Among the many officers and men who fell was an old warrior. Corporal Borstel, although young in years, was very popular with his men. Once more he had been in action with his motor-cycle—one of the few in the battalion that still functioned. He brought back the first wounded and returned with his sidecar full of ammunition boxes through the mine-field on which the artillery's fire was concentrated. Four times he made the double journey, but on the fifth he received a stomach wound so much dreaded in Africa. He had a badly wounded man in the side car. "I must get him to the casualty clearing station," thought Borstel, "otherwise he and I will be dead men." Borstel did not dismount or call for a stretcher bearer but rode with the right hand, his left hand pressed against his stomach wound. He reached his goal and fell off his machine. A few hours later he was dead.

This particular Casualty Clearing Station was on the Trigh Capuzzo, and many German soldiers still remember it today. The historians who assess victories should never forget those stations.

The sun beat down pitilessly on the Trigh Capuzzo. The wounded screamed with pain and moaned for water.

Not until nightfall would the first transport leave for the main dressing station. The Red Cross men could hardly stand on their feet. The junior doctor was on the point of collapse.

At 20.00 hours the column, composed of one hundred light trucks, was ready to start. Very few ambulances were available. It was sixty miles to the main casualty centre at Tmimi.

In one of the trucks lay Captain Eckert of the Kiehl Combat Group. He had been wounded at Got el Ualeb. On one side lay Lieutenant-General von Vaerst, who had been wounded on the 27th, and not far away two privates with chest wounds and a man with a badly smashed leg. Every effort had been made to make them travel as comfortably as possible. It was of no avail, for the driver could not pick his route.

It was a gruesome journey. After the first five hundred yards the badly wounded began to groan and then to scream, but the journey continued over potholes and stones. They must not leave the road or hit a mine. Five tanks and five "recce" trucks escorted the column. Forward, forward.... The British had trained their artillery on the lanes through the minefield. Forward, forward....

It was unbearable. The screams rose to concert pitch. Who could stand it?

The driver stopped. The lightly wounded began to help re-bed those who were in agony, but the shells began to fall round the trucks. Forward.... The column had long since spread out, for the individual trucks had to keep stopping.

The journey took nineteen hours. Those nineteen hours of pain had almost driven the wounded men mad.

At the main dressing station things were nearly as bad. The doctors and nurses were exhausted. They went on working in the dusty tents in the broiling heat. The sweat streamed down their bodies... but there was ice, and there was looted champagne. Anyone fit enough to do so was allowed to drink it. There was red wine, too, and iced lemonade. And new wounded continued to arrive. The faces of the doctors and nurses grew hard.

The instruments tinkled in the large, clammy operation tent. Conversation was laconic.

Fortunate the man who eluded death in that main dressing station and reached Derna—reached the hospital on the Mediterranean.

Major Ehle, the wounded commander of the 3rd Battalion Grenadier Regiment who had forced the 150th Brigade to surrender, reached Derna. In the small room two beds were already occupied—a major-general and a lieutenant-colonel, according to the badges of rank on the greatcoats hanging over the chairs. They were asleep under their mosquito nets. Major Ehle rolled over on his side. As he woke up he saw through his mosquito net Field Marshal Kesselring standing in the room. Now he recognised his two room mates: Major-General Gause, Rommel's Chief of Staff, and Lieutenant-Colonel Westphal, the G.S.O.1. They had both been wounded at Got el Ualeb. Gause had been flung against a tank by the blast of a shell and was suffering from concussion. Westphal had a piece of shrapnel in his thigh.

Kesselring was not in the best of moods.

"My dear Gause, I don't want to upset you but things can't go on like this. Rommel must not cruise about in the front line. He's no longer a divisional or a corps commander. As an army commander it must be possible to reach him. You must make him see this." Kesselring continued to grumble for a long time.

"Herr Feldmarschall, the Colonel-General can't be restrained. He simply drives off and then the wireless truck can't keep up with him or gets shot up. By the time we reach another radio post it's usually too late. But how could he lead here in Africa from the rear? This is the type of warfare where everything has to be decided from the front." At this Westphal broke in: "Herr Feldmarschall, it's impossible to pin Rommel down. In order to make grave decisions he has to have a picture of the terrain." Kesselring was difficult to convince. "One day it might have disastrous consequences, gentlemen."

15

THE HELL OF BIR HACHEIM

"Get into the car, Bayerlein, I'm driving to Bir Hacheim."
With these words Rommel greeted his new Chief of Staff,
Colonel Fritz Bayerlein, who on the 1st June, 1942, replaced
the wounded Major-General Gause on his transfer from the
Africa Korps to the Panzer Army. This was typical of Rommel.
He had just got out of the deadly pincers of the numerically
superior enemy and left the battlefield to Ritchie, only to
launch an attack on a keypoint of the enemy front.

Rommel had formed a combat group from units of the
90th Light, a few tanks of the Afrika Korps, the 33rd Reconnaissance Unit and the Italian Trieste Division. Since the
26th May the Italians had lain in front of Bir Hacheim. They
were supposed to take the strongpoint at the beginning of the
offensive, but had not managed to advance a single foot.
Rommel shook his head: "A whole division," he said, "well—
we'll soon take that." From this simple statement developed
the toughest battle to date in Africa. Bir Hacheim, the
southern pillar of the Gazala front, protecting Tobruk, was
defended by the 1st Free French Brigade and a battalion of
Jewish volunteers under General Pierre Koenig.

General Ritchie had sent these resolute fighting troops
to Bir Hacheim intentionally. This was the key to the Gazala
front. Were this citadel to fall then the whole Gazala line
would be untenable. This was the last bastion before Tobruk.
If Bir Hacheim held, then this coastal strongpoint upon any
advance would represent a constant threat to the German
flank. Ritchie, therefore, was determined that Bir Hacheim
must hold out. For Rommel it was vital that it should fall.

At the outset Rommel tried his famous white flag tactics,
but they did not succeed at Bir Hacheim. The German tanks
were shot up and a furious volley of machine-gun fire greeted

Rommel and the white flag-waving patrols. "Never mind," said Rommel, turning to Bayerlein, "we'll attack."

The three thousand Frenchmen and the one thousand strong Jewish battalion were entrenched in brilliantly fortified positions. The levelled, well-camouflaged machine-gun and artillery emplacements were impossible to spot. Twelve hundred of these nests were counted later. They put up a devastating barrage with enfilading fire from every corner. The French artillery smashed every attack. "Stukas," ordered Rommel, sending a signal to Kesselring. "You shall have them," was the field-marshal's reply. They arrived in due course and dropped their bombs.

But the French sappers had built very small slit trenches and emplacements. Unless a bomb fell on them direct little damage was done. General Koenig then radioed to Ritchie: "Send fighters." Ritchie complied. The Stukas were helpless against the manoeuverable fighters, and things looked very grim. Many of the dive bombers were brought down like flaming torches. Rommel was greatly perturbed at this misfortune.

Kesselring flew in and raged: "We can't go on like this, Rommel. Attack the bloody nest with all available ground troops. Abandon these economical combat tactics."

Rommel sent for the flak, the firing power of the Panzer Army. Colonel Wolz, veteran C.O. of the 135th Flak Regiment, with various detachments and batteries of sister regiments whose names are written for ever in the annals of the African campaign, arrived. Their names recurred in the battle reports: 1/Flak 43, II/Flak 25, 1/Flak 18 and 1/Flak 6. The Flak forces were supported by the 3rd Reconnaissance Unit, 33rd Panzerjaegers, Grenadiers of the 90th Light and the Italian Treiste Division. The Wolz Combat Group led the assault.

But the successful bluff used against the 150th Brigade at Got el Ualeb did not succeed here. When the German sappers cleared a lane through the minefield at night the French had relaid them by the following morning. They slipped supplies and ammunition through the broad-meshed perimeter defences and subjected the attackers to a barrage such as had never previously been seen in Africa. Rommel was livid. He ordered flares to be fired all night so that the enemy positions could be constantly under machine-gun fire in order to tire out the French. But when the German troops attacked the next morning the defence fire greeted them in undiminished strength. Rommel reluctantly agreed with Colonel Wolz that his attacking strength was too weak. Kiehl Combat Group suffered appalling losses. So did the flak. What had started as a simple raid gradually developed into a full-scale attack.

Fortunately for Rommel, Ritchie allowed the Bir Hacheim action to go on without interference. Instead of deliberately concentrating all his forces and staging a diversionary offensive on a broad front against Rommel's north flank where the main body of the Afrika Korps stood, he launched half-hearted attacks against the Italian Ariete Division at Got el Ualeb. The Afrika Korps command naturally seized upon this opportunity, and as a matter of course—since they were out of touch with Rommel—attacked the scattered armoured brigades.

The 15th Panzer Division, led by Colonel Crasemann deputising for the wounded General von Vaerst, attacked from the south. Its 8th Panzer Regiment drove straight through a mined line of barbed wire to Bir el Tamar. The 21st attacked from the east. The British still believed that they were engaged with the armour of the Ariete Division. Suddenly they were involved in a tank battle with the Afrika Korps.

When such a battle of armour is over everything looks quite simple. The mistakes are reconstructed. The orders are assessed and the victory or defeat becomes a well-rounded whole. In reality it is quite different. In a fluid tank battle it is rare for the combatants to have a clear view of the position—neither the man in the tank, nor the regimental commander, nor the staff officer, nor the general. Everything is in constant flux. The reports sent back to headquarters are usually out of date, and when an order comes back it is often too late because in the meanwhile the situation has changed. Those British generals who waged war in the old manner from far behind the front line were in this way completely out-manoeuvred. Rommel and his commanding officers led the battle in commander tanks or in armoured cars. Even then they saw only sections of the main battle. As a result, the responsibility often rested on leaders of all ranks down to tank commanders. In their steel "battle wagons" they had to make their own decisions—alone with their crews, their courage and their fears. Naturally, they knew that Rommel was on the battlefield. Accompanied by his aide he drove into the attack in his armoured car or in his "recce" truck, "Greif." Time and time again an irresolute commander who had halted his tank would hear a loud knocking against his steel giant. When he opened the turret he would see Lieutenant Freiherr von Schlippenback, Rommel's aide, using an iron crowbar as a knocker. Crowbars were always carried in Rommel's car. They were the modern counterpart of the Prussian king's cane. Rommel stood up in the car, and as soon as the tank commander appeared in the turret he shouted: "Get cracking! On your way! Attacks don't succeed by standing still." On one occasion these exhortations to battle nearly ended in disaster. "Once more we had approached a halted tank from behind," Lieutenant von Schlippenback told me. "I had already jumped out of the car with my crowbar. At this moment the tank came under fire. The driver put it into reverse and backed into our car. Rommel only just managed to jump out in time."

The Afrika Korps' attack impressed the Tommies. They still would not believe that Rommel, who had just got out of the difficulties at Got el Ualeb, could already take the initiative once more on the battlefield.

The 15th Panzer Division defeated the 5th Indian Division, and at the same time the 10th Brigade was wiped out. They were encircled in the north by a company of the 5th Panzer Regiment under Lieutenant Riepold. General Nehring took part in this attack in his armoured car and closed the breach in the perimeter with his accompanying 5 cm. antitank gun by firing on the British tanks as they broke out. The eighteen-year-old Corporal Bayer from Neckarsulm in the heat of the battle suddenly had a fleeing Tommy in front of his sub-machine gun. He looked like a private solder. "What's your unit?" asked Bayer. The prisoner shook his head. He was within his rights for he was not obliged to divulge military secrets. "What is your rank?" He was forced to tell this. He replied: "General of an Indian Brigade." The corporal must have looked incredulous, for as proof the prisoner produced a general's shoulder straps from his trouser pocket. It was Desmond Young, commanding the 10th Indian Brigade. After the war he became Rommel's most outstanding biographer.

The 2nd, 4th and 22nd Armoured Brigades suffered the same fate as the 5th Indian Division. They lost 170 tanks. Almost the entire 201st Guards Brigade were "in the bag." Rommel destroyed the 8th Army piecemeal because it insisted on fighting that way.

But the 8th Army was strong—far stronger than Rommel's army. Intact forces were still in position in the northern sector of the Gazala position at Tobruk, Knightsbridge and El Adem. Had there been a resolute leadership in the offensive the position could have been just as dangerous for Rommel as it had been a few days before at Got el Ualeb. His rear was still not out of danger for he had not yet captured Bir Hacheim.

"That accursed Bir Hacheim!" as Rommel so often swore during those days. For a whole week his combat group from the south-east had been attacking the stronghold. Stukas flying more than a thousand sorties had dropped their bombs on the positions but without effect. Rommel then decided to approach the affair in another way. He ordered the 33rd, 200th and 900th Engineer Battalions to attack from the north through the extended minefields between Got el Ualeb and Bir Hacheim.

On the morning of the 8th June, the sappers were some five miles north of Bir Hacheim. Rommel appeared. The commander of the Army Engineers, Colonel Hecker, was ordered to withdraw part of his troops, and with two Italian battalions form the combat group which was now to take Bir Hacheim from the north. "I am not in sufficient strength to carry out this task, Herr General," said Hecker. Whereupon Rommel decided to use stronger forces and promised Hecker part of the Special Commando 288. This élite unit, commanded by Colonel Menton, had originally been earmarked for service in Iraq in March 1942 but had been transferred to Africa. The Alpine Company, the Panzerjaeger Company and the "recce" column were to be used in the attack. Hecker was also given units of the Kiehl Combat Group with eleven tanks, "recce" trucks and 88 mm. battery. And finally, a further artillery company, a heavy battery and Colonel Wolz's flak troops were to protect his flank. It was a considerable force. Hecker split his troops into two fighting units. Both attacked from the north but in a pincer movement. The left wing was led by Hecker and the right by Captain Hundt of the 200th Engineer Battalion.

The show did not start too well. While they were getting into position the artillery barrage from Bir Hacheim increased in violence. Then fighter bombers attacked. The sappers who were clearing lanes for the forthcoming assault came under heavy fire. At 17.00 hours Hecker gave his order to attack.

The colonel drove in an armoured car ahead of the Italian battalions. Clinging on to the turret with one hand he kept waving the other and shouting: "Avanti, Avanzate!" The attack got under way but the enemy artillery and the mines made more and more gaps in the ranks of the attackers. Of the six Italian company commanders three fell very early in the action. The terrain, devoid of all cover, was an appalling death trap. Of the eleven tanks of the Kiehl Combat Group, the superbly camouflaged enemy anti-tank guns put six out of action, while four ran into mines.

Sergeant Karl Erich Schulz stood by his 88 mm. firing with open sights at recognized machine-gun and mortar emplacements.

"Smoke out the trenches with smoke shells," ordered Captain Hundt.

The temporary layer, Corporal Gerhard Schmidt, collapsed at his gun. He had been hit by a machine-gun burst. Another man jumped into his place.

The 4th Armoured Brigade, the British shock troops, tried to make a diversionary attack from the east on Hecker's left wing. But there stood Colonel Wolz. His 2 cm. flak paid an appalling price and the heavy flak had huge losses, but the British armour was repulsed.

By nightfall Hecker's Combat Group had fought its way to within five hundred yards of the outer defences of Bir Hacheim. The Alpine troops launched their attack as soon as it was dark. Together with the engineers they managed to capture the forward machine-gun posts. Captain Thumser, leader of the Alpine company of Special Command 288, leaped with his sub-machine-gun into a trench full of men from the Jewish battalion. "Hands up!" The prisoners were taken to the rear. They were weary men with vacant eyes who had fought to a standstill. Would the Germans spare them? They did.

Night lay over the battlefield, and the wounded were taken down the line. There was a lull the battle. Early next morning, 9th June, Stukas were to launch a heavy attack on Bir Hacheim before the troops made their final attack.

Hecker drove deep into the minefield to observe the effect of the Stuka attack. Dawn broke with African suddenness, and he looked at his watch. Not a Stuka to be seen in the sky! No destructive carpet of bombs fell on the Bir Hacheim fortress. By some error in the transmission orders the attack never took place. This oversight proved highly dangerous for Hecker. The French immediately spotted his "recce" truck; MGs, anti-tank guns and artillery opened fire. The driver made off at full speed, but then the worst happened. Crump! A mine. Hecker was flung against the armoured roof and received a deep head wound. Together with the interpreter, Captain Klemke, whose foot was smashed, the driver and the commander of the heavy battery, Colonel Hecker was able to reach a burnt-out tank and make his headquarters in it.

When Hecker gave his report on the 9th June, Rommel said angrily: "This accursed Bir Hacheim has taken sufficient toll. I'm going to leave it. We'll attack Tobruk."

According to General Bayerlein, Hecker replied: "Herr General Oberst, give me a battalion of German infantry to continue the attack. Now that we have already taken several strongpoints I am convinced that we can bring the battle to a victorious conclusion." Rommel held a council of war with Bayerlein. "You're right," he said as he returned. "I'll give you Lieutenant-Colonel Baade with at least one battalion."

Baade, the commander of the 115th Panzer Grenadier Regiment, had two battalions with heavy weapons, and a regimental staff with all the necessary technical equipment.

Before the Baade Combat Group actually arrived the Stukas at last rained down their bombs on the fortress. The German artillery fired with all its guns.

On the evening of the 9th June both battalions were in position and immediately went over to the attack. But the foe in Bir Hacheim was incredibly tough. In the midst of the German hail of fire, an order of the day from General Koenig was circulated among the twelve hundred nests. "In this outpost of the desert we have to prove that Frenchmen know how to fight and die."

Through the positions of the Jewish Battalion the order of the day ran from mouth to mouth. "Fight to the bitter end. World Jewry is watching us."

On the evening of 10th June, 1942, Baade's battalions and Hecker's intrepid engineers and Alpine troops had penetrated deep into the defence system and reached the ruins of the old desert fort.

General Koenig sent a message to Ritchie: "Am at the end of my tether. The enemy is outside my headquarters."

General Ritchie could only reply: "Try and break out."

The final tragedy began.

Since the 6th June, Captain Briel had lain with his combat group barring the south to Bir Hachiem. The Kayser Panzer Grenadier Battalion, units of the 606th Flak Battalion and the 605th Panzerjaegers, led by Captain Schulz, formed the shock troops of this combat group. An attempt to take the fortress on the 7th by frontal attack had failed. The minefields and the artillery defence had been too powerful for Briel's strength. So this combat group lay before Bir Hachiem with orders to prevent any breakouts or attempts at relief.

On the night of the 10th June a patrol brought in a prisoner who had been caught wandering about the British

MG. 42

minefield. His interrogation produced exciting information. According to the prisoner the encircled troops had orders to break out through a specially swept lane in the minefield and try to join up with the British. "Recce" and armoured trucks were despatched next morning from the south to join the German positions. At the same time runners from the combat group crawled across the terrain. Orders were passed on in whispers. Briel and Kayser ran from gun to gun, from machine-gun to machine-gun. Every gun was trained on the break out position. Tracers were loaded into every magazine and belt. The signallers laid lines up the front line; sentries were posted with flare pistols all over the terrain. The entire combat group was ready for action. Briel had given strict orders that no one was to fire until he gave his flare signal. Only when the green stars—preceded by a red flare—burst in the sky were the guns and the machine-guns to speak.

Briel had prepared a particular surprise in the shape of the first six MG.42s. The 606th Flak Battalion had organised this new miracle "pep weapon" from Army headquarters. Men on leave had brought them back to Africa. In a remote wadi the guns were assembled into a machine-gun column.

Around midnight the advance posts heard the sound of engines being revved up in Bir Hacheim. . . . The rattle of tank tracks. . . . The "ping" of cut wires in the minefields. "Hold it," Briel whispered to his runner. "Hold it!" As soon as the enemy fired smoke shells to make themselves invisible Briel nudged Corporal Batz. "Get going!" The scene was suddenly lit up by beautiful green stars and at the same moment hell broke loose. An inferno of fire, explosions and death. The smoke screen did not help Koenig's legionaries. The tracer bullets hissed into the enemy vehicles. For the first time, too, the German soldiers heard the impressive rattle of the MG.42 with its twenty-five shots a second.

At other parts of the far-flung perimeter, it came to bitter hand-to-hand conflict with the escaping legionaries. Men fought against men with spades, revolvers, bayonets and hand grenades. Only half the fighting troops managed to break through with their general and reach the lines of the 7th Brigade.

At dawn on the 11th the survivors of the garrison at Bir Hacheim waved white flags. When the combat group occupied the battlefield they found five hundred wounded and a small rear-guard party.

With the fall of the Bir Hachiem cornerstone, the Gazala line became untenable for General Ritchie. Now Rommel was in a position to attack Tobruk.

The British High Command was in despair at the loss of Bir Hachiem. Was this German invincible? Was there no recipe against Rommel? This was the question asked at British H.Q. Once more they were amazed by this phenomenon, who fought against all the rules of war and invariably won.

For example, although the laws of warfare maintain that the attackers should always be stronger than the defence, Rommel, the attacker, was often outnumbered. He did not abide by the traditional canons. "Why should I bother about the superior number of British tanks when their commanders always use them in driblets? Against those driblets I am the stronger with my army," Rommel once said to a captured British general. At the outset the British refused to learn this. The great nation of seafarers could not bring itself to stake everything on one card in Africa. Not yet! As a result Rommel decided where the battles should be fought and dictated the rules of the game.

At the very moment Bir Hachiem capitulated he flung his troops to the north. The great battle against British armour was to be fought. A week before Rommel had stood on the verge of a disastrous defeat. Now he already had the elements of a great victory in his hands once more.

Yet again they were on the way. "Double white." Two huge white flares shot vertically into the air simultaneously. This was the recognition signal for the 21st Panzer Division to take up its positions. Stragglers or units which had lost their way were guided in by these flare signals or by radio. A swift compass bearing taken on the flares and then a course on the star above or below them. On their way!

Lieutenant Schulz of the 104th Panzer Grenadier Regiment was one of the stragglers who drove through the desert between Bir Hachiem and Knightsbridge. He had lost his way on patrol.

In the back seat of the truck sat Corporal Müller, his sub-machine-gun on his knee in case of surprises in the desert night. The driver was fully occupied with his engine and the route. Lieutenant Schulz's eyes were glued to the compass which he held steady in both hands. Two degrees left. Okay! A little to the right. Now set your course on the centre star of Cassiopea. Look, there's something dark over there! Go easy! A door opened and someone cried: "Are you British?" Müller slowly raised his weapon but the other fellow had suspected something. He trod on the gas and disappeared. Further—somewhere to the right, they heard the typical rattle and crackle of a Bren carrier—the smallest type of British armour. But what was that noise? Tack-tack-tack-tack. . . . It was a desert rat. Yes, there were such things just as there were desert foxes. In the rutting season the male rats banged their tails on the sand to attract the female.

It was 02.45 hours. Lieutenant Schulz' patrol still had not made contact. Now they had to follow the left outer star of Cassiopea, since to the eye of an observe the sky revolved to the right.

"Halt! Who goes there?"

"Kurfürst."

"You clods! So you've got here at last!"

What a relief to hear those friendly words. Now in company with the regiment they proceeded northwards towards the coast.

16

THE FALL OF TOBRUK

For six months Lieutenant Pfirrmann of No. 2 Company, 361st Afrika Regiment, had been without his Sergeant, Brockmann. Among the former German Foreign Legionaries he had had the reputation of being an organising genius. One day during the November, 1941 battle, he had not returned from a raid. He was posted missing. Missing—that sinister word which can mean so much. What it can actually mean is proved by the fate of Sergeant Brockmann. The 12th June, 1942. The 90th Light was in action at El Adem against the 29th Indian Brigade, which had consolidated in the boxes. Units of the 21st Panzer Division were at the same time fighting their way through to the east. The great decisive battle for the last bastions of Ritchie's defence system round Tobruk was imminent.

At Derna, far to the rear of the front line, in the South Derna airfield mess where Major-General Seidermann's Stuka and fighter squadrons were stationed, they were celebrating Lieutenant von Rantzau's birthday. They sat and discussed God and the universe, even though they received constant warnings to be on the alert for sabotage by the Long Range Desert Group. On several occasions the airfield staff had been forced to take them seriously. Machines were blown up and the sleeping crews were killed. Although no one took these warnings very seriously their weapons were always within reach.

Outside it was pitch black. That night captain James Bray of the Long Range Desert Group drove with two trucks full of heavily muffled men through the desert. His party was a strange mixture of British, French and Germans. Now they halted and split into two groups. Orders were repeated in an undertone: Destroy the aircraft with hand grenades, attack the shelters, cut the telephone wires. At least two prisoners must be brought back. They proceeded on their way. The French lieutenant who led one group was nervous. He kept looking at his compass and telling his driver to drive carefully. "We must be getting near," he murmured. Suddenly the driver stopped.

"What's up?"

"Let me take a look round, mon Lieutenant. I know my way about here." Grudgingly the Lieutenant agreed. "*Ça va, mais fais vite.*"

The man was swallowed up in the darkness. The others crouched in their trucks and waited. After five minutes they were still waiting.

While the French lieutenant of this British sabotage group gave vent to an oath the door of the airfield control room was flung open. A soldier, filthy dirty and in a strange garb stood there panting. "The Tommies are outside. A Commando of ten men. I led them here. They're going to blow up the airfield. Get busy!" In a flash officers and men of the H.Q. staff leapt to their feet. They asked no questions. They did not hesitate. Seizing hand grenades and sub-machine-guns they went outside, accompanied by their strange informant.

"*Merde,*" swore the French lieutenant, "where can that fellow have got to?" "I hope there's nothing fishy about this," one of his comrades said in French. "I never trusted that Boche." "Rubbish!" replied Sergeant Michel. "The German's all right. He was put in a Nazi concentration camp because he had served with us in the Foreign Legion. Then, because they didn't trust him, they stuck him in that damned 361st Regiment. It's not motorised and they have to fight with tommy-guns and grenades." "But—" interrupted another man. He did not finish his sentence, for at this moment they saw shadows making towards them and heard a German word of command. They grabbed for their weapons but they were too late. Hand grenades exploded and the petrol tanks were blown sky high. The ammunition exploded. Men screamed and the wounded moaned. A few jumped out of the truck but a machine-gun mowed them down. Only one man slipped away—the French lieutenant. The Germans chased him but the desert had swallowed him up. He was the only man who, after several days wandering, found his way back to a British unit and was able to relate what had happened.

Three men of the Commando survived and were taken prisoner. In the South Derna mess, however, was the Long Range Desert Group man who had thrown a monkey wrench into their plan—the driver who had brought the Commando to the airfield. His name was Brockmann—Sergeant Brockmann. After being taken prisoner by the British in November 1941 this organising genius had done his best to avoid the vicissitudes of captivity. His former service in the French Foreign Legion inspired confidence. He was able to interest the Long Range Desert Group and volunteered for active service.

The company commander of the 361st who told me of this incident, which is recorded in British documents—I noticed that the sergeant's name had been changed—wrote: "Even today one can argue as to what yardstick we can apply to this deed. One thing is clear—it was the result of the equivocal position in which the ex-Foreign Legionary was placed in the Third Reich. The bond between himself and his adoptive country was loosened by the original abuse he had suffered as a Foreign Legionary, and could hardly be renewed by orders and promotion."

Yes! this was the position among the "gypsies of the desert," as the 361st often called themselves. They may have been worse armed than all the other units—they usually marched through the desert when other regiments drove— but they were fine soldiers and no other unit could surpass them in camaraderie. In contradiction to many stories and assertions it must be stated that the ex-legionaries got on particularly well with their specially selected officers. It was advisable for any officer who did not get along with these men to ask for an immediate transfer.

The 361st took part in all the hottest actions in the Africa war. Whenever they attacked things "began to hum" as they said. They hated sentimentality and had no use for such words as patriotism and nationalism. They fought for no ideals. They were purely and simply mercenaries. When one of them returned with loot he always brought something for the "gang." In no other one did the cook look after his men as well as did Erich Leibenguth of No. 2 Company of the 361st. These human touches held them together. The company was their home and they referred to the desert as legionaries always do—as the Bled.

Major Hardy pushed his cup of tea aside as Sergeant Cooper brought his wireless pad into the room. "Message from Cairo, sir," said Cooper. The Major nodded and read. He gave a start, looked at the date and despatch time of the message and with a shake of his head took the text into the room of the 8th Army commander.

Ritchie stood at the window of the former Italian administration building in Gambut, staring at the ruined houses on the market square. This man, usually so calm, was tapping nervously on the window sill. In front of the great positional map stood General Norrie, commander of the 30th Corps, trying to form a picture of the situation and to give his views on the necessary measures to be taken. What General Norrie had to say that day about the position of his 1st and 7th Armoured Divisions was tragic. Piecemeal, without a coherent plan, the British armour for the last twenty-four hours after the fall of Bir Hachiem had endeavoured to halt Rommel's troops advancing northward to the coast. They had failed. The commander of the 7th Armoured Division, General Messervy, had been captured and his division was left without a commander for a whole day. The results were to be expected. In vain Major-General Lumsden, with his 22nd Armoured Brigade, tried to go to the help of the 7th Division. It took him eleven hours to make contact with his corps commander.

Once more Rommel exploited the muddled leadership of the Allies. His armour soundly defeated the dispersed brigades of the British. Thus, by the afternoon of the 12th June, the British armour was a mere shadow of its former self. The desert was strewn with Grants, Crusaders and Stuarts.

Even if General Norrie could not yet assess the magnitude of the disaster the description he gave to General Ritchie in Gambut was alarming enough: They had been unable to stop Rommel's advance to the coast with any effective armoured strength. If the Germans reached the sea, both fighting divisions in the Gazala position, the 1st South African and the 50th British, would be cut off and lost. He had barely finished his report when Major Hardy, one of Ritchie's staff officers, entered the room with a message from Cairo. "Sir, the C-in-C has announced his departure from Cairo. He will be here in an hour." Ritchie and Norrie exchanged glances. They knew that this would not be a friendly visit.

Sir Claude Auchinleck, the Supreme Commander, did not lose his temper, but anger and bitterness could be heard in his curt phrases. An enemy whom, ten days ago, he had considered beaten, who had been encircled and left without supplies, to whom he had proposed to give the coup de grâce, was on the point of smashing the British 8th Army. Was this Rommel in league with the devil? Were none of the British front-line generals his equal? The generals and staff officers listened with stony faces to this "rocket" from their chief. The younger among them were tight-lipped. They were silent but they would have liked to speak. What they might have said could have been roughly this: "As long as we fight the Second World War with 1914-18 methods we shall never win. Until our generals realise that another epoch has dawned in the art of war in which swift armoured troops have invalidated the static fronts, we shall always be the losers whatever our strength. Our generals argue, dilly-dally and wait for orders in their staff headquarters well to the rear. Rommel, Nehring, Kleemann, von Bismarck, Crasemann and company lead their armour, flak and motorised infantry in person. As a result in any crisis they can immediately give the necessary orders. And what does the British 'top brass' do? Here on the staff it is a quarrel for precedence. There is no single will there, no confidence in victory, no fire—only cold, old-fashioned strategy concocted in Cairo and translated at Gambut into boring orders. But before a message from Gambut to the 13th or the 30th Corps reaches the 7th Armoured Division or the armoured brigades hours go by, and the position has completely changed." Perhaps the younger staff officers would have liked to say this to their commander-in-chief. They would also have liked to tell him that they were in despair at the pointless bravery shown, for example, by the men of the 6th South African Field Battery when they covered the withdrawal of the Scots Guards and were wiped out almost to a man. The battery commander, Major Newman, had manned each gun with an officer, with orders to fire at point-blank range against the tanks of the 5th Panzer Regiment. But of what avail was that? Under the concentrated fire from the German tanks and artillery his eight guns were put out of action and half the crews, including the officers, were killed. Lieutenant Ashley and his wireless operator had manned the last gun until they were blown to pieces by a shell, to no good purpose and for no good reason—except perhaps for the history books.

But Rommel's troops displayed no story-book heroism. The 21st and 15th Panzer Divisions of the Afrika Korps under Nehring continued their advance towards the coast, keeping to the rear of the 1st South African and 50th British Divisions which Ritchie had left stranded in and around Gazala.

No, conservative strategy at this stage of the battle for North Africa lagged far behind Rommel's drive. He and his commanders exemplified the tank warfare of the Second World War—a swift, mobile battle of armour. When they led attacks in the front line they did not do this from any mock heroic motive. It was because they knew how to evaluate correctly the tactics of armour and troop psychology. Rommel stated this quite clearly one day. "The majority of fighting men in a swift exhausting tank battle at a given moment always succumb to a need for rest. No army is composed solely of heroes. They will insist for one reason or another that they cannot go on. The commander with his authority must combat these natural phenomena of weariness, and wrench his officers and men out of their apathy. The man in command must be the galvaniser of the battle. He must constantly be on the battlefield, in the front line, to exercise his control." The young British staff officers had grasped the secret of Rommel's leadership. Many of their superiors had no such understanding.

But in no army in the world are young staff officers permitted to voice their opinions when the generals are talking. Thus they, too, remained silent at Gambut. They listened to Ritchie's words with which Auchinleck seemed to agree as though he had uttered them himself: Rommel was no superman. His troops had suffered heavy losses. Numerically the British were equal to the Germans, and if they continued a war of attrition Rommel must finally pause for breath. If Rommel reached the coast with even weak forces, they had to be thrown back. This optimistic note pleased Auchinleck. All commanders like optimism. The outcome of this long conference was as follows: The battle was to be continued on the Gazala–El Adem front until Rommel had to pause for breath. Before leaving for Cairo the British C-in-C wired to Winston Churchill in London that the enemy intentions had not gone according to plan, and the morale of the troops was good.

Here was a telegram to Churchill's taste. He drafted the following reply: "I applaud your decision to carry on the fight. Your success does not depend upon weapons alone but upon will power. God bless you all. Winston Churchill."

The battle continued in the great desert square formed by Tobruk, Gazala, Knightsbridge and El Adem. The Guards were defeated at Knightsbridge, the Indians at Acroma; the British armour could not take avoiding action. Wherever Rommel's massed armour appeared they had to accept battle, for to weaken meant to open the road to the coast and Tobruk. Rommel, therefore, decided the battlefield.

Where would he attack? At Knightsbridge? At Gazala? Or at El Adem? Ritchie was in a dilemma. If he sent all his armour to one spot there was a danger that Rommel would break through in the weakly held sectors. If he withheld his armour there was the even greater danger that Rommel would reach the outer Tobruk defences. Rommel's advancing armoured divisions defeated the divided strength with which Ritchie opposed him. A trump card which must not be overlooked was the 88 mm.: again and again it hammered the massed British tank attacks. The Afrika Korps rolled on past wrecked and burning British tanks. The weight of the German attack routed the British formations. With uncanny precision, Rommel and the Afrika Korps commander, General Nehring, gave a virtuoso performance of the modern battle—the destruction of the enemy's armour—the only classic tank battle of real importance in the Second World War. The back of the British 8th Army was broken. General Auchinleck's aircraft had not yet landed in Cairo on the night of the 12th June when it was clear to British H.Q. at Gambut that the British armour had been virtually wiped out. The mobile wall of steel which had protected the infantry in the Gazala position and in Tobruk had been pierced. Rommel was master of the desert between Bir Hacheim and Tobruk. General Ritchie, however, still had at his disposal two fully equipped infantry divisions, each of ten thousand men. But of what use were they in 1942 in a tank battle where a few tanks could overrun an infantry regiment's positions because an efficient anti-tank defence was lacking?

On the 14th June General Ritchie issued an order which contradicted the dispositions decided upon by Auchinleck thirty-six hours before. He gave the code word "Free born." This meant that the 1st South African and the 50th British Divisions were to abandon their positions on the northern Gazala front, to try and reach Tobruk or alternatively by-pass Tobruk and reach the Egyptian frontier.

Auchinleck protested vigorously from Cairo. But the situation as it appeared to the C-in-C did not conform to the position in which Ritchie found himself. In London and Cairo all eyes were focused on Tobruk. What would be the fate of the fortress built on sand, the great stronghold at the gates of Egypt? Would it be able to hold out again as it had done a year ago or would it have to settle down to a state of siege?

Rommel now saw his main objective within his grasp. He had fought for a whole year for this situation. After having destroyed the main mass of the 8th Army's infantry divisions and to follow this up with a swift raid and the capture of Tobruk. What could stop him then from marching on Cairo? From there he could attack the Nile and press on to the oilfields of the Near East and the Persian Gulf.

But Rommel's divisions had also taken great punishment. Admittedly the 15th Panzer Division on the morning of the 15th June crossed the Via Balbo on its way to the sea. But the 3rd Battalion of the 115th and six Mark III tanks which were to hold the road were not strong enough. They were overrun by the British who put up a desperate fight to avoid being taken prisoner. German artillery, tanks and Stukas subjected the fleeing South Africans to a heavy barrage beyond the Via Balbo. The old, much-disputed coastal road was a sea of flames.

The 1st South African Division retreated without its heavy arms into Tobruk. The Guards who had defended Knightsbridge retired from that sandy sector eastwards. The whole battlefield was fluid. At night German and British often passed within a few hundred yards of each other. But the 50th Division found a bold way of breaking out. In small groups they forced their way through the Italian lines to the west, not to the east. Flight in reverse. The Italians were flabbergasted by these unexpected attacks. The Tommies penetrated far behind the German supply lines, turned off into the desert, by-passing Bir Hacheim, and finally joined up with their own troops near Maddalena. Saved! But without their heavy weapons. This division was now out of the decisive battle for Tobruk. In London Winston Churchill still believed that the fortress could hold out. His telegram to Auchinleck on the 15th June read: ". . . . Leave as many troops in Tobruk as are necessary to hold the place for certain." When Auchinleck acknowledged this message Churchill wired: "The Cabinet is glad to know that you intend to hold Tobruk at all costs."

Rommel had naturally thought out another ruse for capturing Tobruk. To fox the adversary he allowed his mobile forces to by-pass the city. The infantry alone approached the western sector of the fortress. This was to give the British the impression that he intended to ignore Tobruk and make straight for the Egyptian border as he had done a year before. Rommel was at the head of the 90th Light and reached Bardia on the 19th June. He hastily sent messages in clear. "The Old Man is being pretty frank" grumbled Karl Dorn on his wireless truck with the 200th Panzer Intelligence Unit. Operation "Double bed" was the order of the day. Everyone was convinced that Operation "Double bed" referred to Bardia. The British also believed this. The German listening service reported that the British operational staffs were aware of Rommel's presence at Bardia and had relayed the news to higher quarters. "Attention! Rommel is advancing towards the

Egyptian border." This had been the intention of the operation. Rommel, however, turned back and joined the Afrika Korps assault divisions and the 20th Italian Motorised Corps which were in readiness south-east of Tobruk. They, too, had put about during the night and advanced closer to the fortress.

Shortly before dawn on the 20th June Rommel and his staff arrived at his Tactical H.Q. It was Saturday evening. The sun gleamed fiery red through the mist. Rommel stood apart. He kept looking at his watch. His field glasses hung round his neck and his eyes were half closed, shielded by the peak of his cap. From time to time he focused his glasses on Tobruk. At last he climbed a small sandy hillock well under cover and walked up and down. It was the early morning lull. Slowly the hands of his watch crept forward to 05.20 hours. In the distance a faint drone could be heard and a moment later small black dots appeared on the horizon. Stukas, light and heavy bombers. Every airworthy Italian and German plane in Africa was to take part in a mass bombing attack on the south-eastern sector of Tobruk.

"Major Wolf," called Rommel. A grin appeared on the faces of his Staff. There was no Major Wolf but there was a Major Fox (Fuchs), the Luftwaffe liaison officer. Rommel could never remember his name. The man with the animal name eventually became "Major Wolf". Once more the staff officers echoed the general's call: "Major Fuchs to report to the General."

"Where the hell is Wolf?" growled Rommel. He appeared a moment later. "Major Fuchs reporting." But Rommel stuck to his Wolf. "Listen, Wolf. Has good care been taken to see that the aircraft will bomb accurately?"

"The squadrons have been well briefed, Herr General," replied Fuchs. At this moment they heard a huge explosion from the fortress. Eighty Stukas and over a hundred bombers had released their loads on Tobruk.

The first blow had been struck. The second battle for Tobruk was in progress.

Tall fountains of dust rose from the south-eastern fortifications where the Indian positions lay. Barbed wire, concrete blocks and weapons flew into the air. Wave after wave of bombers and Stukas flew in. The cumulative effect of this shuttle service corresponded to a raid by six hundred bombers. Load after load of bombs destroyed the barbed wire entanglement on the defence perimeter over an area three miles square.

The Panzer divisions now went into action. The 21st, commanded by General von Bismarck and the 15th, still led by Colonel Crasemann, staged a full-scale attack supported by Panzer grenadiers of the independent 15th Artillery Brigade led by its experienced C.O., Colonel Maury

The 1st and 2nd Battalions of the 361st Panzer Regiment earned special praise from Rommel. The 8th Company under Lieutenant Jörns, as leading infantry unit, stormed the harbour. Sergeant Wilshaus's column crushed the resistance of the Marines. The battalion commander, Captain Kleemann, was awarded the Knight's Cross for his men's achievements.

The 8th Company of the 5th Panzer Regiment was again in action. Many of the men still remembered Easter Monday a year ago. Then, too, they had tried to take Tobruk. They had already advanced to the notorious crossroads when the Tommies sealed off the gap and inflicted grievous losses on them. Most of the tank crews had returned on foot only too pleased to be able to save their skins from this cauldron of fire. What would happen this time? The fortress was certainly no weaker than a year before. Broad barbed wire, formidable tank traps, strategically placed gun emplacements were there in defence of this harbour city. The strength of the garrison was approximately the same—thirty to forty thousand men. There was only one difference. The defending troops—mainly Indians and South Africans—were exhausted after the recent battles on the Gazala front. Their morale was low and they did not believe in victory. When the B.B.C. mentioned in one of its broadcasts, "Tobruk is not a decisive factor in operations on the North African front," the South African garrison commander, General Klopper, was justifiably furious at this blow to the morale.

No. 8 Company of the 5th Panzer Regiment still consisted of two columns of Mark IVs. The rest had been put out of action during the previous days and lay as hulks in the desert or were in the repair shops. The steel giants rolled forward cautiously. In the grey morning light the company commander, Lieutenant Koch, looked through his range finder at the sappers laying a bridge over the tank traps under enemy fire. Overshadowed by the assault troops which always got the credit, these first-class artisans and technicians of modern warfare did a magnificent job. With great caution the Panzers stalked forward and were led singly over the bridge. Another few hundred yards and then they would come to the accursed bunkers, strongholds quarried out of the rocks which were invisible until you were on top of them. Koch's men knew this from the previous year.

Actually the promised Stuka support must be forthcoming at any minute. Each tank had been issued with smoke flares to mark the spearhead of the German advance so that the Stukas could pound the concrete artillery and machine-gun nests ahead. In due course the "artillery of the air" arrived. "Fire violet!" echoed in the headphones of the tank crews. They might have been on manoeuvres. The first Stuka formation roared over their turrets and their bombs burst a hundred yards ahead on the enemy positions. Lieutenant Koch put his head inside the turret, a rare procedure in Africa because it was difficult to recognise anything through the silted up visors. In the midst of the bomb explosions the tanks rumbled at full speed into the clouds of dust.

In short, sharp rushes the Panzer Grenadier Regiment's infantry now reached the machine-gun nests and smoked them out.

The 15th Division successfully crossed the broad tank traps at 08.30 hours. Sappers and storm troops had done a first-class job. Empty oil drums and petrol canisters were thrown in the trenches. Rommel appeared while they were working. "Speed it up, boys! We've got our finger on the trigger," was his encouraging remark. Now the first tanks of the 8th Panzer Regiment and trucks of No. 3 Company of the 33rd Panzerjaegers rattled over the trenches. In the meantime the sappers had cleared lanes through the minefields and cut the wire.

They had reached the famous crossroads at Sidi Mahmud where the tarred road of the Via Balbo branches off to El Adem. As they had done a year before. But this time it was no mousetrap. Admittedly anti-tank guns spat fire and death from the edge of the Jebel but a new wave of Stukas appeared. The accurate air support set the tone for the attack. This came as a surprise to the British. The perfect co-ordination of the bombing, the tank assault and the infantry wore down the British resistance in the forward positions

5 cm. Pak Anti-tank Gun

of the Tobruk fortifications. It was a long, bitter and exhausting battle.

The first British artillery observers surrendered. The 5 cm. anti-tank guns of the Panzerjaegers shot up the South Africans' machine-gun nests. More and more men armed with sub-machine-guns jumped out of their vehicles and forced their way into the corrugated iron roofed dugouts. Most of them brought out prisoners—South Africans with their Boer's hats. Corporal Fritz Hoffmann of the 33rd Panzerjaegers emerged with one who aroused great astonishment. A giant with an enormous black moustache. The man was terrified that he was going to be shot, but on being offered a cigarette by Hoffmann his face broke into a smile.

Rommel's calculations had been wrong in one respect. The 20th Italian Motorised Corps still lay in front of the outer line of defence and did not advance a signal yard. As a result the 15th Panzer Division's flank was in the air and the British gunners concentrated on it. Lieutenant Koch's Panzer Company also began to feel the pinch. It came under a hail of anti-tank fire. Moreover, the heavy coastal batteries had trained their guns on the German attackers. The tank turrets were naturally closed. It was safer, but in these boxes of steel the temperature rose to 120 degrees. Leading Wireless Operator Schrödter, in the leading tank, found it hell. His seat was next to the engine. For him the battle was a matter of picking up orders and reports. Tortured with thirst, he opened a British tin of condensed milk but the sticky mess only made him cough. He opened the turret to get a breath of air. At the next moment a shell burst a few yards away and the turret was blown off. Mud and stones poured into the tank but the engine continued to drone. Cautiously, almost feeling its way, the tank went forward. Half left on the ridge were enemy tanks. The British made their usual mistake. They drove straight across the slope, offering their broadsides—an easier target and less well armoured than the bows. "Attention! 10 o'clock. 800 yards. Enemy tanks. Fire!" Koch signalled to his tanks, which were advancing in extended formation. Koch himself took as his target a Mark VI which had a flag flying on its aerial. This denoted the commander of the enemy formation. Strange that the British did not abandon the idea of making their commander tank so obvious. The ridiculous little piece of bunting proved fatal, for without a commander the formation was far easier to fight. "Fire! Armour piercing shells, 10 o'clock! 80 yards!"

"Ready to fire," reported the loaders. "Ready," repeated the gunners. "Fire!" "Up 50!" Direct hit!

The British commander's tank was on fire. Its turret flew open but the other tanks did not wait to pick up the crew. They turned tail and Lieutenant Koch approached the damaged tank. A British lieutenant and his gunner came out with raised hands. Both men were slightly wounded. They were given bandages. "What are we to do with you?" said Koch. Then he decided. "We must take you into our tank or else you'll make a break for it."

They continued to advance. The prisoners sat under cover behind the turret. No. 6 Company was on the left. Lieutenant Frank-Lindheims' tank received a direct hit and was set on fire. Where had the shots come from? A few hundred yards ahead Koch saw the muzzle of a British gun being trained on his tank. "Put on speed! H.E. anti-tank gun at 12 o'clock!" Too late. The British were quicker on the draw and registered a direct hit. The turret was ripped off and could no longer be turned. The driver was wounded. "Abandon ship!"

The crew crawled into a foxhole twenty yards away from their tank. The two captured British officers were still with them. "Have a cigarette," one of them said to Koch with a grin. "Not for the moment, thanks."

They were in an awkward spot. Shells were bursting all round. We must get out of here, thought Koch. Since his driver was wounded he himself made his way in short sharp rushes over to his damaged tank. Climbing into the driver's seat he drove it back to the foxhole. Soon they were all inside it, including the prisoners. Now they were out of the shell-fire. Koch discovered that he had a shell splinter in his thigh. The wireless operator did not discover his slight wound until much later.

In the meantime a recovery truck had driven up. While they were still deciding whether the tank could be made serviceable again a small armoured car arrived. In it was Rommel. Koch hobbled over to the general and reported. "You must get back to the main dressing station. It's at El Adem," said Rommel, and ordered one of his staff lorries to take the wounded tank driver, the commander and the two British to the rear. The driver had to be taken off again for he could not sit and had to wait for the stretcher bearers. Koch was driven off with the two prisoners—straight across the desert in the direction of El Adem. The battle was soon left far behind. Koch suddenly had an idea. In the excitement no one had bothered to search the prisoners for arms. Koch himself had left his revolver in the tank. Suppose one of the British now produced a weapon?

"Tell me," Koch whispered to the lorry driver, Jantsch, "Have we got a revolver?"

"I've no idea. Perhaps there's one behind in the baggage," was the reply. As soon as he had said this he flushed, because he realized the significance of the question and his reply. The British lieutenant smiled. Slowly he felt in his pocket. Had he understood? Had he got a revolver? "Here you are," he said, handing Koch his revolver. "Do you want a cigarette now?" The Players tasted extraordinarily good.

The battle of Tobruk continued to rage. The German artillery had been brought right forward and was firing at the positions with open sights. Shell after shell left the barrels of the 15th Panzer Division Artillery Regiment's guns. Corporal Hans M. Pfaff of the 408th Artillery Detachment stood at his heavy 10.5 cm. Within half an hour eighty shells sped over towards the bunker. Pouring with sweat the men brought up

more ammunition. By some good fortune the gunners had
found a German shell dump from the previous year. What a
bit of luck! They were the right calibre. As the 250-lb. shells
left the barrel the order came through: "Change of position."
And so it went on. Fire—advance a few hundred yards and
fire again. They caught up with the tank spearheads and the
infantry. Now from the shortest possible range they pasted
the anti-tank and machine-gun nests. No defenders could
stand that. By 18.30 hours the 15th Panzer Division had
thrown the enemy out of Fort Gabr Gasem. Half an hour
later Fort Pilastrino capitulated. Two-thirds of the defences
were now in German hands.

At the head of his staff combat group Rommel had taken
part in the decisive break-through by the Afrika Korps. The
combat group, a number of which were under Rommel's
personal command, was the ideal form of rapid fighting unit
which had developed out of the desert war. It had the
approximate strength of a battalion and consisted of a tank
company, a mixed company of anti-tank artillery and flak, 7.5
self-propelled guns, 5 cm. and 3.7 cm. anti-tank guns and 2
cm. flak. In addition to this a column of armoured "recce"
trucks and radio cars. Rommel constantly flung these troops
into the hottest spots of the battle. On the Jebel descent to
the city they had cracked bunkers like nuts; at the famous
crossroads the troops saw the old mine specialist, Rommel,
dig out mines with his men from a tank trap in his path.
Corporal Kurt Kind from Volklingen on the Saar learned at
first hand from his C-in-C the best way of digging out these
"devil's eggs" from the sand.

In the meantime the South African garrison commander,
General Klopper, sat in his headquarters in the centre of the
fortress. At the very start of the German attack his headquarters had been bombed by Stukas. His new H.Q. also suffered
a direct bomb hit. Thus the garrison commander, in the most
critical hours, was chased from one place to another. Communication with his troops was interrupted. From midday onwards Klopper could give no more orders. General Ritchie,
who had flown to Egypt to report, "watched" Tobruk in its
death throes from the Nile. Fires had sprung up all over the
city. Klopper sent a message to Ritchie. "My position is
hopeless, I will try to break out to the west."

In Cairo they waited. In London they were on tenterhooks. Then came Klopper's last message. "Too late. Most of our transport has been destroyed. We are no longer mobile. Shall continue to offer resistance until the most important material is destroyed." The defenders of Tobruk, the legendary fortress, who a year before had resisted twenty-eight weeks of attack by Rommel, were at the end of their tether. The preceding Gazala battle, the devastating bombardment, the Stuka attacks and the relentless advance of the Afrika Korps through the mined and wired perimeter, had exhausted the old campaigners of the 8th Army.

On the morning of the 21st June at 05.00 hours Rommel entered the city of Tobruk at the head of his combat group. He found a pile of ruins. Hardly a house remained intact. The mosque was only slightly damaged. But apart from this the harbour installations and the streets had been transformed into a maze of rubble. In the basin lay the wrecks of several ships, most of which had been sunk by direct hits from the guns of the 21st Panzer Division. Masts and funnels rose pathetically into the air. On the Via Balbo at 09.40 hours Rommel accepted the capitulation of the garrison from General Klopper. Rommel, who had driven past burning vehicle parks and exploding supply dumps, was furious at the work of destruction wreaked by the British demolition squads. Klopper was told: "If you go on destroying your transport I shall have to make your prisoners march through the desert. And if you go on blowing up your food supplies your soldiers will have nothing to eat." Klopper replied icily: "I'm only carrying out my commands, General." In a slightly more conciliatory tone he added: "I have given no orders to blow up the food dumps." Rommel and Bayerlein persuaded the general to drive into the town in their truck column. Thirty-three thousand prisoners streamed, hobbled and staggered to the assembly points. Alan Moorehead gives the following account of the battle: "It was defeat as complete as may be. In equipment alone the enemy had won the richest treasure the desert had ever yielded. Rommel had there enough British vehicles, enough tanks and guns, enough petrol and fuel and enough ammunition to re-equip at once and drive straight on to Egypt. Yes, that was Rommel. Would he soon be on the Nile? Would his officers realise their ancient dream of drinking whisky and soda in the bar of Shepheard's Hotel? It looked very likely and Rommel had great hopes of it. We can read in his order of the day: 'Soldiers of the Panzer Army Afrika! Now we must utterly destroy the enemy. During the coming days I shall be making great demands upon you once more so that we may reach our goal.'"

Our goal!

His goal was the Nile. The victory of Tobruk would serve as a springboard. Rommel as a campaigner was at the height of his fame. From Rastenburg he learned of his promotion to Field-Marshal. From now onwards he was to be known as "Marshal Rommel." The man who had borne the main brunt of the exhausting battles waged with the Afrika Korps armour, Walter Nehring, was promoted General of the Panzertruppen. Rommel presented him with his own Colonel-General's stars to confirm him in his new rank. The Italian Generals, Cavallero and Bastico, were also promoted to Field Marshals by Mussolini.

The rank and file in Tobruk took their promotions and decorations in their own inimitable way and descended upon the loot. The men of the 200th Panzer Reconnaissance Unit were as happy as sandboys when Karl Dorn returned with a crate of real German blood sausage. The British had captured it a year before from a German unit. Now it had returned to its rightful owners. Another symbol in the ebb and flow of victory and defeat.

17

ADMIRAL CANARIS TAKES A HAND

In the Kit-Kat Bar in Cairo life did not start until midnight. At this hour a gentle breeze blew from the Nile and the feathery leaves of the palm trees started to sway. A dark, starry sky looked down on the dance floor of polished tiles. Only the long bar which ran in a half circle round the stage and the dance floor was covered in. The high wall round the smartest of all the Cairo night clubs allowed no opportunity for onlookers. The obsequious porters in gala uniform bowed from the waist before important guests. They arrived in their cars, the men with their note-cases full of money and the women in smart dresses. Arabia and Europe still found here all the pleasures of peacetime in the damp summer night of the year 1942. Egypt was "neutral" although it served as a British military base for the North African war and Cairo was a busy troop centre. But King Farouk and his Cabinet found it opportune to show neutrality in the shadow of the British High Commissioner. In Cairo, therefore, war and peace ruled at the same time. At the outset one saw only the bright side of the war, particularly in the realm of business. At night British and Egyptian officers in mufti went in search of amusement. The jeunesse dorée of Cairo, the sons of the pashas and beys, the big land-owners and the black marketeers all put money into the pockets of the night-club owners. Egyptian effendis with well-stocked note-cases, oil men from Arabia with their expensive girl friends, not to mention the anonymous host of people who lived on the fringe of war, deriving their income from stool-pigeon activities and dangerous missions to the front line as spies. At night they all enjoyed extremely expensive whisky and soda, pernod or gin fizz. Anyone who wished to maintain a reputation drank champagne. Anyone who wished to be regarded as a good Mohammedan stuck to coffee. Admittedly even the most orthodox Moslem is allowed by the Prophet to take a little drink if his brow is feverish or his stomach is out of order, for it is medicine. The Prophet was never averse to a bargain. He knew his Orientals when he wrote the Koran, thirteen hundred years ago.

Coloured lanterns flooded the garden with their gay lights. A hum of conversation . . . the sound of laughter. . . . The Orientals love noise. The dance band played syrupy European tangoes and lively foxtrots. In between the specialty of the house—Arab dances. That night there was a particular attraction. Hekmat Fahmi, the most beautiful belly dancer in the Near East was to appear. Wherever she danced the applause was riotous. Bouquets of flowers were thrown and page boys sped to and fro with the visiting cards of rich admirers. Hekmat travelled like a queen with her court, and her patrons and friends were legion. Her real interest, however, was centred on a young Egyptian bey who had only recently appeared in Cairo society. His name was Hussein Gaafar. He was rich, very witty, a great lover of life with a great deal of time on his hands. All virtues to obtain the friendship of such a famous dancing girl. Everyone took him for a wealthy idler. In actual fact he was a German agent named Hans Eppler, who, with his friend Hans Gerd Sandstede, had come to Cairo on a special mission. Sandstede figured as the American friend, a crazy Irish-American who used his American passport in order to avoid fighting for England. The name on his faked passport was Peter Muncaster and his nickname was Sandy.

The Kit-Kat was full to the last small table. The couple danced to the favourite hit of the moment: *"Le soleil a rendezvous avec la lune mais la lune n'est pas là."* At all the tables people hummed "mais la lune n'est pas là" and made feeble witticisms that she was shining brightly in the sky

Hussein Gaafar looked round for the waiter. His eyes caught sight of a big table near the bar at which a dozen young Egyptian officers in mufti were sitting. Among them was Lieutenant Anwar el Sadat, who was often seen together with a broad-shouldered subaltern named Abdel Nasser, when the latter occasionally came to Cairo from his garrison in Southern Egypt. In the barracks officers winked at each other when these two names were pronounced. Nasser and Sadat were no friends of England. They were biding their time, and they belonged to one of the various cells fighting for Egyptian independence. They wove a net which embraced every discontent. They were even against King Farouk, who supported Great Britain. It was whispered that they wanted a revolution. But the Egyptians so far had not taken them very seriously. No gesture, no nod, no change of expression revealed that Gaafar and Sadat knew each other.

In the middle of the dance there was sudden excitement. It had been caused by the last guests who carried special editions and were talking excitedly. What was that? Tobruk? Tobruk—a copy of the paper suddenly appeared on the Egyptian officers' table. One of them read out the headlines and the news spread like wildfire. Those who did not understand asked the waiters, or the boys—those smart, impertinent youths who are nowhere in the world so gallant and arrogant as in Cairo. They approached above all the tables where British officers were sitting and did not wait to be asked twice. "Rommel has taken Tobruk in a single day. The 8th Army is on the run and is being chased by the Germans across the Egyptian border. They're coming here, sir, here to Cairo." With arrogant boredom the boys raised their eyebrows and said with emphasis: "Maybe the Allemanis will be here the day after tomorrow and Rommel Pasha will be drinking whiskey with his officers at this table." They were impertinent, and their eyes twinkled with delight on seeing the surprise on the faces of their British audience.

"Well, I'm damned," murmured the serious-looking grey-headed gentleman who, a few minutes before, had joined Hussein's and Sandy's table. Gaafar, alias Hans Eppler, nodded sympathetically. "Bad news," he said.

"Very bad," replied the gentleman who at a hundred yards could have been recognized as a British officer in mufti. "Incredible," he added. His embarrassment could be felt, but the head of the British Intelligence Service in Cairo could disguise his feelings.

Hussein shrugged his shoulders. "But the 8th Army is still intact. Thirty thousand men have been captured in Tobruk. All right. But Egypt is full of British soldiers. And finally, there's the 10th Army. What has that got to do in Syria? It must come to our"—he stressed the word 'our' —"defence here. You can't possibly let Cairo be taken."

The Intelligence officer could not resist saying: "You can console yourself. The 10th Army won't remain in Syria looking on when Rommel comes."

There was a smile in Sandy's eyes. "That's fine," he said. "Good news. By God, that's good news." "Moreover, we've also got the Egyptian Army," put in Hussein. The British officer took out his packet of Players.

"The Egyptian Army? Forgive me, I don't want to offend you, but look over there behind you. Do you think that the fall of Tobruk has upset them?" He pointed to a table where Sadat was sitting with his friends.

Sandy was about to reply but Hussein put a hand on his arm. "Hekmat Fahmi is just coming in," he said. At this moment there was a burst of applause. Conversations ceased. Hekmat was already on the stage. "One of the wonders of the world, like the hanging gardens of Semiramis," said the Major.

The woman was really beautiful. An Arabic type, with luscious curves, feline movements and magnificent eyes. A genuine Egyptian profile and a spectacular dancer. . . . No, outside Cairo one never saw such a figure—neither in the Winter Garden nor the Scala in Berlin, the Follies Bergères in Paris nor the Café de Paris in London. Nobody at the Kit-Kat and very few people in Cairo knew that this woman was one of the Abwehr's most important sources of information.

When Hekmat finished her dance the applause was tremendous. The audience shouted and flowers were thrown. But then something unusual happened. A cry rang out through the hall. It came from the young Egyptian officers' table. They cried: "Dance the Tobruk Waltz, Hekmat!" The cry was in Arabic but many of the British had understood it. In a lightning flash the whole Egyptian problem had been brought out in the open here in this bar: the problems of a nation rattling at the chains of colonialism. And the lightning flash was Rommel. It had struck throughout Cairo. Special editions were rushed out. Groups of people discussed the news; there was shouting and singing beyond the Nile. On the Schari Wagh el Birket there was a demonstration of students. "Press on, Rommel!" they yelled.

It was also hot that night in Washington on the 21st June, 1942. At the White House, seven thousand five hundred miles from Cairo, Winston Churchill and Roosevelt were in conference. The British Prime Minister had flown to the U.S.A. in order to discuss the war situation with the President. There was little encouraging they could say to each other. Europe was in German hands, from the Franco–Spanish frontier to Narvik. In Asia the Japanese were pursuing their victorious march. Singapore had capitulated and Hitler's U-boats were sending thousands of tons of shipping to the bottom. In Russia the German divisions were attacking the Volga. Stalin was sending desperate SOS's for a Second Front to be opened. But where could America and England attack Hitler?

Nevertheless, they were pleased that they could give each other mutual support. In the American President's study Roosevelt and Churchill, accompanied by General Ismay, discussed their plans. Presently a telegram was handed to Roosevelt. The President read it. His face was frozen to stone. There was silence. Roosevelt handed the paper to Churchill. No one could describe this dramatic moment better than Winston Churchill himself has done in his memoirs: ".. it said, 'Tobruk has surrendered, with twenty-five

Sherman Tank

thousand men taken prisoner.' This was so surprising that I
could not believe it. I therefore asked Ismay to inquire of
London by telephone. In a few minutes he brought the
following message, which had just arrived from Admiral
Harwood at Alexandria: 'Tobruk has fallen, and situation
deteriorated so much that there is a possibility of heavy air
attack on Alexandria in near future, and in view of approaching
full moon period I am sending all Eastern Fleet units south of
the Canal to await events. . . .'

"This was one of the heaviest blows I can recall during
the war. Not only were its military effects grievous, but it had
affected the reputation of the British armies. At Singapore
eighty-five thousand men had surrendered to inferior numbers of Japanese. Now in Tobruk a garrison of twenty-five
thousand (actually thirty-three thousand) seasoned soldiers
had laid down their arms to perhaps one-half of their number.
If this was typical of the morale of the Desert Army, no
measure could be put on the disasters which impended in
North-East Africa. I did not attempt to hide from the President the shock I had received. It was a bitter moment.

Defeat is one thing; disgrace is another. Nothing could exceed the sympathy and chivalry of my two friends. There were no reproaches; not an unkind word was spoken. 'What can we do to help?' said Roosevelt. I replied at once, 'Give me as many Sherman tanks as you can spare, and ship them to the Middle East as quickly as possible.'"

Not only the Germans were a threat to Great Britain's power in the Middle East. In the old quarter of Cairo, in the garrisons throughout the land, were the resistance groups which wanted to free Egypt from British domination. At the moment they were only small cells—political, military and religious cliques. As yet they were united only in their hatred of England and in their dream of a free Egypt. At any time they could become a dangerous organisation. If the Germans were to exploit the conspirators for their own ends, then the fanatical officers round Sadat and Nasser, the friends of General El Masri Pasha, of Major Sulfikar and Abdel Rauf could become a Fifth Column. At German headquarters they had harboured these thoughts since 1940.

In the spring of 1940 a major in the German Secret Service had devised a bold plan. In Budapest this Abwehr agent had met an officer of the old Austro–Hungarian Army, Captain Laszlo, Count von Almaszy. He was a desert expert and had worked for years as a surveyor to the Cartographical Institute of the Egyptian Government. He had flown over the Sahara and made many friends in Cairo. Almaszy was won over for the German intelligence and made a Captain in the Luftwaffe. His first suggestion at the beginning of 1940 was to recruit for the German cause the Chief of the General Staff of the Egyptian Army, El Masri Pasha, who had been dismissed by the British.

El Masri was an enemy of Great Britain. He sympathised with officers like Abdel Nasser and hoped, as so many other did, for a German victory, because in this event he envisaged the liberation of Egypt. This man could be a powerful trump card on the German side.

At the Berlin headquarters of Admiral Canaris some surprise was caused when the Luftwaffe Major and Abwehr officer, Nikolaus Ritter, suggested bringing General El Masri to Germany and, if need be, kidnapping him. At first Canaris thought the idea was crazy. But then this imaginative plan revised his opinion. He gave "Plan El Masri" a three weeks' trial.

Ritter founded a special Commando within the framework of the 10th Flieger Korps. He made contact with the Hungarian Ambassador in Cairo who was making a report in Budapest. This intelligent diplomat was not immediately let into the secret. It was a question of contact with El Masri, he was told, and they needed a secret transmitter in Cairo for important weather reports. This last detail was true. The ambassador was prepared to help.

In the meantime Major Ritter had increased his special Commando to ten. Including von Almaszy, they were all Abwehr men—wireless operators, decoders, interpreters and drivers. All specialists from the interpreter companies or from the Foreign Broadcasting Station of the German High Command at Stahnsdorf.

In Budapest the ambassador packed Ritter's agent's transmitter in his diplomatic bag and brought it safely to Cairo. With diplomatic caution he refused to have it installed in the Embassy but gave it to an Austrian priest in Hungarian pay. The priest was a keen, intelligent man. "I shall have a lot to account for to the Good Lord if I have to confess my activities in Cairo," he was wont to say to his friends. For the installation of the secret transmitter he chose the safest place that could possibly have been envisaged: beneath the altar of St. Theresa's in the Shoubran district of Cairo.

The ambassador and his wireless operator became asssiduous church-goers, for only in this way could they go to their "place of work" and remain unsuspected. Only during a service could they transmit and receive. Thus a sinister fact comes to light in the history of the secret war: in St. Theresa's Church in Cairo, while the Te Deum rang out through the nave, the operator tapped out his messages under the altar. "Attention, attention, RBQX calling Central. Come in please." And when the Abwehr in Derna replied, the transmitter gave his message: "Point 1: Weather forecast." Then followed an accurate report of the weather. "Point 2: Pasha reports..." and then followed the information from El Masri whose code name was Pasha.

El Masri proposed at first that he should be fetched by a German U-boat from Lake Berollo in the Nile Delta. This was impracticable. It was finally decided that a German aircraft should fetch him from a pre-arranged spot in the desert not too far from Cairo.

After the capture of Crete on the 20th May, 1941, Ritter at last obtained two He 111s from the 10th Flieger Korps for the Pasha missions. The machines were attached to No. 26 Battle Squadron. Almaszy, who knew the desert like the palm of his hand, had chosen as rendezvous a spot near the Red Jebel on the oasis road.

The Pasha could reach this point by car in a few hours from Cairo. He was to report an hour before sunset and fly a wind cone. Ritter's He 111 would land and pick him up while the second remained in the air to give him cover.

The machines were all ready to take off when the message arrived from the St. Theresa Church via Derna that El Masri had had a car accident and could not be there on time. By Saturday, 7th June, 1941, he was well enough to take off at 15.00 hours. Captain Haller flew the escort machine with Major Ritter as passenger and Captain Blaich as observer. Captain von Almaszy flew the second machine which was to pick up El Masri. Both machines showed German identification markings.

At 16.00 hours the agreed landing place was reached but nothing could be seen. Almaszy glided down and flew low along the road in the direction of Cairo, to ascertain that El Masri was on the way. Nothing! After fifteen minutes the pilot turned back. The minarets of Cairo could be seen in the light of the setting sun. It was a bus ride to the Egyptian frontier where British headquarters lay. But where was El Masri Pasha? Had the plan been betrayed?

The following morning at the appointed time the transmitter in the St. Theresa Church reported: "Pasha probably arrested. Treachery suspected. Fear that our transmitter and our own position is in danger. As a result we are breaking of contact. End of message."

What had really happened? Not until long after the war could I find the answer to this question.

El Masri wanted to fly to the rendezvous in an Egyptian Air Force plane. He confided the plan to Squadron-Commander Hussein Zulfikar, who arranged the day for the flight when he was on duty at the Heliopolis airfield. Naturally the pilot also had to be informed. While the machine was being refuelled

the latter went over to the tower to report. The British
control officer was apparently suspicious and questioned him.
They took off and a few minutes later the pilot lost height. A
British aircraft had appeared on the scene. Did the pilot lose
his nerve or could he not get his machine into control again?
Whatever the case, he prepared to make a forced landing. He
hit a group of trees and crashed into the top of a palm. The
machine was a write-off and the pilot fled. The general was
rescued from the treetop by an Egyptian M.P. Fortunately
the man on duty was loyal to the group of revolutionary
Egyptian officers. By the time the British control officer, after
a telephone conversation with Heliopolis airfield, arranged to
arrest the general an elderly major, who was also in the
resistance movement, had doubled for El Masri and was
driven away under arrest. El Masri escaped. Not until three
months later did the British notice the mistake when they
caught and interned the right man. The Egyptians were to
keep an eye on him. But what Egyptian at that time would
not have been prepared to close both eyes when El Masri
Pasha took an extra long walk or did not return to camp for
the night? Thus El Masri was able to keep in contact with
Nasser and his conspirators. Not until much later was he
interned in Palestine.

Ritter's commando, however, learned nothing of this
although there was an efficient Italian spy net in Cairo, led by
an officer named Nani. The Abwehr had introduced "Roberto"
from their Athens branch into this net, and from May 1941 to
January 1942 profited from his information. But Italian intelligence was not always reliable. In the middle of June a new
council of war was held on the Tirpitzufer in Berlin, at which
Canaris himself presided. "Rommel needs reliable information from the British base in Egypt," began the Admiral. "His
strategy is based on ruse and surprise. Any information that
helps him is worth more than twenty tanks, which, by the
way, he is not getting anyway because they are being sent to
Russia," stressed Canaris.

A new, bold coup was planned. Two special agents were
to be infiltrated into Cairo and Haifa.

Shortly after this Berlin conference two new faces appeared
among Ritter's special commando in Derna. One was a
friendly man of about fifty, jovial and very Jewish-looking,
called Klein. He was nick-named Patachon. His friend was a

blue-eyed very sporting looking man called Mühlenbruch. Both of them spoke perfect Arabic and Mühlenbruch knew several dialects. Both had lived for many years in Arab countries—Klein in Alexandria, Mühlenbruch in Haifa. They were to return to these cities, install secret transmitters and build up their spy centres by recruiting further agents and contact men from the Egyptian resistance movement. This was the first step taken to infiltrate German spies into Great Britain's Egyptian base.

There were long discussions as to the route to be used. U-boat? No. By car across the desert? Impossible. All that remained was to drop them by air.

A caravan route leads from the Farafrah Oasis to Beirut on the Nile. About sixty miles from the river, Almaszy knew of a hill which stood out as a landmark in the desert. South of this was a broad strip of firm serir soil on which an aircraft could easily land. It was exactly four and half hours by air from Derna and in consequence from nine to ten hours for the double flight. But how were the agents to cross the sixty miles of desert to the Nile valley? On foot it would have been certain death. Almaszy knew an alternative. He had done this trip in a car before the war. A car of course could not be carried in an aircraft but what about a motor-cycle? That could easily be stowed. Everything was measured and calculated—E.T.A., weight, fuel, provisions, clothes, money, etc. The calculations continued. After a long search a light motor-cycle was found. The aircraft flew in and everything was ready by the 16th July, 1941.

The air over the Derna field was like a furnace. Things did not start well. The aircraft which was to land the agent had a burst tyre. Ritter had to decide whether to postpone the action or alter his plans.

"The action must continue," he said. "The escort aircraft will carry the agents and the damaged machine will take over the covering rôle in the air." They took off, at first maintaining a low altitude. On entering enemy territory they climbed to six thousand feet but finding the air full of sand they went higher, to between nine and twelve thousand feet. An hour passed, two hours, three, four.... After nearly five hours' flying the observer pointed to a hillock. The machine was brought down to a few hundred feet. The sun was already low on the horizon. They had to hurry. The escorting He circled at three thousand feet. "Why doesn't the fellow land?" they grumbled. "Why aren't we landing?" asked Major Ritter, but the young pilot was still looking for a suitable terrain. "Put her down, man," ordered Captain Liecht. Klein and Mühlen-bruch, who were sleeping on their packs in the bomb bay, were wakened.

Landing flaps lowered. Keep her steady. . . .

Now the machine must settle. But the pilot continued to roar across the track.

"For God's sake, land!" shouted Liecht. But the pilot did not land and the daylight was running out. In a few seconds night would fall and then no one would be able to decide whether there were rocks on the hard serir, which is a natural runway.

"Put her down, man! Put her down!"

They could see the wind direction from the trail of a smoke bomb they jettisoned. The pilot prepared to land, but once more pulled up the nose of the machine. "What's the matter?" shouted Ritter. They soon saw for themselves. On the horizon a British scout car was driving slowly and throwing up a cloud of dust. The He, from which the extra fuel tanks, cannon and armour-plating had been removed before the flight, could not risk an encounter. So it must get out of the way. They flew back in a broad sweep. Then the pilot prepared for the second time to make a landing. The setting sun cast strange shadows on the undulating ground. Now the He had to land. All the occupants held on tight, but once more the pilot gained height. Captain Liecht cast a question-ing glance at him.

"The ground's too bumpy," he said. "We shall crash." He was red in the face.

"Rubbish, they're only shadows. In the dying sun's rays every inch of muck looks like a three-foot hedge. The ground's as flat as a runway at Tempelhof," shouted Liecht. "Put her down!"

Too late.

The pilot had already started a new sweep. By the time his nose was into the wind the sun had disappeared. Never-theless he made another attempt.

By now the ground was a sheet of black cloth. The

African night had descended. The young pilot did not dare to land. "I can't do it," he muttered. Ritter and Liecht stared at him.

"Flight Sergeant-Major, do you realize what you are doing?" Ritter asked sharply. At this the N.C.O. pilot grew obstinate. "I'm responsible for the machine, Major. If I crash..." He did not complete the sentence but they all knew what he was about to say. If he crashed he would be blamed and he had not been ordered to land his machine. He had only been ordered to fly as escort. Above them at three thousand feet was an experienced pilot whose orders had been to effect a landing.

"The agents must jump," said Leicht.

"What about the bicycle?" replied Ritter. "They can't walk sixty miles on foot through the desert to the Nile valley. We only arranged water and food for three days, not for a week's march through the desert." Klein and Mühlenbruch, lying in the bomb bay, did not understand a word.

The latter went forward and approached Ritter. "What's the trouble, Major?" Ritter shook his head and turned to Leicht. "No, no, they can't jump. We must postpone the affair. Let us hope that the squadron will give us the machines for a second attempt."

"Let us pray," said Captain Leicht grimly.

"Back to Derna," snarled Ritter. Mühlenbruch shook his head and crawled back into the bay to inform Klein. Not a word was spoken. Captain Leicht drummed with his fingers on the arm of the observer's seat. Ritter was furious with himself for having changed machines. He could visualise the disappointment on Almaszy's face when he learned of this piece of bad management.

The roar of the engines and the vibration made them feel sleepy. A thousand stars in the African night twinkled through the cockpit perspex...

The wireless operator fiddled with his set and prepared for reception. The agreed signal reached them. Yes, that was the Derna station. Dot-dash-dot-dash! His pencil sped over the paper. Then came the voice of the operator. "No permission to land at Derna. Enemy attack. Fly to an alternative field."

And now this, to make matters worse! All eyes were turned to the fuel indicator on the instrument panel. Had they enough juice to reach Benghazi two hundred miles away? "Perhaps we can do it," said Leicht, but while they began to calculate, the port engine began to splutter. The adjustable propeller was not functioning and the motor had almost died.

Now only one course remained to them—to fly to Derna in spite of the British air attack. At this moment the rear gunner fired at a British bomber. The pilot put the machine into a dive and took avoiding action. Had everything conspired to defeat this undertaking?

"Reception out of action," reported the operator. "Look for an emergency landing strip on the coast."

"Impossible, Major. How shall I find the narrow coastal strip?" he went down still lower.

"We're over the water," said Leicht.

"We have juice for another twenty minutes' flying."

"Operator—send an SOS to the Air Sea Rescue." And Leicht added coldly: "Pilot, don't forget to keep your tail down when you land on the water."

It was now pitch dark. There was a deathly silence. The engines had ceased firing.

A hard impact—far too hard—but the He 111 floated. The empty tanks gave her buoyancy.

The wireless operator, engineer and the two agents had crawled to the rear hatch. Since the He hit the water tailfirst the cockpit bounced and was drawn under the water. The whole crew got away with it, except Mühlenbruch who had been pinned beneath a sliding crate. In the darkness and the first excitement the others did not observe this. They opened the hatch and were soon on the top of the cockpit. They hoisted out the dinghy. The pilot came swimming toward them. But where was Mühlenbruch? Where were Ritter and Captain Leicht?

The wireless operator crawled back into the machine, stumbled over bent struts, the motor-cycle and the boxes of supplies. He felt a leg. "Mühlenbruch!" he shouted, tugging at his leg. Not a sound. Not a movement. Mühlenbruch's head and chest had been crushed. He was already dead. Since the operator could not make his way through to the cockpit he crawled back.

What was happening in the cockpit? There the water seeped through the hatch, through which the uninjured pilot had escaped. Ritter was sitting there in a daze. He had hit his head against the side as they landed. The water was already up to his knees. He tried in vain to stand up but his right arm had been crushed. In front of him, in the observer's seat, was Captain Leicht up to his chest in water. He, too, was trying to extricate himself, but his arms continued to fall back in the water. His head fell forward. "Leicht!" shouted Ritter. "Leicht— we must get out of this. What's the matter with you?" Leicht murmured something, came to his senses and dragged himself over to the hatch. Ritter gave him a helping shove with his shoulder. Leicht was free. He slipped into the water and was pulled into the boat by the others.

Ritter now climbed into the pilot's seat and knelt for a moment in the cockpit to get his breath. He heard Leicht shouting: "Come on, Major, the cockpit's going to break up at any moment." He had no Mae West and only his left arm with which to swim. The right hung down like lead and was very painful. He could only float on his back. He cried out loudly, trying to contact the men in the dinghy. At last they had made the rubber dinghy seaworthy and rowed across to him. With a gurgle and a hiss the plane sank. For Mühlenbruch it was a coffin.

They were twelve hours in the water. Four men in the boat and two hanging on to the safety lines in the water, for there was only room for four in the little craft. Ritter's right arm was broken, Klein had a crushed shoulder and Leicht a few broken ribs. The three uninjured men paddled throughout the night and until the following midday when the swell cast them ashore between Barce and Derna. After an appalling march through the desert they reached an Arab village almost dying of thirst. There they were fetched by a Storch of the Desert Rescue Squadron. The second machine reached Benghazi with only a few drops of petrol left in its tank.

Thus ended the first attempt on the part of the Abwehr to infiltrate two agents into Alexandria. The O.C. Air Forces Africa gave vent to his anger. They would not be given any more of his aircraft in a hurry. Ritter was flown back to hospital in Germany and Almaszy took over his commando.

18

OPERATION "CONDOR"

The former Egyptian specialist, Almaszy, knew better than anyone else what Cairo meant as an intelligence centre. He knew, for example, the value of the radio messages sent by the American military attaché in Cairo to Washington, which were intercepted and deciphered by the German and Italian intelligences, thanks to the ingenuity of the Italian spy, Bianca Bergami. Through this channel Rommel had received, since August, 1941, the most valuable information which proved decisive for many of his military coups in North Africa.

One day, however, Almaszy said to himself: "This source can dry up. No military leader can tolerate a constant leakage of news to the enemy for any length of time. A trifling mistake, an indiscretion, a piece of treachery and the source will be closed."

Rommel was still learning a lot of secrets in the winter of 1941, but Almaszy trembled at the thought that the German armour might one day be without the decoded information from Cairo. Finally, on Rommel's agenda for 1942 was the advance of the Panzer Army Afrika to the Nile. Rommel required from Abwehr detailed reports of the enemy in the Egyptian sector, of preparations for the occupation of important strategic and economic points, security from surprise dangers and protection from sabotage actions once the Germans entered the Nile delta.

With his usual obstinacy Rommel insisted that his requirements be met. After their experience of the El Masri Pasha action and Ritter's attempts to convey the agents Klein and Mühlenbruch to Cairo, experienced men like Count Almaszy saw only one possibility—the agents must be brought straight across the desert by the land route to Egypt.

Canaris appointed Almaszy as chief of this undertaking.

As agents, two were chosen from Abwehr H.Q. in Berlin who had spent many years in North Africa: Eppler and Sandstede. The transport and technical details were left to the 800th Brandenburger Lehr Regiment. This intelligence contingent, directly responsible to Admiral Canaris, took its name from the city of Brandenburg from where in 1939 the first company was despatched to the Polish front. In October, 1942, it became a regiment, and by December, 1942, had swelled to a division. In the various theatres of war wherever special missions, commando raids and operations in enemy territory were needed, the Brandenburgers went into action. Its members were mostly Germans living abroad who had learnt one or two foreign languages in addition to their mother tongue. Many of them still possessed the original passports issued to them by enemy countries. The Brandenburgers had many successes, as did their opposite number on the British side, the Long Range Desert Group.

The men taking part in Operation Salaam, the code name for Almaszy's march through the desert, were from the Brandenburg Regiment or had been temporarily attached to it. With few exceptions they were men who had lived for many years in the East. They knew the customs of the country and were in a fit state of health for undertaking very fatiguing expeditions.

The preparations for this operation took about three and a half months. As a result of the military setback in the winter of 1941 which forced Rommel back from Tobruk, Sollum and Halfaya Pass to El Agheila, the originally planned point of departure had to be pushed further back. Eventually from Tripoli, about seventeen hundred miles of country had to be crossed before the agents reached their destination—Assiut, on the Nile. Seventeen hundred miles is the distance from Madrid to Moscow, or from the North Cape to Sicily. A great part of it ran through enemy territory and through desert which no human foot had ever trod. In addition to this the transport column had to hide for days on end. It was equipped with supplies for six weeks. The Luftwaffe provided special nourishment which the army did not possess to overcome the obstacles in the great sand sea of the Sahara. Flexible ladders were made for the trucks. With strong rungs specially ordered by the Wehrmacht from a Berlin firm. These ladders were to be unrolled whenever the wheels threatened to sink into the sand. In addition to this, a mass of special equipment was needed, the procuring of which caused great difficulties in the third year of the war.

A particularly difficult problem was a suitable radio set. It had to have a long range, but also be able to be used at short distances. It could not exceed a certain size and weight. It was a magnificent achievement on the part of the technicians at Wehrmacht headquarters broadcasting station in Stahndsdorf to develop and make these sets within the appointed time.

At the beginning of February, 1942, the two agents and three wireless operators, under the leadership of Cavalry Sergeant-Major von Steffens of Berlin, set out with all their equipment on their journey to Tripoli. They went by train to Naples and were to be flown on the next stage of their journey in two Ju 52s. That was easier said than done. The whole of air transport was devoted entirely to supplies for the African army. The sergeant-major traveled to Rome and procured the two necessary machines from the local air fleet. Secrecy was essential. It made everything very difficult but a top Abwehr man knew the "open sesame."

In Tripoli a villa was requisitioned to serve as headquarters for the undertaking. Then work began on the vehicles. Captured English trucks were found—two Ford de luxe heavy trucks and two Ford half-ton personnel trucks, known as Flippers. They were carefully overhauled and run in. For armaments they had light machine-guns mounted in the cabin next to the driver.

Since the greater part of the expedition was through unknown territory, they had to navigate by compass. Three of the trucks were equipped with Ascania global compasses and the leader's truck carried a sextant in case of emergency. The column sported the black and white crosses normally used on German military trucks. Nevertheless they were so sprayed with sand that they were almost unrecognisable even at close quarters. In this way the terms of the Hague Convention were observed. The agents wore German uniforms to prevent them being shot as spies should they be captured.

By the 29th April, 1942, they were ready to start. The comparatively easy stretches were covered as far as the Gialo Oasis which was occupied by Italian troops. At Gialo they were due for their first unpleasant surprise. The Italian maps were inaccurate. They all recorded serir, hard, smooth sand on which a car could drive fast, as far as the British military station, Dachla. According to the statements of natives and the experience of Almaszy, about thirty miles east of the Gialo–Kupra track there must lie a girdle of dunes, one of the so-called dune corridors which could only be crossed by zig-zagging, involving loss of time and fuel. A reconnaissance flight by Almaszy confirmed that the huge sand dunes extended a few hundred miles in depths. This would have completely upset the fuel calculations. New calculations had to be made, and the necessary increases provided for. Then came the second surprise. The oasis drinking water was not fit for transportation. The canisters had to be refilled at wells twelve miles away.

Almaszy was convinced that it was a matter of life and death. They set out at sunrise, two men in each truck. Almaszy and Eppler led the column. The commando consisted of eight men.

The serir was as firm as a concrete road. The wind of centuries had swept the loose sand away from the hard gravel underlay. They could travel at sixty miles an hour without a care. There were no telegraph poles, no ditches and no pavements. The road stretched as far as their eyes could see. The drivers kept the steering wheel with two props on the compass course. They trod on the accelerator and off they went. On the second day the fun was over. Like the waves of the ocean in a heavy wind, the great sand dunes barred their passage. Here no man's foot had ever trod and no car had ever driven.

There is a particular art in negotiating the sand dunes in the Sahara. The car is set at right angles to the crest of the dune. Then it drives up at full speed to the top of the dune. But not too far or else it falls down into the trough—ten, twenty or sixty feet. Then it would never get out again. Shortly before the crest therefore you have to pull over the wheel and speed down the other side aslant the crest. Full throttle and swing are necessary to negotiate the dune. The game is repeated as on a scenic railway.

They continued like this for two days and advanced a bare twenty miles. And all this at 120 degrees. During the night the thermometer fell to 20 degrees and the men froze. On the third day the junior doctor succumbed to desert colic—an illness caused by exhaustion, which results in loss of balance and fainting fits. With a serious invalid, and particularly the doctor, they could not continue their journey. No speedy recovery from his delirium could be hoped for. To waste time by pitching a camp would have been absurd. To complete their misery, von Steffen's heart let him down. For months on end he had been the driving force in procuring equipment and dealing with the technical preparations. He had been the genius of the technical side of operation Salaam. He had calculated everything, wrestled with the services for each tin of sausage, coffee beans and even for margarine rations. In addition he had even checked the water. It was lucky he did—for Almaszy, accepting Italian reports, would have had his canisters filled at the Gialo wells. An Arab voluntary helper, however, asked them if they intended to keep the water for a long time. "Naturally," growled Steffens. "Is that any business of yours?" The son of the desert gave a start and replied: "Oh, no, sir. I only meant that this water won't keep. In three days it will be undrinkable."

Although Almaszy relied on the Italian specialist's report, Steffens sent a specimen to be analyzed by the experts of the 659th Hydraulics Company. "It won't keep for more than three days," was the verdict. Hence their cans having to be filled at Bir Butafall, twelve miles away.

Sergeant-Major Steffens had worked twenty hours a day. Now the Sahara had presented him with the bill . . . and with a doctor who could not help. Almaszy decided to do what anyone in the same predicament would have done: to turn back. Five days later they were back at the Gialo Oasis.

Taken all in all this misfortune turned out to be to their advantage. Almaszy knew that he could not conquer the great sand sea. Therefore, after taking on more provisions, he tried another route.

They set out once more on the 11th May, this time without the doctor and without von Steffens. Sergeant Boilharz was also left behind as a sick man. They travelled along the famous Balificate, a route marked by the Italians with tall iron posts and surveying pyramids skirting the sea of sand. The broiling Sahara sun was once more their companion.

On the sixth day they met something which the German explorer, Friedrich Hornemann, saw for the first time in 1798 and described as follows: "We travelled for seven days through a black, rocky desert which must certainly be one of the dreariest regions in the world. This desert plateau probably owes its horrific appearance to a volcanic eruption."

The Almaszy commando also entered a similar field of black basalt blocks. The Bedouins call it Garet. These lava fields were produced by eruptions which took place before the dawn of history. The boulders which covered the ground as though flung there by some giant's hand were, in places, as large as motor cars, while among them lay small boulders ranging from the size of a fist to a man's head.

Almaszy reconnoitred and was absent for several hours. He returned at last, having found a moderately passable route. Wearily, at five miles an hour, the commando wended its way through this maze. They crossed it in six hours. Ahead, majestic and bizarre, loomed the Kebir Mountains. They consisted of a huge plateau rising in the west to twenty-five hundred feet but sinking away in the east to join the desert sand.

Once more Almaszy went on ahead. This genial adventurer whose name will always remain closely associated with the Panzer Army, moved about the Sahara like a Bedouin, as though he had spent his entire life there. His sense of direction was phenomenal. Anything that he had once seen remained impressed forever in his memory. In his soft Hungarian accent he told his comrades: "I wandered round here in 1930. Two years later I was the first European to cross the Gilf Kebir from the east to Kufra. I was accompanied by an English friend, Clayton. Today he is with the Long Range Desert Group waiting to capture me. In those days we were the best of pals and together we explored the legendary Zarzura oasis—the oasis of the Little Birds. I found it and thus enabled the poet, Arnold Höllriegel, to put a fairy story in his book. A fairy story from a past age set among the age-old grazing grounds of the pastoral Tibbus and a once flourishing vegetation. In the autumn of 1932 I acted as guide to Professor Leo Frobenius, the great African explorer, and showed him the marvellous cave drawings of the Gilf Kebir. They are near here on the west slope—over there in the hidden Surawadi, the Valley of the Pictures, as I called it, and the name it now bears on the map. I was the first white man to see these centuries-old cave drawings. Their description by Professor Frobenius caused a revolution in the assessment of

African cultures. If we had time we could go and look for the stone pyramid carved with my name which I erected in honour of the Egyptian prince and explorer, Kemal el Din Hussein, in 1933." Almaszy related all this as casually as though he had earned his living as a travel guide in Central Europe. A delightful man, Almaszy—cavalryman, Hungarian monarchist, revolutionary and partisan of the Emperor Karl after the First World War, adventurer, aviator, racing car driver, desert explorer, now fighting for Germany on one of Rommel's desert patrols.

Now they had to find the pass over the mountains. "I came down here in 1937 from the east, so I now have to find the entrance from the west side," said Almaszy. Yes, he had always started his expeditions from the east, from the Nile delta. As a pathfinder for the Egyptians and the British, for explorers, globe trotters and strategists, this Hungarian count had been the best guide in the Libyan desert. But they had never been grateful to him. They had always snubbed and despised him and now he was taking his revenge. Now his direction was from west to east, against England and towards the Nile.

With his sixth sense, Almaszy soon found a water store which he laid down in 1937 at the foot of the Gilf el Kebir. The buried water in its airtight cans was still drinkable. Almaszy opened one of the cans and poured it into the outstretched palms of his men. They tasted it cautiously. It was certainly not pure spring water. It was warm, but it tasted no worse than the stuff they had in their cans. They drank it with a laugh and then defiantly poured a few handfuls over their faces. Costly extravagance!

Directly behind Almaszy's water store, the leading Flipper was secreted in a rocky nook to serve as depot for the return journey.

A radio message in code informed Gialo and Rommel's Panzer Army wireless post as to the progress of the march. The signallers, Aberle and Weber, both Brandenburgers, picked up the message in a tent near Mameline in Cyrenaica. In this way the Panzer Army could follow the route of the secret Salaam commando.

After three hours Almaszy had found the pass over the Kebir Mountains.

He called a halt on the top of the plateau and calmly

began to survey the hundred and twenty mile long Gilf el
Kebir. "What a wonderful natural airfield," he said. "This
struck me in 1937. A whole air fleet could land here, four
hundred miles from the Nile." Almaszy continued his survey.

On the evening of the 22nd May, a Saturday, the little
group saw the lights of Charga Oasis glittering in the hollows
at their feet. Since they could not light a fire, for fear of
betraying themselves, they satisfied their appetites with a
cold meal. Tinned tongue, black bread, cold tea and chocolate sweet. Anyone who wanted to smoke had to sit in one of
the cars. Then they crawled into their sleeping bags and for
the first time a guard was posted.

The morning sun rose in all its glory. Charga lay below
like a fairyland. An extensive cluster of oases where there was
plenty of fresh water, green vegetation and human beings.
But the men down there in their wooden huts were the
enemy. It was impossible to by-pass this oasis, but presumably not all the clusters of little palms were occupied by the
military. They decided to drive straight through it.

Now they drove in two trucks containing six men each,
Almaszy in the leading truck. The main pass forked. They
took the narrow route to the smallest oasis. "We must hope
for the best," grumbled Almaszy, but the worst transpired.
The little oasis to which the pass route led was occupied. A
few trucks and soldiers stood under the dusty palms. There
were no help for them now, for they must already have been
spotted. "Press on," ordered Almaszy. "Remove your safety
catches." But they were Egyptians, garrison troops guarding
the oasis.

The sentry raised his hand.

"Halt!"

"Go on, Eppler. Tell them that we're the advance guard
of the divison," Almaszy said in English to Eppler. He leaned
out of the truck and said in Arabic: "Advance guard of the
divisional commander." Then he pointed to the plateau behind him. "Maybe the general will be coming this way
himself."

Why should an Egyptian sentry be suspicious when,
nearly a thousand miles away from the front line in one of the
remotest outposts, a soldier announced the arrival of a general in Arabic? He merely waved them through. Almaszy and

Eppler heard him grumble: "Let us hope we are spared a visit from your general."

"I hope not," murmured Almaszy thinking of Rommel.

They drove on at full speed and early next afternoon, after crossing the Japsa Pass at the edge of the desert, were staring down on Assiut in the Nile valley.

The palms swayed in a light breeze. The fields of cotton gleamed and seemed to nestle close to the glittering ribbon of the Nile. Almaszy took out his camera which he had used constantly throughout the journey. He photographed a signpost: "Assiut—5 miles." Next to it stood a notice in Arabic and English. "Danger. Seep gradient. Drive slowly."

"Danger," Almaszy said to Eppler, trying to sound unconcerned. They smoked their cigarettes in silence. Then the two agents took their civilian clothes from their packs. Weber H.Q. in Berlin had not forgotten to sew the tabs of Cairo firms into their jackets and trousers. Nothing had been overlooked. Their notecases were also well provided with personal letters and photographs, bills, hotel receipts. There were also a key ring with ignition keys and the key of an American Buick, Egyptian small change, a diary of the Cairo Automobile Club full of notes, appointments, etc. In short, everything that two young men should carry in their pockets when arriving with the tale that they were returning to Cairo after a car trip in the desert. Then the suitcase with the transmitter was fetched from the car, and a second one containing the money—£20,000. When the paymaster, Gertner, had packed the money in Berlin it had made his heart bleed. These were no forged pound notes, such as crop up even today in Egypt. They were good, solid British pounds.

The farewells were short and swift. "No time for sentimentality," said Almaszy. "See you soon in Cairo. Find us decent digs."

"We'll do that," replied Sandstede. "Of course," said Eppler. Then the two men marched off, each carrying a suitcase.

Almaszy put about and led his men back fifteen hundred miles through the desert. They surveyed the land as if on an expedition. They drew maps and sketches. They stalked past a British column. On the way they found a Long Range Desert Group dump consisting of trucks loaded with water, petrol and tinned foods. They took as much as they wanted. The remaining petrol was poured out into the sand, and sand was also put into the engines. Sergeant Woermann proudly sent the pre-arranged success signal to Mamelin. Rommel's head-quarters replied: "Message received." It was the last message they could send: from now on they received no answer. Not until Almaszy in person reported the return of his commando to Rommel at Bir Hacheim did he learn what had happened. Saluting smartly, he reported to the C-in-C: "Herr General, Operation Salaam successfully concluded. Operation Condor can now begin." Rommel made no secret of the fact that this was a painful subject. It appeared that at the beginning of the May offensive he had fetched Aberle and Weber from Mamelin and included them on his signals staff. Every man was needed and these two, Rommel said, could wait for messages from Cairo just as well at his staff headquarters as anywhere else. But then came the disaster of the 27th and 28th May. Those were the days when the Afrika Korps was in grave danger behind the Gazala line. The Tommies arrived from all directions and one morning Rommel, half-shaved and with the soap still on his face, had to beat a swift retreat. In the confusion Rommel's intelligence staff was taken prisoner in-cluding the truck with Aberle and Weber and all the details of Condor. Almaszy gasped as he heard this news. How could a beautifully devised plan, on which the head office in Berlin had taken so much trouble, be risked in such a manner? And all because two men had to be found employment. He tried to dispel the embarrassment of the meeting by telling of Sa-laam. "Herr Generaloberst, I could have taken a whole regiment with me to the Nile." Rommel slapped him on the shoulder, promoted him on the spot to major, and said with a laugh: "Count Almaszy, I hope to arrive there soon with my whole army by a far shorter route." With all his charm the Hungarian count replied: "Herr Generaloberst, our men will certainly have prepared a villa there for you if the British haven't captured you in the meantime."

Eppler and Sandstede duly arrived after their adventur-ous trip with their secret transmitter in Cairo. They hired a houseboat on the Nile. Eppler successfully played the rôle of the rich young Egyptian Hussein Gaafar, Sandstede that of the crazy Irish-American Peter Muncaster. They erected their aerials on the roof of their houseboat and got in contact with

the Egyptian resistance movements. Anwar el Sadat, now a
Minister of the United Arab Republic in Cairo, was one of
Eppler's contact men. Sadat was a lieutenant in an Egyptian
intelligence unit. He was a good friend of Abdel Nasser,
today President of the United Arab Republic and at that time
a lieutenant on active service in the Sudan. Sadat functioned
as Nasser's deputy in revolutionary, anti-British officers' circles in Cairo. The erstwhile lieutenant Sadat arranged contact
for the two German agents with the former Chief of Staff of
the Egyptian Army, el Masri Pasha, the man whom Major
Ritter had tried to abduct by air. Eppler and Sandstede
received first-class secret information from these anti-British
military cliques. The ace agent was the most famous dancing
girl in Cairo, Hekmat Fahmi. Her good relations with British
officers produced fabulous intelligence material. The much
admired "belly dancer" hated England, and was ready to
commit any act of sabotage against the enemy. Eppler was
not shy in exploiting this. Hekmat informed him of the
transfer of elements of the British 10th Army from Syria and
Palestine to Egypt. She informed both German agents of the
delivery of one hundred thousand mines for the El Alamein
front, where it had been decided—although at this time it
was not clear—that Great Britain's vast defence line was to be
built. Eppler also learned from Hekmat of the transfer of
General Freyburg's 2nd New Zealand Division to Mersa
Matruh long before the division marched off. Wireless Operator Sandstede, alias Peter Muncaster, always sat at the appointed
hour by his radio set listening. Nothing! At his side lay the
messages which had been carefully coded from the English
edition of Daphne du Maurier's novel "Rebecca." The Abwehr
had procured three copies of the same edition from Portugal—
one for the Condor Group, one for Abele and Weber and
one for the Abwehr secret broadcasting station in Athens.

Hussein Gaafar and Peter Muncaster, the two German
agents who were to have acted as Rommel's eyes and ears, sat
sulkily in their plush chairs drinking whisky. What use had
been their fifteen hundred-mile march with Almaszy through
the desert? What had happened to the hopes that Berlin and
Rommel had set on Salaam and Condor? A great game had
been ruined.

The two men had arrived safely in Cairo. They had
rigged up their aerials in the houseboat. The Fifth Column

was already in action. The dancer, Fahmi, gave them brilliant information. Their contact with the anti-British resistance movement was good. But none of this bore any fruit.

And why?

Various answers have been given to this question. Nasser's present Minister, Anwar el Sadat, mentions it in his secret diary of the Egyptian Revolution. Eppler had informed him that his transmitter was not in order and that he could get no contact with the German station. Sadat, himself an officer in an intelligence unit, a specialist in radio contact and radio sets promised to look at this one. "When I visited the two Germans in their houseboat," reported Sadat, "I looked in vain for the transmitter. I had spotted the obvious aerials on the roof of the boat, but I could not discover the secret apparatus. Then Eppler took me over to a radio gramophone cabinet. On pressing a spring the wooden lid rose and, behold, there was a hollow in which the transmitter and operator's seat had been installed. There was even a lamp inside it so that the transmitter could be used with the musical instrument shut and while the gramophone was still playing. The keenest-witted informer would hardly have suspected that a German transmitter was hidden and being operated by a German agent in such a piece of furniture." Sadat inspected the transmitter thoroughly but could find no fault. Is it surprising that the suspicious revolutionary entertained the idea that perhaps the two Germans did not want to send messages?

Abdel Nasser's fanatical partisan goes on: "The houseboat was a set straight out of the Arabian Nights, where everything suggested the enjoyment of the senses and relaxation. It was a disturbing setting, and perhaps the two young spies had rather forgotten what a tricky task they had been given." This is Sadat's version.

But none of the parties involved knew that the German station had heard the first calls from Condor but refused to answer.

The solution of the problem was given me by the head of all the German special missions in the Middle East, Major S. He was the man who under the code name of Angelo was well known to both sides of the espionage services. His real name has not yet been released and I shall not be the one to unmask him.

When Angelo learned the fate of Abele and Weber he gave orders to all radio stations not to receive any more reports from Condor and to have no traffic with them. It was clear to this master spy that sooner or later Abele and Weber must betray their limited knowledge of Operation Condor. If their radio code had fallen into British hands—which was to be feared and afterwards proved correct—then the British specialists had evidence enough to pick up the two wireless operators and subject them to third degree. If the British learned enough they could then send messages themselves to befog the Germans. In this way any information from Condor had become useless. Angelo's order to avoid all contact with Eppler and Sandstede was intelligent and necessary for the safety of both agents. Only in this way had they any chance of surviving. The question was, who would win this race against time? Would Rommel's armour arrive in Cairo before the British security forces visited the houseboat on the Nile? The British were the quicker. Sandstede and Eppler were arrested on their houseboat in September, 1942.

19

FORWARD TO THE NILE

To bathe in the Mediterranean was the dream of every soldier in Africa, from the private to the general. On the 22nd June, 1942, therefore, the commander of the Afrika Korps, General Nehring, and his Chief of Staff, Colonel Bayerlein, celebrated the German victory at Tobruk with a bathe. The bathe nearly ended in disaster, for when Sergeant-Major Voller pulled up his truck outside a small, apparently abandoned house two desperate, half-starved, British soldiers suddenly appeared with revolvers in hand. They had fled from Tobruk and had been in hiding. None of the German party had a weapon, but Nehring kept his head. He spoke calmly to the two Tommies and bluffed his way through a critical period. During the conversation the general's wireless truck, which always accompanied him but had lagged behind, arrived. The trouble was over. Since neither Nehring nor Bayerlein felt inclined to ruin their outing by taking in prisoners they disarmed the Tommies and sent them back to the city. They were ordered to report to a prisoner-of-war camp. The British were quite determined not to go into the bag. They turned off into the desert. As a result, the British history of the war was enriched by the gallant story of Lieutenant Bailey and Sergeant Norton, who reached the British lines after a thirty-eight day march along the coast.

But let us return to the beach at Tobruk. Hardly had the two officers finished their bathe than a runner summoned them back to headquarters. A radio message had come through from the field-marshal that they were to report immediately. What awaited them was Rommel's controversial decision, alternately admired and deplored, to push on to Alexandria without a pause after his Tobruk victory.

After the British defeat at Tobruk Rommel believed that his main goal was within his grasp. Admittedly both the German and Italian detachments had paid for the capture of Tobruk and the preceding victories with a heavy sacrifice in men and equipment. A pause seemed inevitable, not only on practical but on other grounds. As usual the problem of supplies was the greatest headache. And this problem of course hinged on the island of Malta. Only with the island in German hands could Rommel continue to wage war in that part of North Africa unhindered. To leave Malta in British hands was to challenge fate with any further advance to the east. Rommel's brilliant G.S.O.3 (Q), Lieutenant-Colonel von Mellenthin, discusses the problem in his book *Panzer Battles* and sums up as follows: "A serious decision had to be taken. In the original plans agreed upon by Hitler and Mussolini at the end of April it had been laid down that after the capture of Tobruk the Panzer Army should halt on the Egyptian frontier until all available air and sea forces were ready to subdue Malta. The island was to be taken by airborne troops. This was the right idea, for with the fall of Malta lines of communication to North Africa were secured and an attack on the Nile delta could be carried out without any undue worry about supplies. On the 21st June, the day Tobruk fell, Field-Marshal Kesselring flew to Africa and I was present in the commander's car at his conversation with Rommel. The latter proposed to carry on his victorious advance and not wait for the capture of Malta. Kesselring insisted that an advance into Egypt, in view of the proximity of the British base, could only be successful with the full support of the Luftwaffe. If this was to be afforded the Luftwaffe could not continue its successful operations for the reduction of Malta. It was inevitable that Rommel's long lines of communication would be seriously threatened. Kesselring, therefore, stood by the original plan and demanded a postponement of the invasion of Egypt until Malta had been taken. Rommel strongly opposed this and the argument grew heated. The two German marshals could not agree. The Italian General Staff, the German naval chiefs and Field-Marshal Kesselring continued to oppose Rommel. The latter radioed to Hitler demanding a decision. Hitler telegraphed to Mussolini: 'Duce, the Goddess of Victories usually only smiles once.' Thus the grave decision was taken to postpone the attack on Malta until September and to place all available forces at Rommel's disposal for his offensive in the Nile delta. Was this decision correct?"

It is interesting to hear upon what Rommel based his decision. Lieutenant-General Bayerlein related to me the field-marshal's arguments. "I must do everything in my power to see that the British do not open a new front or bring fresh troops from the Middle East to this front. The 8th Army is now extraordinarily weak. Its backbone is two British infantry divisions. The armour which could be brought up from the Eqyptian rear could not possibly possess any great striking power."

Rommel had a second argument on his side. "When would the Italians be ready with their preparations to land on Malta?" Had the operation not already been adopted and then postponed because the Italian preparations had not been completed? In no circumstances did the Duce want to leave the capture of Malta to the Germans alone. Hitler, as a result of the heavy losses suffered in Crete, was quite prepared to let the Italians play their part. Thus the question of the invasion of Malta was largely dependent upon the Italian General Staff. And here once more Rommel had his own private doubts.

The Desert Fox, moreover, was very confident. He knew that the British had withdrawn elements of their 10th Army from Syria for active service on the North African front. He also knew that American armour could be expected at any minute in this theatre of war. He knew the British did not intend to hold Mersa Matruh. He knew it from the decoded messages from the American military attaché in Cairo. As we have already mentioned, the latter's lengthy radio communications with Washington were betrayed by the Italian agent, Bianca Bergami. Bianca, the daughter of a high-ranking officer in the Fascist militia, had "borrowed" the code from the American Embassy in Rome.

In addition to this information, the listening companies on the African front furnished Rommel with accurate information on the enemy positions. Several serious crises in this campaign (up to the Battle of Alamein) were overcome, thanks to the achievements of the listening companies. The latter picked up the British messages, tuned into every station, followed the troop movements and finally broke the British code. Rommel, therefore, knew a great deal about the plans, intentions, armament and troop concentrations of his opponents—and he knew how to exploit them. These priceless sources functioned until the end of June, 1942—until the day Rommel launched his offensive against Alexandria. Then they dried up. The code was suddenly altered. Now by rights Condor should have been functioning in Cairo. Now the situation had arisen which Almaszy had foreseen and feared, and which had made him so eager to deliver Eppler and Sandstede to Cairo. But the Condor's wings had been clipped.

As a result of this Rommel failed to discover one vital piece of information: in what strength the British had built their defence position, the Alamein front, sixty miles from Alexandria. It was a defence line forty miles wide between El Alamein and the impassable Qattara depression in the south. This was the last bastion before the Nile. Nor did Rommel know that the British had used Italian prisoners-of-war, some of whom were highly qualified sappers, to build these positions. The Italians, so skilled in building earthworks, had laid good minefields and built dug-outs, trenches and strongpoints.

On the 22nd June Rommel's armour rolled eastwards. On the following day the field-marshal himself crossed the Egyptian frontier which the 90th Light Division had already left far behind. Captured documents and decoded British messages had shown that Auchinleck's Eighth Army was to hold a position at Mersa Matruh. Rommel harried his divisions until their fuel ran out. At Habata station, however, an important British oil dump was captured, enabling him to send his armour even farther east—towards the Nile!

They were crazy days. German and British truck columns were often traveling only five hundred yards apart in the same direction: eastwards.

Various seasoned units whom we have already met continued their trek through the desert.

Lieutenant Servas, of the 104th Panzer Grenadier Regiment, was there with his self-propelled guns, so was Lieutenant Hans Schulz of the 15th Motorised Infantry Battalion. On the 24th June he shot up a tank and a light truck from a British passing column. Schulz drove over with his men, hoping to capture some booty and exchange the monotonous *Alter Mann* for British corned beef, bacon and mixed pickles. But they found a number of badly wounded Tommies. There were also unwounded soldiers there ready to give them medical attention. They were not stretcher-bearers, but armed to the teeth.

The British did not use their weapons or throw hand grenades. They were too busy with the sufferings of their wounded comrades. Schulz and his six men were likewise moved by their plight. They jumped out of their vehicle, produced their bandages and helped to tend the wounded. A few moments later another section of British trucks appeared. There was a quick exchange of glances between Schulz and a British sergeant. The lieutenant called to his men: "Remount!" He saluted and the N.C.O. returned his salute. One of the men quickly slipped Corporal Miller a packet of cigarettes. No one fired at them as they left. No one called: "Hands up!" Both sides would have found it absurd at that moment.

Rommel advanced with his three combat groups into the Mersa Matruh area. He used the old tactic of engaging the enemy armour and encircling the infantry. The destruction of the British armour was the task of the 15th and 21st Panzer Divisions, which advanced south of Mersa Matruh. The 3rd Battalion of the 104th Artillery Regiment, under Captain Reissmann, captured a decisive point in the defences on the road from Mersa Matruh to Siwa Oasis under heavy British artillery fire. At first things appeared to go badly. The British made a counter-attack with tanks. Corporal Susenberger had just sent a message to the regiment: "Enemy tanks attacking us. Please send reinforcements." The bullets were soon whizzing about his ears. Before he had taken off his headphones a Tommy stood there with his sub-machine gun. "Hands up! Get going!" Susenberger was the only one they caught. They took him over to their position, put him on a truck after his first interrogation and he went off with the transport of the strongpoint in the direction of Mersa Matruh.

In the meantime it had grown dark. They had barely been travelling a quarter of an hour when a mad fireworks display broke out. The Tommies had run into Colonel Wolz's flak unit. They all ran for cover. The German corporal seized his opportunity and slipped off into the camelthorn bushes. At the next salvo he flung himself into a pothole and fell on top of a British soldier. Susenberger grabbed the man's tommy gun and pointed it at his belly. They sat like this by the glare of the flak shells until a lieutenant of the 6/18th Light Flak discovered them.

During the 26th and 27th June Rommel's divisions bypassed Mersa Matruh. The 15th and 21st Panzer Divisions destroyed the massed British armour in the south. There was a grim battle with the 2nd New Zealand Division. Rommel had suspected that General Freyberg's crack division would be in Mersa Matruh. Until quite recently this error was perpetuated in many of the German histories of the war. In actual fact General Freyberg, with a head wound, was leading his men against the 21st Panzer Division. General Kippenberger led the 5th Brigade and directed the fire of his yelling Maoris. The 90th Light Division in the meantime turned northwards and the Marcks Combat Group, together with the 1/6th Flak, closed the coastal road to the east. Apparently the last stronghold before Alexandria had been encircled. Inside the iron ring lay the greater part of the British infantry—the 10th Indian Division, elements of the 5th Indian, the 50th and the South Africans. If Rommel succeeded in capturing these forces his victory would be complete, for the backbone of the 8th Army would be broken and the road lay open to Alexandria.

Everything depended upon preventing the enemy forces breaking out of Mersa Matruh and out of the cauldron in the south. But it proved too difficult in the wide desert, with the few weakened divisions at Rommel's disposal to form a ring of steel round a superior opponent. With mighty blows the well-motorised New Zealand infantry under General Freyberg broke through the 21st Panzer Division. The R.A.F. gave their full support to this break out.

The fighting here was particularly bitter. Freyberg's New Zealanders, clinging on to their trucks, advanced with their knives and shouting their war cries. In appalling hand-to-hand fighting there were heavy losses on both sides.

The detachments of the 90th Light Division which had encircled Mersa Matruh met with resolute break-out attempts by the British 10th Corps. Rommel himself was in the thick of the fighting. His officers had to act as machine-gunners. The Kiehl Combat Group once more acted as his bodyguard.

The 361st suffered heavy losses. No. 4 Company under Lieutenant Stahler ran into a British anti-tank and mortar position. The company was in danger of being wiped out. Most of the vehicles were already on fire. The wounded screamed loudly for the Red Cross sergeant, Busch. A real Foreign Legion coup rescued the rest of the company. On their own initiative Sergeant Rosenzweig and Corporal Schwarz, firing their sub-machine-guns from the hip, rushed the British positions. The Tommies put their heads down and the company was given a breather to search for cover. Both these N.C.O.s paid for the rescue of their company with their lives.

The Holzer Combat Group from Special Unit 288, under Colonel Menton, bore the brunt of an attempt to break out by the 50th British Division and South African artillery units. Staff officers, the paymaster and the signallers fought with revolvers, hand grenades and bayonets. Lieutenant Kiefer's group was encircled. It formed a hedgehog, shot up the British trucks until they were on fire and prevented the break out through a wadi. The men fought desperately against the advancing Indians and South Africans. Corporal Johannes Müller of No. 8 Company, Quartermaster Sergeant Tauch, Sergeant Langer and Lieutenant Kiefer, hiding behind a truck, flung their hand grenades among the South Africans. The few attackers who got through ran into fixed bayonets or into the barrels of sub-machine-guns.

Such scenes were frequent in many parts of the encirclement front. The 7th Flak Battery, 11/25 was ordered to close off the telegraph track, the line of communication between

Mersa Matruh and the Siwa Oasis in the south. The six guns of the battery took up their positions to the east of the road. A sapper commando was detailed to cover them. Staff-Sergeant Frey and sixteen men carried out this order. They had one machine-gun, two Tommy guns, rifles, a few revolvers and bayonets. During supper the alert sounded. The South Africans and Indians attacked. Corporal Heinz Britz blazed away with his machine-gun at the first truck. The Tommies halted and opened fire. Suddenly the German machine-gun was silent. "Give it to them, Heinz!" shouted Corporal Anton Staudenmeyer. But Heinz did not reply. A burst of machine-gun fire had killed him. The Tommies continued to advance. Then from behind came the cry: "Make way for the anti-tank guns." The German 88 mm. batteries wreaked havoc among the British trucks. They fired from the right flank. A battle suddenly developed along the telegraph track. British night-flying aircraft dropped their Christmas trees and followed with their bombs. Many of the British vehicles got away. Others flamed like torches. In these wounded and trapped men were burned to cinders.

Those who accept the constantly reiterated opinion that the British successful break-out from Mersa Matruh was the fault of the Italians are quite wrong. Rommel's encirclement ring was too weak. The British troops which broke out were well motorised and fought with the courage of despair. The R.A.F. from the near-by Egyptian airfields could give real support. The Italian units fought with great courage. This is even more remarkable since their equipment was for the most part appalling, their tanks mere cardboard boxes and their heavy weapons too few in number. The Ariete Armoured Division and the Trieste Motorised Division were reduced to 14 tanks, 30 guns and 2,000 men. But they stood firm. The commander of the 20th Italian Corps, General Baldassare, and the Corps Artillery Commander, General Piacenza, fell at the head of their troops in a British bombing attack.

I wish to take this opportunity once more of saying something in favour of the much maligned "Eyeties," particularly in view of the coming events at El Alamein. Anyone who wishes to judge the achievements of the Italian soldiers must start from the premise that too many demands were made on them from the very start. Mussolini had promised

Italian Tank

that they should retake their Empire with seven million
bayonets. But the bayonets were fixed on ancient blunderbusses.

The Italian High Command despatched a single armoured
division to Africa. This was the Ariete, which bore a proud
name from a glorious past. Aries is the Latin for a ram, and in
antiquity this name was given to the gigantic battering ram
with which the Romans broke down the fortresses of the
ancient world from Spain to Syria. The Ancient Roman
Arietes aroused the admiration and terror of the nations. The
Ariete tanks of Mussolini, however, aroused only the con-
tempt of their enemies and the compassion of their allies.
They terrified their own crews. Weighing twelve tons with
inadequate armour and a 4 cm. gun, what could they do
against the British ack-ack and the British armour? The
sandbags packed round the door were intended to give the
unfortunate crews in these travelling coffins a little extra
safety. "The chance of surviving an attack in such a tank, not
to speak of success, lay beyond the realms of courage which
can morally be demanded." This is what Dr. Monzel, chief
German interpreter of the 20th Italian Corps wrote to me.
He was right.

Their other types of weapons were hardly better than
their tanks. In many respects the Italians were in the same
position as our People's Army at the end of the war when the

Americans arrived. Every German soldier, however, knows that the Italian, despite this wretched equipment, was often surprisingly tough and fought with great bravery. The 9th Bersaglieri Regiment, in common with all the Bersaglieri, was irreproachable from the military point of view. One more thing is worth while mentioning. The many Italian labour battalions achieved wonders. The approach road to Tobruk was a magnificent example of the Italian building art. Even if the average Italian did not show the same inclination to heroism in battle and to death as the soldiers of other nations, thousands of them in North Africa displayed a great capacity for hard work in the most invidious conditions.

In the Second World War the American G.I.s, even in the most advanced positions, were served with a splendid menu. Our German field kitchens produced a decent, satisfying meal. But what the Italian soldier had from his mess tin was under-nourishing, tasteless, pauper's food. In spite of all this he fought and died, and the word *camerata* had a real meaning for him, as many German soldiers can testify.

On the 28th June at about 17.00 hours the 90th Light Division with the 580th Reconnaissance Unit, a host of combat groups—among them the Kiehl, Captain Briel with the 606th Flak Battalion, the Special Group 288 with elements of the 10th and 21st Italian Corps, launched an attack on Mersa Matruh. In the fortress about eight thousand South Africans and Indians put up a stout defence from well-prepared positions.

But in the early morning hours of the 29th June the last shot was fired. Forty enemy tanks were destroyed within the perimeter of the fortress and six thousand men were marched off as P.O.W.s. The last stronghold west of Alexandria with a satisfactory harbour had fallen. It was a great victory and the 90th Light were mentioned in the Wehrmacht communiqués. It was not, however, a final victory over Auchinleck's army in the field.

Rommel's aim had been to capture the mass of the British infantry in Mersa Matruh and prevent the occupation of a new British defence line before Alexandria. He did not succeed. The British C-in-C was able to withdraw the best part of his infantry to the Alamein position, and with it to form the last line of resistance west of the Nile.

The men of the Briel Combat Group were searching for

booty in the British supply dumps in Mersa Matruh: beer, jam and cigarettes—and looking forward to a few days' rest, when the alert was given.

At 11.00 hours Sergeant Schmidt, in charge of a radio section, had brought a message from Rommel to the commander of the combat group. The text read: "Captain Briel with his combat group to 586—left 9. Rommel." Five minutes later they fell in ready to march to the spot indicated on the map. Rommel appeared.

He folded up his map and began: "Well, Briel, you will advance with your men to Alexandria and stop when you come to the suburbs. The Tommies have gone." The field-marshal paused, smiled and continued: "When I arrive tomorrow we'll drive into Cairo together for a coffee."

Captain Briel, the first man in the Army Flak to win the Knight's Cross and the first holder of the German Gold Cross, had received many strange orders from Rommel during his time in Africa but this one took his breath away. This meant victory. The Westphalian go-getter raise himself to his full height and said: "Jawohl, Herr Feldmarschall. What support am I to be given?" He expected certain reinforcements. His 60th Flak Battalion had suffered losses; as armament he still had a 4 cm. gun, one 5 cm. anti-tank gun, four 2 cm. guns, 2 mortars and seven 10.5 cm. batteries of the 33rd Artillery Regiment. Lieutenant Greb's gun was missing and only joined the battery later.

Rommel smiled and said: "Off with you, Briel. I'll send you everything I can scrape together." In actual fact the detachment was scantily reinforced. Two self-propelled guns, Czech 38-ton tanks with German 7.5 cm. anti-tank guns from the 605th Panzerjaegers. They had already fought with the Briel Combat Group at Bir Hacheim. In addition the whole Kayser Panzer Grenadier Battalion, which had fought side by side with the Briel Combat Group and beaten off the French break-out attempt. And, finally, two Panzer "recce" trucks. They set off. What had Rommel said? They were not to halt until they reached Alexandria.

It was a mad dash. Whenever they met a British unit they surrounded it in a pincer movement until it retreated or surrendered. No heed was paid to forces on their flanks.

At tactical headquarters of the Panzer Army the G.S.O.3 kept shaking his head when he read the hour-by-hour reports from Briel. "It's impossible," he kept growling. "Repeat the message," he ordered the signaller.

There was no mistake: 14.30 hours, first objective reached.

14.50 hours, second objective reached.

15.35 hours, encounter with enemy scout car. Three tanks destroyed. Losses: one 4 cm. gun, one 2 cm. gun, a small car and a 10.5 cm. gun.

18.02 hours, day's objective reached. Combat group digging in.

Anyone who knew the first, second and the day's objectives as points on the map knew that Briel and his men had reached El Daba. "If things go on like this there'll be no need to dig in," said Rommel. Briel Combat Group was given orders to attack El Daba and the stronghold was duly taken.

At 22.10 hours Briel reported: "El Daba captured, pushing on to Abd el Rahman." The Panzer Army followed Briel's report. "He is really pulling it off—he will reach Alexandria," said the officers, shaking their heads.

In the meantime the main body of the 90th Light was assembled on the coastal road preparatory to advancing east. The tracks of the 21st and 15th Panzer Divisions rattled eastwards through the abandoned Mersa Matruh line—direction Alexandria and Cairo.

Briel was far ahead.

But even the boldest undertaking has its natural limits as represented by the physical strength of the soldiers. No commander can exceed these. When limbs are heavy as lead, when the brain will no longer function clearly, then no words, no gulps of captured gin, however large, and no orders can help. Then it is time to call a halt. Then the men fall to the ground or sit at the wheel with their heads on their chests and fall asleep.

Late in the night Briel ordered a halt north-east of Abd el Rahman. Not only were the soldiers deathly weary, but the vehicles began to strike. The men rolled themselves in their blankets and flung themselves under their trucks.

"How far have we still to go?"

"About sixty miles."

Sixty miles to Alexandria! Of El Alamein that lay between them and the Nile delta Briel only knew what was drawn on the Arab map: that it was a small place with a station, and that the British had presumably assembled their troops there.

The German staffs knew nothing of the minefields round El Alamein. They were unaware of the mines which had been laid in depth for weeks on end by Italian prisoners-of-war and British Sapper units south of El Alamein on the Ruweisat crest and along the Qattara depression. Admittedly these positions were weakly manned at the outset. The 1st South African Division had held the stronghold for a week reinforced by the 6th New Zealand and the 18th Indian Brigades. That was all. If Rommel gave the British no time to concentrate their retreating divisions in this stronghold then the Alamein front would not hold out very long. . . . If!

Captain Kayser's battalion secured the coastal road. Patrols were sent out during the night. Next morning the Briel combat group remained in their position to overhaul their weapons and vehicles. Reconnaissance patrols advanced to the east. They passed the famous White Mosque and came to the station. A few trucks stood on the rails. Nothing else. No British units had dug in here. Briel nosed his way forward as far as the mine belt in front of El Alamein. Here he met with the first resistance: strong defensive fire. The "recce" trucks put about, and through his field glasses Briel saw columns on the coastal road. The British were moving up from Alexandria and Cairo: everything they could lay their hands on was being used to occupy the last bastion before the Nile delta.

"How far is it now?"

"Fifty miles."

Fifty miles to Alexandria.

"We'll be there tomorrow, then," laughed Briel's men. But nothing matured next day. When on the morning of the 30th their vehicles were ready for action once more, the 15th and 21st Panzer Divisions had already crossed the El Quseir–El Daba line. In the coastal area the 90th Light had fought its way beyond Fuka, through the retreating British, and after neutralising a minefield and wiping out some British artillery batteries reached the El Daba sector. R.A.F. fighter bombers and low-flying aircraft began to strafe them. Rommel, once again leading his spearhead, made his tactical headquarters in the huts of the El Daba supply dump. He was bombed out. He withdrew his staff but again bombs fell. For the first time they felt a new threat—the massed strength of the R.A.F. which took off from the Cairo and Alexandria airfields and fought with determination. The R.A.F. were to stop Rommel's advance "irrespective of losses," Churchill had ordered from London.

The war in North Africa hastened towards its climax. Would the German armour reach the Nile? Would Britain's position as a world power be destroyed? It was a breathtaking strategic chance for Germany: Syria, Iraq and Persia in German hands; Turkey outflanked and forced in on Germany's side; Russia's eastern flank threatened.

On the 30th June, 1942, all this appeared credible. Between himself and his objective Rommel saw only the apparently routed British army which was being reinforced at El Alamein to offer its last resistance. This resistance must be broken.

In the course of the afternoon the field-marshal summoned his local commanders to his tactical headquarters on the coastal road between El Daba and Sidi Abd El Rahman to discuss future operations. Colonel Bayerlein from Nehring's tactical H.Q. in the southern desert had to trek thirty miles through the retreating columns of the 1st British Armoured Division. For hours on end he drove in the British wake. A sandstorm obscured the sky.

At this conference the attack on the Alamein position was set for the following day, 1st July. The orders for the Afrika Korps were: advance at full speed through El Fajade to Cairo. When Bayerlein tentatively mentioned the exhausted condition of the division, the chief of staff of the Panzer Army said with exuberance: "The men will make it. But make sure that the British won't have time to blow up the big bridge over the Nile in Cairo." This showed their degree of optimism.

A message was sent to Briel: "Halt your advance. Retire and join the 90th Light. Await further orders."

Briel received this order when he was with the battery of heavy 10.5s. Lieutenant Greb had just given the order to fire. The 10.5s hammered the British positions in front of El Alamein. "Our coffee is getting cold, captain," Wireless Operator Schmidt remarked slyly. Briel laughed. "Well, we shall have to drink it cold, Schmidt."

The British aide, Lieutenant Blenton, of the 3rd South African Brigade, sped along the coastal road in the direction of Alexandria. With orders for the supply units and the naval commandos he brought the grim news: "The Germans are already shelling El Alamein." He had no idea that it was the advanced Briel Combat Group and not the Afrika Korps—not even the 90th Light—and that in front of Alamein it was only an artillery skirmish. But in those days anything seemed possible.

"The Germans are attacking." The report ran through Alexandria like wildfire.

"Rommel is at the gates." As once the citizens of Rome had raised the cry: "*Hannibal anta portas,*" the report of the German attack on the advanced positions at El Alamein sounded just as sinister to the ears of the British staff. The Royal Navy was given orders to leave Alexandria for Port Said and Haifa. The Egyptians saw the ships leave and composed lampoons; the British troops shook their heads.

No German is in the position to describe the drama of those days in Alexandria and Cairo. Only an eye witness can make it sound credible. The British war reporter, Alan Moorehead, was in Cairo at the time. His wife was also there working at British H.Q. "When will he arrive?" was the question that they and their friends asked each other. "Into the Middle East for three years the British Empire had poured every man, gun and tank it could spare. Here alone the British had a front against the enemy. The loss of Egypt would precipitate a chain of misfortunes almost too disastrous to contemplate. It would force England back to the dark days of the Battle of Britain.

"With Egypt would fall Malta and all British control of the Mediterranean. The Suez would be lost and with it stores and equipment worth fifty Tobruks. Suez, Port Said, Alexandria, Beyrout and Syrian Tripoli might go. Palestine and Syria could not then hope to stand, and once in Jerusalem and Damascus, the Germans would be in sight of the oil wells and Turkey all but surrounded."

In Alexandria the quays were abandoned; demolition troops stood by ready to blow up the harbour installations. Nearly all the British troops had left the city.

And how did things look in Cairo? The streets were jammed with cars which had streamed in from Alexandria and the countryside. The city was in a state of siege. In front of the British consulate stood a huge queue waiting for transit visas to Palestine. The exodus from Cairo was like a full-scale migration. Anyone who showed optimism or called for calm was told to look at the column of smoke that hung above the British Embassy in the residential quarter. The British were burning their documents. Anyone who wanted further evidence only had to go and look over the fence. Soldiers were shovelling piles of maps, documents, code books and personnel lists on to a huge bonfire on a building site between the general staff buildings.

Long columns of trucks loaded with office equipment drove off in the direction of Palestine. The American staff left for Somaliland. The Information Service, A.T.S. and all the female secretarial staffs were sent south. The women and children of the British military had been given orders to evacuate the city and sat waiting on their packed suitcases. The military police held at bay the host of European refugees who had fled from Hitler.

Outside the city, past the pyramids, the transport rolled in from the front with wounded soldiers and stragglers who had lost their units and their equipment. Alan Moorehead wrote: "Guns of all sorts, R.A.F. wagons, recovery vehicles, armoured cars and countless lorries crammed with exhausted and sleeping men, were pouring up the desert road into Cairo . . . an immense lizard over a hundred miles in length. We asked ourselves: 'Is the whole army in retreat?' . . . A good deal of the traffic going back, it transpired, had been ordered into the delta to prepare defences there."

Defence positions in the Nile delta! We know today that General Auchinleck had already envisaged giving up the Nile delta and withdrawing the remains of the 8th Army to the Sudan, to Palestine and Iraq. So nearly within reach was a German victory in Africa.

The plan which the German C-in-C divulged that day to his commanders—an advance against the last British bastion before the Nile delta—was a repetition of the tactics he had used at Tobruk and at Mersa Matruh. The Afrika Korps was to advance south in the direction of the Qattara depression as though it intended to break through at the southern tip of the forty-mile wide Alamein front. At dusk it was to turn north-east and fight its way ten miles to the El Alamein railway station. Under cover of night the Afrika Korps divisions were then to take the British in the rear between the strongpoints Alamein and Deir el Abyad. The 90th Light—again as at Mersa Matruh—was to sweep round El Alamein from the south, reach the coastal road, blockade it and in this way encircle the stronghold. "When Alamein is encircled and our Panzer divisions are to the rear of the main enemy forces in the south, the enemy will collapse as he did at Mersa Matruh," said Rommel.

In the light of their experience at Mersa Matruh this operation had every chance of success. The German forces, after five weeks' heavy campaigning, were too weak to fight an exhausting war of attrition, but they were still in a position to out-manoeuvre the enemy. According to all experience it seemed probably that the 8th Army would finally collapse if Rommel brought up his divisions in the rear of the British main forces behind the Alamein front. But fortune suddenly deserted Rommel. The daily telegrams from the American military attaché in Cairo to Washington, which the Abwehr had been able to decipher, could no longer be read. On 29th June the code had been changed. The British had learned that the Germans were reading them. The last telegram which the deciphering experts in the Prinzregentenstrasse in Berlin could decipher was in the old Brown code, a five-letter code consisting of about eight thousand word groups. It stemmed from the American military attaché in Rome and read: "A high Italian official mentioned in conversation to an absolutely reliable informer that the code messages from our military attaché in Cairo are being read in Rome and Berlin. Suggest that the code be changed."

With this an important source of information had dried up. But misfortunes rarely come singly. The Panzer Army reconnaissance had not functioned well. The Afrika Korps was behind its time-table because the advance from El Quseir to the turning point before El Alamein led across difficult terrain and was delayed by a sandstorm. When the Panzer divisions arrived at Deir el Abyad on the morning of the 1st July they found no occupied British strongpoints. Reconnaissance, however, reported that the British were holding a heavily mined stronghold at Deir el Shein, three miles away. Since Nehring's reconnaissance also reported that a second British strongpoint was being held north of the Ruweisat Ridge by the 1st South African Brigade there was no other alternative than to attack Deir el Shein in order to achieve a break-through of sufficient breadth. Rommel agreed. That afternoon the Afrika Korps broke through the mined positions and the 18th Indian Brigade was wiped out. With exemplary bravery the 21st Panzer Division captured the Deir el Shein box. But—and it was a very large but—the Afrika Korps lost eighteen of its remaining battle-worthy tanks and Rommel's striking power was thus severely impaired.

During the afternoon the 90th Light Division advanced according to plan and tried, as ordered, to by-pass the fortifications of El Alamein—a tactically impossible undertaking because it ran into devastating fire from the 1st, 2nd and 3rd South African Brigades and suffered heavy losses. When Rommel heard the news he drove at once to the 90th to lead the division forward, but he himself had to admit that it was impossible.

With these setbacks Rommel's plan came to grief. It had been based on not becoming involved in costly battles but in outmanoeuvring the enemy. It is hair-raising today when one reads in the British general staff documents that on the morning of the 1st July, due to a misunderstanding, the 1st British Armoured Division had not yet taken up its positions south of the Ruweisat Ridge. Had Deir el Shein not held out so gallantly it would have been child's play for Nehring at Ruweisat and he would have achieved his objective of coming up behind the British 13th Corps. But Nehring had no chance because of the obstinate resistance put up by the 18th Indian Brigade. When the remains of the German Panzer divisions attacked Ruweisat on the following day they found an enemy which could not be dislodged. The task was simply beyond the strength of the German troops—not to mention the R.A.F. mastery of the skies above the battlefield. On the 3rd July Rommel abandoned hope of getting behind the 13th Corps. He now tried to carry out an encircling movement round El Alamein with the Afrika Korps, the 90th Light and the Italian Littorio Division, but a mass attack by the New Zealanders from the Quaret el Abd box defeated this plan. Freyberg's New Zealanders overran the Italian Ariete Division and captured its entire artillery. Rommel's flank was now exposed and threatened. But the field-marshal still did not give up. He threw his heavy guns into the attack—the 88 mm. batteries were sent up to the front. But the British position could not be taken with twenty-six tanks. As the fatal night of the 3rd July broke over the desert Rommel ordered his soldiers to dig in where they stood. Every man, from the divisional commanders to the private soldiers, realised that the attack which had begun so victoriously on 26th May and was to end in Alexandria had come to a standstill.

When Rommel telegraphed to Kesselring that he had been compelled to halt his offensive, the latter had just learned that the British fleet had left Alexandria and that the British staff had been evacuated from Cairo. But although in the two Egyptian cities a swift German victory was still feared, Great Britain's crisis in North Africa had passed.

In the old quarter of Cairo the leaders of the Egyptian resistance movement sat and waited in vain for orders to strike. King Farouk continued to discuss with the politicians how the throne and the government were to behave when Rommel entered the city.

What happened throughout the whole of July before El Alamein was an ebb and flow prior to the approaching great battle for the Nile. Rommel's military strength was exhausted and his position more than dangerous. With his weakened forces he lay day after day in front of the ever-increasing British might. The British line of communication to their main dumps was sixty miles. The Germans, on the contrary, had to bring up everything over three hundred miles from Tobruk—provided anything at all arrived in that harbour. The Italian staff usually ordered the supply ships to put into Tripoli on security grounds. From there to the front line it was twelve hundred miles—the distance from Düsseldorf to Moscow.

That the German–Italian Panzer Army survived that critical July, 1942, was due to the bravery of the troops, and also to the British staffs' belief that Rommel was powerful enough to withstand a full-scale offensive. Rommel's G.S.O.3, Lieutenant-Colonel von Mellenthin, summed it up as follows: "There is no shadow of doubt: we could not have withstood a full-scale attack by the 8th Army."

Rommel's army, therefore, survived the 4th July with the utmost difficulty. The Tommies attacked the 21st Panzer Division as it retired on Rommel's orders. The German artillery was pasted, but batteries of the Zech Group halted the British attack.

Rommel held on throughout the 5th July. The 15th

Panzer Division had sixteen tanks left, as opposed to the 1st Armoured Division's one hundred. The 4th New Zealand Infantry Brigade attacked, but a well-planned raid by Stukas put the entire brigade staff out of action. The troops, left without direction, broke off the engagement.

The following day Rommel regrouped his forces. Mines had arrived and were laid in all haste. 88 mm. batteries were brought up to the most vulnerable points in the line. Captured British 25-pounders were made ready for action. Supplies eventually arrived from Tripoli for the 90th Light and the two Panzer divisions. The Afrika Korps now had forty-four tanks again! General Auchinleck, who had personally led the 8th Army in the field since the end of June, thus missed his chance of putting an end to Rommel.

On the 9th Rommel again took the initiative. He wanted to get out of his dangerously exposed position His reconnaissance had discovered a weak point in the British lines to the south. German and Italian armoured forces took the important Quaret el Abd position. The Tommies surrendered with amazing celerity, but a trick lay behind this British surrender. Auchinleck wanted to encourage Rommel to use his forces in the south, for he proposed to deliver a counter-blow in the north.

05.00 hours on the 10th July. Rommel, who had not retired to bed until three a.m., was still asleep, but his orders were being put into force. Zero hour for the attack was 06.00 hours. The troops were to advance to the east and try to take the Alamein stronghold from the rear. At that moment the sound of heavy artillery fire began in the northern sector of the front. What now happened was a disaster and influenced the entire further progress of the campaign.

This is Colonel von Mellenthin's account of the tragedy: "Our tactical headquarters lay only a few miles behind the front. As I drove up to the front hundreds of Italians streamed towards me in a panic-stricken rout. They were men of the Sabratha Division, and it was not difficult to see that the whole division had been over-run. Something had to be done to stop this huge gap. I immediately got in touch with headquarters and scraped together everything I could in the way of staff personnel, flak, infantry, supply units, field kitchen companies . . . and with these heterogeneous troops faced the Australian attack. In bitter hand-to-hand fighting, in which staff officers manned machine-guns, we managed to halt the first enemy rush."

Colonel von Mellenthin closes his report with the sober statements: "Unfortunately the brilliant leader of the listening post service, Captain Seebohm, fell in this action and most of his important information was destroyed or captured." Behind this laconic statement lay a tragedy. The listening company, NFAK, 621, was invaluable to Rommel's judgement of the enemy positions. Its achievements cannot be over-praised. It was Rommel's ear placed against the wall of enemy staff, since it listened to the telephonic communications of the enemy with special apparatus tuned in to the conversations between enemy units and broke code messages. Many of the bold Afrika Korps manoeuvres which are recorded in the war histories as "lucky" or "strokes of genius" were only made possible by the information furnished by the listening companies.

The last situation report sent by the 621 Company on 9th July ran as follows: "Australian Division recognised. Whereabouts as yet unknown." This was the 9th Australian Division which attacked on the 10th July, over-ran the Sabratha Division and wiped out the listening company. With this loss and the drying up of the Cairo telegrams Rommel had no sources of information left. This handicap could not be overcome during the decisive battles for the El Alamein positions. The tragedy of the loss of this important company was that Captain Seebohm, in the defence battles of 10th July, had only tried to hold a hopeless position because at Mersa Matruh he had been give a "rocket" by a superior officer who had no real appreciation of the importance of this troop. Misplaced courage led to an irreparable loss for the whole army.

During this stout defence battle on the 10th, a new unit of the Afrika Korps appeared on the scene—the 164th Light Afrika Division. It had been flown to Africa without its vehicles. It was largely composed of Saxons, and the divisional emblem was the crossed swords to be seen on Meissen porcelain. The 382nd Grenadier Regiment and No. 3 Company of the 220th Engineer Battalion were flung into the battle direct from their point of embarkation. They fought with the Hecker Combat Group, which had halted the enemy breakthrough with flak and weak armoured forces. The 382nd was largely responsible for stopping a British break-through on the northern flank of the Panzer Army.

What the 10th July had dramatically revealed was proved on the following days. The Italian troops were no longer up to the great efforts demanded by this exhausting combat. Rommel had to bring up more and more German forces from the south flank to stiffen the Italian front-line sector in the north. He made one more attempt to alter the position. In the afternoon of 13th July he stormed towards the Alamein strongpoint with the armour of the 21st Panzer Division. He failed. The attack was brought to a halt by the defensive fire of the 3rd South African Brigade. Rommel obstinately repeated his attack on the following day. The tanks attacked late in the evening. Kesselring's bomber squadrons gave them support. The coastal road was reached after bitter fighting. A flank attack by the Australians from the Alamein position put paid to this attempt. Rommel's forces were too weak. A full-strength armoured division, perhaps a single division, might have changed the fortunes of war, but it was not available. The Russian front had consumed the German military strength.

On 15th July the New Zealanders and Indians broke through at Ruweisat Ridge. The 15th Panzer Division and the 3rd and 33rd Reconnaissance Units counter-attacked and recaptured the lost terrain. The following day the Australians mopped up the rest of the Italian Sabratha Division at Tel el Eissa. The 382nd Grenadier Regiment held the position and prevented a catastrophe.

The following day the Trieste and Trento Divisions were over-run. Only by assembling all his forces could Rommel seal off this gap.

That evening Kesselring and the Italian chief of staff, Cavallero, visited Rommel. The field-marshal declared: "If something is not done about supplies soon we shall collapse." He was right.

Kesselring could now congratulate himself that he had been right. His argument had always been "Malta first . . . then an advance to the Nile." But warfare is no mathematical calculation but a special art in which the imponderables play an important rôle. Examples of this are legion. We quote but one of them.

On the smoking stage of the July battles before El

Alamein appeared a Panzer Grenadier whose name has been engraved on the roll of fame. His picture appeared in all the German newspapers. He was a lad of nineteen with a boyish face called Günther Halm. He was one of a hundred thousand other youths whom war took too soon into its bloody arms. He was neither an aggressive type nor a go-getter, and was in fact rather a sober youth. His sergeant in the barracks would have bet any sum that this pale young man, born in 1922, would never become a hero and certainly not a man whose name would always remain associated with the story of the desert war.

And yet the ex-machine-tool fitter, Günther Halm, after Hubert Brinkforth from Westphalia was the second and youngest soldier to be awarded the Knight's Cross. Rommel personally hung the order round his neck. At this ceremony a fly persisted in sitting on Halm's nose, and he says today that the effort of standing to attention in front of the field-marshal with a fly tickling his nose was a worse torture than the whole battle which had brought him fame and this high decoration.

For Günther Halm was not killed in the desert as so many reports and books maintain. He is alive, and I heard his story from his own lips. The present-day owner of a coal merchant's business in Bad Munder, and father of four beautiful daughters, told his tale slowly and shyly in the way one recounts half-forgotten stories. He speaks with a broad, Brunswick accent. No one in the neighbourhood knows that this Günther Halm is the man whose portrait appeared fifteen years ago in all the German papers. "Why should they?" said Halm, shrugging his shoulders. He had enough trouble with his fame. That after the war this gallant soldier was not allowed to study mechanics at Brunswick University was the least of these. He has built up his business with his wife and today he is prosperous.

On the night of the 21st/22nd July Auchinleck launched his strongest storm brigades in a large-scale attack against the central front of El Alamein. They were to break the back of Nehring's Afrika Korps. Wave after wave of Australians, Indians and South Africans were hurled against the German front. The 15th Panzer Division, with its remaining strength, fought bravely against the British armour. Then Auchinleck played his trump card. The 23rd Armoured Brigade, which

Valentine

had just arrived from England, was thrown into the battle in
conjunction with the 161st Indian Brigade to over-run the
21st Panzer Division.

On the edge of a three-hundred-yard long wadi a few
miles from the tactical headquarters of the 21st Panzer Division stood the anti-tank column of the 104th Panzer Grenadier Regiment with its two Russian 7.62 cm. flak guns, each
weighing 14 cwt. The Battery leader was Lieutenant Skubovius;
Sergeant Jabeck was in charge of No. 1 gun; Günther Halm
was the layer. On Halm depended whether direct hits were
registered or not.

Throughout the morning the British artillery pounded
the slopes of the wadi. The gun crew lay under cover behind
their gun. The fountains of dust from the shell bursts covered
them. Skubovius stood like a statue with his field-glasses
behind the protective shield and observed the wadi. Suddenly there was a burst of fire. When the smoke-screen lifted, his
voice could be heard shouting: "They're coming!" As though
galvanised the men jumped to their action stations.

An enormous formation of British Mark IIs, Mark IVs
and Valentines was rolling through the wadi as if on parade, a
hundred and fifty yards from the slope where Halm's gun
stood. The men at the gun did not know that a spearhead of

five tanks had already over-run them under cover of the smoke screen. Soon they would reach the division's tactical headquarters. Five tanks. These first five had to be knocked out. But if the others got through, ten, twenty, thirty . . . , it was "goodnight Marie," as the German soldiers used to say.

"Open fire!" said Skubovius. Now everything depended upon whether Günther Halm kept his nerve and aimed correctly. If the leader could cold-bloodedly feed the 14 cwt. gun with shells. If Nos. 3 and 4 guns rested firmly on their carriages and did not roll back when fired, for they could not be embedded in the rocky soil.

Not a word was spoken. Halm, as the layer, sat on the left. On his right was the loader.

Halm nodded. Pressed the button. The muck flew round their ears and the smoke enveloped them. The rails quivered. A wheel jumped back and pinioned Halm's leg. They righted the gun and he said he could feel no pain. "Direct hit" called Skubovius. The gun was reloaded. Halm aimed. A second direct hit!

Within the space of two minutes four burning Tommy tanks lay ahead. The others stopped to discover the whereabouts of this dangerous enemy. They spotted him and now it was hell let loose.

The tanks fired and shells fell all round, but the men paid no attention. They loaded, aimed, fired and registered direct hits.

A hurricane raged around them. A tank shell sped between Halms' legs. A second tore off the loader's thigh. "No. 3 to act as loader." The boy in question jumped into position. Load, aim, fire, direct hit!

Six . . . seven . . . eight . . . Now the ninth British tank was on fire. The others broke off the engagement. Obviously the tank commander had decided that they could not get through. One of them turned off and climbed the jebel slope to take the dangerous anti-tank gun from the rear. But the second gun was prepared for this. Two shots and the turret of the Mark II was blown to pieces.

The attack by tanks had failed. It had been brought to a halt by a single anti-tank battery. The nerves of a few men, the eyes and hands of a nineteen-year-old boy had halted the brigade.

The regimental commander, Colonel Ewert, had watched

this bloody duel from his armoured car. He drove at full speed to the rear, for he knew that the gun could not hold out very long. Stukas were alerted and the tanks of the 21st Panzer Division were directed towards the spot. It was high time. Halm's gun was now under fire from the repulsed tanks. The protective shield was smashed. The loader, with a temporary bandage, tried to make his way back to the main dressing station. He collapsed from loss of blood a hundred yard behind the position. Nearly all of them were wounded or had severe contusions from the recoil, but they went on firing. Then a direct hit destroyed the gun sights. The shield flew into the air and the men lay there among the wreckage.

That was the end of the Cavalry. The second gun was still firing from the other side of the jebel. Stukas roared overhead; Mark IV tanks from the 21st Panzer Division arrived. A British eye-witness reported the end of the story. "The Brigade, which had taken a false route, came under accurate fire from the German anti-tank defence. The spearhead was shot up. Nine tanks, including the C.O.'s, were on fire within a few minutes. Six others were put out of action. The whole brigade was in confusion. Before they could regroup they were attacked by Stukas. The rest were finished off by German Mark IVs. A whole brigade had been annihilated. Two years' training, a voyage half way round the world, and in half an hour it was all over."

Gordon Radford, a Londoner, was one of the few who brought their tanks back.

"It was a nightmare," he said. "We lost ninety-six tanks."

The British attempt to break the back of Nehring's Afrika Korps had failed. To five gunners and a lieutenant belongs most of the credit.

Günther Halm received his Knight's Cross from Rommel. He was promoted to corporal. He fought in many battles and was eventually promoted to lieutenant. In 1944, as a prisoner on the way to the U.S.A. in the *Mauretania*, he met a British officer who had lost a foot. In conversation, one of those astonishing coincidences that happened to so many soldiers came to light. The British officer had been in one of the tanks which Günther Halm, on 22nd July, had put out of action in the wadi below the Ruweisat Ridge. "He gave me his address, but later my papers were taken away from me by the French in a prisoner-of-war camp. I was never able to write to him, although I promised to do so."

20

ALAM HALFA—THE STALINGRAD OF THE DESERT

With inflamed eyes, plagued by a nose infection and a swollen liver, Field-Marshal Rommel sat in his omnibus poring over maps and aerial photographs. He kept repeating: "When we advanced at Alamein at the beginning of July, against all reason and despite our exhaustion, I wanted to prevent the British from consolidating before Alexandria and bringing up new material. I wanted to prevent the war from becoming static with a fixed front line. The British troops, both officers and men, have been trained for such a war. The stubbornness of the Tommy bears fruit in such a position where his chronic rigidity works for him."

Rommel had tried to prevent this but he was never able to carry out his plan of making a thrust past El Alamein. London and Washington had expected Rommel's armour to appear off Alexandria. That had been the beginning of July— to be more accurate the evening of 3rd July. Since then he had been held up at El Alamein.

From the 26th May to the 30th July 60,000 British, South Africans, Indians, New Zealanders, French and Australians were marched off to the German–Italian prisoner-of-war camps. Two thousand British tanks and scout cars had been shot up. The wreckage of a whole British offensive army lay scattered about the desert. Rommel's Panzer Army supplied itself for weeks on end with captured provisions; 85 per cent of his trucks were now Anglo–American. But the German losses between May and September were very high—2,300 officers and men killed, 7,500 wounded and 2,700 taken prisoner.

Their fighting strength in August had still been 34,000 men. The losses of the Italians amounted to 1,000 killed, 10,000 wounded and 5,000 prisoners.

Cairo had not been reached. They were pinned down before El Alamein, running the very danger which Rommel had wanted to avoid. The British grew stronger every day. Their supply lines to the front were from 50 to 125 miles. The Allied shipping brought everything round the Cape. New divisions had arrived from Syria, India and Iraq. And what did Rommel receive? One division, the 164th, and the Ramcke Parachutist Brigade—without vehicles. Not more than a third of the necessary supplies reached the front and they had to be brought up from Tobruk, Benghazi or even from Tripoli, along roads constantly under attack by the R.A.F. What the octopus, Malta, together with the British Naval and Air Forces did not devour on the crossing from Italy, the British bombers destroyed on its way up to the front. On the other hand over 2,000 vehicles and 100 guns awaited Rommel in Italy. A thousand trucks and 120 Panzers lay in Germany waiting to be despatched. But they did not reach Africa. The Italian Navy failed them. The calculation was simple and Rommel, a man who understood simple calculation, said to his officers: "The successes of our Panzer Army in the last weeks have spread gloom and panic in Washington and London. It is quite clear that this alarm will encourage the Allies to make even greater efforts to prevent the loss of the Nile delta and the Middle East." Rommel brought his hand down hard on the reports of the reconnaissance and the German intelligence. "Vast convoys are sailing with powerful escort round the Cape. Already the first of these are in the Red Sea, but that is only a beginning. More and more will arrive. Churchill and Roosevelt both know what is at stake in North Africa. It is obvious that by the middle of September the British 8th Army will be so strong that we shall not be able to deal with it."

The middle of September, Rommel had said.

What was to be done? The German general staff officers produced statistics. At the end of August the ratio of strength was three to one in favour of the British. In the air it was five to one.

Two hundred and fifty-nine efficient German and 243 almost useless Italian tanks faced 700 British tanks.

The British minefields were incredibly strong. Their artillery was superior and they had unlimited ammunition to expend.

And then fuel. In Rommel's Panzer Army there was none available for trips of more than eighty miles. The British had as much petrol as they wanted.

But general staff officers are naturally cautious. Rommel knew the miserable calculations they produced before each offensive. He had conquered in spite of them. Throughout the night the field-marshal sat in his omnibus thinking matters out.

On the other side the British were also reflecting. Winston Churchill flew to Cairo at the beginning of August. He was on his way to Moscow to pacify Stalin, who was in a panic as a result of the German summer offensive in Russia. The Germans were thrusting to the Caucasus, were already on the Don and before Stalingrad. Something must be done.

"Something must be done," Churchill growled in Cairo, and things were done. General Sir Harold Alexander, the best strategical brain in the Empire, was appointed C-in-C, Middle East Forces. The 8th Army was also given a new commander. Churchill's choice fell on General Gott. But this formerly aggressive and wiry man, who was known to the troops as "Strafer," had grown tired. Rommel could not have wished for a more congenial opponent. General Gott would have been no problem for the Desert Fox. But Churchill stuck to his choice. He did not care at that time to entrust the leadership of the 8th Army to an untried general from England called Montgomery.

But if proof were needed that the Gods sway the history of wars then the name of Montgomery should be quoted. General Gott had been chosen. Then, one afternoon, a lone German reconnaissance plane, flying slowly back to the German lines after a flight over Cairo, spotted a British transport machine without air cover. A bust of fire and the British machine crashed in flames. General Gott lost his life.

Montgomery was chosen to lead the 8th Amy. The die had been cast. The man who was to defeat Rommel took the stage.

As soon as Montgomery's appointment became known to the Germans Rommel sent for all the information known about this general. That evening he read the reports. "At

Dunkirk Montgomery made a name for himself as a divisional commander and organiser." Rommel muttered to himself, as he read, "That man is dangerous."

And how dangerous he was. He brought with him from England a few officers who were deeply attached to him, above all Lieutenant-General Brian Horrocks, to whom he entrusted the 13th Corps. These young military leaders obeyed orders and did not wage war on their own initiative, merely in the interest of their troops. Montgomery immediately cancelled all instructions and plans for a further retreat by the 8th Army from the Alamein position. "It is out of the question that we should abandon the Alamein front," was his thesis.

He ordered the individual divisional commanders only to engage their troops in massed strength. "We are finished with this splitting up of our forces which has enabled Rommel to win his victories," he declared. "In future, tanks and artillery will only be used en masse." After this Monty informed the Cabinet of his minimum requirements. "I shan't attack until they are fulfilled, but I will hold Alamein until you have fulfilled them." Naturally the German war leaders heard of this, but what was to be done?

"Was Rommel to sit still," General Nehring said to me, "and wait for this threatened offensive which would doubtless have been carried out with a great superiority of forces and careful planning? Or should he try to forestall it? Or should he retire to a more favourable position such as that which he held in 1941 on the Italian–Egyptian border?

"After the event it may be said that a withdrawal to a more favourable defence position with better scope for supplies would have been the correct solution. But it would have been a retreat. Berlin and Rome considered such strategical withdrawals unacceptable on political grounds, although such a decision would have given Rommel mobility and a chance to exploit his tactical superiority." This was the judgement of the cool-headed, cautious Nehring, the man who in the course of his career had so often aroused resentment by his impartial criticism of a position.

The German High Command, Hitler and Mussolini, ordered Rommel not to retreat. They instructed him to stand firm, leaving only one course open to him; to attack; to assemble once more all his forces and gamble everything on a single card. The plan was worked out accordingly and incorporated into the order which Sergeant-Major Mankiewicz of No. 9 Company, 104th Panzer Grenadier Regiment and the staff sergeant-majors of the Panzer Army passed on to the various company headquarters on the 30th August.

> Panzer Army, Africa.   Tactical H.Q. 30.8.1942
> ARMY ORDER OF THE DAY
> Soldiers,
> Today the Army, strengthened by new divisions, is embarking on the final destruction of the enemy in a renewed attack.
> I expect every soldier under my command during these decisive hours to give of his utmost.
> Signed: ROMMEL. Field-Marshal
> Commander-in-Chief.

The battle plan was "genuine Rommel." The opening of the offensive was to be an attack by the Afrika Korps, the 90th Light Division and the 20th Italian Motorised Corps, on the south flank of the army from the sector round Jebel Kalakh to the north-east. After crossing the Ruweisat Ridge the British north flank and the reserves were to be encircled and destroyed.

The 164th Light Afrika Division and the Italian divisions north of Ruweisat, to which the Ramcke Parachutist Brigade was attached, was to pin down the enemy on the coastal road by a limited attack. The 20th Italian Corps and the 90th Light Division were to stay between this more-or-less static force and the Afrika Korps, acting as a kind of hinge. By a similar attack they had to safeguard the north-west flank of the Afrika Korps at the same time. The latter, as usual, had to bear the brunt of the action. If this planned destruction of the 8th Army succeeded, the second part of the plan was to be carried out. The Afrika Korps, together with the 15th Panzer Division and the 90th Light, was to attack Suez via Cairo. The 21st Panzer Division was to capture Alexandria.

Before me lies General Nehring's sketch of the plan which he endeavoured to carry out.

The success of Rommel's offensive depended upon a few major hypotheses. Firstly, there was his idea of not launching the attack with the motorised strength of the Afrika Korps in the good going of the northern part of the front but on the rough terrain to the south at the edge of the salt pans. The guile lay in the fact that the British leaders would least expect the attack here, and in addition the Afrika Korps armour would be recognisable to the air reconnaissance from its position on the north of the Alamein front. To protect the tanks and vehicles against bomb splinters they were built into boxes and covered with camelthorn, captured British camouflage and other aids to concealment.

Rommel ordered the same number of boxes and artillery positions to be built behind the south wing of the Alamein front for purposes of deception, and in such a way—and this was a brilliant ruse—that the enemy by careful observation would recognise these installations as dummies. Were the enemy to recognise these installations as dummies he would expect even less an attack on the south front. If he mistook them for Panzer positions he would have to estimate Rommel's army reserve as being twice as strong as they actually were. This would once more lead the enemy to the conclusion that they could expect an attack from the north.

The second important point of the plan was that the advance of the assault troops, the crossing of the mine fields and the break-through to the rear of the British southern front must be carried out at lightning speed in one night. Only in this way could the vastly superior enemy be prevented from regrouping his forces.

Under cover of two short nights of full moon—the 29th and 30th August—the Afrika Korps was transferred to the south. The dummies in the north hid the departure of the tanks from the enemy reconnaissance.

But did these dispositions really remain a secret? Had the first and most important requisite for success been effected?

In the memoirs of the Chief of General Staff, Field-Marshal Lord Alanbrooke, concerning his visit to the 8th Army in the second half of August, 1942, can be read: "Montgomery had only been in command for a few days and he knew that Rommel would attack on a certain date, and in actual fact on the southern front with the aim of a subsequent turn to the north. He explained to us in detail how he would beat off this attack with his artillery. His assertions were so confident that the Prime Minister considered all his plans and precautions water-tight."

Montgomery, too, in his memoirs, proudly admits his conviction that Rommel would attack from the south. Lieutenant-General Sir Brian Horrocks, the commander of the 13th Corps, also admits that the British defence precautions had been planned in detail on the basis of Rommel's cunningly thought-out plan. The German offensive, both as regards its time and nature, came as no surprise to the British leaders in Africa. From the very start Montgomery considered the Axis attack on the northern part of the front as a feint and made no extra dispositions to counter it.

He waited in the right spot and at the right time.

General Horrocks, whose corps faced the line of the main German attack, even retired to sleep after the report that the offensive had started.

He had not the slightest doubt as to what Rommel would do. With his Afrika Korps he would attack the 13th Corps positions between the New Zealand division and Himeimat. When he had pierced the front of the 7th Armoured Division he planned either to attack in a wide sweep round Alam Halfa or to make a small sweep against the Alam Halfa rear.

The British generals do not mention treachery. This is not particularly significant. Rommel, in his diary, did not always reveal the sources of his secret intelligence.

Montgomery and his generals say that they had deduced Rommel's plan from the weather conditions, the strength and the fuel position of the Afrika Korps, from Rommel's tactics, the German mentality and normal reconaissance. But the following story gives food for thought.

On my table as I write lies a map which General Bayerlein, at that time a Colonel and Chief of Staff to the Afrika Korps, placed at my disposal. It represented the secrets of Rommel's offensive and showed clearly in colour and text the routes, the going and the state of the soil behind the British southern front. The objectives and time-table of the German offensive were worked out according to this map. It was a treasure. It had solved all the difficulties which the German command had envisaged before the offensive. The rough going in the southern sector of the front was not known to the German staff. Reliable German reconnaissance had, however, discovered a belt of minefields. But what lay behind these? Italian maps of the area gave little information. Interrogation of the natives was unreliable. An armed reconnaissance was out of the question for fear the opponents might become suspicious. Bold forays into the enemy hinterland could only bring back reliable information of the ground they themselves had covered. As a result every unit was ordered to pay special attention to captured British maps of this area. Such booty had often been of the greatest help since it stemmed from the first-class British map-making studios.

One night the sound of fighting came from the German minefield on the southern sector of the front. Mines exploded and the German sentries gave the alert. The machine-guns were trained and flare pistols fired. There was a scuffle in the minefield. Apparently a British reconnaissance troop was taking back its wounded.

"German reconnaissance patrol, forward!" A smashed British scout car was found in the minefield. The soldiers searched it for loot. What was that lying on the seat next to the driver? A blood-stained map case. They picked it up.

There was great jubilation among Rommel's staff when, in the pocket of the case, they found a route map of a sector of the southern British front. It was well printed with serial and code numbers. Crumpled and dirty from teastains and inkspots. A host of entries. . . . The staff were naturally cautious and suspicious. They checked it and made comparisons. "It's genuine," was the verdict. Now they had what they needed. The firm serir routes were shown and the soft impassable sectors of dunes and drifting sands. Also the treacherous wadis and the broad open patches of desert. The open sesame to the keypoint of the British positions, the Alam Halfa height, was as good as in German hands.

This prize booty was immediately made the basis of maps showing the going. The details were not all accepted without criticism. Nevertheless a few dangerous errors must have crept into the map of the proposed route of the British armour.

General Horrocks has since confirmed this story.

"The Jerries have emptied the scout car," reported the 7th Armoured Division to the commander of the 13th Corps, the morning after the German patrol had captured the British scout car. Sir Brian immediately phoned to Montgomery's Chief of Staff, de Guingand. "Hallo, Freddie, they've picked up your egg."

Monty's chief merely replied: "Let's hope they'll hatch it."

What did this mean?

In order to facilitate Rommel's decisions the British thought out a magnificent trick. De Guingand had worked out the route map in which complete distortions of the going were recorded behind the British front. The map was carried into the German minefields. A few "S" mines were detonated to damage the car, then the patrol retired to see what happened next. A German reconnaissance patrol searched the car and found the map. It was made the basis for the plans of attack and the prototype for the German route maps. This faked map had an important influence on the course of the Alam Halfa battle.

I have seen the general staff map of the fighting round El Alamein and have been able to follow once more the coloured lines, representing our own and the enemy positions. I could read the numbers of the strategically important points and run my finger along the tracks. Fritz Bayerlein, Rommel's travelling companion, sat at my side and explained.

In the battle of Alam Halfa Bayerlein was Chief of Staff to the Afrika Korps, commanded by General Nehring, who was wounded on the 31st August and replaced by General von Vaerst. He and General von Vaerst are two of the few surviving witnesses of the Afrika Korps' disastrous August offensive known as the "six days race". This fast attempt to pierce the Alamein front and capture the delta lasted exactly that period.

Bayerlein drew a few pencil lines to describe the various situations and the course of the battle. "This is how we wanted to act. While the Ramcke Parachutist Brigade, the 90th Light Division and the 20th Italian Motorised Corps were to pivot from the Alamein front to the north, it was the task of the Afrika Korps armour to encircle the 8th Army and finally to destroy it by an armoured attack from the rear. That was Rommel's familiar tactic. He had used it at Tobruk, at Mersa Matruh and at Gazala. Here, too, in Alamein this recipe was to bring him success. Finally the plan was to have a psycho-logical effect—a broken front, the enemy in his rear, causing the British troops to panic. Admittedly the huge sweep that the Panzer divisions had to make while fighting demanded considerable petrol supplies. It also demanded an element of surprise and a fast thrust so that the opponent had no time to counter this operation and to deal with it by regrouping. Petrol supplies, therefore, and surprise were the two premises for the success of this offensive.

"On the 27th August a decisive conference took place at Panzer Army headquarters between Rommel, the Italian Supreme Commander, Marshal Cavallero, and Field-Marshal Kesselring, the Commander-in-Chief south. Rommel demanded six thousand tons of fuel as a minimum reserve for his offensive. 'The outcome of the battle depends upon the punctual delivery of this fuel,' he explained. 'You can start your battle, Field-Marshal,' replied Cavallero, 'the fuel is already on the way'."

Rommel knew from past experience how much store to set by such remarks. He knew the pitfalls of the long supply line and remembered the disastrous occasions when the Italian convoys had run, as though according to plan, into the arms of the Royal Navy or into a hail of bombs from the R.A.F. Rommel at the time did not know everything we know today, but he knew enough to be suspicious. He did not know, for example, what the Italian pilot, Antonio Trizzino, revealed in a sensational book. He gives some astonishing details, as for example the following: In the summer of 1942 an Italian naval officer sat in a specially erected radio post near Mersa Matruh giving the most important military intelligence day and night to his chief, Admiral Maugeri of the Italian Secret Service who, after the war, was awarded a high American decoration. The same officer later organised the landing of American agents on the Italian coast and saw to it that they were put in touch with high-ranking staff officers of the Italian Admiralty. There is a whole chapter on the collaboration of senior Italian naval officers, who knew the details of the African convoys, with the British intelligence. It is corroborated by what the American frigate captain, Ellis M. Zacharias, writes in his book *Secret Mission*. "We were just as well informed on the intentions of the Axis naval command regarding the African war as on the conversations between the German and the Italian Navies." It would be wrong even in the light of this disturbing information to cry "Treachery!" after every lost battle.

The Axis also had their agents and this murky business

was not confined to one side alone. But it can safely be maintained today that the supplies for the Panzer Army dependent upon the Italian naval authorities were especially open to treachery. Rommel's last great offensive also stood in the shadow of this betrayal. Since 1941 the field-marshal suspected something and we know of conversations in which he expressed his anxiety. It was, therefore, a great solace for him when Kesselring, at that important conference on the 27th August, assured him that the German Second Air Fleet would transport the necessary fuel for him should the Italians fall down on their deliveries.

On the 30th August at 20.00 hours, about nightfall, the Panzer divisions left for the southern sector of the Alamein front. A full moon shone on this noisy armoured procession. The 15th Panzer Division was in strength and went into battle with seventy Mark II and Mark IV tanks. The 21st Panzer Division attacked with a hundred and twenty tanks. The advance proceeded on a wide front. Shortly before midnight the spearhead of the 15th Panzer Division made contact with the British defences in the mine belt. But where only weak forces had been expected they found a spirited defence. The 1st Battalion of the 115th Panzer Grenadier Regiment, under Major Busch, drove into a British minefield defended by tanks, artillery and infantry. There was a grim battle. The 2nd Battalion, under Captain Weichsel, managed to save the situation: they attacked through the minefield, formed a bridgehead and made possible the clearing of a lane through which the tanks of the 15th Panzer Division could drive.

The 21st Panzer Division also ran into a British minefield. The battalion staff of No. 3 Battalion, 104th Panzer Grenadier Regiment, ahead of the armour, reached the minefield and waited to direct the tanks through the lane. Then suddenly along the whole line trucks flew into the air as the mines went off. Like a ghost, a sapper lieutenant stood there and tried to stop the tragedy by waving. Here, too, the advanced elements of the division had driven into an unmarked British minefield. The grenadiers climbed cautiously out of their trucks. "S" mines were exploding everywhere. "Halt! Lie down!" came the order. Now the British machine-guns began to rattle. The tracers buried themselves in trucks and in men. That was the first surprise of this offensive. And while the call for stretcher-bearers rang out and staff officers tried to bring some order into the chaos there came a new blow. The R.A.F. arrived. The sky was lit up with parachute flares popularly know as Christmas trees. In addition to these the British pilots were using a new type of ground-marker. They dropped a magnesium flare which only lit up on reaching the ground. It was extremely difficult to extinguish and the battlefield was as bright as day.

General Walter Nehring, commanding the Afrika Korps, drove round the 21st Panzer Division. In his commander's truck were his chief of staff, Colonel Fritz Bayerlein, his aide, von Burgsdorff, two drivers and three signallers, including Wireless Operators Halcour and Gummersbach. Mines continued to explode, shells burst and machine-guns raked the ground. The battle raged and Nehring received the first unwelcome news: the commander of the 21st Panzer Division, Major-General Georg von Bismarck, had been killed at the head of his division while breaking through the British minefield. Major-General Kleeman, commanding the 90th Light Division, was wounded.

It was past midnight on the 31st August, and the divisions were still fighting in the extensive, well-defended British minefield. Heavy bombs crashed down out of the brilliantly lit sky. Fire from the cannon of British fighters and bombers wreaked havoc among the German motorised forces. A British pilot dived like a hawk on to the brilliantly lit battlefield. He had spotted Nehring's commander truck. The general's staff fired with all its guns but the pilot refused to be diverted. He dropped his bomb at low level. It fell just in front of the car and exploded, killing several men and officers near the truck. The shrapnel pierced the armour plating and Nehring was wounded. Outside, von Burgsdorff was dying and the corps supply officer, Walter Schmidt from Würzburg, was dead. Sergeant Franz Voller drove up in his Volkswagen, took the general aboard and drove him to the field dressing station. Of the four generals leading the attack three were killed at the beginning of the battle. Bayerlein climbed into a tank and led the corps until General von Vaerst took over.

It was not until shortly before dawn that the British resistance in the minefield was broken. Thus the spearhead of the Afrika Korps and the reconnaisance group were only able to reach a sector eight to ten miles east of their own minefield at daybreak on the 31st August. Rommel's intention of advancing his motorised troops by moonlight thirty miles east, and turning from there for a further attack to the north had failed. It failed because of the unexpected resistance and because of the surprise "going" difficulties which had not been shown on the route map—Freddie de Guingand's egg. Where the troops had expected tracks they found only heavy sand dunes. Where impenetrable dunes were marked they actually ran into British strongholds.

"We now considered whether we should break off the battle," Bayerlein told me. "The British knew where we stood. Rommel discussed the position with me and we decided to continue with the attack. But one thing was clear: the main plan, the encirclement of the 8th Army, was now no longer possible, for the enemy had had time enough to prepare counter-action. The surprise element had gone. Moreover, in daylight it was no longer possible for us to by-pass the fortified heights of Alam Halfa. The enemy forced us to take the second alternative. This was to turn north as previously planned and make a frontal attack on the important Height 132 on the Alam Halfa ridge."

The German reconnaissance had reported that Alam Halfa was strongly fortified, but it did not discover that a whole British infantry division, the 44th, recently arrived from Great Britain, was in position there with heavy armour and dug-in tanks.

At the outset the attack of the 15th and 21st Panzer Divisions made some progress, but the Ariete and Trieste divisions lagged far behind. Fortunately a sandstorm raged throughout the day which, although it made life unbearable for the troops, prevented the R.A.F. from entering the battle. On the evening of the 31st the fuel position of the divisions was precarious. Where was the fuel that Marshal Cavallero had promised to send? It must be remembered that he had assured Rommel: "You can begin the battle—the fuel is under way."

A host of legends has sprung up about this fuel tragedy behind the battle of Alam Halfa. Some tell of sabotage, others of inefficiency and the third of devilish luck.

I have gone into this question very carefully and honestly believe that I have cleared up all that can be explained.

On the 27th August the tanker *Picci Fassio* sailed from

Leghorn. Two days later it joined the tanker *Abruzzi* from the Piraeus and set course for Tobruk. Both these tankers were sunk near Derna by British torpedo-carrying aircraft. On the 27th August Cavallero had reluctantly despatched the 12,000-ton tanker *Pozza Rica* from Naples. It was torpedoed. A second tanker and a cargo vessel loaded with oil drums, the *Tergestaere*, left with a destroyer escort. Their journey can be traced as far as their arrival off Tobruk harbour. There there are two conflicting versions of its fate.

The one maintains that an Italian escort vessel gave the Captain orders to reduce speed to five knots for fear of magnetic mines. While a German merchant ship ignored the Italian order and reached port at fourteen knots, the Italian ship was attacked by British aircraft as it idled along and was sunk outside the entrance to Tobruk harbour.

The second version maintains that the *Tergestaere* reached Tobruk safely but was ordered to leave harbour during a bombing attack and was sunk by a British submarine just outside the entrance. Whichever version is correct, Cavallero's fuel was lost. Kesselring now went into action and despatched his transport aircraft to Africa. But the carrying capacity of these aircraft was relatively small.

On the 1st September the 15th Panzer Division, under the brilliant tank commander, Colonel Crasemann, attacked the Alam Halfa ridge and after bitter fighting advanced to within striking distance of Hill 132. The battle was in its decisive phase. What the infantry, sappers, gunners and tank men had to suffer is indescribable. They fought in a hail of bombs and had to assault the slope under murderous artillery fire. In addition, strong armoured attacks were launched by the 7th Armoured Division against the east flank of the German divisions storming Alam Halfa. But Rommel was determined to reach the sea. The 8th Panzer Regiment had already pierced the enemy line and by the afternoon of the 1st September was ten miles from the coast with its spearhead to the rear of the Alamein front. But on the left the 5th Panzer Regiment was pinned down and could not get through the British defences. Throughout the day the R.A.F. pounded the tanks and the Grenadier Regiments. In the Afrika Korps staff alone seven officers were killed. Supplying the advance armour with fuel and ammunition was difficult. The troops lay for the most part immobile from lack of fuel in the enemy's rear. Relentlessly the R.A.F. squadrons pounded them. The troops and their staffs cowered beneath a hail of bombs in the open desert. On the evening of the 1st September Rommel decided to break off the attack and to retire by stages to the points of departure, north of the Qattara depression. This grim rearguard action lasted another three days and the "six day race" was at an end.

Time and time again the question had been asked: "Why did Rommel lose the game in this decisive phase of the battle for the Nile?" The reply is invariably the same: it was due to lack of fuel. This theory cannot be supported. There was a shortage of fuel, but in the retreat very few vehicles were abandoned on this score. General von Vaerst explained this fallacy to me. The tanks of the reserve vehicles were emptied and the Luftwaffe came to the rescue with deliveries of fuel. The general stressed that Rommel's forces were too weak. The new British commander, Montgomery, aware of the German plans, was well provided with artillery and armour and superior in strength. Possibly a more favourable fuel position for the Afrika Korps and the resultant improved mobility and manoeuvrability could once more have turned the tables against the obstinate British defense. *Possibly*. But it cannot be denied that the British air supremacy was also a decisive factor in the battle. For the first time in World War II the German leaders were forced to recognise that enemy superiority in the air was a fatal handicap in an operation. It was the writing on the wall. But the German command in Africa was powerless against this. Field-Marshal Kesselring even contrived that squadrons from the Eastern front should be released for Alamein. Three flights of the 210 Bomber Squadron flew on the 17th August from Taganrog to Tobruk. But this was only a drop in the ocean. German air strength was on the wane in Africa. In addition to this the Luftwaffe radar posts which tuned in to enemy ground and air traffic, giving invaluable information to the air defence as to the enemy's movements, suddenly went silent. The British, for their radio conversations, had suddenly changed from short to ultra-short wave. Combined with the sudden failure of the army's listening posts, this sudden silence on the part of the air defence proved fatal.

Alam Halfa ended that period of the Africa war which had been determined by the boldness, cunning and courage of the German C-in-C and his men. Rommel lost to an enemy superior in equipment, air support and artillery. But above all, to a new military commander, who, even as a newcomer was confident of victory and had overwhelming material at his disposal, the man who altered the course of the war in Africa—Montgomery.

From now on, Bernard Montgomery dictated events. The over-taxed German troops experienced their inevitable defeat in all its bitterness. In addition to their heavy losses their confidence in victory had been shaken. Nor is it a coincidence that the turning point at Alam Halfa was contemporary with the setback of Stalingrad. That is why Alam Halfa has rightly been called the Stalingrad of the Desert.

21

THE BRITISH RAID ON TOBRUK

"Egypt is the most beautiful country in the world, and it is at its most beautiful from the terrace of the Royal Yacht Club in Alexandria," is a saying among the inhabitants of that city. Those who visited it during the war found it a fairytale city. They sat in the shade with a view of the turquoise blue sea and the white sails of the yachts. The guests were officers, wealthy people and smart women.

Off shore at the beginning of September, 1942, the 10th and 15th M.T.B. Flotillas carried out manoeuvres. They had small landing craft in tow. They practised disembarkation and re-embarking. It was a great success. The Egyptian ladies who took tea every afternoon on the yacht club terrace brought their opera glasses so as not to miss a single phase of this regatta. The British Naval Staff frowned but their faces brightened when they heard one of the women say: "What nationality are those naval officers' uniforms?"

"Greek, my dear, Greek. I heard it from my husband," replied her friend.

"Greek?"

"Yes. Greek instructors."

Her friend was a trifle obtuse. "Where have the Greeks come from?"

"From Greece."

"Oh, of course."

The Greek instructors taking part in the M.T.B. exercises off Alexandria had been a good idea on the part of the British Secret Service. The Axis troops in the Meditarranean were soon instructed to be on the alert. "Beware of an attempted invasion of Greece."

The exercises at Alexandria had nothing to do with Greece.

The affair had started at the beginning of July, 1942, when Colonel John Haselden, chief of the Long Range Desert Group, conceived the idea of dealing a heavy blow to Rommel's fuel supplies. He proposed to blow up the large oil-storage tanks in Tobruk. Since the staff in Cairo that summer seized upon anything which gave them a glimmer of hope, Haselden's plan found many supporters.

The original plan was soon enlarged. Not only were the oil-storage tanks to be blown up, but also the important German repair workshops in Tobruk. The Legendary 548th Recovery Regiment, which repaired Rommel's tanks and vehicles, had to be destroyed. These capable fellows ran the finest German tank factory on African soil. This was the opinion of the R.E.M.E. chief in Cairo. At the same time the ammunition dumps and the harbour installations were to be destroyed. Then they must liberate the British prisoners, and . . . and . . . thus Haselden's sabotage plan developed into a G.H.Q. affair, a combined land–sea–air operation with its goal three hundred miles behind Rommel's lines.

On the 21st August the heads of the three British services, air, land and sea, sanctioned the plan. It was the middle of September. The danger to the British front was actually past, for the battle of Alam Halfa had destroyed Rommel's striking power. But the operation was not abandoned.

On the 13th September the Medical Service Corporal, Albert Goldmann, who had been transferred from Crete to the 2/220th Company, North Africa, was marching with five of his men into Tobruk. They had just landed on the airfield and were looking for quarters. A few captured 3-tonners drove past them. The men were about to stop these trucks

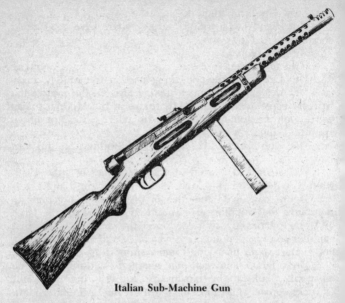

Italian Sub-Machine Gun

but saw that they were full of ragged British P.O.W.s who had obviously come from the desert—in actual fact from El Alamein. In the cabins the German sentries sat close together.

Goldmann waved to the Tommies and one of them waved back. "Poor bastards!" thought the N.C.O.

They saw the German sentries lift the barrier for the trucks at the advanced post. A Fieseler Storch hovered over the road and accompanied the convoy for a time. Then everything was swallowed up. Albert Goldmann and his men marched past the old barbed wire entanglement and the débris of the war. The sea gleamed ahead of them and there was no gunfire. The war and the front line were far away. Night fell swiftly. Goldmann and his squad stumbled into an abandoned flak emplacement. "We'll stay here," said the corporal, "make yourselves comfortable."

In the meantime the trucks with the British prisoners had driven down the main street towards the harbour. They turned to the right. "Halt!" Two M.P.s stood there with torches. "Your papers, please," they cried to the German officer in command. "Coming!" was the reply. He dismounted, accompanied by a tall grenadier. The British in the truck suddenly fell silent. It was almost sinister. Then two torches fell to the ground; there was a faint moan and a stifled scream.

"Press on," ordered the man in the German officer's uniform, replacing a long knife in the pocket of his trousers.

An Italian officer at his sentry box stopped the column. In the middle of the conversation three flak shots were fired: the signal for an air alert. A scream was suppressed and an Italian oath was drowned in the noise of the anti-aircraft fire. The huge German grenadier handed an Italian sub-machine gun to one of the British prisoners in the truck. "He won't need this where he's gone."

The sky suddenly sprang to life. The R.A.F. were there—punctual to the minute. But today there were many more bombers than usual.

As on every evening about 20.00 hours the men of the Heavy Flak Unit 114 on the Tobruk promontory waited for the routine attacks by the British. The aircraft arrived on time. First the normal formations. They were fired on and turned away. But then the radar recorded further formations flying in. Wave after wave appeared. The twelve 88 mm. guns hurled their shells into the air. The Flak had no idea that it would use up all its ammunition that night; 3,500 rounds were fired by the first battery alone.

"Operation Agreement" was supported by nearly two hundred aircraft. For four hours Wellingtons bombed the city. They destroyed the telephone lines, attacked flak positions, kept officers and men in the bunkers and thus prepared the way for Haselden's commando raid. The commando which had driven through Tobruk in the guise of a convoy of P.O.W.s was trying to form a bridgehead on the Umm-Esc-Sciause Bay. The orders of Special Commando Y1 were as follows:

Colonel Haselden was to drive with ninety men, disguised as British prisoners-of-war, in three trucks to Tobruk. German-speaking members of the commando in German uniforms played the part of guards. Under cover of the air attack Haselden was to occupy a bridgehead to the south of the harbour bay. The coastal artillery and flak located there had to be captured. If this succeeded, the naval forces off Tobruk would be given the signal to land by flares. Marines

were to be landed on the north beach of Tobruk from
destroyers, and storm troops from M.T.B.s south of Haselden's
occupied bridgehead. About six hundred and fifty men were
to be landed and together with Haselden's group were to
capture the city, held by German supply units, flak and
Italian coastal artillery. All important installations were to be
destroyed. The return journey was to be made in M.T.Bs and
destroyers. A special unit under Captain Lloyd-Owen, which
had driven with Haselden through the desert to Tobruk, was
to wait outside the city and penetrate the fortress during the
air attack. Owen's task was to seal off the entrance road,
capture the German radio and radar stations, carry off the
most important material, put the staff headquarters out of
action and cut all communications. That was the plan.

It was not lacking in audacity. Haselden's Long Rangers
travelled fifteen hundred miles from Cairo through the desert. It was by the same route, though in the opposite
direction, which Captain Count Almaszy had taken four
months earlier with his Brandenburgers to drop Rommel's
agents, Eppler and Sandstede at Assiut.

Offshore, units of the British Mediterranean Fleet waited.
The two destroyers *Sikh* and *Zulu*, eighteen M.T.B.s, eight
Hunt class destroyers and the cruiser *Coventry*. The maps
which Colonel Haselden carried were accurate, and the aerial
photographs correct in every detail.

They found the wadi which split the proposed bridgehead in two. Major Campbell took thirty men to the east and
Haselden the remainder of the men to the west. Campbell
disappeared into the darkness. Haselden's men opened the
door of the first Italian hut where the staff of an Italian coastal
battery sat by candlelight with blacked-out windows, drinking
Chianti. The Italians looked up in surprise. Before they could
understand why men in German officers' uniforms stood in
the doorway revolvers in hand, it was already too late. Hand
grenades burst and machine-guns rattled. There were screams
and groans. They were drowned by the din of the air attack as
the bombs rained down on Tobruk. The Tommies carried the
corpses outside and settled in their new headquarters. The
signallers rigged up their sets and Colonel Haselden had his
staff headquarters.

The next hut was a quarter of a mile away. In spite of the

air raid alert the Italians were asleep. David Sillito kicked open the door, flashed his torch and gave orders to fire.

The commando leader, Macdonald, spotted the subterranean gun emplacements. He heard the Italian gunners snoring. He gave his order in a whisper. Hand grenades were thrown down the ventilators. Screams and explosions. His men went on throwing their grenades until there was silence.

Things proceeded in this manner on the west side of Umm-Esc-Sciause Bay. Only on one occasion did a few Italians offer resistance in a guardhouse. Lieutenant Graham Taylor was wounded in the arm and chest. His bodyguard, Mackay and Allardyce, threw so many hand grenades into the small building that there were no survivors.

Everything had gone according to plan. The personnel of an entire Italian unit lay dead in their huts or at their guns.

"Fire the green flares," ordered Colonel Haselden. This was the signal that the west side of the bay was in British hands. Lieutenant Scott was posted at the end of the promontory. He saw the signals, turned to the east and waited for Campbell's flares. As soon as these were fired he had to inform Haselden's headquarters by flare so that a signal could be sent to the fleet. This signal meant: "The bridgehead is ours". Scott would then fire his flares out to sea and the waiting M.T.B.s could sail in under cover of darkness. Campbell's flares were never fired.

At 01.30 hours waves of Wellingtons were still arriving over Tobruk. For half an hour they had dropped no more Christmas trees over the northern part of the harbour because the destroyer invasion fleet needed the darkness.

Colonel Hartmann's heavy battery on the point had, by this time, fired 6,500 shells. Twenty-three bombers were brought down. The first telephone calls sounding the alarm came through: "The Tommies have landed."

The G.H.Q. staff had foregathered in the Director of Military Intelligence's headquarters in Cairo. They kept looking at the clock. The landing had been timed for 01.00 hours. Now it was nearly an hour later. If by 02.00 hours the code word had not been given the Naval commando was to return from the mission.

Ten minutes before zero hour...five minutes...

The duty aide brought in the order to cancel the operation. Without a word he laid it on the table. The buzzer went... The message was decoded. It was the long awaited message. The staff officers left at once.

Major Campbell had finally given the signal that he had captured the Italian batteries on the eastern side of the bridgehead. Things had not gone as smoothly for him as for Haselden. Campbell could not hold the captured battery positions and had been forced to blow up the guns. Nevertheless, the bridgehead was firmly in commando hands, although they were a little behind schedule. The Navy could begin. But now fate took a hand. Campbell's signaller, Tom Langton, who like Scott in the Haselden contingent was to light up the eastern corner of the bay, had lost his portable searchlight. The M.T.B.s missed the little bay. Only two of the eighteen found it. The others circled out to sea or round the harbour entrance.

What had happened to the destroyer flotilla? The Tribal destroyers *Sikh* and *Zulu*, camouflaged as Italian warships, had been crusing close inshore off Tobruk. After receiving the code word they sailed with a delay of one hour to the coastal sector north of the harbour entrance to land the marines before entering the harbour and attacking the shipping and coastal targets.

The first trouble started with the lowering of the clumsy landing-craft. In spite of this, the first wave went ashore, though half an hour late. The destroyers retired offshore; forty minutes later they were still waiting to lower the second wave into the returning landing-craft. But the landing-craft did not return. A signal was received that the leader of the first wave had been driven ashore with engine trouble. The other craft had no leader and lay beached waiting for orders.

The destroyers now went close inshore to speed up the action. But suddenly the 60 cm. searchlight of No. 1 Battery 1/46th Flak Regiment, under Lieutenant Muller-Frank, turned its beams on the water. It picked up the destroyer *Sikh*.

The destroyer began to fire its pom-poms. Italian coastal artillery returned the fire and the ship's guns replied.

In the meantime the signals sergeant of the Vieweg Battery had mobilised his Lieutenant with the report: "Our set registers three warships at six thousand yards."

Now, for the first time, at 04.00 hours the Tobruk staffs

were alerted and the German commandant received his report. Now they believed the first excited reports of the fugitive Italian gunners from Umm-Esc-Sciause Bay that British forces had landed. They had laughed then. Now their laughter was silenced. They could see that a British flotilla lay off Tobruk.

But where was the Owen special unit—the Group Y2? Was it not yet in Tobruk? To Haselden's chagrin it was not. Owen and his men had been in the city. They, too, had been allowed to pass by the German and Italian posts. Wherever they encountered difficulties the dagger and the wire noose proved effective. Owen, however, waited in vain for radio communication with Haselden, for the code word indicating that the first blow had succeeded. He felt that the time-table of the plan was irreparably delayed. At 01.00 hours, when the British landing-craft had not come ashore, he turned about and left Tobruk. He was the only man to save his commando. But the vitally important 88 mm. batteries on the point and the airfield were not captured. The radio and telephone centers remained intact. As a result Haselden and the fleet had already lost half the battle.

At 05.10 hours Lieutenant Veiweg opened fire on the destroyer *Sikh* with his gun Dora. The first shot was beyond the target but the second was a direct hit.

Firing orders for all guns with open sights! This was the best target practice they could possibly hope for, although the flak gunners were slightly out of practice.

Vieweg controlled the whole battery by radio, and lobbed flak shells to burst a few feet above the deck of the *Sikh*. The British warship returned this fire but Captain Ruhau's No. 3 Battery alone received direct hits

The *Sikh*, on fire with a slight list, sheered off. *Zulu*, although damaged, tried to take the *Sikh* in tow, but a lucky hit from an 88 mm. shell broke the tow-line.

The crew of the *Sikh* abandoned ship. Their commander and a part of the ship's company were picked up later. The *Zulu* was also sunk by flak and an Italian battery firing a captured 75 mm. gun. Only the small Hunt destroyers got away in this action, although some of them were very heavily damaged.

At 07.00 hours three British M.T.B.s entered the harbour at full speed. Before the flak could fire an Italian freighter arrived, and, in a low level attack, sank the British craft. It was a nightmare.

At the southern end of Tobruk and in the wadi of the little bay Haselden's men lay under withering machine-gun fire and a hail of hand grenades. And here at last died Colonel Haselden, the guiding spirit of the Long Range Desert Group, his head resting on a Tommy gun. It was the end of a great adventurer. Major Campbell also lay dying on the beach of the little bay, weapon in hand.

By the afternoon of the 14th September it was all over. Commandos of the German recovery and supplies units combed the neighbourhood and took prisoners. The German High Command issued the following communique:

"Last night in the Tobruk sector the enemy attempted to land in several places with land and naval forces. The attempt failed as a result of immediate action taken by Italian and German troops."

Half a dozen of Haselden's men and a handful of Marines took to the desert.

Five weeks later, almost dead with thirst, filthy dirty, thin as skeletons, seven men fell into the arms of a British reconnaissance unit. Exactly two months after the action another British patrol found Lieutenant David Lanark wandering, like a half-crazed ghost, through the desert. The last man from Haselden's Tobruk raid had reported back.

22

THE "DEVIL'S GARDENS" AT ALAMEIN

The stony desert, waterless, barren or rocky land, interspersed with patches of sand and a few stunted camelthorn bushes. That was the Alamein front. In the north the sun beat down on the rocky height of Tel el Eissa and in the south on the 600-ft. high Himeimat on the fringe of the impassable Qattara depression. These were the cornerstones of the front, and they lay forty miles apart. Sixty miles separated the line from Alexandria. Here in the autumn of 1942 the two warring armies faced each other, both of them exhausted by the tough battles of the past five months.

Lieutenant Freidrich Pfanzagel was a veteran mine specialist. Nevertheless in Africa he had to start again as an apprentice, for what held good in Poland, France and Greece, where Pfanzagel and his men of the 220th Engineer Battalion had won their spurs, did not hold good in Africa. Here a new set of rules applied to the minelaying.

Rommel's engineers had developed the technique into a great art. The engineer commander in Africa, Colonel Hecker, and his units cannot be excluded from any history of the desert war. The 220th, 33rd and 900th Engineer Battalions, the special units and army detachments have remained too long in the shadow of military fame. But their achievements went a long way towards bringing about the German victories in the Africa campaign.

El Alamein saw the climax of the war of mines. No such quantities of mines were laid in any theatre in the Second World War as here.

When the three companies of the 220th Engineer Battalion arrived on the northern front, they relieved the famous 900th. These were Major Kuba's men who had been trained at the Dessau-Rosslar Sapper School. What the 200th was for the 21st Panzer Division and 33rd for the 15th, the 900th was for the 90th Light Division, acting as pathfinders, fighters of rearguard actions and aids to advances. The 220th were attached to the 164th Light Afrika Division. When Lieutenant Glück initiated Freidrich Pfanzagel and his men he said: "Here in Africa the sapper is an important figure. He is probably the most important weapon in Rommel's present armoury. That, however, does not make it any better to be blown up by a mine!" Weeks later Glück's name figured in the casualty list.

Rommel's six infantry divisions (one German and five Italian) and the Ramcke Parachutist Brigade had dug in on the forty-mile broad Alamein front. Behind them lay the mobile reserves of the German and Italian armour.

The 90th Division was initially held in support in the north on the coastal road.

The 21st Panzer Division stood in readiness on the southern flank.

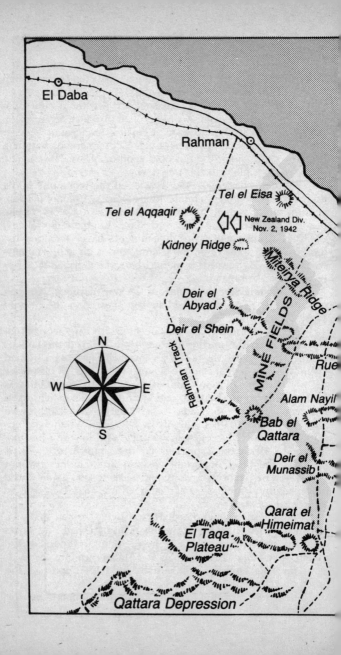

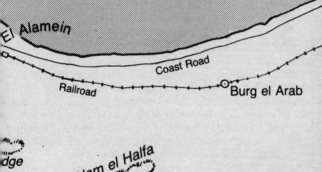

MEDITERRANEAN SEA

El Alamein

Coast Road

Railroad

Burg el Arab

dge

Alam el Halfa

Deir el Agram

EL ALAMEIN

Scale of Miles

| 0 | 10 | 20 | 30 |

The 15th Panzer Division defended the centre.

The Desert Foxes had been forced to adopt positional warfare. The 15th Panzer Division had formed a defence line and dug in behind a broad minefield. The grenadiers and the anti-tank gunners lay close behind the artillery. It entailed an enormous effort to camouflage the tanks in the rocky ground and surround them with walls of stones. Exactly the same thing applied to the other side. Montgomery's eleven divisions had dug themselves in, too. The two armies, totaling a quarter of a million men, lay watching each other. Who would make the first move? That was the question.

The German leaders were under no illusions. They knew that Montgomery's 8th Army was growing stronger day by day. A stream of supplies and reinforcements flowed into Africa from England and the U.S.A.—tanks, guns, fresh troops and, above all, fuel. The German supplies, on the other hand, were being sent to the Caucasus and to Stalingrad.

Rommel cursed, sent SOS's, radioed and threatened. He appealed to the German High Command and the Duce. All of them promised help but none of them kept their promises. In Rome and Rastenburg they were obsessed by the thought: "Everything has gone all right so far in spite of Rommel's grousing. Why shouldn't it be the same this time?"

The Panzer Army commanders were convinced that the British would be ready for an offensive before the Axis forces. What would be the result?

The Alamein front, on account of the terrain conditions, offered both sides the sole hope in all North Africa of being able to defend a comparatively small line, with every prospect of success, without being encircled or outmanoeuvred. To the south the front rested on the salt pans of the Qattara depression and in the north on the sea. Any attempt to pierce the line had to be done by frontal attack. For Montgomery there was no other way, and Rommel had to do everything in his power to prevent him.

Rommel and his officers knew that the British army in the field were better equipped to withstand or carry out a resolute frontal attack than for open battle in the desert. The training of British soldiers was still partly based on the experience of the battles of the First World War. "This caused us great anxiety," General Bayerlein said to me. "The New Zealand and Australian infantry were also trained for frontal attacks and the superior British artillery, with its vast supplies of ammunition, could be very destructive. It was a great headache. For us, it was a question of not allowing our positions to be broken, for the Panzer Army was no longer in a position to fight a mobile defence battle. The shortage of fuel and, above all, the vast superiority of the R.A.F. ruled this out. Our plan, therefore, was to hold the front at all costs. Any penetrations by the enemy were to be ironed out by immediate counter-attacks so that a salient could not be developed. Rommel had devised a method alien to his nature, a special device known as the 'Devil's Gardens.'"

Lieutenant Pfanzagel and his company commander, Lieutenant Junkersdorf, were summoned to the headquarters of the 443rd Panzer Grenadier Regiment. Rommel had arrived to hold a C.O.'s conference, and eagerly propounded his idea of protecting the Alamein position not only with the normal minefields but by huge fields of great defensive strength which he called "Devil's Gardens."

"What do the sappers think of the idea?" asked Rommel. He had already discussed the matter with their commander, Hecker, and worked out the plans. Pfanzagel and Junkersdorf replied: "To lay special minefields should entail no difficulties for the sappers, but where are we to get the material and the mines, Herr General Feldmarschall?"

"I'll attend to that," replied Rommel. "The main thing is that the sappers have to build efficient 'Devil's Gardens' through which no British soldier can pass and which no mine-sweeping squads can clear."

"Don't worry, sir," chuckled Junkersdorf, mentioning a few tricks he had learned with the 220th and had used with some success.

If, for example, a few telegraph poles were laid with the wires down on a road, the British scout car drivers would get out to remove the obstacle. If the harmless-looking wires were attached to a charge of high explosive built into the road, detonated when the wire was moved, not only the men but the car would be blown sky high.

Such booby traps made an opponent nervous and unsure of himself. This effect was perhaps more valuable than the actual losses. Hecker's sappers thought out new stunts daily for this infernal psychological war.

Karl, a corporal from one of the engineer combat groups,

produced the most diabolical ideas. Since Mersa Matruh he had been consumed by hatred. In the summer of 1942 the British had left cunning booby traps in the hotels and officers' quarters. In the toilets, for example, the plug was attached to detonators so that when it was pulled a mine exploded. Mines were even built into the drawers. There were many casualties. Among these was Karl's best friend, the battalion commander's orderly. Since then Karl had concentrated his ingenuity on these instruments of mutilation.

"You must approach the matter psychologically," was his eternal cry. He could not stand for a long time in front of a house. "Attach a mine to the door handle? That's for kids! The British did it until they got bored. It no longer takes anyone in and does not affect the adversary's morale." On the wall of a room a picture hung crooked. "A Tommy wouldn't bother at all about a crooked picture," Karl declared, "but it would annoy the British officer who saw it. He would go over to it and put it straight. But that would be his last action on earth. Therefore, attach a fine wire to the picture leading to a charge in the plaster wall, put in at breast height."

A few days after the conversation between Rommel and the engineer officers at the headquarters of the 433rd, the G.O.C. Engineers Afrika issued orders to lay the "Devil's Gardens." In the sector of the 164th Division their task was as follows: the building of four huge minefields to protect the northern front. The base of each box was to be between two and three miles long and the sides about two and a half to four miles. Each box was naturally open to the enemy front so that the attacker could run into the trap.

The first "Devil's Garden", Box H, was built in the coastal sector held by the 125th Saarland Grenadier Regiment. Here Lieutenant Drexel of No. 3 Company, 220th Engineer Battalion, gave full rein to his imagination. The second and third boxes, I and L, were in the sector of the 382nd Grenadier Regiment. Lieutenant Laurenz, with No. 2 Company, laid his death traps. The fourth box, K, was built by No. 1 Company in the sector of the 433rd Grenadier Regiment. The operational group was led by Lieutenant Pfanzagel who later took over No. 2 Company and built Box L. Rommel had kept his promise that he would provide the material. Everything from the famous Egyptian Libyan frontier fence in the way of poles and barbed wire was dismantled and taken to the front. It was astonishing how many iron struts, rolls of wire and poles came to light. Wire and stakes were used to surround the base of the big U-boxes, to make a fence for the "Devil's Gardens." Finally, the mines arrived—truckloads of French and Egyptian tank mines. These were laid in horseshoe pattern ten yards from the wire fence. But this was only the subterranean fencing. The actual content of the "Devil's Gardens" was as follows: first came simple "T" mines. The sappers laid them in tiers of twos or threes. If an enemy minesweeping squad forced its way through the field and removed the top mine the second exploded, and on very careful sweeping which might have revealed the second, the third proved fatal.

Special minetraps were formed by Italian hand grenades secured to "T" mines. As a special feature 50 and 250-lb. Luftwaffe bombs were added. These were laid in chessboard pattern and covered with the débris of demolished trucks surrounded by trip wires. These wires lay like a net round the spider, and the slightest touch detonated the bomb.

Naturally these bombs were not live at the start. Rommel had withheld the order as to when the dangerous content of his "Devil's Gardens" were to be made "active." This was essential because at the outset the main battle line lay in front of these boxes. Only after the completion of the "Devil's Gardens" were the troops to be withdrawn behind the boxes.

Infantry, intelligence and tank men could only gape in astonishment at the achievement of the sappers and the way they had busied themselves, banging and digging in constant proximity to death. Bundles of hand grenades and captured artillery ammunition were equipped with detonators as in a precision tool workshop and secured together with small charges of explosive. Harmless-looking wooden poles were coupled to huge charges of explosives so that an enemy tank which drove past one of these poles would touch off a heavy, well-camouflaged charge and be blown sky high.

All this work was carried out in the broiling sun of the late African summer. The sappers laid half a million mines in the sands before El Alamein. They worked not only by day—that was tolerable. But it was far worse at night. Everything had to be organised down to the last detail so that accidents should be reduced to a minimum.

The sappers paid out telephone wire from the regimental

headquarters to the forward company in the line. The vehicles followed at walking pace. They were covered by a machine-gun section which went on ahead. Then work started. One squad fetched the mine from the light truck. Another prepared it and a third laid the mine. Finally, another squad covered it in. The last men in action made it live and finally the whole field had to be measured and recorded on the map.

The laying of a thousand mines during one of these night shifts was not unusual. A thousand mines! The sappers flirted with death, with the confidence shown by steeplejacks. But sometimes their very familiarity proved fatal. There was a sergeant in No. 2 Company who liked scaring the infantry by laying live French tank mines. Unlike the German mines of this category they did not explode except under a pressure of seven hundred pounds. To lay his mines, the sergeant marched once more through the French field, but he had forgotten that sensitive German "S" mines had been mingled with them. He was buried near the White Mosque.

Rommel had a particular affection for this war of mines. He used to maintain that he himself could spot a mine from ten yards away. This was not difficult for a specialist, because a slight depression in the sand round the mine usually betrayed it. The field-marshal watched the progress of his "Devil's Gardens" daily. When Colonel Hecker explained the special traps to him, Rommel always looked pleased. His confidence that these minefields would prove an insurmountable obstacle for the 8th Army grew stronger.

After the battle of Alam Halfa, the doors of the Alamein front were finally bolted and barred by the engineers. The main front line was withdrawn behind the "Devil's Gardens." The horseshoe shank stretched far out into no man's land. Naturally these boxes had to be covered by infantry fire. An uncovered minefield is valueless. The opponent can sweep it. The defenders have a false sense of security. Thus, companies or sections were left behind in the old positions where the battalions had recently lain. They were suicide posts and in army slang they were known as "cannon bait."

The gaps between the "Devil's Gardens" were also closed with a barrier of "T" and "S" mines. Small lanes known only to the initiated were left so that liaison with the outpost companies could be maintained. But here special tricks were used. Freidrich Pfanzagel related: "We buried iron staves in the lane. If one of the British sweeping squads came his detector registered and he was bound to think that he was over a mined part. We observed the Tommies one night sweeping a lane for a reconnaissance patrol to slip through the girdle of mines. We let them continue. Hardly had the British commando retired than we crawled in and laid new mines. Naturally we left the Tommy's markers. The recce group got a nasty surprise!"

A particular sport was devised by Lieutenant Huntz's men of the 200th Engineer Battalion. They crept into the British minefield, removed the detonators and then reburied the harmless eggs. If the British controlled their minefield with electro-magnetic detectors everything was in order. But imagine the unit's horror when suddenly a German reconnaissance patrol made a sortie and German soldiers stormed through the minefield without a single explosion taking place!

23

JOCHEN MARSEILLE

The route from Tripoli to El Alamein led past many mosques. Nearly all of them had a white, pointed minaret and a white dome. But only one of these did soldiers and generals alike refer to as the "White Mosque." Every soldier who fought in Africa knows which one is meant—the little mosque of Sidi Abd el Rahman just outside El Alamein. A yellow hill, a square building and a crescent on the white dome. Everyone took his bearings from this for five months during the struggle for El Alamein. "Our unit lies eighteen miles south of the 'White Mosque.'" That was information enough. They knew where they were.

At that time it was empty and badly damaged. No surah was read in its cool interior. No muezzin called to prayer from the minaret. The Koran lay for some time at the foot of the chancel steps. Then it disappeared as so much disappeared from that silent, ravaged house of prayer.

Today once more from its minaret rings out the muezzin's cry: *"Allah il Allah. Allah ho akbar!"* The sand is no longer ploughed up by tank tracks or pitted with shell holes. But the memories remain. And the memory, too, of the fate of Germany's most popular fighter pilot who met his death here. He was 22, but he was known throughout the world: Jochen Marseille. In the newspaper reports he was called "The African Eagle." Young girls wrote their letters addressed simply to "The Star of the Desert," and these letters always arrived.

Much has been written about Jochen Marseille—a mixture of truth and legend. But this great pilot needs no legends and will remain one of the most fascinating figures in the history of the Second World War.

On Christmas Eve, 1940, Marseille, as a Cadet Pilot, joined No. 3 Flight of No. 27 Fighter wing in Berlin-Döberitz. On the 13th December he celebrated his 21st birthday. His active service over the Channel had revealed his daring which had been rewarded by a score of eight bombers to his credit. But this record was no indication of his ultimate flying skill.

Berlin could not produce any adventures for Marseille, for in those days, at the beginning of 1941, there was not very much to hunt over the capital of the Reich. Time was spent in practice flying, playing cards and drinking coffee. The squadron was delighted when it was sent to Africa at the end of April, 1941, after a short mission to Jugoslavia. No. 3 Flight commander at the time was Oberleutnant Homuth. (The story of Homuth's bitch, Kitty, is amusing. He had brought her from France and she had become the mascot of No. 3 Flight. The trip across the Mediterranean was to be carried out at 15,000 feet, but since no one knew whether dogs could stand high altitudes, Homuth asked his squadron commander, Neumann, to change the height to 12,000 feet, "Because I have no oxygen mask for Kitty." His request was granted and Kitty landed in splendid fettle.)

When the 21-year-old Cadet Pilot Marseille landed in Africa he was merely one of many young men eager for experience and for action, and intent upon bringing the war to a victorious conclusion. His record was not particularly encouraging. Embittered C.O.'s had recorded in his conduct sheet pranks which in the Luftwaffe were termed as "lack of flying discipline." When shooting down his eight bombers over the English Channel he had baled out nearly the same number of times. This medium-sized youngster with the well-chiselled profile and long, fair hair recalled Manfred von Richthofen, the German ace of the First World War. Both had a great passion for flying. Marseille needed but a bare six months to turn his flying into a real art.

During Rommel's 1941 summer offensive the name of Marseille was prominent in despatches for shooting down enemy aircraft. But there were still better fighter pilots— even in Africa. In defensive tactics against the British offensive in the winter 1941-42, Jochen became one of the squadron aces. He had acquired the right to certain privileges and always flew "Yellow 14." A fighter wing consisted of three squadrons and each squadron had three flights. The numbers painted on the aircraft were as follows: No. 1 flight of each squadron had white numbers; No. 2 flight red and No. 3 yellow. If, by any chance, there happened to be a fourth flight the figures were painted blue. The staff aircraft carried black double or single, broken or straight lines as recognition markings. A flight often consisted of between twelve and sixteen machines, a squadron forty to sixty and the wing of about a hundred and fifty fighter aircraft.

"Yellow 14" soon became synonymous with audacity and flying kill. In the spring of 1942 the squadron artist, Ständler, from Munich, painted a mural in Captain Homuth's quarters to correspond with his squadron commander's private hobby. Each pilot in the squadron was portrayed as an organist playing an organ. Each enemy machine brought down was an organ pipe. Many of them sat with forlorn faces at their organs with no pipes. But Marseille was the virtuoso and trod on his pedals with his hair waving in the wind. His organ was already decorated with a very respectable number of pipes.

The flying technique by which Marseille achieved his successes with such apparent ease was held to be the model for fighter pilots. He was the prototype but no one could approach him. Three to six machines were his normal kill if it came to a dog-fight. His log book, for example, records that on the 1st December, on three sorties he had seventeen victories, sixteen of which were officially recognised. In the morning of this particular day he shot down nine of the enemy in twelve minutes. Captain Franzisket, himself the possessor of the Knight's Cross, climbed out of his machine and shook his head. "I forgot to fire as I watched Marseille wading into the enemy formations."

Sergeant-Pilot Reiner Pöttgen, who for months had flown with Marseille as "winger," described to me in detail how difficult it was to keep in formation with his flight commander, cover him and at the same time check the machine he shot down. Marseille exploited the confusion into which the enemy formations were thrown by his sudden attack, making certain that one of them broke out of the safety chain and then shooting him down in tight turn back. His eyes were focused entirely on the enemy machine when he pressed the buttons of his cannon and machine-guns. He flew almost mechanically. Pöttgen insisted that Marseille, in a tight turn fight, throttled his engine back to the minimum. In this way he flew in a tighter turn and managed to arrive beneath his opponent's belly. His aiming was obviously a special gift. In addition to this he had an amazingly quick grasp of a situation.

After the toughest dog-fights Marseille, with the greatest number of victories, held the lowest record for ammunition expenditure. He once used only ten 20 mm. cannon shells and a hundred and eighty rounds of machine-gun ammunition to bring down six planes.

It is difficult to analyse the technical and tactical abilities of Marseille, for he himself gave very few indications of them. He would pull the throttle back in the middle of the enemy stream, then fly at reduced speed in a tight vertical turn. When he fired it was usually a bull's eye. A fraction of a second later he did a half roll, zoomed and waded once more into the enemy formation.

His technique can only be explained as superb, inborn skill, a mixture of experience, instinct and resolution. He flew his machine with the same ease that other people put on their clothes, and he flew as though he himself had wings.

When the German armour reached the Egyptian frontier and stood before El Alamein, Jochen Marseille, after Rommel, was the most discussed figure in Africa. He had won the highest German and Italian decorations—the Knight's Cross with Oak Leave and Swords and the rarely awarded Italian Gold Medal for Bravery which only three soldiers won in the Second World War—Marseille, Captain Müncheberg and the Duke of Aosta. Rommel and Nehring themselves only wore them in silver.

Marseille represents a type which may soon become extinct—a chivalrous adversary who had perfected a technical specialist's art and was, at the same time, a romantic. But before long his face grew hard from his constant battle with death. It was pale and pinched as he clambered out of the machine after each landing. His first gesture was to take out a cigarette which he could only hold with trembling hands. Anyone who saw Marseille at such moments got some idea of the expenditure of energy and nerves which each of these missions under the hot African sun cost. But he withstood the danger of becoming a neurotic by sheer health and youthfulness. He shook off his experiences as a dog shakes off water. Generals and high-ranking officers of the Axis staffs were daily guests in his quarters. When you entered his tent among African dunes you might have been in some Bohemian café in Rome or Paris. Against one of the tent sides was a tiny bar and behind it a South African Negro, Matthias. The stools were made from the finned tails of British bombs. Old rolls of telegraph wire served as tables; sofa and chairs were made of sandbags and mosquito nets. Gramophone music rang out until late into the night—Argentine rumbas, Italian songs and every evening, "Lili Marlene." Here Marseille and his fellow pilots sat and smoked and drank to forget the war.

Jochen Marseille had 158 victories to his credit. After the 125th he was awarded the diamonds to his Iron Cross. Hans Rudolph Marseille, his brother, told me that he never actually received this highest of all German decorations, however, which was made to a special pattern according to Hitler's personal instructions. Nor was it presented to his family after his death.

Jochen Marseille succumbed to no enemy pilot. The malice of man-made machinery caused his death. Reiner Pöttgen, who flew with him on his last mission, described his death to me. "It was the morning of the 30th September, 1942. My altimeter registered 4,500 feet. We were returning with No. 3 Flight from a sweep of the Cairo area without having made contact with the enemy. The wings of my Me were close to the wings of the Captain's 'Yellow 14' as they had been a hundred times before.

"The clock on the instrument panel showed 11.35 hours.

"We hadn't a care in the world. What could happen? What could possibly happen?

"I was thinking of Jochen's bitterest fight three days before on the 27th September. At six thousand feet he had met a British ace who, with thirty-five victories was the recordholder in the North African theatre. Jochen needed twelve minutes to shoot him down. On landing, he said: 'That was the toughest adversary I've ever had,' and added in admiration: 'His turns were fabulous.'

"Jochen's voice in my headphones interrupted my thoughts. 'There's smoke in my cockpit.'

"I looked across the few yards that separated us and could see the captain's face. It was snow white under the glittering cockpit roof. His left hand opened the ventilator and smoke poured out. I looked at the map. We were still three minutes flying time away from the German lines at El Alamein.

"The ground station had picked up Marseille's first SOS. Now voices chattered over the air. 'What's the matter, Elbe 1? Come in, please.' 'I can't see clearly,' Jochen kept calling. Our flight closed in. We took him in the centre and guided him over the R.T. Our cries: 'Starboard!' 'Port!' were constantly interrupted by his complaint 'I can't see anything.' I called to him: 'Only two minutes to El Alamein.'

"The ground station gave the order 'Bale out' but Marseille refused to abandon his aircraft over the enemy lines. He could not envisage being taken prisoner.

"The second hand of the instrument panel clock had made three complete turns: 11.38 hours."

Below, in "Devil's Garden L" at one of the mobile guns of 707 battery, the leading gunner, Sergeant Bauer, put his field-glasses to his eyes and looked up at the German fighters. He called to his comrades: "One of them's on fire!" Thick black smoke was pouring from the machine.

But up in the air at four thousand five hundred feet Pöttgen stared alternately to starboard at Yellow 14 and then ahead. There was the "White Mosque", the German lines. Would he make it? The cockpit was full of smoke. What did

Jochen say? His words came in gasps: "I . . . can't . . . hold out . . . any . . . more", and once more: "I must get out of this. I'll fly in a broad left hand turn." As Pöttgen told me this the beads of sweat stood out on his forehead as they must have done at the time. "Marseille pulled the machine over on its back and the cockpit roof was torn away as if by a giant fist. Now he must bale out.

"'Jochen's baled out,' I said over the R/T.

"But what was wrong? Hell for leather, his machine descended in a shallow dive. It would not release the body. It flung him against the tail unit when he finally baled out.

"He fell. Fell like a stone. Where was the white rescuing blossom of the parachute?

"A quarter of an hour later we landed behind the dunes. One of us was missing. One from No. 12 flight. . . .

"Captain Franzisket fetched him. He lay four miles to the south of the White Mosque."

The members of the flight sat at the table in silence. Matthias, the Negro from the Transvaal, Marseille's batman, had disappeared. From the kitchen where he usually worked no sound could be heard. Not until evening did he return from some hiding place or from out of the desert. He was carrying a necklace of shells. He handed it to Pöttgen.

"What is that, Matthias?"

"Fifty-seven shells, sir. Fifty-seven victories since I came to the captain at the end of August. I have looked for them all one by one. Sometimes it was a long time before I found one that matched, white and beautiful."

Matthias was proud but the tears ran down his black cheeks. "Lay the chain in his grave," he said, as he turned away and left the tent.

Three years later Matthias was captured by the men of the Maquis in France and shot. His necklace of shells lies in Jochen Marseille's coffin. When they buried him it lay on his chest like a glittering order, more brilliant than diamonds—a token of love from a black man.

24

MONTGOMERY ATTACKS

Autumn 1942. Rommel had been eighteen months at the head of his army. Eighteen months in the desert without leave.

Professor Halster, his doctor, had already looked anxious during the battle of Alam Halfa. Each day he examined the general's swollen liver and observed his constantly inflamed throat.

In Mauerwald, near Rastenburg, Hitler's headquarters, news had reached them of Rommel's ill-health. On the 19th September Hitler sent General Stumme to Africa to deputise for Rommel. The field-marshal left on a well-deserved spell of leave.

In the entry of 22nd September, 1942, in the flying log-book of Lieutenant Giesen, Rommel's pilot, stood the entry: "Flight to Derna". The following day they flew on to Rome. On the 24th Rommel broke his flight at Forli to visit the Duce in his summer residence.

When Rommel said goodbye to Marshal Cavallero after this conversation with the Duce the latter asked: "Can Italy count upon your immediate return if Montgomery attacks?"

Rommel turned to his pilot: "How long should we need, Giesen, to reach Africa if the Tommies attacked?"

"Eight hours in direct flight. Ten via Rome, Herr Feldmarschall."

"Does that satisfy you?" asked Rommel. Cavallero nodded, shook him by both hands, and said: "Thank you."

Before Rommel returned to Semmering south of Vienna he was presented with a field-marshal's baton on the 25th September at the Führer's headquarters by Hitler. Weary and depressed, he returned to Berlin where Goebbels invited the home and foreign press to meet him in the theatre of the

Ministry of Propaganda. The old Desert Fox fell for a propaganda trick which later he was bitterly to regret. Acting on
instructions, the field-marshal came to a halt as he entered
the hall and held the door handle in his hand. The expectant
silence was broken by his voice: "I have my hand on the
handle of the door to Alexandria."

Four weeks later the handle was wrenched from his
grasp . . .

"Tomorrow is full moon," said Colonel Markert. He
wanted to add: "Monty does not appear to be ready; this
would be the most favourable time for an offensive." But
Markert never uttered his thoughts. A mighty roar like a
thunder clap tore the silent, moonlit, desert night. It rumbled through the huge roofed dugout which served as tactical
headquarters and sleeping quarters for the staff of the 164th
Light Afrika Division. The officers were drinking with the
divisional commander, General Lungershausen. It was as
though a giant had banged his fist down on the table. Colonel
Markert, the divisional G.S.O.1, ran up the steps of the
dugout to his commander truck. The G.S.O. 2, Major Elterich,
just had time to steady a bottle of wine. The soda water
siphon rolled from the table. General Lungershausen looked
through the slits towards the front. He saw a single golden
flashing strip of fire—a barrage trained on the whole division.
"Monty's offensive has started," said the general. He looked
at his wristwatch. It was 20.45 hours on the 23rd October,
1942.

Five days before Colonel Liss had come from Rastenburg
to Africa to inform them that according to intelligence
Montgomery could not possibly attack in October.

Montgomery had managed to deceive the leaders of the
Axis forces. He had cunningly staged a feint attack south of
the Alamein front while making preparations for a thrust in
the north. The British general had learned this from Rommel.
He had even created an intelligence cell for his southern
front, the reports of which were designed purely for the
German listening posts. Moreover, he had a pipe-line, with
fueling stations and petrol dumps, built slowly, very slowly, so
that the German intelligence would form the opinion that it
would take another four weeks at the least before he was
ready. He foxed the German General Staff so cleverly that
even the arrival of two new divisions with two hundred and

forty guns and a hundred and fifty tanks had taken place unobserved.

Montgomery's trump card lay in attacking the Alamein front at its strongest point instead of at its weakest. According to all the principles of strategy he should have launched his main assault in the south. But he attacked in the north, in the very spot where the sappers of the 164th Light Division had for weeks on end been laying Rommel's "Devil's Gardens." Was this not bound to fail?

It would have failed had Monty attacked with his tanks and tried to drive through the minefield, but the British general had thought out a new tactic.

The orthodox principle was: first destroy the enemy armour with tank attacks then overpower the enemy's unarmoured forces. Montgomery reversed the process.

He had decided to flout experience, Montgomery told his staff. In a vast battle of material he would proceed to destroy the Axis infantry in their defence positions. He would break down Rommel's fortified wall stone by stone and draw the teeth of his front line. Then he would break through with tanks and destroy the enemy Panzers.

This was Montgomery's new recipe, and he could afford to use it.

The battle opened with a five-hour heavy barrage. A thousand British guns poured their shells on to a front-line sector five miles broad, between Bir el Atash and Bir Abu Sifi, where the 164th Light Division and Italian infantry lay. One thousand guns on a ten thousand yard stretch, which meant virtually a gun every ten yards firing at the opposite ten yards of the German front. The Axis troops were subjected to an inferno of explosions, smoke and dust. All communications were disrupted.

At 22.00 hours the British guns were switched to the "Devil's Gardens." The result was unimaginable for anyone who was not present. Each shell was followed by the explosion of mines, the detonating of the aircraft bombs and the explosive charges. The "Devil's eggs" which Colonel Hecker and his sappers had so carefully laid flew into the air. They had been designed to destroy the attacking British tanks or infantry. But now Rommel's minefields were ploughed up. Montgomery was strong enough to shoot corridors through the minefields with a wealth of American made shells. Rommel had not envisaged this.

When the British infantry divisions of the 30th Corps attacked they did not believe that they would find a single living creature in front of and in the German minefields. But they were wrong. In "Devil's Garden H" lay the survivors of the battalions and companies of 125th Panzer Grenadier Regiment. They lay in wretched holes among torn wire and ploughed up minefields, and they fired—fired with their anti-tank guns, fired with their machine-guns. The British infantry attack was halted for a while. No. 2 Battalion under Captain Wendel bore the brunt of the defence.

But south of the 125th, in front of and behind the boxes J and L, things looked serious. In the sector of the 382nd Panzer Grenadier Regiment the incorporated Italian Battalions I/62, II/62 and III/62 abandoned their positions. The 382nd defended their sector desperately against the assaulting 9th Australian and 51st Highland Divisions.

Captain Krupfganz with his battalion waged a hand to hand conflict with the Australians and Highlanders. The British tanks gave the attacking Tommies artillery support and machine-gunned the German positions. But when the British infantry attacked with fixed bayonets, the German battalion replied with hand grenades and sub-machine-guns. Then the British tanks rolled forward. The battalions were over-run. The badly wounded battalion commander and a handful of wounded men were taken prisoner.

Things were not much better for the 1st Battalion under Captain Piper.

The British had broken through. Behind the main front line a battalion of the 433rd together with a detachment of divisional artillery managed to seal off the attack.

A little farther south between "Devil's Gardens L and K," the New Zealand and South African divisions had forced their way through the minefield. In "Devil's Garden K" the British armour suffered heavy losses from exploding aircraft bombs. But of what avail was this? The great mine belt had been overcome.

In the southern sector of the Alamein front, too, the divisions of the 13th Corps tried to force a break-through. Here, too, artillery and R.A.F. bombers had softened up the

German–Italian positions, wiped out the outposts and blasted the strongholds in the mine lanes with artillery fire. But Rommel's teeth had not been drawn. Sir Brian Horrocks could make no appreciable impression at this stage.

The Kiehl combat group repulsed every enemy attack. The battalions of the 104th Panzer Grenadier Regiment and artillery units of the 21st Panzer Division fought to a standstill. The 10th Company, under Lieutenant Ringler, held off the attack of a whole battalion of the 44th Division for twenty-four hours between the mine belts. The men lay there for twenty-four hours without water or food, constantly under fire. The wheel of an anti-tank gun was blown off by a direct hit. Two men lay under the axle to enable the gun to go on firing. In this way they destroyed two heavy tanks. The Ariete Division, the Bersaglieri Battalion and units of the Brescia and Folgore Divisions fought magnificently. Montgomery's 13th Corps was able to make minor break-throughs in the eastern minefield, but did not reach the main front line.

In the north, on the other hand, things were getting worse. By dawn on the 24th October the British had opened two breaches. Behind the three spearhead infantry divisions the British C-in-C now despatched the 1st and 10th Armoured Divisions with seven hundred tanks and thrust with this mighty force to the west. Was this the end of the Panzer Army Afrika? Would the Axis front collapse?

But Montgomery never risked everything on a single card. The Germans were given a chance of recovering from this dangerous crisis. Their leadership, however, seemed cursed with ill luck that day. General Stumme, temporarily in command of the Panzer Army, a very brave man who had been only a short time in Africa, thought it only right to follow the Rommel tradition and be up in the front line. Accompanied by an intelligence officer, Colonel Büchting, he drove over the "alert road" to the front. He drove straight into the crisis position near Hill 28. British machine-guns and anti-tank guns opened fire on him.

Colonel Büchting received a fatal head wound. The driver tried to get his car out of the line of fire. Stumme, who had leaped out on to the road, held on to the fast travelling car. He fell without the driver noticing it and remained lying there. A reconnaissance troop from the 1st Battalion of the 125th went to rescue the general. Sergeant-Major Holzschuh and Corporal Kiehl of No. 2 Company found him. He was dead. General Ritter von Thoma took over command of the Panzer Army.

On the evening of the 24th October, the German High Command demanded from Westphal within the hour a report as to whether this flare-up was a reconnaissance in strength or a full-scale attack. Westphal replied: "Undoubtedly the long-expected full-scale offensive. Rommel's return essential."

Montgomery's infantry continued to attack in new waves. The artillery thundered almost without a pause and the R.A.F. bombed the front night and day.

Lieutenant Bernard Orth had his night field-glasses to his eyes. He lay with No. 1 Battery of the 31st Panzer Artillery Regiment some five miles behind the advanced line. He was attached to Combat Group South of the 15th Panzer Division, led by Lieutenant-General von Vaerst with the old campaigner, Heinrich Müller as G.S.O.1. Colonel Teege, commanding the 8th Panzer Regiment, led the combat group. When the early morning sun of the 24th October broke through the smoke of gunpowder and shell-bursts Lieutenant Orth, from his armoured observation truck, saw now to his horror that the Italian infantry was in flight. "Front kaput! Front kaput!" they screamed as they fled to the west. Behind the stragglers the first enemy tanks appeared. They were brand new American Shermans and General Grants. "Enemy armour advancing!" went the message over the radio. The hour had arrived for the artillery, which, with its guns, mortars and field howitzers, formed the backbone of the Panzer divisions. The guns were well trained. The first tanks were immobilised and set on fire. The armoured spearhead was halted. This was the moment for a counter-attack by No. 1 Detachment of the 8th Panzer Regiment under Captain Stiefelmayer. His powerful thrust with armour forced the British tanks back into "Devil's Garden L". This was fatal for the British, even though many of the mines had been detonated during the night bombardment. For now it appeared that many of the dangerous "Devil's eggs" were still intact. One column of flame after the other rose to the sky. Aircraft bombs exploded, causing consternation among the enemy

Grant

tanks. Thirty-five of them remained in "Devil's Garden."
The rest retired. Montgomery's break-through in the northern-
most corridor was halted.

For the Panzer Army Afrika, however, the term "poor
man's war" still held good. Montgomery himself had material
to spare. Above all he used his air forces to the full. The
R.A.F. now had air supremacy in the African theatre of war.
The German ground forces were constantly bombed. The
usual British raid was with eighteen bombers escorted by
fourteen fighters. The German soldiers got to know the
"pig-headed eighteen." They never veered from their course
and bombed map square after map square. They always
arrived in eighteens.

At dawn on the 25th October, Montgomery, after powerful artillery preparation and renewed air bombardment, launched

another attack. Hill 28 was the crux of the battle. This is where the Tommies wanted to break through.

While the shells were bursting round this miserable hummock in the sand dunes Erwin Rommel was in Wiener Neustadt standing by his He 111 with the markings: DHYA. It was 07.50 hours. His pilot, Lieutenant Giesen, was still arguing with the "weather frog" for permission to take off. The wireless operator, Staff-Sergeant-Major Hahne, reported the machine airworthy and mentioned the argument with the men. "We're taking off," said Rommel. He stood by this order although Giesen returned and reported: "We have no permission to take off, on account of icing danger at 18,000 ft."

Giesen and Hahne exchanged glances. "Bazi" Wolf, the engineer, and Sadrich, the observer, were already in the machine. They took off for Rome and from there, after a short stop, landed at Heraklion in Crete. A Do 217 took them to Africa. Rommel landed at El Daba at 17.20 hours. He immediately climbed into a Storch and flew to the front. Before nightfall the field-marshal was in his tactical headquarters hearing a report of the situation from Westphal.

The following morning General Ritter von Thoma, a lean, ascetic-looking, pedantic man gave his report. He closed with the words: "The position, Herr Feldmarschall, has greatly deteriorated. The overwhelming enemy artillery has destroyed our 'Devil's Gardens.' We have been able to halt the enemy but not to repulse him. The fuel position is static. Artillery fire and repeated bombing attacks have decimated our troops. Only thirty-one Panzers are battleworthy in the 15th Panzer Division."

It was a gloomy report. Rommel looked at the map with his hand up to his chin and a scowl on his face.

He immediately ordered all his mobile forces on the northern front to mass for a counter-attack. But he could not make up his mind to fetch the 21st Panzer Division from its reserve position in the southern sector of the front. He was not sure whether the British northern offensive would not be supplemented by an attack in that sector. Montgomery's stratagem had worked.

In the meantime the British C-in-C brought infantry brigades and armour from his southern front and threw them into the battle in the north. On the 27th Rommel decided to withdraw his 21st Panzer Division and half his artillery from the south. He was gambling, but what else could he do? The gap in the northern front must be sealed or else he was faced with total defeat.

The 21st Panzer Division attacked through the holding elements of the 15th. General von Randow with his G.S.O.1, Major von Heuduck, who was killed two months later on Christmas Eve by a mine laid by the Long Range Desert Group, led his division into the breach out of the dust and smoke which lay over the battlefield. The commander of the 8th Panzer Regiment, Colonel Teege, joined in the attack with the rest of his tanks. This thrust met with heavy artillery fire. The battle raged against the new British tanks which were superior to their predecessors in firing power and range. British infantry often appeared behind the fighting detachments in front of the heavy artillery positions. Here only rifles were of any help. The gunners became infantry men like the men of the 10.5 cm. guns of the 408th Artillery Detachment. Twice they flung Tommies out of their positions in bitter hand-to-hand fighting. But the enemy was too strong.

For the Panzer Army it was in the truest sense of the word a hopeless battle. The most successful of Germany's military commanders was confronted with the material superiority of the Western Powers against which no courage was of any avail. "Even the bravest soldier can be killed by a bomb," commented Rommel, with a note of resignation in his voice.

On the night of the 31st October Montgomery launched "Operation Supercharge," the great break-through to the north. After an hour's heavy barrage the Australians made a frontal and flank attack on the 115th Panzer Grenadier Regiment. British armour over-ran an Italian artillery detachment. On the morning of the 31st the British stood with their heavy tanks on the coastal road. Rommel flung the 33rd Reconnaissance Unit into the battle to prevent the northern salient being closed. The last Stukas were sent into action. The 90th Light and the 21st Panzer Divisions launched a counter-attack. They succeeded in closing the broken line on the north wing, but no decision could be reached.

Then Montgomery produced his great blow. All the tanks which he had left from his original eight-hundred strong armada were massed and flung into the battle. Four hundred British tanks opposed eighty to one hundred German and Italian Panzers.

25

THE FÜHRER'S ORDER: "VICTORY OR DEATH"

When the night of the 1/2nd November, 1942, descended on the North African desert, the Battle of El Alamein was entering its ninth day. Rommel's minefields, the famous "Devil's Gardens" were almost entirely in the hands of the enemy. The northern sector of the German front had been pushed back and broken at many places. The new front was held with few guns, little armour and the telescoped remains of decimated divisions. The 125th, 104th, 382nd and 433rd Grenadier Regiments had been in action without a break for nine days.

Montgomery's night attacks were carried out on well-established lines. For three hours the shells from four hundred to five hundred British guns pasted Rommel's main battle line. Carpet bombing attacks by the R.A.F. exhausted the troops. Then the British infantry supported by tanks went into action. The result was inevitable; the front south-west of the famous Height 28 was broken. About four hundred enemy "battle wagons" poured through the gap to the west. Montgomery had another four hundred tanks in reserve to the east of the minefields.

"Prepare to counter-attack," was Rommel's order. The remains of the German armour assembled. Grenadier Regiments, the flak, the artillery, combat groups consisting of sappers, the staffs and reserve units. The tank battle of Tel el Aqqaqir developed. It was one of the toughest battles of armour in the history of the African war. Without respite the R.A.F. formations and the British artillery attacked with inexhaustible supplies of ammunition. The advanced German artillery, on the other hand, was frequently short of shells.

This was not because there were none left in Africa—they were there in Tobruk or in the depots far to the rear—but there was a shortage of transport and of petrol to bring them to the front. Even field cookers were used by General Krause to carry shells up to the front line. No. 2 Battery of the 11th Artillery Regiment fetched shells for their 21 cm. mortar with their supply trucks from Tobruk. Ten shells could be carried by a three-tonner and the trip took three days. This was indeed a poor man's war.

Nevertheless, the German troops managed for a while to seal off a gap made by the British on a front of over two and a half miles. Montgomery now threw in his reserve tanks. The Afrika Korps had only thirty-five serviceable "battle wagons" at its disposal.

The guns of the 33rd Armoured Artillery Regiment shot as on manoeuvres at the attacking British armour. No. 2 Battery was over-run; only the presence of mind of Oberleutnant Orth saved No. 1 Battery. He withdrew out of the range of the medium and light British artillery and took up a more favourable firing position. Only thanks to the fire support of this battery and of an 88 mm. could three guns of No. 2 Battery be rescued from the enemy hail of steel and be used as anti-tank defence. The proud 33rd Armoured Artillery Regiment which had fought under its first C.O., Lieutenant-Colonel Crasemann in all the victories and suffered all the crises of the armour in Africa, was now reduced to seven guns. The famous 8th Panzer Regiment was wiped out. The C.O., Colonel Teege, was one of the last to fall. The grenadier regiments, pioneer battalions, flak and signal units, reconnaissance sections, and other troops consisted only of exhausted soldiers, wounded, desperately weary men without water, lying in their foxholes. This was the situation on the 3rd November, 1942. Lieutenant Ralph Ringler, in command of No. 10 Company, the 104th Panzer Grenadier Regiment, wrote in his diary:

"3rd Nov. 1942. On the Telegraph road, the desert road from Sidi Abd el Rahman. It is morning again. I'm hungry and cold. Corporal Franken was blown to bits. It is growing lighter. The sun is piercing the smoke. The cold has passed but hunger remains. And now in addition comes thirst. We are here, a few grenadiers in our foxholes. Every twenty yards and in places at about fifty lie a few men. Two anti-tank guns, that is all. No. 9 Company must be somewhere to the left. Eight miles away is the sea, and behind us, nothing! And to the south, nothing! And facing us an armada of tanks. They came yesterday. Two . . . four . . . eight . . . ten—they attacked. Alert!

"Four tanks sped towards my position.

"Why don't the anti-tank guns fire? In my periscope I could see the men working desperately at the breach.

"The four tanks were on us. In Africa there was no such thing as close in-fighting with armour. We had no explosive charges or shrapnel. Now the first tank had reached the machine-gun post. It drove over the two apertures and came to a stop with a squeaking of its tracks. It turned and buried the crew alive. It crushed the emplacment and then a Mark II made for my position. I crouched in terror in a corner. Would that squeaking noise of the tracks over my foxhole ever come to an end? When would the driver stop and turn? Crush me to pieces? As soon as he had passed I jumped to my feet. A third tank approached from half right. The C.O. was so sure of himself that he was looking out of the hatch. I pulled a hand grenade from my belt, drew the pin and threw it. It bounced against the turret and exploded with no effect. The tank commander grinned at me. He had merely ducked a little. Now he waved his arms as on firing practice: 'Near miss,' and drove on. On the left wing of my position five of my men ran with arms above their heads towards a British tank and clambered on to it. It was the sergeant-major from the Russian front with four of his men. He had just arrived. Last night their nerves collapsed. So this is the end. Will it be the end for me today, too?"

And it was the same story all along the northern sector of the El Alamein front on the 3rd November, 1942. Everywhere the British were advancing. Rommel made the right decision: surrender of the El Alamein position and withdrawal.

The field-marshal, in his strategical report of 2nd November, had already warned the Führer's headquarters of this possibility. By reason of the fact that so far Rastenburg had allowed him a free hand to make decisions he thought that this time, too, he would meet with no opposition. Nevertheless, he had an unpleasant feeling, for he knew Hitler and Mussolini, and realised that both of them considered a withdrawal a disgrace. Rommel's intention here was not merely a retreat to the much-quoted Fuka line, to the old Mersa el Brega position or to Tripoli. He took a far more serious view. It was a question now whether Africa could be held at all. Would they recognise this in the East Prussian "Wolfsschanze" 2,000 miles away?

Rommel decided to send his aide, Reserve Captain Ingmar Berndt, a councillor from the Ministry of Propaganda, particularly popular with Hitler, to the Führer's headquarters. "Make our position quite clear to the Führer and suggest that the African theatre of war is presumably lost for us. Try and get full negotiating powers for our armored divisions," said Rommel. Then he drove eastwards along the coast road to the front line.

Berndt's mission has been constantly over-dramatised. In actual fact it was merely an episode. That Rommel used the political officer for this important task instead of an officer from the General Staff shows that the Swabian Fox knew how much Hitler distrusted the latter. When Colonel Westphal offered to undertake the flight to Rastenburg Rommel replied, quite rightly: "He won't listen to any of your arguments."

At about 13.00 hours Colonel Westphal was having lunch at Panzer headquarters surrounded by telephone reports, maps and petrol cans. Suddenly the aide de camp, Captain von Helldorf, burst in with a paper in his hand and announced: "An order from the Führer, Herr Oberst."

"What does it say, Helldorf?"

"It's the death warrant of the army, Herr Oberst."

"What?" growled Westphal, seizing the message. After reading it he flung the sheet of paper on the table. "Now they've gone completely mad back there."

At this moment Rommel arrived in his commander's tank. The field-marshal jumped out and Westphal handed him the telegram.

"An order from the Führer," he said curtly.

Rommel raised his eyebrows but Westphal did not utter another word. Rommel read it. The rumble of the front line seemed to stress the silence that reigned round the field-marshal. His officers' eyes were focused on him and they saw the muscles of his face twitch as he read. Then Rommel laid the telegram on the table, turned round and stared out of the window. Now they could all read it for themselves:

"I, your Führer, and the German people have complete

confidence in your personality as a leader and in the courage of the German and Italian troops who are fighting a heroic defensive battle under your command in Egypt. In the situation in which you find yourself no other thought is possible than that we must stand firm and throw every weapon and every fighting man into the battle. Despite his superiority, the enemy will come to the end of his strength. It would not be the first time in history that a stronger will triumphed over more powerful enemy battalions. No other path lies open to your troops except victory or death. Adolf Hitler."

Should they carry out his order or should they ignore it? Should they send a telegram in reply: "We shall obey but we should like to point out that. . . ." Or should they merely telegraph: "Retreat already underway"? These were the questions which were discussed in the next four hours by Rommel and Westphal. The cool-headed, analytically-minded Westphal was of the opinion that the pathetic telegram could hardly have been concocted in full knowledge of the strategical report of the 2nd November.

"It's just a pep talk to keep up the morale," said Westphal. "Who knows how many days ago the damned thing was worded?" But to contradict Westphal's argument they had only to observe the despatch time of the telegram from G.H.Q. Obviously the order had been sent after the receipt of Rommel's report of the 2nd November. Nevertheless, the colonel tried to persuade the field-marshal to ignore the Führer's order. But Rommel's military code rebelled against such a solution. For an army commander the problem was far more difficult than for the general staff officer.

"So far I have always insisted upon unqualified obedience from my men . . . Even if they do not understand my orders or consider them to be wrong. Personally I cannot depart from this principle and I must submit to it," he said to Westphal.

"That means the end of the army," replied the Colonel.

"I am a soldier," was Rommel's only comment.

The discussion continued in this vein for some hours. The field-marshal could not conceive that Hitler had given his "Victory or Death" order without some knowledge of the front-line position before El Alamein. He was not in a position to know what a tragi-comic error lay behind Hitler's order.

Rommel ventured to send a reply to Wehrmacht head-quarters. But what other arguments could he call upon beyond his report of the situation of the 2nd November? Captain Berndt was summoned to explain the position once more to Hitler personally. But let us see what happened in the meantime.

Late in the night of the 4th November Rommel decided to stop the retreat and gave the order: "Fight to the last shot."

In what a desperate situation this order was given is shown by the fact that Rommel himself ordered his army staff to be issued with hand grenades and sub-machine-guns for hand-to-hand fighting. It was no longer possible to cancel the order in question. The events followed in swift succession

On the morning of the 4th November the position was as follows: The remains of the Afrika Korps and the 90th Light Division held a thin front line on either side of the sixteen feet high dominating sand dune, Tel el Mampsra. To the south stood the much-battered Italian Tank Corps with the survivors of the Ariete, Littorio and Trieste Divisions. The southern front line sector was occupied by the Italian Trento Division, the Ramcke Parachute Brigade and the 10th Italian Corps. At 08.00 hours Montgomery attacked after a one-hour artillery bombardment. The remainder of the Afrika Korps divisions fought under the orders of General von Thoma and defended themselves desperately against the British who attacked with two hundred tanks.

When Colonel Bayerlein took leave of General von Thoma, at dawn to establish his headquarters some way behind El Daba to the south, he noticed that the general was wearing all his orders, an unprecedented occurrence in Africa. "Bayerlein," said Thoma, "the Führer's order is madness. It is the death warrant of the army. How can I explain it to my men?"

Thoma then looked at the colonel. "Go to El Daba. I shall remain here and conduct the defence of Tel el Mampsra in person." And he added with resignation and not without irony: "As Rastenburg orders."

Bayerlein was struck by the general's state of depression and he reflected that it boded no good as he set out for El Daba. Does the General want to die, he thought.

The weight of the British attack was directed initially on

Tel el Mampsra. Hell was loose in the sand-dunes of the sector. Ritter von Thoma was in the front line at the head of his troops.

At 11.00 hours, Lieutenant Hartdegen, von Thoma's aide, arrived at Beyerlein's headquarters and reported: "The general has sent me back with the radio transmitter. He says he does not need me any more. At Tel el Mampsra our tanks, anti-tank guns and flak have been wiped out. I don't know what's happened to the general." Anxiously Bayerlein jumped into his small armoured "recce" car and drove eastwards. He was suddenly caught in a hail of tank shells. In the midday mirage he could see hosts of black gigantic tanks. He jumped out of his car and ran in the broiling heat towards the crest of the dunes. There he discovered a holocoast. Burnt-out tanks, destroyed flak guns, shot up anti-tank guns, dead men everywhere. Only a few of the badly wounded were still alive. Bayerlein flung himself into a sand hole and looked around. Two hundred yard ahead was a burning tank. Next to it, standing in a hail of fire, was General Ritter von Thoma. The tall, haggard man stood there like a ghost outlined against the sky.

Ritter von Thoma. Twenty times wounded in two world wars. The epitome of courage and gallantry. His valour in the First World War had won him the highest decoration, the Bavarian Medal for Bravery, the Max Josef Order. He had fought with the Condor Legion in the Spanish Civil War and had driven his tank through Russia's white wastes. A few days ago still a tank commanding officer in Africa, he was now standing like a statue quite alone next to a burning tank in the midst of the battle. British Sherman tanks had closed in round him in a half circle. The barrage that they put up on the sand dunes was so heavy that Bayerlein had no prospect of reaching the general alive.

Suddenly the firing ceased. The British tanks moved off. Von Thoma stood there as though frozen to stone with the small sailcloth haversack of provisions, such as every general carried, in his hand. His face was turned towards the retreating English tanks. A jeep followed by two Sherman tanks came up to him. Captain Grant Singer of the 10th Hussars was carrying a sub-machine-gun. He called out. The general looked up, strode over to the jeep and climbed in. Bayerlein jumped out of his hole and ran westwards. It took him a long time to reach El Daba headquarters, find Rommel and tell him what he had seen. Huge dust clouds to the south and south-east of El Daba served as a background to Bayerlein's gloomy story. Back there another tragedy was being played out. Here a battle was raging between the badly armoured Italian tanks of the 20th Corps and about a hundred British tanks. The Italians had been outflanked but they refused to surrender. They defended themselves as Rommel had ordered and the corps was destroyed to the last tank. With the report of this disaster an intelligence officer also brought a radio message which a German listening post had picked up. It had been sent in clear to Montgomery by the 10th Hussars and read: "We have captured a German general. His name is Ritter von Thoma. Signed: Grant Singer, Captain."

During the morning of this tragic 4th November, Field-Marshal Kesselring arrived at Panzer H.Q. from Italy. The greeting between the two field-marshals was extremely cold because Rommel was afraid that Kesselring had been sent as a kind of supervisor from Hitler's H.Q. Rommel was very surprised when Kesselring in the presence of Westphal announced that in view of the situation he considered that the Führer's order could not reasonably be carried out.

Rommel decided to send a radio message to Hitler and to try and have the order cancelled. Kesselring supported Rommel's request in a message of his own to the Führer's headquarters.

Thus everything was done which a general in such a position can do. But Rommel showed that he could do more than merely obey orders.

As a result of the events of the past few hours he had come to the conclusion that no moral or military argument could justify compliance with Hitler's order. A soldier could be ordered to die, an army could be ordered to sacrifice itself. But can one order a soldier to die pointlessly and an army to sacrifice itself for no good reason?

Rommel's answer was: No!

The field-marshal drove to the Afrika Korps headquarters. Taking Bayerlein aside he said: "Our front is broken, and the enemy is pouring through to our rear. The Führer's order has become meaningless. We'll fall back on the Fuka position and save what we can." And he added: "Colonel Bayerlein, I hand over the command of the Afrika Korps to you. If we have to face a court-martial for disobedience we must stand by our decision. Carry out your job well. All your orders to the troops are to be issued in my name. Tell that to the senior officers if you run up against any difficulties." There was a brief silence. Rommel had decided to disobey the C-in-C. Of his own accord and in full knowledge of the possible consequences Hitler's field-marshal decided to take this step.

"I shall do my best, sir," replied Bayerlein.

Rommel climbed into his car and was driven back to the H.Q. of his beaten army where Westphal was waiting for him with the plans for the withdrawal. Late that night a telegram arrived from Hitler's H.Q.: "In reply to your message No.135/42, Top Secret, of 4.11. I have acquainted the Duce with my opinion. In view of the developments I agree with your decision. The necessary orders have been issued by the Duce through the Commando Supremo."

How was this message to be understood? What had happened at the Führer's H.Q.? I have endeavoured to find the real answer to this important question.

"Why has this report only been given to me now?" Hitler snarled to General Jodl at midday of the 3rd November, 1942, as the Wehrmacht G.S.O.1 handed him Rommel's report of the 2nd November. Jodl could have replied: "Because you lie abed too late, mein Führer," but naturally the general refrained from doing so.

Rommel's strategical report of the 2nd November, revealing the disastrous situation on the El Alamein Front and the British break-through, and suggesting the retirement to the Fuka line sixty miles behind El Alamein as the only salvation for the armour of the Afrika Korps, had arrived during the night of the 3rd November at Hitler's H.Q.

The officer on duty at the Wolfsschanze was a certain reservist major, in civilian life the director of a large industrial concern. In those weeks of bitter fighting for Stalingrad he had grown accustomed to alarming news and saw no good reason to wake either Hitler or Jodl on account of this message from North Africa. The two men had just retired to bed as the message had been decoded. It was Hitler's custom to spend half the night in discussion and plans or to pore gloomily over the campaign maps. As long as he was wide awake generals, aides, secretaries and liaison officers to the most important ministries had to remain on call. Thus they were all on duty. But as soon as it was known that he had retired to bed all the sycophants and police spies relaxed their weary limbs on the camp-beds in their shelters. Following Hitler's example they, too, slept on late into the following morning.

Jodl and Keitel had risen at nine o'clock on the morning in question. About ten o'clock Jodl read Rommel's message and was immediately worried. What was all this about a Führer's order? Had it been sent? Had Rommel obeyed it? For days this order had lain on Hitler's desk. The previous night before going to bed the Führer had appended his signature, Jodl had given it for coding and despatch. This appeal from the Führer, as Westphal had judged correctly, was designed as a piece of bravado to keep up the morale. It was assumed that the situation on the El Alamein front was tense but by no means disastrous. Jodl picked up the telephone and got through to Radio H.Q. "Yes, the Führer's order was despatched during the night," was the reply.

Jodl hurried over to the Führer's quarters in order to report to Hitler before the daily discussion on the war position. But he had to cool his heels until close on midday before he was received. Hitler had risen at 11.15 hours.

"What's the trouble?" Hitler asked Jodl suspiciously.

"Bad news from Rommel," replied Jodl, handing him the report of the previous evening. Hitler read it. His face turned scarlet. "This on top of everything else," he murmured. His eyes as they always did at such moments stared into space. A dangerous sign. "Was my special order sent off to Rommel?" he asked quietly.

"Yes, mein Führer, it went off last night."

"Why have I only just received Rommel's report on the situation? Why was it not shown to me last night? Why wasn't I woken? Why?" His voice was raised to a scream.

Jodl replied that the message had arrived very late during the night. "The major on duty thought—" Jodl was not allowed to finish.

"The major thought—" echoed Hitler. "Who is the fellow? Couldn't he see that the order I had just sent put myself in the wrong over the African position?" Since Jodl remained silent Hitler shouted: "Another instance of stupidity and indifference. I'll make an example of him. The major is to be court-martialled." Hitler's wrath could be heard in every room in the hut. Officers and secretaries cowered.

Three hours later the major was facing a court-martial. The sentence was pronounced the same evening: reduced to private soldier and to be sent at once to a Labour Battalion. A scapegoat had been found and punished. But the order remained in force.

Hitler raged throughout the day at the inefficiency of his staffs, but it was not in his nature to cancel his order. The telegrams from Kesselring and Rommel enabled him to do this without losing face. Had Rommel waited for some move on his part the catastrophe would have been complete. His well-timed appeal saved the remains of the German armour from destruction.

"A victory has many fathers but defeat is an orphan," the Italian Foreign Minister, Count Ciano, once wrote in his diary. When applied to the war in North Africa this means: if the victories between Mersa el Brega and the "White Mosque" of Abd el Rahman were Rommel's victories, then the defeat of El Alamein was his defeat. But it is just as certain that with the strength possessed by Rommel in autumn 1942 no army commander in the world could have won a victory over Montgomery's 8th Army. The opposing forces were too unequally matched. What Rommel's troops achieved in spite of this inequality during the twelve days of the battle of El Alamein is quite astounding. Montgomery's victory at El Alamein was inevitable. But what was a victory in the desert? In the course of nineteen months many battles had been won and lost by both sides. What made Rommel's defeat at El Alamein so disastrous was the delay caused by Hitler's order. This resulted in serious losses which made it impossible for him to pull out in time in the face of Montgomery's superior armour. Many guns, too, which could have been saved during the retreat and brought into action once more against the British tanks were lost.

The extent of Rommel's defeat and the degree of his losses have remained a matter for controversy. The theories are very conflicting. On the Italian and also on the German sides losses were often played down, and the field-marshal has been reproached for not having retreated quickly enough and for failing to fight a stout rearguard action. But all the reports from Rommel's entourage insist that it was impossible to stop the rout until the 6th November. The speediest possible retreat was then expedient. It took place at breakneck speed past scenes of former victories farther and farther westwards. To get out of range of the R.A.F. was the order of the day.

Other critics maintain that Rommel was convinced that all was lost and only a retreat to Tripoli and departure from North Africa was the right course to pursue. That is why he took no further risks, did not weaken the British by stout resistance but allowed them to advance too rapidly on his tail.

This reproach is accentuated tragically by the fact that on the 8th November, General Eisenhower landed with an Allied Expeditionary Force in Morocco and Algeria, preparatory to attacking Tunisia. To keep Eisenhower and Montgomery from joining forces was now the main goal of the Axis strategy. It is understandable that Rome, Rastenburg and the C-in-C Southern Command, Kesselring, insisted that Rommel should give battle to Montgomery's 8th Army between Fuka and Tunisia. Was this possible under existing conditions? Could Rommel have taken up his positions and pulled the chestnuts out of the fire? This is a question which still remains unanswered.

The last Motorised Supply Corps Officer of the Panzer Army, Lieutenant-Colonel Dr. Muller, managed to rescue a part of his papers which showed clearly the losses of El Alamein. Dr. Muller lent me these documents to make my assessment. They reveal that aspect of modern technical warfare which is waged with ink instead of blood, with workshop calculations and logistics. Victory or defeat is calculated in tables and graphs. Here a Panzer II was not so much a weapon in the hands of a brave or cautious commander as a machine which needed eighty gallons of petrol for sixty miles. Eighty gallons! In the Supply Corps offices all the details for getting the armour into the field were worked out to the last decimal.

Dr. Muller's work was typical of the military organisation of today, where the winners of battles are the engineers and the soldiers are glorified mechanics. In Dr. Muller's documents we can read the true armament situation of the German Panzer troops, before and after the battle of El Alamein.

On the 23rd October, when the British offensive began, Rommel's armour—according to the records—consisted of

285 tanks, 89 commander's tanks and one mobile gun. By 18.00 hours on the 2nd December the following total losses had been reported: 221 tanks, 8 commander's tanks and one mobile gun. Thus on this date he had left only 64 tanks, 11 of which were in the workshops undergoing repairs, leaving only 53 ready for action. In his report to the Q.M.G. and to Rommel we read: "The heavy losses suffered on the 4th November are due to Hitler's order to hold the El Alamein position. Since, as the result of this order, the repair shops were overwhelmed with work. In No. 5 Panzer Regiment 40 damaged tanks had to be destroyed to prevent them failing into enemy hands."

The preservation of at least a remnant of Rommel's armour was due entirely to the efficiency of the tank repair shops and the reserve tank columns.

Winston Churchill referred to Rommel's technical service as a pillar of the German victory in Africa. He was right.

The tactical badge of the repair service was a Negro's head with a cog in his left ear. Every African soldier was familiar with it.

But of what avail was the technical skill of the specialists if the front could not be held, if the damaged tanks fell into enemy hands, if ramps and workshop benches had to be blown up because the retreat had become a rout?

That accursed El Alamein! The despair that descended upon officers and men alike because the sky was black with Allied bombers and the desert teemed with British tanks!

Against this retreat even the burning sun lost its terror— despite the hosts of sand flies, the dysentery and jaundice. El Alamein was grim; and El Alamein lay on the victorious route to Cairo. Now El Alamein was lost. It lay far to the rear. The "White Mosque" was out of sight. The countless graves were left behind to be neglected. How did that old saying run: "Forward over the graves"? Now they were retreating over them.

26

THE DOOMED ARMY

Military retreats after a defeat are always harrowing. Fear and the spirit of *sauve qui peut* loose all the bonds of discipline, and nothing is more horrifying than an army, the criterion of discipline, which becomes a rabble.

As the 5th November broke the remains of the Panzer Army was retiring through the desert and along the coast. Their objective was the Fuka position, sixty miles behind El Alamein. But what had been envisaged as salvation was only a short respite. Montgomery attacked the routed German–Italian forces with two hundred tanks. Rommel saw himself forced to make a further retreat if his army were not to be overtaken in Fuka by the disaster which he had avoided with such great difficulty at El Alamein.

The R.A.F. located Rommel's staff through intercepted radio messages. A carpet of bombs. Rommel and Westphal had to take cover in a foxhole.

Forward... under the whine of bombs, along jammed roads, through minefields, behind which the vehicles piled up.

Forward! Rommel's soldiers were soon on Libyan soil once more, looking down on to the Egyptian coastal plain across which four months ago they had sped eastwards towards the Nile delta in English captured trucks with British fuel and British supplies. Now Tobruk lay far behind them. The sappers were once more the tail light of the Panzer Army. They blew up the hairpins at Derna, laid their mines in the Italian colonial houses by the roadside, making the road through Cyrenaica almost impassable. Demolition troops could be seen squatting by the roadside, pressing on, hurrying, groaning—the veterans of Tobruk, Sidi Rezegh and El Alamein. Volkswagens, motor-cycles, self-propelled guns, a few Panzers and ever fewer 88s. Time for a cigarette. . . . The columns thinned out and then more troops arrived.

"What's behind you?"

"Nothing but Tommies."

"Then be on your way," ordered the sapper officer.

With Arab roadworkers under the orders of an Italian N.C.O. the sappers tore up the roads. Then came the usual business: death laid in chequered pattern. But Rommel's sappers had devised new tricks. For some days they had been commanded by General Bulowius; the old army sapper officer, Colonel Hecker, had gone down with jaundice and dysentery.

The new booby traps were just as ingenious and infernal. In the first belt it looked as though real mines had been buried in the road. Filled-in holes in chessboard pattern were clearly visible. And the same five yards ahead, and again at another five yards. But in these holes were merely piled up tins and an occasional "T" mine without a detonator.

The English advance units arrived and the leading scout car spotted the holes. There was a halt. Mine detectors forward! British sappers with the most modern mine detectors which looked like brooms started to work. They searched the road and the warning buzz betrayed the presence of metal. Cautiously hole after hole was cleared and nothing appeared except old tins. After the fourth row of old tins the sweeping appeared a waste of time. They climbed into their car and drove on. After twenty yards they ran into the real, well-camouflaged mine belt. Screams and casualties.

Now the column stopped in front of every hole in the road. Again they continued digging out old tins until once more it seemed too ludicrous and once more there was a tragedy. Radio Cairo reported: "The advance of the 8th Army is meeting with little resistance but is being greatly hampered by the German engineers."

Any man who had a seat under him in this retreat was lucky. The infantry, of course, were the unfortunates. They had to go on foot. The lack of motorisation of the Panzer Army proved fatal in the retreat from El Alamein. For Rommel the question was: do I leave the infantry to its fate or by saving it overtax the motorised troops, rendering them incapable of fighting and manoeuvring? Since the Italian foot-sloggers could not be saved, Rommel naturally could not transport the German infantry units—not even crack troops such as the Ramcke Parachute Brigade. Moreover, there were no vehicles available even for these special units.

"We shall have to write off Ramcke's boys," said Rommel, when he received the report that the Italian 10th Corps to the south of the Alamein Front had been over-run and taken prisoner. But Rommel was due for a surprise.

It is still a matter of controversy whether Rommel should have given vehicles to his paratroopers in order to save this important special troop. General Ramcke was of this opinion, and later complained bitterly to Goering that this had not been done. Rommel's lack of consideration may be deplored, but the records of Lieutenant-Colonel Doctor Muller show that Ramcke had a considerable fleet of vehicles at his disposal whereby at least a part of his men could have been transported. The trucks had driven off in the general chaos without waiting for the front-line troops. The battalion and company commanders also took to their heels, but the parachutists had by no means given up the struggle. With a few Volkswagens and motor-cycles they set out on their march on the 3rd November. An artillery detachment, under Major Fenski, covered their retreat. A British armoured attack was beaten off. The brigade's radio car was put out of action. The water column had not arrived and the field cookers, for lack of towing machines, had to be blown up. Each man still had half a pint of water left and sixty miles to go to Fuka.

The old swashbuckler, Major Burckhardt, led the rear-guard battalion. He took an Italian artillery detachment under his wing, and in this way brought his men safely to the west. He was a lucky fellow, this veteran commander, but his luck did not hold. He was taken prisoner. A few of his men, however, slipped through the British lines, repaired an old German Zundopp and, travelling by night and hiding during the day, reached the Siwa Oasis on the thirteenth day. Here their odyssey too was at an end. It was heart-breaking and infuriating, for eventually Egyptian police captured Heinz Friedrich and his two comrades. Five-and-a-half years of captivity lay ahead of them—this is only one of many stories.

Major Fenski, with his artillery, caught it earlier than Burckhardt's group. After a battle with British armour, in which he defended his positions to the last shell, the British put them in the bag. The same fate overtook Lieutenant Haseneder, of the Parachute Anti-tank Company, but the majority of the brigade got through. More than this: just before Fuka, during the night, a British transport column was spotted. The parachutists crept among them with sub-machine guns and revolvers.

Before the crews of the accompanying British armour had noticed anything the column had gone. An anti-tank gun held the armour at bay and the "Green Devils" left in the captured British trucks. It was a splendid haul—not only serviceable trucks but useful contents. The trucks carried petrol, water and tinned food, from corned beef to pineapple. And cigarettes . . . Ramcke's men had high-jacked the complete supply column of a tank unit.

"What's that approaching?" Rommel asked at about ten o'clock next day at his tactical headquarters, on the coastal road behind Mersa Matruh. Westphal put his glasses to his eyes and scanned the desert in the direction of a dust cloud. A light car drove up. With several days' growth of beard and a grimy face General Ramcke reported the return of his brigade.

Rommel forgot all his troubles as he greeted the six hundred parachutists. They had fought their way two hundred miles through the desert. A stirring chapter in the history of a resolute body of men.

But there were many stragglers.

Medical Corporal Dr. Otto Buchinger flung himself down behind a small sand dune as a squadron of Hurricanes flew low over his positions. Seconds later he heard the rattle of the enemy's guns as they strafed the airfield. In the past few days such attacks had taken place every few hours. Buchinger's hospital tent stood alone and abandoned in a small depression. Not a soul to be seen. Sergeant Otto Boddien had evacuated the last wounded men in his ambulance. Corporal König had ridden off to the flak batteries on his motor-cycle. "Try and get hold of a light truck," said Buchinger, "so that we can salvage the tent and the medical supplies." He did not want to be put in the bag by the advancing Tommies. Montgomery was pressing on with unusual speed, chasing Rommel's troops towards Fuka. His men were marching on a parallel course to the Germans giving them no time to reorganise or dig in for a defence—not even in Fuka. The British High Command seemed to be fully aware of the disastrous position in which Rommel found himself. It is to be presumed that some of the captured officers, distraught after their defeat, when closely interrogated by the British had given information about the collapse of the Panzer Army. Montgomery must also have known from his air reconnaissance the limitations of the fleeing army's striking power. In any case the boldness of the British pursuit was conspicuous and forced Rommel, who had nursed great hopes on speedily clearing the Fuka position, to by-pass it because Montgomery was harassing him. The 580th Reconnaissance Unit, which had remained in Fuka under Captain Voss, was in a tricky position.

Doctor Buchinger, in the dunes behind Fuka airfield, naturally knew nothing of Rommel's decision. Nor did he know that his last motor-cycle combination had been shot up by fighter bombers and lay on the track before Mersa Matruh. All he knew was that the British could not be far away.

Staff-Sergeant Krol, from the flak position on the airfield, had arrived that morning with his motor-cycle and said: "Doctor," they all called Buchinger doctor, "we won't go without you. We'll send a light truck to fetch you." Then Krol drove back to the airfield. Shortly after this there was another air attack and Buchinger could hear only the light flak. "That's funny," he thought, but he did not worry unduly. He waited. He did not hear that Flak Lieutenant Schmidt's 4th Battery had been bombed out, that Krol nervously gave orders to retire, that to make matters worse a heavy truck caught fire and burnt out with its whole load, and finally that Krol fled with the rest of No. 4 Battery. They had forgotten Buchinger.

When the doctor climbed on to the dunes and put his hand up to his eyes he could still see the barrel of an 88 mm. gun pointing up at the sky. He was too far away to see that this gun had been put out of action and had been abandoned. The desert was silent.

The Red Cross flag fluttered lazily in the midday breeze which usually blew in about that time from the sea. "In Bad Pyrmont it's chilly autumn now," thought Buchinger. Pyrmont ... the house of the well reputed Buchinger Sanatorium, founded by Father Otto. But of what use was a good reputation in the German provinces when the local gauleiter deduced ideological unreliability from the family documents? As a result, in the army papers of Doctor Otto Buchinger, Junior, in spite of good credentials, experience in gliding and an excellent military record stood the entry: "unsuitable to be promoted to officer." This is why Doctor Otto Buchinger, the son of a First World War general of the Medical Corps, became first a light truck driver and then, after a few bold missions, an ambulance lance-corporal and finally a full corporal. But—and this is why I am telling the story in such detail—with Rommel in Africa people paid very little attention to the ideological pronouncements of gauleiters in the far-off Fatherland. The orders could not be changed, but they were simply ignored or circumvented. Thus, Doctor Buchinger, who had been awarded the Iron Cross, 1st and 2nd class, for bravery, still only wore the stripes of a corporal. But he had been promoted by his superior in the 6th Flak Regiment and by the divisional doctor of the 19th Flak Division to doctor for special service in the field. When Buchinger appeared every officer and man, including the commanders of the 90th Light Division and the 19th Flak, greeted the corporal doctor with particular friendliness.

Behind the airfield of Fuka, Dr. Otto Buchinger tested his field telephone, which was relayed to the flak position. It went dead. Instead of a reply he saw strange scout cars bumping over the dunes in the direction of the coastal road, and tanks with round turrets. "British! I must get going," Buchinger said to himself. He quickly assembled his hospital equipment, carried it outside the tent, placed a British water-proof sheet over it and sprinkled it with petrol. Before he set out into the blue he threw a match into the pools of petrol. For a whole hour when he looked back he could see a column of smoke rising behind the dunes of Fuka.

He marched parallel to the coastal road, keeping his eyes open for the enemy. At night he bivouacked in small wadis. His overcoat served as mattress and blanket. To the west he could see in the bright moonlight the flashes of artillery and the Christmas trees dropped by the bombers. The battle had overhauled the doctor. He followed in its wake, although he need not actually have done this. But the German Desert Expeditionary Force had its own code of life and comradeship. It must not be forgotten that with Rommel in Africa the following four things did not exist—the S.S., the shooting of hostages, political brain-washing and front-line brothels. Things were different on the other fronts. On the other hand there were stricter forms of what we usually understand by the much misused word duty. The corporal doctor, in spite of all the humiliations he had experienced at home from over-eager party members, did his duty, for the Panzer Army Afrika was not a régime but the better part of Germany. So he followed in the wake of his comrades, slept in caves and sandholes and after four days, just before Mersa Matruh, finally waved to a German "recce" car. It was a happy reunion. A long pull at a flask of coffee and the advice to carry on to the town off the road, for the British fighters occasionally strafed stragglers. This was a good tip. When the doctor at the roadside outside Mersa Matruh waved to a troop of German infantrymen, they gesticulated in horror. Not until the good man joined them did he understand what they meant. He had been lucky: he had wandered into a minefield which the German sappers had just laid. A good angel must have guided the doctor's steps. He joined the 90th Light Division in time to take part in their rearguard action. Ever farther to the west.

27

EISENHOWER ARRIVES

"At times it is a disadvantage to have a great military reputation. A man usually knows his limitations, whereas others always expect miracles and attribute any defeat to pure malicious intent." A deep resignation can be read in these words of Rommel. He knew that his defeat at El Alamein was neither ill-luck nor inefficiency but the vindication of his warnings, threats and demands which Rome and Rastenburg had completely ignored. Montgomery had broken the German front because the 8th Army was stronger and better equipped and, above all, because he had air supremacy over the battle area. It became clear that the greatest gallantry on the part of the land forces was of no avail against enemy air supremacy. Two examples spring to mind—El Alamein in 1942 and the Ardennes offensive of 1944. On both occasions the vital armoured forces were immobilised and the land forces paralysed by air power.

In Africa Rommel had to accept many defeats in order to build up to new victories. But he realised that his defeat at El Alamein was more than a lost battle. He knew that he had lost the North Africa campaign. His opinion was reinforced when he learned on the 8th November that the Americans had landed in Morocco and Algeria.

Now there were eighty thousand Americans and twenty-five thousand Tommies determined to crack Rommel's weakening army in a pair of mighty pincers. The German Panzer Army was to be brought to its knees. With little interference from the French, General Eisenhower, the American C-in-C, landed his guns, aircraft and troops on the north and northwest coasts of Africa. It was a long way from there to Tunis, Tripoli or Tobruk, but it was merely a question of time. Who could stop the Americans? Berlin and Rome had not been able to strengthen Rommel's army sufficiently in eighteen months to defeat one British army. How were two armies to be dealt with?

On the night of 8/9th November, 1942, Rommel sat in the armoured car of General Lungershausen, commander of the 164th Light Division. The nearby wireless truck relayed Adolf Hitler's usual speech from the beer hall in Munich. The Führer spoke of victory. At Capuzzo, however, the men of the 90th Light, the 164th Light and the Afrika Korps lay exhausted in the desert sand. When No. 2 Company of the 220th Engineer Battalion arrived Sergeant-Major Ohler reported to the company commander: "Company reporting with 28 men." Six months ago they had arrived in full complement and fully armed from Crete.

The Führer in Munich ignored these signs, but Rommel could not ignore them. With great bitterness he spoke that night to Lungershausen of his fears. "The campaign in Africa is lost. If Rome and Rastenburg don't realise it and take measures in time to rescue my soldiers then one of the bravest German armies ever will take the long road to the P.-O.-W. camps. Who will then defend Italy against the threatened invasion?"

This was Rommel's great anxiety and a bold plan began to mature in his mind. He would carry out an African

Dunkirk. Anything that was seaworthy and everything the Italian navy could muster as escort was to be used to save his soldiers. He discussed the matter with Colonel Westphal. He also discussed it with Bayerlein and made himself quite clear to his aide, Berndt—a fanatical Nazi. He propounded the following theory: "What is the significance of the equipment that we leave behind? Most of it is captured British war material. The rest is only of use to the breaker's yards. But a hundred and fifty thousand men, seventy thousand of them well-seasoned troops who could still win battles in Sicily or the South of France, could save us from total defeat."

Rommel had the courage to admit in front of his officers that the British retreat to Dunkirk in 1940 had been not only a brilliant feat of organisation but a courageous and far-seeing decision, although in Germany Goebbels had termed it "a disgraceful rout." What would have happened to Great Britain's military strength had she not had the officers and N.C.O.s from Dunkirk at her disposal to build up a new army for further battles?

But the German High Command had never had the courage to use the strategical withdrawal, and it certainly contributed to their being denied final victory. This may sound paradoxical but it was so. And the reckoning was very bitter.

The 21st Panzer Division had been badly mauled on the 6th and 7th of November by enemy armour in the Fuka sector, and only four of its thirty tanks which had survived the Alamein battle were intact.

The 2nd Detachment of the regrouped 2nd Afrika Artillery Regiment before El Alamein under Captain Duval de Navarre was sacrificed as a rearguard at Trigh Capuzzo. One hundred men had survived.

The battle-seasoned No. 3 Company of the 606th Flak Battalion had been over-run while putting up a stout defence at Fuka. The battalion had been virtually wiped out and only a transport led by Lieutenant Dany had avoided capture.

Tireless shock troops, like the C-in-C's staff combat group consisted now of only exhausted, half-moribund men. And yet they continued to shoot their way out of encircled positions.

During those last November days, General Graf Sponeck's 90th Light Division had put up an amazing defence against a

vastly superior enemy and covered the retreat of the German–
Italian troops.

Only thanks to the skill of its commander did the 90th
Light escape destruction at Halfaya Pass. When an Italian
battalion laid down its arms on the Pass, a whole British
armoured brigade was able to break through. But Graf Sponeck,
who was on reconnaissance, spotted the enemy armour in
time, alerted the support division and deployed it successfully against the advancing enemy.

But Halfaya Pass, which had changed hands three times,
was now irrevocably lost.

The Gazala line, the battle scene of 1941 and 1942, was
left behind. On to the tracks round Mechili, past Benghazi—
and Cyrenaica was lost.

By the 13th November the spearheads of Rommel's
defeated army had retreated six hundred and fifty miles. The
advanced elements reached the Mersa el Brega position.
Now Rommel was back at the old point of departure from
which he had twice advanced on his victorious marathons to
the Nile. Would El Agheila and Mersa el Brega once more be
the turning point? This time it was quite different. Two dates
and two places left their mark on that African November—
the 24th November at Arco dei Fileni and the 28th November
at Rastenburg.

On the 24th November a conference took place between
Rommel, Kesselring and the Italian Marshals Bastico and
Cavallero at Arco dei Fileni, the desert gate dividing Cyrenaica
and Tripolitania, a signpost for every German soldier. In the
shadow of a monument which was to introduce a new Imperial epoch in the Fascist colonisation of Africa, the German and
Italian marshals exchanged views. "The Mersa el Brega position must be held. Preparations must be started at once for a
new offensive against the 8th Army." That was Mussolini's
order. But Rommel was obdurate. He revealed the situation
to the Italians and demanded the immediate evacuation of
Tripolitania. Kesselring tried in vain to act as mediator.
Rommel saw no more hope of a victory in Africa. He saw only
that with the utmost effort he had brought his troops back to
the Mersa el Brega position. More than once Colonel Bayerlein,
who had led the Afrika Korps during those weeks, had been
faced with grave decisions. Should or could a certain spot be
held or was it not high time to slip out of the British pincers?

Montgomery in his memoirs expresses his amazement that Rommel's troops succeeded time after time at the last moment in slipping out of the famous bottleneck. How difficult a responsibility it was is revealed by the fact that even Bayerlein, Rommel's most trusted colleague, was once threatened by the field-marshal with a court-martial because he did not obey an order but acted on his own initiative.

Rommel could see only one reasonable solution: to retire as fast as possible to Tripoli or to Tunis in order to rescue his army by evacuation to the European mainland.

On the 27th November Rommel's pilots received the order: "Transport machine and accompanying aircraft to be ready to take off from Arco dei Fileni on the night of the 28th." The log book of the wireless operator, Staff Sergeant-Major Richard Hahne, shows that the pilot Giesen landed at Arco dei Fileni after the last incendiary bombs had been dropped by British bombers. Rommel was there fifteen minutes later. They took off at 02.50 hours for Hitler's headquarters, the Wolf's Lair at Rastenburg. Rommel wanted to visit the Führer unannounced and obtain his permission to evacuate Africa. Before he decided to make this flight he had discussed it at length with Westphal, exposing all the pros and cons. Rommel envisaged the rescue of substantial numbers of the army for further conflict on the Continent.

"I won't see anyone, Giesen," Rommel said curtly, before they landed at Grottaglie near Taranto. Sergeant-Major Hahne closed the curtains of the portholes. While they took on fuel, Rommel remained in his seat with eyes closed. Was he asleep or was he running over in his mind the arguments he would lay before Hitler? Rommel's aide, Berndt, perused some old numbers of *Oasis*, the Panzer Army's newspaper.

At 08.15 hours they landed at Wiener Neustadt; Rommel paid a swift visit to his wife, and four hours later was seated once more in his plane. At 15.15 hours he landed on the airfield near the Führer's headquarters. A staff car took Rommel through the East Prussian oak forest to Hitler's Wolf's Lair. The guard at No. 2 Gate saluted, the barrier was raised, the car took the main drive, turned off left on to a by-road and pulled up at the barracks where Field-Marshal Keitel was quartered. In a conversation which lasted almost an hour Rommel gave his report on the military situation in

North Africa and proposed evacuation. Keitel, Jodl and Hitler's Chief of Military Staff, Major-General Schmundt, listened in silence and with very great interest. They seemed to be in agreement with Rommel's proposals. The Field-Marshal was full of optimism as he made his way to Hitler's quarters. He had been summoned to a Führer conference at 18.00 hours.

Hitler had not waited for Rommel on his own. Goering was present. "How are things in Africa?" asked Hitler. Rommel gave the reasons why the British had been able to break through the Alamein lines: "They have better material, more powerful artillery, more tanks and supremacy in the air."

Rommel went on to explain why he was no longer in a position to take the offensive after the British break-through. "We had no fuel," was Rommel's first argument. Goering piped up like a monkey: "But your trucks fled back in their hundreds along the coastal road. There was fuel enough for that." Hitler looked at Rommel but did not say a word.

Rommel: "We also had no ammunition."

Goering: "Nevertheless, you left 10,000 artillery shells behind in Tobruk and Benghazi."

A red flush mounted to Rommel's cheeks. Should he ask Fatty how he would have got these munitions away? How he could have brought them up to the guns? Hitler still said nothing. Had he arranged this farce of exchanging rôles with Goering? "We also had not enough weapons," Rommel said, emphatically.

"And what happened to the weapons?" asked Goering. He made a little theatrical pause, then continued with a raised voice: "The weapons were thrown away on your flight." Now, as if in a prearranged dialogue, Hitler broke in: "But anyone who throws away his weapons deserves to rot."

Rommel jumped up from his seat. He was scarlet in the face. "Mein Führer . . ." he began. But Hitler banged his fist on the table and repeated: "Anyone who throws his weapons away and has no gun left to defend himself with must be left to rot."

The ghost of Stalingrad was present in that room. Stalingrad which had been encircled ten days before on the 19th November. Stalingrad, which the maniac Hitler had sworn to hold against all common sense. And now he was being asked to withdraw from Africa?

"Never!" shouted Hitler, turning to Keitel. "What arms have we in Naples?"

"Six thousand rifles lie there ready to be transported, mein Führer."

"Send them all over at once." But Rommel was not to be appeased with the promise of six thousand rifles. "Of what use would they be, mein Führer?" Then, despite Hitler's threatening tone, he developed his theory that North Africa after the Allied landings in Morocco and Algeria could no longer be held. "Let me withdraw the Panzer Army to Italy, so that it can defend the Continent against Eisenhower's anticipated invasion," pleaded Rommel.

But Hitler replied icily: "I no longer want to hear such rubbish from your lips. North Africa will be defended as Stalingrad will. Eisenhower's invading army must be defeated at the Italian front door and not in the Sicilian parlour." It sounded good. It sounded heroic and it was correct, provided sufficient troops, armour and aircraft were sent to Africa. But for the past twenty months not enough had been sent to conquer one army, and now they proposed to try to defeat two. In Rastenburg for two years, and in spite of the warnings, they had looked upon the war in North Africa as a colonial expedition and not as a theatre of war where decisions affecting all Europe could be made.

Rommel tried to continue but Hitler silenced him: "North Africa will be defended and not evacuated. That is an order, Herr Feldmarschall!"

"That is an order, Herr Feldmarschall!" Yes, Adolf Hitler knew the magic of those words. He knew how to handle his marshals.

"That is an order..."

In the Prussian tradition Rommel accepted this old formula against which there was no argument. He obeyed half-heartedly and sorrowfully.

From that moment his belief in the Führer was destroyed, and with it his own luck as a campaigner. Exhausted and in despair he traveled in a special train with Goering to Rome. The Reichsmarschall wanted to handle the affair personally with Mussolini, Kesselring and the Italian Supremo Commando. "In order," as he said smilingly, "to ensure the further defence of Africa."

After a great many fruitless talks at which unkept promises were made, Rommel flew back to his army, which was now at Mersa el Brega. Here at the kilometre stone in front of El Agheila the war had started for the Afrika Korps twenty months before. The first victory had started from here. It was here they had halted after their defeat in November, 1941. And here, once more, the trusty divisions had set out in January, 1942, and forced their way to the gates of Alexandria. Now they had been flung back again to this fatal spot on the Cyrenacian border. Would the famous El Agheila kilometre stone for the third time be the starting point for a new victorious offensive, direction Egypt? Rommel's troops hoped so. But while the men of Heyde's Combat Group in the eastern half of the Libyan desert were fighting against Montgomery's 8th Army spearhead and holding the front line of the Brega position, the second North African war had already broken out to their rear in Tunisia.

In the early hours of the 8th November, General Dwight D. Eisenhower—whose name most of them now heard for the first time—had appeared with a mighty invasion fleet off Casablanca, Oran and Algiers, and landed his assault troops safely. His divisions came partly from England and partly direct from the U.S.A. Roosevelt and Churchill had christened this bold action: "Operation Torch." Did I say bold? I should have said adventurous, for Morocco, Algiers and Tunis were French and France had signed an Armistice with Germany and no longer considered herself at war. Marshal Pétain, the French Chief-of-State, and his Prime Minister, Laval, had embraced Franco-German collaboration. For this "Co-operation" they had received the assurance that Hitler would leave their North African territories, as an economic source and a political empire, untouched. French divisions were garrisoned there.

The British and American secret agents had prepared the landing well. The French Military Commander in Algiers, General Juin, who had been released from German captivity as a reliable adherent of Pétain, was won over to the Allied cause. The general was prepared to flout the orders of his Chief-of-State and go over to Eisenhower's troops. But since the most carefully thought-out plans sometimes go wrong, a coincidence disrupted this particular one. On the day of the landing the Vichy Admiral of the French Fleet, Darlan, happened to be in Algiers. He was visiting his son who had

caught polio. This personal tragedy was the starting point of a
political drama with sinister developments.

Darlan's presence by pure coincidence resulted in his
being temporarily C-in-C instead of Juin. London and Washington were horrified. Darlan was pro-German and hated
both the British and the Americans. The worst that London
and Washington feared had happened. Darlan ordered armed
resistance against the invasion. In vain General Juin tried to
win the officers over to his side. Only a handful followed him.
The majority of the French forces fired on Eisenhower's
troops. Instead of the enthusiastic reception for which an
American regiment had optimistically brought its band, two
British destroyers were sunk in Algiers harbour; in Oran one
of the assault battalions of the 1st American Armoured Division was decimated by French marines and another two
destroyers sent to the bottom with all hands. After a twenty-
four hour battle the French resistance was broken.

In Casablanca it was even worse for Eisenhower. Here,
too, the British Secret Service had won over the French
Commander, Béthouart. But again things did not run smoothly.
The Resident-General, General Noguès, remained loyal to
Pétain. He arrested Béthouart and gave orders for resistance.
American naval forces had to sink seven French ships before
the shock troops could land. A thousand Frenchmen met
their deaths but General Noguès fought on. Pessimists in
London foresaw a catastrophe. They feared that the dead of
Casablanca, Oran and Algiers might prove grounds for a
Franco-German military alliance. Everything hung by a thread.
A magnificently contrived diplomatic coup ended the crisis.
The dangerous Darlan, who had hampered Roosevelt and
Churchill's invasion time-table, was rendered harmless—even
more—he was "converted."

Churchill had always known how dangerous this anti-
British admiral was. Shortly before the invasion he had
intimated to Eisenhower the enormous advantages to be
derived from winning Darlan over to the Allied cause. Churchill
did not have to wait long.

Admiral Darlan had spent the whole afternoon and half
the night of the 8th November at conferences and briefings.
Then he had visited his son's sick bed. He had slumped
wearily on a sofa when the telephone roused him. An officer

requested him to report immediately to General Juin. It was extremely urgent—a matter of national importance.

Darlan, overtired and not on the alert, drove over to see Juin. The former United States Consul-General, Robert Murphy had conceived the bright idea of luring the admiral into the general's hands and having him arrested. The plan succeeded.

What actually happened that night has never officially been put on record. In Churchill's memoirs one can read that Darlan, when he realised that he had fallen into a trap, turned to Murphy, scarlet in the face and said: "I have known for a long time that the British were stupid, but I always believed that the Americans were more intelligent."

Strangely enough, that same night orders signed by Admiral Darlan arrived directing the cessation of French resistance. These orders naturally came to the ears of Hitler. Since he did not know the sinister background of the trap he quite naturally attributed this to treachery on the part of Darlan. His suspicions even fell on the aged Marshal Pétain. In his rage Hitler ordered the occupation of the previously unoccupied Vichy Zone. This was a crazy short circuit: for now Marshal Pétain appeared in the eyes of the world as a puppet Chief-of-State, no longer ruling from unoccupied territory but a dotard, a prisoner, acting under the threat of German bayonets.

Unfortunately Hitler also forced Pétain to pronounce the death sentence on the "traitor Darlan". This, in addition to his personal worries, forced the bewildered admiral to continue on the side of the Allies.

After discussing the matter with Murphy, Eisenhower hurried in person to see the "hateful rogue", as Churchill had called Admiral Darlan a few weeks before, and by honourable assurances swung the admiral over on to the side of the Western Powers. Thereby, the official C-in-C French Forces became allied with Eisenhower. A brilliant stroke on the part of Anglo-Saxon diplomacy. The man whom the British and American press a few days before had called a traitor, a Fascist and a black-hearted bandit was now worth more than an army to Eisenhower.

The admiral played his tragic rôle fairly. But on Christmas Eve he was murdered in mysterious circumstances.

Within forty-eight hours his murderer was tried by court-martial and shot. Winston Churchill writes of it in his memoirs:

"Darlan's murder, however criminal, relieved the Allies of their embarrassment at working with him, and at the same time left them with all the advantages he had been able to bestow during the vital hours of the Allied landings."

And now the improbable had become reality—an Anglo-American army now stood in Rommel's rear.

Unlike Mussolini, Hitler had not expected this landing in North Africa and had taken no steps to prevent it. On the morning of the 8th November, Goering was still of the opinion that the objective of the sighted Allied invasion fleet was the South of France. "Let them come," he remarked. They came—but not to the expected venue. The telephone wires from Berlin and Rastenburg to Kesselring in Rome were kept busy.

"What can you send to Tunis in the way of land forces, Kesselring?" Hitler asked his Commander-in-Chief South peremptorily. "A handful of paratroopers and my staff company," was Kesselring's reply. "Send everything you can across," implored the Führer.

28

THE RACE FOR TUNIS

On the 11th November there was more activity on the Italian airfields of Naples and Trapani than had been witnessed for a very long time. Forty Ju 52s took off with a valuable cargo aboard. Kesselring had ordered the 5th Parachute Regiment, under Lieutenant-Colonel Koch, to Tunis. He intended to form a bridgehead and prevent this city with its 220,000 inhabitants and its important harbour falling into Allied hands.

It was a gallant body of youths which flew across to Africa in the ancient Ju's. Hardly one of them was more than twenty, and the most experienced N.C.O.s were twenty-one at the most. The officers were battle-tried, for Koch's regiment had been formed from the famous Meindl Assault Parachute Regiment. Liége and Crete figured in its battle honours. After its reformation in Grossborn, the regiment was transferred to France to be trained for the invasion of Malta. But this operation never took place.

At Tunis the aircraft landed one after the other as though it had been Tempelhof Aerodrome. The parachutists could dispense with their "umbrellas" this time for Kesselring and two skilled diplomats of the Wilhelmstrasse, Ambassador Rudolf Rahn and Consul-General Friedrich Möllhausen, had taken their revenge on their American opposite number, Murphy, for the Darlan coup. Rahn was sent to North Africa by the Berlin Foreign Office as "political representative" for Tunis. As an expert in French problems, he was to be a kind of political fireman. Rahn succeeded in persuading the French Resident-General, Admiral Esteva, to preserve strict neutrality.

Upon orders from Colonel Harlinghausen, O.C. Air Forces Tunis, the airfield of El Aouina was occupied on the 9th November. Harlinghausen landed at midday in an He 111 escorted by two Me 109s. A few moments later three Focke-wulf Condors landed and at 10.55 hours a few Ju's carrying the technical personnel of the 53rd Fighter Squadron, taxied up the runway. They were followed by the first Stuka formations and elements of the 53rd Fighter Squadron as well as transport Ju's with petrol, oil, light flak guns and their crews. Among these was the veteran transport unit, KG 105, which had been withdrawn from Russia. Rahn then went to see the President.

The French were in their trenches round the airfield but they did not fire. After an hour's conversation with Rahn, Admiral Esteva, towards midnight, gave orders that the German troops were not to be looked upon as enemies. The French divisional commander, General Barré, therefore withdrew his troops from the airfield. Thus twenty-four hours later Koch's paratroops could land at El Aouina airfield as if on manoeuvres and march in column of fours through Tunis to the famous Marshal Foch Barracks. The Germans had arrived. It was a single regiment—one regiment to protect a city of 220,000 inhabitants. But it was a fine regiment as we shall soon see.

The 1st British Army, under General Kenneth Anderson, approached from the west. Attacking force "B" of the 1st

American Armoured Division, under General Robinett, advanced on Tunis. General Eisenhower considered the capture of the city merely a question of days.

It was the American's bad luck that it was raining and the roads became waterlogged. By the 15th November, however, no German army had yet occupied Tunis but the German High Command had at least sent a General—Walther Nehring. This experienced, capable desert specialist who had half-recovered from his wound, was to have built up the Mersa el Bregha position but he was now sent to Tunis. He took over command in Tunis as G.O.C. 90th Korps. The 90th Korps! It was not even a division. In addition to Koch's regiment, Nehring was given Major Witzig's parachute engineer battalion, which was despatched in all haste to Bizerta.

To Nehring's forces we must finally add an armoured reconnaissance company under Lieutenant Hämmerlein, and as the *pièce de résistance* an 88 mm. flak battery from the 20th Flak Division.

No Medical Corps, just one doctor.

No vehicles apart from a few Tunisian taxis.

The staff of this remarkable 90th consisted of a general and an aide-de-camp. Its chief of staff was supposed to be the capable Colonel Pomtow, but he was still serving with the 3rd Panzer Division in the Caucasus as G.S.O.1 (Ops). Snowstorms prevented his machine from taking off. The German High Command obviously had no other Chief of Staff for their freak 90th Korps. Nevertheless this ghost formation performed some magnificent military feats. They afforded a shining example of courage, boldness and the art of improvisation.

The first German landing in Bizerta was also in the nature of a bluff. The 15th Foot, which was to be transferred from Laibach via Athens to Rommel's front, was hastily diverted to Rome. There the C-in-C South transformed it into the 1st Tunis Field Battalion. Lieutenant Werner Wolff, with No. 1 Company, reinforced by the Ahrendt parachute engineer column, landed on the Bizerta airfield on the 11th November. To Wolff's surprise a Ju was already there with supplies. It had left the formation and, together with two parachute sections of the Ahrendt column, had more or less captured Bizerta airfield.

After the war American and English commentators often complained that an Allied landing had not also been made at

Bizerta. But it is by no means certain whether Eisenhower's invasion forces could have landed, as the Germans did, without heavy fighting. This vital strategic harbour off the third largest town in Tunisia was occupied by Admiral Dériens' Marines. They were fourteen thousand strong. Dériens, however, was a loyal Vichyite. The 30 cm. guns of the fortress batteries would hardly have remained silent in the face of any Anglo-American attempt at landing. Eisenhower, therefore, was not so far wrong in refusing to take Bizerta from the sea. He wanted to capture it from the land side. But—and herein lies his fault—he should have been a little quicker. The Commander of the 1st British Army, General Anderson, received orders to occupy the city with troops which had landed in Algiers. But General Nehring thwarted this plan with his paratroops. Admiral Dériens obeyed Vichy's orders to offer no resistance to the German troops. Major Witzig's airborne sapper battalion immediately took up defence positions along the Mateur-Abiod Road. They advanced boldly to the west, reached the sector east of Abiod and barred the way to the spearhead of the strong British 78th Infantry Division. The Tommies were very surprised to meet the "Green Devils" from Crete. Two Italian guns which Witzig had at his disposal fired ceaselessly until the British scout cars beat a retreat.

But General Anderson wanted to know a little more and advanced with strong armour. Witzig fought a brilliant rearguard action, came to a halt at the Jefna Tunnel and repulsed all subsequent attacks. Until January 1943 the British did not advance a single yard from this spot. The battle for the Jefna Tunnel became a Tunisian Verdun on a minor scale. The Tunis battalion which relieved the paratroopers in bitter fighting won many Iron Crosses.

At dawn on the 17th November, 1942, Sergeant Rudolf Bohn, with men of the reinforced cyclist column, stood shivering on the rain-drenched airfield of Tunis. The paratroops had their gear and all their arms for a mission behind the enemy lines. They also took their cycles with them. Naturally no one knew anything precise, but rumours ran round the ranks. After the briefing of the second-in-command by Lieutenant Kempa it was clear that they were to take Gabes airfield. It was to be a surprise attack by airborne troops.

Gabes was an important strategic point selected for the

joining up of the Tunis bridgehead with Rommel's army. Should the Tommies or the Americans arrive first from the Algiers–Bougie sector, the whole of the Tunisian promontory would be cut off. By exploiting the French fortifications in the Mareth Line they could bar the way to Rommel's Panzer Army which was nearly a thousand miles away. In the meanwhile the Allied main forces could have over-run Tunisia and prepared for the invasion of Sicily. Gabes must, therefore, be occupied by the Germans to prevent such a development. At the time it was held by French units under General Barré. No one knew on which side he stood. In various places his troops had barred the way to German reconnaissance forces, taken them prisoner and sent them to the rear unarmed. Was the general already in league with Eisenhower?

In twelve Ju's Lieutenant Kempa's raiding party of fifty men, together with the 3rd Guards Company of C-in-C South roared toward Gabes—the "White City." The leading flight turned in towards the town. Muzzle flashes and tracers... What was that? The fire came from tank machine-guns. The French were firing at the German aircraft from their reconnaissance trucks which were defending the airfield. A couple of the Ju's were hit. The company commander of the Guards Company, Lieutenant Salg, who was in the third machine, gave the order over the long-wave not to land. The machines gained height, turned off and flew back to Tunis. But as a result of the firing and the interrupting landing manoeuvre, the formation had been broken. Only the six Ju's carrying Kempa's paratroops and Captain Grund, the intended station commander of Gabes, reassembled swiftly. A seventh Ju, which was on the way to Tripoli with oxygen tanks, joined them. About twenty-five miles west of the Sfax–Gabes road the flight commander spotted a suitable airfield. Lieutenant Kempa informed the other machines over the R/T and ordered a landing. Everything went smoothly except that one Ju broke its undercarriage on landing.

What were they to do? Were they to ride off on their cycles and attack the tanks in Gabes? Lieutenant Kempa did the right thing in the circumstances. He despatched a "recce" troop to explore the position. Finally he gave his orders. "The airfield of Gabes is to be taken in a raid. Airborne troops arriving tomorrow are to be guided to the landing place with white-green-white flares."

The reconnaissance troop set out. Outside the city they ran into a French scout car. With great difficulty, protected by a camel caravan, the parachutists were able to avoid capture. Without their cycles and in a bad mood they bivouacked in a depression.

On the morning of the 18th, at about 10.00 hours, the Ju's carrying airborne troops for the Gabes sector flew over them. The men below waved but their comrades in the air mistook this for a greeting and simply wagged their wings. Everyone expected disaster. But then something strange happened. From behind a cluster of palms in the direction of Gabes white-green-white flares rose into the sky and the Ju's prepared to land.

At full tilt the six men rushed to the next Arab village, requisitioned two donkey carts and drove to Gabes. On the airfield they found everyone in high spirits. The hero of the day was a certain Corporal Beder.

What had happened? Chance had once more taken a hand in a battle. When the first "recce" troop did not return Lieutenant Kempa, in accordance with military practice, sent out a second patrol. But these seven men under Corporal Beder drove straight into a French patrol. They could not flee like their comrades. They were taken prisoner and driven back to Gabes.

Here they were interrogated by the French commander. "What do you want here?" Corporal Beder adopted a firm attitude. He was there with orders that the airfield was to be surrendered, otherwise it would be subjected next morning to a Stuka attack. The Frenchman was furious. "Very well—" he said. "We shall see. If no planes arrive tomorrow morning I'll have you shot." He locked the seven men up in a corrugated iron hut and placed a sentry outside. Beder and his comrades spent an anxious and uncomfortable night.

Next morning the Frenchman had the seven men fetched from their prison, obviously with the intention of interrogating them further. But at this moment the Ju's approached with fighter cover. The French major assembled his troops at all speed and fled. Beder and his six men were left to their own devices. The corporal was now able to fire his white-green-white flares signifying airfield clear of enemy troops. The key-point for a line of communication with Rommel's army was in German hands.

It was none too soon, for three days later the first American tanks appeared off Gabes. Eisenhower's staff had also grasped the importance of this place. But they were too late. The German paratroops received the Americans with rapid machine-gun and light gunfire, pretending to be a complete regiment. The American advance troops halted just long enough for two battalions of the Italian Superga Division to be brought up at all speed. They relieved Koch's paratroops and held Gabes.

Every German who served in Tunis knew the name of Barenthin. His paratroop regiment was the third pillar of the improvised defence during the first weeks of November. The Barenthin Regiment, called after its commander, Colonel and Korps Engineer Commander Walter Barenthin, was hastily formed for the Tunisian war from various elements of the Parachute Korps. It was well motorised and equipped with 5 cm. anti-tank and flak machine-guns. On the 20th November the first transport arrived in Bizerta with the staff, the motorcyclist column, sapper column, intelligence, and Medical Corps detachments. The staff and the 3rd Battalion immediately advanced in the Mateur sector. Here, to a certain extent, at the back door of the marine fortress, Colonel Barenthin took over command as C.O. of the Mateur combat group. This little spot soon became as important a spot as was the little town of Tebourba, farther south, for the city and harbour of Tunis.

The situation in Mateur was less hectic. In the little town lay two battalions of Italian infantry and an Italian artillery battery. But they were of little use. Barenthin immediately ordered defence positions to be prepared on the heights outside the city. The Witzig battalion secured his right flank. Motorised infantry and sappers protected the left flank and acted as liaison with the Koch Regiment. In this way a very thin front now existed around Bizerta and Tunis in the Jefna-Mateur-Tebourba-Massicault area. They had settled down quite nicely in their positions when the fireworks started.

On the 26th November, the 36th British Brigade attacked. The Italians were over-run and threw up their hands. Barenthin, however, put up a magnificent show with his anti-tank guns. The British grew cautious.

When would they launch their full-scale attack? A single

battalion could not stop an entire brigade. If the Tommy attacked, Bizerta was lost. Would he do this before Barenthin could bring up the rest of his regiment? The Tommies did not come. Colonel Barenthin told me the exciting story: "On the 28th November, to our great surprise, we could see the British building breastworks. They were doing this quite openly. At this moment the Caid of Mateur appeared at my H.Q. With great pride he told me that the British would not attack. 'And why not?' I asked. The Caid had sent one of his sheikhs to the British and told them that a strong, particularly aggressive parachute regiment from Crete with heavy weapons were entrenched round Mateur. This had dissuaded the British."

The rascally Barenthin was naturally not blameless for this piece of intelligence which the Arabs had passed on to the British. Barenthin, on the orders of his C-in-C, had fostered a particularly friendly relationship with the Arab population. The result was that he soon had a dozen Arab volunteers to each company: they served as soldiers, runners, jacks-of-all-trades and for special missions behind the enemy's lines. In this respect they rendered excellent service and arranged contacts with Arab notables. Barenthin's policy, as one can see, was profitable. It paid dividends all along the Tunisian front, for during the whole of the campaign there was not a single act of sabotage committed by the Arabs against the Germans. A very remarkable achievement.

When General Anderson resumed his attack on Barenthin's positions on the 29th November the 1st and 2nd Battalions had arrived. A whole regiment of the "Green Devils" was there and the British brigade was repulsed.

Although things had turned out well at Mateur, they had gone badly on Barenthin's left flank in the Medjez el Bab sector. Koch's paratroops had advanced far beyond Tebourba to Medjez el Bab. Here they met French forces under General Barré which disputed their passage. German reconnaissance troops were killed and some taken prisoner. Kesselring gave orders to parley with the French in order to free the road to the west.

When this failed he sent Stukas to attack the spearheads of the French division. But time had been lost and the Brigade of Guards with elements of the American 1st Armoured Division arrived and attacked Medjez el Bab on the 20th

November. The American troops, under General Robinett, fought magnificently and Koch's "Green Devils" went berserk. The railway station of Medjez el Bab changed hands twice, but then the regiment was beaten back step by step. It was a bitter pill, for now the important road north of the Medjerda River to Tebourba was open to the enemy. And as troubles never come singly, an American armoured troop consisting of sixty tanks and scout cars suddenly appeared over the Chougui Pass north of Tebourba, crossed the Tine River and rolled towards Fred Hämmerlein's weakened armoured reconnaissance company. The company was thrust aside and the 2nd U.S. Armoured Battalion sped past Tebourba in its Grants. A company of Barenthin's Combat Group closed in and pushed on towards Djedeida. The light German flak holding Djedeida air-strip was suddenly faced with a strong contingent of enemy armour. It was over-run. Fourteen Me's and twenty-four Ju's on the field could not take off on account of the wet soil. Armour-piercing shells smashed them to pieces. The Americans pressed on in the direction of Tunis. It was obvious that they wanted to capture the city and the harbour in a swift raid.

The American tank men could already see the minarets of Tunis. The city on the plain was only six miles away.

But in such situations General Nehring invariably kept his head. He had posted two 88 mm. guns of the 20th Flak Division at the entrance to the city. He set all his hopes on these two guns. They shot up the American spearhead and laid down a barrage ahead of the attackers. This was too much for the inexperienced G.I.s. The contingent halted and beat a swift retreat to Djedeida. Tunis had been saved, but the crisis was by no means over.

The 88s also averted a dangerous situation at Tebourba. Staff-Sergeant Wilhelm Voigt, of the 3/52 Flak Battery, contrived that the olive grove of Tebourba should be recorded in the history of the war. On crawling through this olive grove with his battery commander, Captain Welte, on a reconnaissance to find a new position for his gun, he saw, a bare three hundred and fifty yards away, heavy American tank concentrations making their way through the plantation to Tebourba. "This is the right spot," said Welte and ran back to the old position to have Voigt's gun brought up. In the meantime, the N.C.O. had erected a camouflaged fence of branches and twigs between two olive trees. The 88 mm. was towed up by the heavy tractor.

The gun was not yet in position before two American tanks appeared out of a clearing. Their 75s, 3.7 pom-poms and five machine-guns were pointed the other way. Had the Americans noticed what was brewing behind them they would have been a trifle less careless. By the time they realised it was too late. At the first shot—this was the first shot fired from Voigt's gun on African soil—a Pilot tank was put out of action. A column of flame and an explosion and the driver of the second tank immediately fled at top speed. The famous sharp report of the 88 mm. echoed once more through the olive grove and a second column of flame rose into the air. Two men sprang from the turret, shed their burning jackets and ran for cover behind a hill.

This salvo in the olive grove was the prelude to a two-day duel of armour fought by the batteries against heavy tank forces for Tebourba. Twenty tanks were destroyed. Twelve of these were claimed by Lieutenant Happach. Wilhelm Voigt bagged four. But this was only one episode in the battle in which General Nehring frustrated Eisenhower's first large-scale attempt to pierce the Tunis bridgehead and cut off Rommel's retreat and supply bases.

Hardly had this danger been averted than two new crises seemed to be building up. On the 28th November Arabs reported the landing of two thousand Allied troops at Cap Serrat. They were presumably intended to surround the Witzig Combat Group and neutralise the defence of Bizerta.

The second alarming piece of news came also from an Arab report. A thousand American paratroops had landed north of Zaghouan. This meant that Eisenhower wanted to break through at the weakest spot in the defence front round Tunis with his crack troops.

Nehring flung his infantry against the troops which had landed at Cap Serrat. He was successful. The newly landed men were either taken prisoner or driven back in their landing craft. There were not two thousand but only 500 men.

To counter the dangerous landing of the American paratroops in the Zaghouan area, Nehring again used Hämmerlein's armoured reconnaissance company, the "fire brigade" of the bridgehead. Fortunately here, too, the Arab report was exag-

Russian T - 34

gerated. Five hundred men had jumped at Depienne, north of Pont du Fahs. Because of their heavy arms and equipment they were not particularly mobile. Hämmerlein's company and Italian elements of the Superga Division encircled the "Amis" and took the majority of them prisoner. About a hundred escaped. Unfortunately we shall meet them again.

For weeks on end Nehring waged this kind of hand-to-mouth war with his meagre forces. Finally, on the 29th November, strong elements of the 10th Panzer Division, under Major-General Fischer, arrived in Bizerta and Tunis. Something else arrived at the same time—three of the new miracle Tiger tanks. These fifty-five-to-sixty ton monsters with 88 mm. guns wore armour such as had never been seen on any front. However, they also consumed a hundred and eighty gallons of petrol for a sixty-mile trip and Tunisia in the winter with its rivers in spate, muddy roads and mountain passes was not an ideal terrain for them.

The Tigers had actually been built for Russia to counter Stalin's T-34s. When they went into action in Tunisia it was found that they were still suffering with teething troubles. Some of the engines broke down after a hundred and fifty miles. There were faults in the wireless apparatus and there was great trouble with the gears.

Nevertheless, the Tigers proved decisive in the battle for Tebourba. The powerful, good-looking tanks inspired confidence in the infantry. They came from Fallingbostel in Lower

Saxony, where Major Lüder had formed the first 501st Tiger Detachment. Lüder brought his "charges" in person to Tunis. His No. 1 Company Commander was the brilliant tank commander, Captain von Nolde.

Nolde, like the parachute Commanders, Barenthin, Koch and Witzig, and the C.O. of the Armoured Reconnaissance Company, was a fine leader. These were the men who formed the old guard of the Tunisian combatants.

In the meantime elements of the 10th Panzer Division had assembled in the Bizerta–Tunis area ready to be despatched in any direction required.

On the 1st December Nehring gave orders to attack the advanced British–American forces at Tebourba.

Colonel von Broich was in command in the northern sector to the west of Bizerta. The centre was under the commander of the 10th Division, Major-General Fischer. Italian forces guarded the front south of Tunis. Everything which had legs or could travel on four wheels was flung into the battle; the 7th Panzer Regiment, the 86th Panzer Grenadier Regiment, the 10th Motorised Infantry Battalion, the 90th Panzerjaegers, elements of the 90th Signals, the Tiger Company, the 88 mm. batteries and the infantry. A harbour guard of only thirty men remained behind in Tunis to keep watch on the 220,000 inhabitants. Two 88 mm. guns guarded the entrance to the city.

General Nehring's aim was to encircled the enemy's advanced forces in the Tebourba sector. Still surrounded in the city of Tebourba itself were a company of Barenthin's paratroops and his sappers. All attempts by a Guards Brigade and the American Combat Group B to remove this thorn in their side had failed. The "Green Devils" had defended themselves stoutly since the 25th November and now formed a hedgehog in the enemy's rear. Lieutenant-Colonel Koch, whose regiment had closed in from the south-west to attack Tebourba, now flung in his sapper column commanded by Sergeant-Major Ahrendt. He forced his way through the British support troop and made contact with Barenthin's sappers in Tebourba. United, the parachute sappers closed the vital main road between Tebourba and Medjez el Bab to the Allied troops. The first act of the battle for encirclement at Tebourba was over.

Sergeant-Major Ahrendt was in his element. He had

posted two machine-guns on either side of the road bridge over the Medjerda River, two miles west of El Bathan. He mined this single bridge over the Medjerda River with gunpowder charges for lack of T.N.T. The first British light truck appeared. A mighty explosion and the truck lay on its side as a natural barricade on the bridge. Anyone who tried to clear it came under devastating machine-gun fire. For three days and two nights Ahrendt held this key position during the battle for Tebourba, preventing the bulk of a British brigade and elements of the 1st American Armoured Division from bringing up supplies or withdrawing. In the meantime, General Fischer's 10th Panzer Division entered the fray. A bold raid seemed to have been successful, but as so often happens in the history of a war "General Coincidence" took a hand.

The "Ami" paratroops who had escaped on the 28th November at Pont du Fahs had made their way north-east. They arrived at Medjez el Bab just as elements of Koch's Regiment thrust to the south-west to close the cauldron behind the encircled enemy forces in Tebourba. Koch's battalion did not recognise this unit which suddenly appeared on the road, took up its position and started to fire. The Americans, for their part, had not the slightest idea into what operation they had fallen, but they fought like hell because they thought their lives were at stake. This unexpected battle delayed the timetable of the German encirclement movement and gave the Allied troops at Tebourba a chance to slip out of the bag and to retire on Tebourba–Sidi Nsir and the Medjez el Bab sector. This was entirely due to these errant paratroops.

The battle of Tebourba, which lasted four days, resulted in a complete German victory. They had won the first round in Tunis. The battle experience of the German troops, despite their inferiority in numbers and equipment, had beaten the British–American newcomers to Africa. The 11th British Brigade and the American Combat Force B lost their entire equipment. The 18th Infantry Regiment of the 1st American Armoured Division suffered heavy losses. A British battalion was completely wiped out. Eleven hundred prisoners were sent back to Tunis. A hundred and thirty-four burnt-out tanks lay on the battlefield. Forty guns were captured and forty-seven enemy aircraft shot down over the battle area. It was a heavy defeat for General Eisenhower's invading army.

There were heavy losses, too, on the German side. Among the fallen was the greatly beloved leader of the Tiger Panzers, Captain von Nolde. He fell after leaping from his armoured car in the bitterly contested olive grove north-west of Djedeida, to give an order to Captain Deichmann in his Tiger. A shell took off both his legs. Captain Deichmann destroyed the two American tanks which had caused Nolde's death, but when he opened the turret of his Tiger to take his bearings a bullet from a British sniper hidden in the grove killed him.

Sergeant-Major Ahrendt was among the fallen. He had been awarded the Knight's Cross in a special message from Führer headquarters, but it could not even be laid on his coffin. Ahrendt had been shot through the head, fighting a rearguard action against dispersed enemy troops. The sappers had placed him in a hayrick which caught fire during the fighting. The sergeant-major's corpse was burnt with it.

Many other men of the same calibre were killed, but the victory seemed worth the sacrifice. Tebourba was one of those murderous battles, like El Alamein and Stalingrad, but the victory saved the German bridgehead in Tunisia. The campaign of General Nehring, that bold improviser, was brought to a successful conclusion. The American general staff account of the North African war published in 1944 remarks soberly: "The Germans won the race for Tunisia."

29

CONFERENCE AT THE FÜHRER'S HEADQUARTERS: THE 5TH PANZER ARMY IS BORN

The Germans had won the race for Tunis. The bridgehead held. The back door for Rommel's retreat remained open for the moment. But Eisenhower's reinforcements from the States rolled out from Casablanca, Oran and Algiers. Any

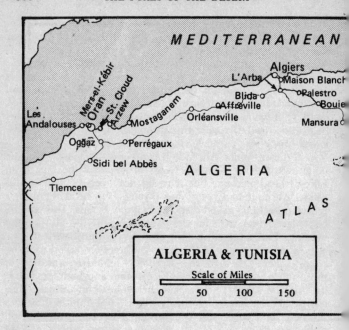

German soldier in Tunisia could see what the Allied Supreme Commander intended to do. He did not need to know the terms of Roosevelt's and Churchill's pact at the Casablanca Conference. The Allied aim was to smash the Tunisian bridge-head; to advance in the south to the Tunisian coast, to bar Rommel's retreat into the bridgehead and to establish contact between Eisenhower's invasion army and Montgomery's 8th Army.

This was the ABC of strategy. But by the beginning of December, Eisenhower had not got very far with his ABC. His armour, paratroops and infantry were held up until the 12th November in Bone, on the 15th in Tebessa, in the north, and on the 25th in Medjez el Bab. On the 28th November he had finally occupied the Sbeitla, Gafsa, Kasserine Pass area. Here his advance came to a halt. Nehring had stopped him with a handful of troops. Here we must not forget a fortuitous ally of the Germans—the weather god. The unaccustomed difficulties of the going and the terrain for

the American troops considerably delayed the Allied plans.
Eisenhower's report of this in his memoirs is a long complaint,
illustrated with many examples of motor-cycles sticking in the
mud, of tanks sinking to the midriff in filth. The German
soldiers who had been used to the mud of Russia knew how
to cope better than either the Americans or the Tommies.
Colonel Berenthin can give many examples of how experience beat the novice. During the battle for Tebourba, for
example, Berenthin's Jaegers, with two anti-tank columns
south of the Tine Bridge, beat off a British armoured attack
with forty tanks. Berenthin's trick was to fire four consecutive
shots with an 88 mm. at the greatest possible speed in order
to make the enemy think that it was faced by a whole battery.
He trained his fire alternately on the attacking tanks, which
were confined to the road, and then again on the famous
Ghost Farm, a French property in no-man's-land. With the
first four shots a tank was hit and an ammunition dump near
the farm destroyed. This multiple artillery fire surprised the

Tommies. After ten salvoes the tanks drew off. Berenthin could finally eliminate the enemy road block on the important Chouigui–Tebourba branch road. Whether we take this episode or the cunning stratagems of the Witzig battalion at the Jefna Tunnel, the bold surprise attacks of Lieutenant Börger with a company of paratroops on the dominating heights of Sidi Nair, or the disarming of twelve thousand Frenchmen on the 8th December with their heavy coastal artillery in Bizerta—it was all brilliantly executed and displayed an admirable courage and leadership. But no general staff officer could help realising that sooner or later this war of trickery and bluff must cease. Time and time again General Nehring drew the C-in-C South's attention to the fact. His reports of the situation disguised nothing. Nehring saw very little chance. But what did Hitler want? What did the German High Command want? Was Rommel's army to be evacuated from Africa and was this the reason why the Tunisian bridgehead had been created? Or did Hitler want to return to the offensive in Africa?

On the 3rd December, 1942, a very enlightening conversation took place at Rastenburg which provides the answer to these questions.

Hitler had summoned Colonel-General von Arnim and Lieutenant-General Ziegler from the Eastern front. Ziegler, who had arrived somewhat earlier than von Arnim, was received at once by Hitler. The Führer revealed to him that in Tunisia the 5th Panzer Army was to be created. Colonel-General von Arnim was to be in command. Ziegler was to be his permanent deputy with full powers. It is interesting to see why Hitler created this new post of "permanent deputy with full powers". According to Hitler, he did not want the same conditions to exist as in the case of Field-Marshal Rommel, where everything depended upon his personality as a leader. The commander of an army must have the possibility of discussing things with an officer of the same rank. Above all, this new arrangement would ensure that on trips to the front by the C-in-C—which in Africa, as a result of the great distances involved and the fluid front lines, took on a different character than in the European theatres of war—a deputy with full powers would be on the spot. In this way, decisions could be taken at any time by the high command in Tunis.

General Ziegler was a capable officer and a cool-headed

realist. He immediately asked what troops would be released for this new Panzer army. Keitel, who took part in the conference, replied: "Three armoured divisions and three motorised artillery divisions will be sent to Tunis in March, including the crack Luftwaffe Hermann Goering Division."

General Ziegler asked whether they could be brought safely in such numbers across the Mediterranean. "Naturally," replied Hitler. Under these conditions, said General Ziegler, it would be possible to resume the offensive in North Africa. The general produced his plans for such an offensive— to advance out of the Bizerta–Tunis area to the west and to reach as quickly as possible the mountains of the Tunisian–Algerian border. The capture and elimination of the Bône and Philippeville harbours, followed by the capture of the Algerian harbours farther to the west. General Ziegler counted upon a rising of the Arabs in favour of the Germans. With the support of an Arab resistance movement he considered it possible to advance as far as Oran. In this way the last and most important harbour in North Africa would be in his hands. Eisenhower's army would be given the choice of being taken prisoner or re-embarking. The vital premise for such a development, according to Ziegler, was a guarantee of constant supplies and the capture of the island of Malta. The possession of this island, as has already been proved, was the alpha and omega of successful trans-Mediterranean supplies. These were bold words and bold plans.

After his conversation with Ziegler, Hitler received Colonel-General von Arnim, who had arrived in the meantime. He came from Rjev, where he had been in command of the 39th Panzer Korps. Arnim asked the same questions. How many divisions will my new Panzer army have? Will the supplies be guaranteed? On receiving a positive reply from Hitler, he produced the same tactical solution as General Ziegler. Upon this Hitler agreed to the plans of both generals, who left with high hopes for Tunisia.

On the 9th December Nehring, in an order of the day, said farewell to his troops of the former 90th Korps. "Our position," he wrote, "was unique in the history of war." He was quite correct.

On the same day Colonel-General von Arnim took command of the new 5th Panzer Army.

The new Q.M.G. Tunis, Colonel Heigl, and the experienced Chief of Staff, Colonel Pomtow, from the Russian front began—as many of Rommel's officers had done—to pester the German and Italian G.H.Q.s day after day for supplies. In vain. Neither tanks nor supplies came in any quantity, and there were no new divisions.

The burden of waging war against Eisenhower's invasion army continued to fall on the paratroop regiments, the 10th Panzer Division and elements of the 334th, which had arrived in Tunis with General Weber. The 765th Alpine Jaeger Regiment in particular distinguished itself in the December battles, in the first weeks of January on the Chouigui Pass, on the notorious Jebel Lanserine and the hotly contested Christmas Hill. The Americans called this tactically important height Longstop Hill. The men of Lieutenant-Colonel Burcker's combat group of the 10th Panzer Division would never forget Christmas Eve of the year 1942. Festivities for them consisted of a bloody conflict against a British brigade which was holding the hill. It was thrown out and three hundred prisoners taken, but on Christmas Day a Guards Brigade counter-attacked. Once more the German combat group was flung down the hill. The 1st Battalion of the 69th Panzer Grenadier Regiment—formerly the 69th Wandsbeker—stormed once more with the 5th and 8th Batteries of the 90th Panzer Artillery Regiments and the 2nd Detachment of the 50th Artillery Regiment. They threw out the Guards after hand-to-hand fighting and held the heights, which secured the Tunis bridgehead to the west.

In the ensuing battles for Longstop Hill, the 86th Panzer Grenadier Regiment and the 754th Infantry Regiment particularly distinguished themselves. For the Allies the name Longstop Hill was very apt, for until near the end of the Tunisian campaign they never captured the heights.

30

BRANDENBURGERS IN ACTION BEHIND THE FRONT

The hand grenades were still bursting in the Christmas battle for Longstop Hill when in the Beurat position, one hundred and twenty miles from Tripoli, a young captain stood with Colonel Bayerlein poring over the map of the southern Tunisian sector. Three points had been marked with blue crosses behind the enemy lines—three bridges over rivers and wadis on the Oran–Algiers railway line in the Tebessa, Gafsa, and Tozeur sector. The railway could become an important lifeline for the Allied supplies. Along the track also ran telephone and telegraph wires: supply and intelligence leads. They must be put out of action.

In his general report of the battles waged by his 90th Army Korps in Tunisia, General Nehring mentioned the various operational and tactical actions. "Additional precautions: sabotage and fighting commandos were sent far to the west. Unfortunately no records of their successes against railway bridges and supply dumps are available."

No records. This was a good thing, for the Allied Information Services made a lengthy search for them at the end of the war. These dashing commandos were to be put under lock and key.

Today, at last, some of the details can be given of these bold missions.

Captain Fritz von Koenen was a farmer's son from South-West Africa, and spoke English as well as his mother tongue. He led the 13th Company of the Brandenburg Regiment. The first half company arrived with Koenen in Tunisia at the same time as the first paratroops. The second half company was flown over from Naples on the 5th December. They were quartered in idyllic Hammamet by the sea, in a villa among

371

the orange and lemon groves. But they had no opportunity for relaxation. When things got hot during those first few weeks of the Tunisian campaign, the Koenen Special Commando could be seen in action although, as a rule, the Brandenburgers were not used in the fighting line. Their business was quite different. Brandenburgers sat behind the enemy lines and acted as observers for their own artillery. They cut communications, altered signposts, rendered tracks impassible and achieved a great deal more besides.

About midnight on Boxing Day, 1942, the Brandenburgers set off once more. From Bizerta airfield three Ju 52s took off for the south, each with a glider in tow.

Towed gliders were not particularly comfortable contraptions. The passengers sat one behind the other on a board with hand grips. For the feet there was a wooden thwart.

From time to time Captain von Koenen, who sat behind the glider pilot, looked round and took stock of his men. There was Sapper Sergeant Hans Neumann who had been on many missions. Behind him sat the interpreter, Reginald Dade. Then came Sergeant Sloka and five other men. The glider could not take any more. There was no conversation. Everyone knew the plan and his own particular rôle. Each of them knew that under their seats were crates full of weapons, tools and four hundred pounds of explosive.

The tow line twinkles in the moonlight; deep below them gleamed the Mediterranean. In a wide sweep the three parent machines made for the land at seven thousand five hundred feet. It had been agreed that the gliders were to be released thirty-five miles before the objective. The light signals flashed from the leading plane. The pilots released the hawsers; the sound of engines died away and Koenen's gliders continued noiselessly on their way. Below in the moonlight lay the railway line and the bridge which crossed the Wadi el Kebir in a wide arc.

The pilot continued to glide for a while then put his nose down. The wind whistled as they dived at breakneck speed for the ground. The men clung on like grim death. Every man's thought was: Well, let's hope we get away with it. They could not forget that they were sitting on four hundred pounds of explosive. The pilot flattened out at the right moment. The perspex cockpit was opened and the skids scrunched on the gravel. They were bound with barbed wire, which made a good brake.

A little way off the second glider had landed. He, too, had landed without breakage. The third was nowhere to be seen. Not until their return did they discover that the Ju towing this glider had joined up with another formation. The pilot noticed his error too late.

Captain von Koenen, Sergeant Neumann and the runner, bent double, ran over to the three-hundred-yard long bridge. "A fine piece of engineering," said Koenen. Cautiously they crawled closer. They suspected enemy sentries, but the French were sitting on the far side in the small station building, drinking Algerian wine. Perhaps they were asleep. Koenen peered through his night field-glasses. He could read the black letters of the station's name: Sidi bou Baker.

"The coast's clear."

The runner hurried back. Sergeant Sloka came up with the others, panting heavily. They were carrying the explosive. Koenen removed the safety devices.

Neumann directed the setting of the charges. Two charges of eight pounds on the bridge upperworks. Six pounds at each end of the bridge on the track. Two huge charges of one hundred and sixty pounds lashed to the broadside of the centre pile. In the meantime a man climbed up a telegraph pole to cut the wires. Since he had no pliers he smashed the wires with a mattock. The copper hummed, and as the last wire broke the mast toppled to one side and nearly took the man with it. Now for the fuse!

"Where are the fuses?"

They were in the third glider which had disappeared.

Neumann had spares with him. These infernal machines with their ripcord had the disadvantage of burning for only sixty seconds. That gave very little time. They must be careful. Neumann blew his whistle as a signal to pull the cord for both the main charges.

The moon was bright. The whistle rang out, the three men on the upper works pulled their cords and ran. Neumann listened. No. 1 burning. A hiss from the next. Okay. Twenty seconds had gone. Now he must get going. At that moment his foot caught in the telegraph wire. He fell. Sergeant Sloka jumped fifteen feet from the bridge into the wadi to rescue

Neumann, but sprained his ankle in the attempt. Fortunately Neumann had struggled to his feet and could now rescue his helper. He picked Sloka up and dragged him to the edge of the wadi. They flung themselves on the ground. At that moment the first charge exploded on the rails. But what had happened to the other two? They should all have exploded at the same time. Neumann stood up and looked over towards the bridge. Then fresh columns of flame rose in the air. The blast tore his legs from under him and flung him to the ground. Fragments whistled overhead but the men felt no fear, only triumph. They had succeeded.

When the dust cloud had subsided, the bridge stood in the moonlight like a jagged tooth.

Originally, the assembly place after the action was to have been in a little depression to the south. But this turned out to be too near to the station building from which the French were now firing wildly with their machine-guns. Koenen ordered them to assemble at the gliders.

"Everyone here?"

"No."

Two men were missing. Sergeant Sloka volunteered to go and look for them. The others made for the hills. Charges had previously been secured to the girders. Seconds later they blew up as the shadowy figures moved away.

By daybreak the Arab guides had found a little wadi in the Jebel bou Ramli. The men flung themselves down on the ground to sleep. They could only continue their journey at night.

Towards midday there was an alert. Arabs entered the little wadi. The interpreter was sent forward. He was seen to gesticulate. Then they all came running. One threw off his burnous. It was Berger, one of the two missing men. As a Palestinian German he had been able to make himself understood by the Arabs in a near-by village, and with unerring instinct they had led him to the right hiding-place. Proudly they palavered with Reginald Dade, Koenen's interpreter, and offered to bring the column safely out of the danger zone. As soon as darkness fell they broke camp. The Arabs led the men through the Jebel on a long trek of forty miles past the city of Gafsa, and then by shepherds' tracks through the Jebel Orbata. On the sixth day after their action, Koenen entered

Maknassy. Twelve hours later an Arab troop brought in the second missing man, the Bavarian Hannes Feldmann. He was riding on a donkey and looking the picture of health. It must not be forgotten that the Arabs risked the death penalty for helping a German. Sergeant Sloka never returned. Agents reported that a French patrol had found and shot him.

On the night that Captain von Koenen flew with his twenty men to Wadi el Kebir, ten other men of his company, led by Lieutenant Hagenauer and the sapper Sergeant, Poldi, flew in a glider to blow up the bridge of Kasserine. But this expedition was ill-fated. They crashed on landing. Finally the whole group was captured by a French armoured reconnaissance patrol. Only two men, Corporal Franz Wodjerek and Sergeant Willi Clormann, escaped and reached the German lines after an eleven-day march. All they had between them were sixty-seven cigarettes, a bottle of Coca Cola and two revolvers, each with seven bullets. They, too, were helped by Tunisian peasants.

A fortnight later, on the 10th January, another commando was despatched to blow up a bridge in the Tozeur sector in Southern Tunisia, the third blue cross on the map. Captain Bisping in charge of the commando and Sergeant-Major Klima decided to do the job in a truck from Kibili, since their objective lay north of the Schott Jerid salt pan and there was an advanced Italian strongpoint in the Jebel Morra. But the approach of the commando was spotted by French security forces. Only with great difficulty could the Brandenburgers save themselves by flight. Shrewdly they made a second attempt the following night and this time they succeeded. Sergeant-Major Klima calmly secured the explosives to the central pile. A charge was laid on the girders and the rest between the rails. Klima lit his ten-minute fuses and the commando set off at full speed in the truck. After ten minutes they halted at the edge of the Jebel. Night field-glasses out! The bridge looked majestic in the moonlight. Fifteen minutes went by.

Klima grew nervous.

Twenty minutes.

"Something wrong—I must go and have a look."

Captain Bisping restrained him. At this moment they heard a train in the distance. The locomotive's whistle blew as it approached the bridge. They all stared intently and then came the explosion. The men jumped into their truck and drove off at top speed.

The aerial photographs taken the following evening showed a locomotive and the smashed coaches of a train between the débris of the blown-up bridge.

The British attempted a reprisal action. A British submarine landed a commando at Hammamet with the object of blowing up Koenen's headquarters. But Koenen's second half company were on the alert. Hermann Müller, who was on guard on the beach, heard the sound of a grinding boat and then the click of barbed wire being cut. He fired three white flares. By their light they saw shapes moving. A wild chase ensued. The commando made off, but within the next forty-eight hours the eight men who had been landed by the submarine, including a British captain, were tracked down and caught by Colonel von Hippel's newly formed Arab Legion. A lieutenant of the Long Range Desert Group who had tried to swim back to the submarine was washed up dead on the shore.

31

PANZER ATTACK ON THE FAID PASS

On the 1st February, 1943, the last units of the German 6th Army in Stalingrad surrendered.

Four days later in Tunisia Lieutenant-General Fischer, commanding the 10th Panzer Division, drove over an Italian mine while on patrol. The Italian "Devil's Eggs" were often duds but when they did explode they caused appalling damage. Both the general's legs and his left arm were blown off. With iron self-control he called for a notebook and began to write to his wife. He completed a page and a half. Death did not leave him time to finish. The last words were: "It will soon be over."

Of General Fischer's party the G.S.O.1 of the division,

Lieutenant-Colonel G. Bürrklin, was badly wounded; the aide and the driver were killed outright.

As a result of this tragedy, a man appeared on the scene whose name was to be on every tongue eighteen months later: Lieutenant-Colonel Count Stauffenberg. He became G.S.O.1 to the 10th Panzer Division, which was taken over by Major-General von Broich. Bold, with an outstanding talent for organisation, Stauffenberg was active in North Africa until he was badly wounded and invalided home. History had reserved another rôle for him. This man, who had fought so passionately in Africa for a German victory, later placed the bomb designed to kill Hitler in Rastenburg.

At the beginning of February, 1942, General Eisenhower was still a long way from his goal—the destruction of the German Tunisian bridgehead. Von Arnim's paratroops, Panzer grenadiers, infantry, and gunners, not only held their position in the mountains of Tunisia but actually extended the bridgehead. In the middle of January units of the Weber storm troop—mainly elements of the 334th Infantry Division—in operation "Special Messenger 1," had flung back the French Foreign Legion to the south-west of the bridgehead. In this way the danger that the Italian flank would collapse was averted, though the French did over-run the Superga Division's mountain position on 12th January. With "Special Messenger 1," von Arnim's troops delivered a hard blow against the French corps. Four thousand prisoners were brought in. The dominating heights and passes between Pont du Fahs and Pichon were in German hands.

"Special Messenger 2," the continuation of the operation, with the object of taking Pichon and rolling out the entire French front, failed.

On the 31st January the Weber storm troop arrived. It advanced along the Pont du Fahs–Rebaa–Ousseltia road without incident for five miles. But it was soon obvious that the French corps had been reinforced by American units equipped with the latest anti-tank guns and heavy artillery. The 501st Tiger Detachment suffered casualties.

Heavy fighting developed southwest of the Jebel Chirich. The Jebel Mansur was taken and recaptured by the Guards, captured once more by the men of the 334th Infantry Division—and held. But not much further progress was made. The 47th Infantry Division stormed Pichon, but under pressure from strong enemy forces Weber had to withdraw his troops to the heights east of the town. The aim of destroying the French forces in the Pichon area was a failure. Von Arnim's assault troops were too weak and too short of munitions.

It was the same old trouble from which Rommel had suffered.

In the meantime, since the middle of January, in the southern sector the 5th Panzer Army had at least been given a chance to avert a constant threat which had hung like the sword of Damocles over the German bridgehead. Since December the Allies had sat on the strategically important Faid Pass. Any day the American tanks could leave Sfax, cross the Pass, close Rommel's supply road to the Panzer Army and irrevocably split the two German armies.

But how was von Arnim to dispel this danger? Until the end of January he had not the strength.

Then, as if he had won a prize in a lottery, the 21st Division of the Afrika Korps came under his command. Of Rommel's columns retiring from the Burat front to the Mareth Line, the 21st was the first division to cross the Libyan–Tunisian border. It was taken out of the line for a rest and placed in reserve. But since the position at Faid Pass was growing ever more serious, von Arnim decided to employ this seasoned fighting division there.

On the 30th January the division, led by the Italian 30th Corps, approached the Pass. It was captured the following day and held against all counter-attacks. "My nightmare is over," von Arnim said to his G.S.O.1.

In the defiles near Maknassy a German–Italian combat group under the Italian general, Imperiali, fought bravely in a to-and-fro conflict. The defiles were held and Eisenhower missed his opportunity of forcing his way through to the sea. On the 31st January, new American reinforcements arrived at Maknassy and the German troops withdrew. But on the 9th February the Americans were thrown out of Gafsa and the Germans once more advanced. It can be seen from these events how raw Eisenhower's troops were. On the other hand, in the bridgehead, after three months of campaigning, the Germans were still living from hand to mouth.

But the enemy grew stronger and more dangerous. Something more had to be done. Both von Arnim and Rommel nursed far-reaching plans.

Although they each judged the position and the possibilities differently, on one point they were fully in agreement: the greatest threat came from the southern sector of the Allied Tunisian front. Something must be done. Eisenhower must be thrown out before Montogmery, advancing from the desert, could become dangerous.

At the beginning of February, the 5th Army Headquarters received constant reports of a progressive concentration of American troops in the area Tebessa–Sbeitla–Sidi bou Zid. The Arabs, too, brought in information of American troop movements in this area. The 5th Army came to the conclusion from the enemy dispositions that in a few weeks they would have to reckon with a major attack. It could have but one objective—to reach the sea and to separate the German–Italian armour from the 5th Panzer Army.

Rommel had left Tripoli with his armour on the 22nd January and retired to the Mareth Line on the 12th February. In Rome, both the Fascists and the Monarchists held their breath. Tripolitania, the pearl of their Colonial Empire, had

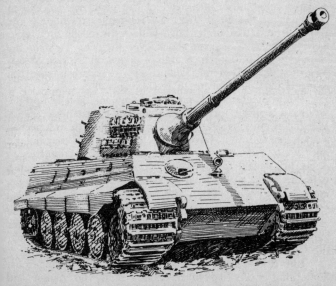

Tiger Tank

gone. Rommel would never be forgiven for that. The field-marshal would never receive the Gold Medal for Bravery, which Mussolini had thought of awarding him. The German-Italian Panzer Army and the 5th Panzer Army, however, were now almost in contact. And that touch must never be lost.

Colonel-General von Arnim, General Ziegler and the army staff, with its capable leader, Colonel von Quast, and its experienced G.S.O.1, Colonel Pomtow, concocted a plan which with two divisions would bring them a decisive success against Eisenhower's Tunisian front. Colonel Pomtow lent me his documents which give an accurate picture of operation "Spring Wind."

The plan was as follows: the 10th and 21st Panzer Divisions were to launch a surprise attack against the reported American concentrations west of the Faid Pass. If the American armour was destroyed by a concerted attack the combined forces would advance northwards and roll up Eisenhower's front before Tunis. It was not an over-ambitious offensive designed to seal the fate of Eisenhower's army but a cleverly planned attack with the forces available which promised a decisive relief. The spearhead of the offensive was No. 1 Company of the 501st Tiger Detachment, attached to the 10th Panzer Division. Its huge tanks with the 88 mm. guns were to make a surprise attack over the Faid Pass on the enemy concentration. In charge of operation "Spring Wind" was Lieutenant-General Ziegler, with a staff from the 5th Army H.Q. Colonel Pomtow led the assault.

While Ziegler and Pomtow were making their last preparations in their tactical headquarters at la Fauconnerie, Field-Marshal Rommel made contact with them. His troops had already reached the Mareth Line. Since the field-marshal did not have to reckon at the moment with an attack from the 8th Army he offered to support Arnim's offensive in the south with the Afrika Korps from the Mareth Line. Admittedly the Desert Fox had something else in mind. The field-marshal did not see eye to eye with von Arnim's cautious planning. His idea was to advance far in the rear of the opponent on the supply and traffic centre, Tebessa, to speed from there to the Mediterranean coast, cut off Eisenhower's invasion army from the Algerian harbours and cause a collapse of the Allied front. This was the old audacious Rommel desert strategy. It had been the principle of his great raids on Gazala, Tobruk and

Sollum. Von Arnim and his Staff were not keen on such an operation. Their main objection was that the forces at their disposal were too small and in consequence the action was too risky. Von Arnim told me that he still sticks to his original view—and he had many supporters among professional strategists—that such an advance, which would have led them far into the impassable Tunisian–Algerian mountain country, would have demanded a smooth-running supply system which was not available. Moreover, Tebessa was protected by three consecutive mountain ridges. What is happening in this sector today in the Franco–Algerian war where the rebels can hold in check a regular French army, one hundred thousand strong, reinforces von Arnim's theory. Be that as it may, von Arnim at that time insisted upon the "close objective" for his operation "Spring Wind," and since the German High Command could not make up its mind to relieve Rommel of the command in Africa, there was now a split in the leadership of the two armies and as a result divergent plans.

On the 14th February at 04.00 hours the 10th and 21st Panzer Divisions were in position. In two battle formations the 10th crossed the Faid Pass. The 21st came sweeping in from the south. The flying sand stung the men's eyes. It was cold and the road was muddy. But the attack made good progress. By 15.00 hours the armour of the U.S. 2nd Crops in the Sidi bou Zid area had been encircled. The 10th Panzer Division turned south and captured the place. A classic tank battle developed. The German armour waded into the deployed enemy tanks on the flank and in the rear. The commanders drove with open turrets. Shells whined and tracers described a picturesque pattern between the weaving tanks. The 88 mm. guns from the Tigers roared mightily. The Americans put up a stout defence. Even the crews of immobilised tanks continued to offer resistance. Sixty-eight American tanks were immobilised. The American Battle Group "A" tried to relieve the encircled elements of the 168th Regiment by a counter-attack, only to become encircled itself.

The following day, the 15th February, Ziegler advanced in the direction of Sbeitla. The 1st American Armoured Division attempted a counter-attack which was repulsed with heavy losses. By the evening a hundred and sixty-five American tanks and armoured vehicles lay burnt out on the battlefield, and two thousand prisoners wended their way to Tunis. The American crack Battle groups "A" and "C" had been beaten. Battle Group "B" alone remained intact. In the Pentagon at Washington they were horrified, and at the White House Roosevelt cross-examined his military advisers as to what had happened.

In accordance with von Arnim's plan the 10th Panzer Division was now diverted north to Pichon. During the night this important strongpoint was to be taken in a surprise assault, and the French combat group defeated in order to cause a collapse of the Allied front. But the break-through was unsuccessful. General Ziegler was, therefore, given reinforcements in the shape of the 47th Infantry Regiment under Colonel Bühse, the Lüneberger whom Colonel-General von Arnim still calls "The Tunisian Fireman". The regiment was ordered to make a frontal attack on Pichon. But on the night of the 16/17th operation "Spring Wind" had blown itself out. The Ziegler assault group was relieved. The 10th and 21st Panzer Divisions came under the command of Rommel. The staff of this combat group returned to Tunis to the 5th Panzer Army H.Q.

What had actually happened? This is one of the most controversial and most exciting questions in the whole history of the war.

As the records of the Deputy G.O.C. Afrika Korps, Freiherr von Liebenstein show, Rommel had suggested on the 5th February to the Commando Supremo that he should advance from the Mareth Line on Gafsa to avert this threat to his flank. But his plan was rejected. The Italian Supreme Command did not wish to interfere with the prearranged operational sectors of the two armies. The demarkation line was latitude 34 degrees. A really fantastic administrative absurdity in modern warfare, when one sees the difficult questions of competence which could arise from the lack of a united African command. Naturally Rommel was furious at the rejection of his proposal. On the 8th February he ordered von Liebenstein to prepare for the advance with elements of the 164th, the 15th Panzer Division and the heavy artillery of the Afrika Korps—all in one formation. During the night of the 14/15th, however, the Americans—as a result of operation "Spring Wind" and their disastrous losses in the battle for Sidi bou Zid—abandoned Gafsa without a struggle. Rommel immediately attacked. He occupied Gafsa with the Afrika Panzergrenadier Regiment, Colonel Menton's famous old Special Unit 288. At the same time he despatched a reconnaissance troop to Feriana. Elements of the Afrika Korps occupied this key point on the road from Gafsa to Tebessa on the 17th February. Thus they were now deep in the flank of the American armour which was defending itself at Sbeitla against von Arnim's divisions.

Rommel was bound to take this development to be a sign from the Gods. His bold plan of taking Tebessa and advancing north, beyond the Allies' crucial supply centres far in the rear of the American front, now looked more attractive.

The Führer's headquarters also grasped at this favourable development and saw a chance of realising Rommel's plan which they had previously considered too bold. Jodl gave way to Rommel's persistence. On the night of the 16/17th February the German High Command transferred Ziegler's combat group to Rommel's command and gave him permission for a further attack in the direction of Tebessa.

This was the reason, then, for the relief of Ziegler's combat group.

At first everything went according to Rommel's plan. The 21st Division took Sbeitla and the 10th Panzer Division was directed to the Kasserine Pass. Far to the south German–Italian forces occupied Tozeur. On the 18th elements of the Afrika Korps and the 15th Division robbed the Americans of the important Thlepte airfield. The following day Rommel's reconnaissance forces groped their way forward to the Kasserine Pass. In the meantime "recce" units were pouring along the main road from Thlepte airfield towards Tebessa. Now Rommel ordered an attack on the approaches to Tebessa—the Kasserine Pass, the gateway to the Tunisian mountains. Still on the night of the 19/20th elements of the 3rd Reconnaissance Unit forced their way to the top of the Pass to wrest the road from the enemy. But this attempt failed. Rommel flung in his seasoned Afrika Panzer Grenadier Regiment commanded by Menton. But this attack, too, was halted by American artillery fire.

On the morning of the 20th February, the 21st and 10th Panzer Divisions, elements of the 15th Panzer Division and the Ariete were massed before the Pass on a seven-mile-long and three-mile-wide front. Smoke-throwing batteries of the

71st Mortar Regiment fired against the enemy positions. The shells made an infernal din as they exploded. They tore the earth and rocks to pieces. By 17.00 hours Major Stotten controlled the pass with a section of armour. The 8th Panzer Regiment streaked over the Pass road, formed a bridgehead and prevented an American counter-attack. Then the mass attack started across the Pass.

In American publications there are accounts of the chaos that was caused among the American troops and staffs by the loss of the Kasserine Pass. No one, including Eisenhower, had envisaged a German attack on this position. No defences had been prepared.

On the 21st Rommel despatched the 21st Panzer Division round the mountains and the 10th to the north on Thala in an attempt, by encirclement, to open the iron ring of hills before Tebessa. Since the 21st met with strong enemy resistance, the planned junction with the 10th did not materialise. The battle had already achieved a remarkable success. Three thousand prisoners were taken, a hundred and sixty tanks, ninety-five armoured cars, thirty-six self-propelled guns and sixty other guns were destroyed or captured. But Eisenhower was not waging a poor man's war. He had plenty of troops and equipment. The 10th Panzer Division was still able to take Thala but resistance increased. The German advance came up against the strong enemy reserve positions of the 6th British Armoured Division and the Guards Brigade. The Panzer division on its own was too weak. Thala had to be evacuated. The combat groups of the Afrika Korps, under General Bulowius, who had replaced the wounded General von Liebenstein, tried to forge west and take Tebessa from the American Battle Group "B". The latter fought like men possessed and did not yield a foot. British low-flying aircraft and American bombers joined in the fray. The enemy had now recovered from his panic and was fighting back. He had plenty of material with which to do it. Eisenhower was in command of more than an army. He had fighters, bombers and artillery. Von Arnim, at Rommel's request, had tried by constant assaults to pin down enemy forces on the 5th Army front. The reinforced 47th Infantry Regiment, under its seasoned commander, Colonel Bühse, attacked stoutly to the west, took Pichon and advanced twelve miles beyond it. But then he was brought to a standstill. It was on the 22nd February that the Afrika Korps attack had been halted by the American Battle Group "B". Once more the enemy had proved to be too strong. He was too strong everywhere. The Germans suffered heavy losses. Rommel himself fell into an artillery ambush and was chased through a cactus grove. With shells bursting all round, Colonel Bayerlein, who had had plenty of experiences of this kind, managed to guide them safely through the cacti. His staff also escaped with slight losses.

On the 22nd February Rommel was forced to realise that he had made no progress either in the direction of Thala le Kef, according to Italian ideas, or toward Tebessa which had been his own plan. He was far too weak. The mountainous terrain was too difficult for swift operations and, as usual, supplies were tardy. It transpired that for the planned operation—particularly in the direction of Tebessa with a subsequent swing to the north—more time would have been necessary than they had thought. In the meantime, the threat to his rear from the 8th Army, about to attack through the Mareth Line, had increased.

As a result of this situation, Rommel, after a council of war on the Kasserine Pass at which Kesselring was also present, called off the battle.

32

ARMY GROUP AFRIKA

On the 23rd February, the day after the offensive had collapsed, the German High Command finally decided upon a unified command in North Africa. Field-Marshal Rommel was given command of the new Army Group Afrika—a combination of the 5th Panzer and the German–Italian Panzer Armies. It was understood that Rommel should temporarily relinquish this command to Colonel-General von Arnim in order to go on a well-earned rest to restore his health.

It is fruitless to discuss whether the Tebessa operation would have been successful had Rommel held the supreme command in Tunisia from the start and been allowed to carry out his plans without interference. Rommel himself thought later that swift action and a full-scale attack on Tebessa would have brought about a collapse of the American front. A host of American reports on the reactions to his attack of the raw American troops and staffs corroborate Rommel's theory. On the other hand, far behind the British battle fronts were at least three new divisions intended for Sicily, and it has been proved without a doubt that the German–Italian supply system was inadequate. Only with an enormous amount of luck and bluff could Rommel have achieved his hoped-for success.

Possibly. But in the long run how could the situation in Africa have developed in the light of the supplies position? Obviously that is a question for the historians to answer and not the generals. Rommel was first and foremost a general. A bold leader of men who never gave up even after suffering a crushing defeat.

This was proved more than once. In a lengthy conversation with Colonel Pomtow, the G.S.O.1 of the 5th Panzer Army, in a wadi near Sbeitla, Rommel agreed to Arnim's plans for continuing the battle with the 5th Panzer Army to gain more favourable jumping-off positions and to forestall Eisenhower's expected attack in the spring. This offensive bore the code name "Oxhead."

Rommel stated quite clearly that, in his opinion, the Axis resistance could not be carried on longer than the middle of May. And then it was necessary that the Army Group Afrika should confine itself to a small bridgehead. The line of resistance of this bridgehead must be west of Tunis, somewhere on the original course of the German positions. In any case, they needed to improve their line and must deploy south from Tunis to the foothills of Enfidaville.

"Oxhead" was the last German operational attack in Tunisia. Its main objective was to occupy important heights to close the supply route from Beja to the notorious Medjez el Bab to Eisenhower, and to win a suitable terrain for armour in the north near Abiod. But even for these very limited objectives, von Arnim was not strong enough. His 10th Panzer Division had been removed from the 5th Panzer Army and was now under Rommel's orders. His remaining forces, including elements of the Hermann Goering Division, under Major-General "Beppo" Schmid, were exhausted and no longer battleworthy. In order to have at least a seasoned combat group, the 47th Infantry Regiment was withdrawn from the Pichon area and inserted between the "Manteuffel Division" and the 334th Infantry Division, where there was already a dangerous gap.

Von Arnim was given an additional division—or at least parts of one—for Berlin had despatched the 999th Infantry Division—a "probation unit": soldiers who had been sentenced for listening to enemy broadcasts, black-market activities and heaven knows what else. Among the personnel were degraded officers and N.C.O.s, and pardoned prisoners from the concentration camps. All of them, therefore, men who had no particular reason to support the Fatherland and the Hitler régime. Let me say at once that the division, whose commander was shot down on the flight over the Mediterranean, fought surprisingly well—above all, the artillery regiment, under Lieutenant-Colonel Wolf. Fewer than ten per cent of them deserted to the enemy. Others tried by personal acts of bravery to make good their criminal record. But instead of a crack division, a "probation unit" for the final battle in Africa! This is all that materialised from the promise made at the Führer's headquarters.

As to how the 5th Panzer Army stood with regard to fighting strength is best shown by its dispositions for the attack. In the north stood the "Manteuffel Division" with the 10th Italian Bersaglieri Regiment, the Witzig Parachute Engineers Battalion, the Barenthin Regiment, the battalion-strong special group under Captain von Koenen and a regiment newly formed from two Tunisian battalions. To these must be added four or five artillery batteries. The term "division" was a piece of bluff designed to deceive the enemy.

In the centre and in the south stood the Weber Korps Group. This was formed of the Lang Brigade with the 47th Infantry Regiment, the 501st Tiger Detachment with thirty Tigers and the main body of the 334th Infantry Division. In addition, elements of the Hermann Goering Division and a few Tunisian battalions. Four detachments of the 334th Artillery Regiment, with twelve batteries including six mountain howitzers—10.5 cms. drawn by mules—formed the artillery armament of the whole group. That was all!

In this formation it entered the battle of the 26th February against Eisenhower's invasion armies. Strangely enough it had an initial success. On the north wing the Manteuffel Division managed to surprise the enemy. Cap Serrat was taken in conjunction with weak combat troops landed from E-boats. But then came the rain—the endless downpour of the second rainy season which begins in Tunisia in the middle of February. The roads were transformed into morasses and the wadis into raging torrents. The country was flooded into one huge marsh. The Tiger tanks could not leave the road and became good targets for anti-tank batteries. Börger's Jaegers from the Barenthin Regiment quite rightly grumbled that their experience of more than a hundred reconnaissance patrols on the heights of Sidi Nsir were of no avail and that the staff expected to take with Tiger tanks what a well-trained infantry detachment could do much better. But in the end the Jaegers had to pull the chestnuts out of the fire—on the heights of Sidi Nsir and at the crossroads of the Jebel Zebla.

The southern group also managed to break through at Goubellat. But here, too, it began to rain and lack of artillery limited their operation.

In the centre, the Lang Brigade had attained its objective, the closing of the road to Medjez el Bab. Grenadiers of the 47th Infantry Regiment entrenched on the heights and plastered the road. At night mines were laid so that the enemy had to abandon all traffic to Medjez el Bab. But here, too, far too much had been demanded of the troops. They did not succeed in capturing all the heights.

The operation was a complete failure on the south flank. Extremely difficult country and strong resistance prevented the Hermann Goering Division, despite great efforts, from making any progress. The 3rd Jaeger Regiment stormed the enemy positions but had to retire after a three-days' battle. The calling off of operation "Oxhead" was the obvious conclusion. The last German offensive in Tunisia came to an end.

33

THE BETRAYAL OF MEDENINE

•

Anyone who has studied Rommel's strategy and tactics knows that it was always his habit to attack enemy concentrations and defeat them. How often had he done this in the twenty-five months of the African war! Rommel wanted to repeat this old technique after the failure of the Tebessa offensive and at the end of operation "Oxhead" against Eisenhower's army, and to turn now to west of the Mareth Line against his old enemy Montgomery. Once more all his strength, cunning and boldness was to be used against the victory-conscious 8th Army, to try to put a stop to its advance for a long time and to destroy a considerable part of it.

The German–Italian Panzer Army after Rommel's appointment as C-in-C Army Group Afrika, came under the orders of the Italian Colonel-General Messe. He had been awarded the Knight's Cross on the South Russian front while leader of an Italian corps. His Italian Chief of Staff was the very capable, clear-sighed General Manzinelli. He was given as his German Chief of Staff, Fritz Bayerlein, who in the meantime had been promoted to Major-General.

This was the position: The 90th Division as a stiffener astride the Medenine–Gabes road. To the left, as far as the sea, the stout-hearted Italian Young Fascist Division, one of the veteran divisions of North Africa which had fought bravely in every battle in which it was engaged. To the right, as far as the Matmata Mountains, the Trieste and Pistoia Divisions. The 164th Light Division on a broad front secured the passes of the Mareth hills. Italian contingents and an Army reconnaisance unit protected the deep flank west of the El Kebili Mountain. The 15th, 21st and 10th Panzer Divisions, reinforced by Army artillery, were also at the disposal of the Axis Panzer Army. The rear north of the salt pans—still under the command of the 5th Panzer Army—was secured by the Centauro Division, under Graf Calvi, and at Sened elements of the Imperial Brigade.

The terrain had certain defensive advantages in the shape of the deep wadis of the Qued el Zeuss and the towering heights of the Mareth hills west of the plain, which could only be crossed by the passes. These passes were protected by French strongpoints which had been dismantled after the Franco–German Armistice. For the enemy only Metameur, a high ridge in the plain to the north-northwest, was a suitable artillery position. The disadvantages of this defence position, however, lay in the possibility of being encircled by an enemy advance through the open desert west of the Matmata Mountains. As experience had so often shown, the desert was no obstacle to motorised columns. In addition to this there was still danger of encirclement by Free French Forces from the Sahara.

It was therefore to be presumed that in these circumstances no lengthy resistance could be put up against a full-scale attack by the 8th Army in the Mareth Line. This was Rommel's reason for the decision to attack Montgomery while he was still on the march. General Ziegler, temporarily in command of the Afrika Korps, was ordered by Rommel to work out a plan of attack and give his views.

In the course of these preparations there were great differences of opinion as to how the attack should be staged. The controversy still rages today, with the inevitable question: what would have happened if . . . ?

Ziegler wanted to attack from the west of Medenine against the forces to the south of the Mareth Line. A long approach march by the armour facing enemy air superiority was the weakness of this plan. General Ziegler wrote to me as follows on this problem: "At the decisive briefing, which took place in a private house on the Gabes–Mareth road, Field-Marshal Rommel, who was accompanied by Major-General Gause, accepted the proposal to attack from the west with the hub in the direction of Medenine with many misgivings. It was not easy to convince the field-marshal of the tactical impossibility of his proposed attack from the north. Again and again the premises had to be discussed and it nearly came to resignations. Even as to the conduct of the attack on Medenine itself there were differences of opinion. Rommel saw a danger that in an attack with the central point south of Medenine the forces engaged there might swiftly be cut off or at least pinned down by enemy reserves brought up from the south-east. In no circumstances did he wish to take such a risk. In consequence he ordered further consideration of the plan that the central point of the armour wing should lie north of Medenine and be directed against the probable enemy artillery dispositions in the highlands north of Metameur. The 10th Division was also to pass north of Medenine in the direction of Metameur. A new meeting was set for the 2nd March. On account of the long and difficult approach route to be covered by the 10th Panzer Division, a further postponement of the attack was unfortunately necessary. It had originally been planned for the 4th March and it was now postponed by two days. This delay boded ill."

In the early morning of the 6th March, the 15th, 21st and 10th Panzer Divisions were in position. They were supported by Major-General Krause's Army Artillery, the 90th and 160th Light Afrika Divisions and the Ariete Armoured Division. General Cramer, the former commander of the 8th Panzer Regiment, had taken over command of the Afrika Korps the day before the battle.

It was a beautiful sunny day and zero hour for the attack was 06.00 hours. The battle began with a mighty bombardment from the Afrika Korps batteries. The 17 cm. field guns and 21 cm. mortar batteries poured their salvoes into the Medenine–Metameur Sector. Then the armour was despatched. From his headquarters on the Jebel Tebarga the commander of the Afrika Korps could see his tanks manoeuvring far below—on the left the forty tanks of his old 8th Panzer Regiment, led by Colonel Irkens; in the centre, on a broad front the 5th Panzer Regiment, led by Colonel Gerhard Müller, and on the extreme right the 7th Panzer Regiment of the 10th Panzer Division, under Colonel Gerhard—a regiment of the former 4th Panzer Brigade. Behind Gerhard's tanks came the 86th Panzer Grenadier Regiment, followed by the 90th Panzer Artillery Regiment, which went from their march straight into action.

There was no chance of surprise. Fighter bombers attacked, and this was most disagreeable in open country. Gunners and grenadiers flung themselves to the ground. A tank battle developed. The grenadiers, laden with ammunition boxes, had pushed their steel helmets on to the back of their heads. Many of them had cigarettes in the corners of their mouths. They had looked exactly the same in front of the Maginot Line, on the Bug, on the Dneiper and before Stalingrad.

When General Cramer visited the tactical headquarters of the 21st Panzer Division, its commander, Major-General Hildebrandt, stood under shell fire with his armoured reserve looking very grave. "We're making no progress," he said. But Cramer could see for himself that ahead lay a heavy barrage of fire. British batteries kept up an infernal bombardment against the attacking armour. The stony ground produced a rain of shrapnel with deadly effect on grenadiers and gunners. Major Schlicke's men of the 326th Observer Detachment lay far ahead with their sound-rangers and range-finders, trying to pinpoint the artillery positions.

General von Broich with the 10th Panzer Division looked gloomy. His Panzer Grenadiers were under direct artillery fire from the British and sustaining heavy losses. The batteries of his artillery regiments had suffered heavy casualties

Nebelwerfer 41

from low-flying aircraft. Far in advance of his front, too, were the troops of the observer detachment, the "Gnomes of the Arillery." They tried feverishly to direct their own artillery fire and to spot the positions of the enemy batteries. What these observers discovered was bad enough. The first aim of the German attack had been to take the strong enemy artillery groups from the flank and at the rear. Now the German attack was a frontal one. As it turned out later, the guns had been in position for two days. There was no question about it: Montgomery had learned of Rommel's plan of attack and had grouped his artillery accordingly. Treachery had been at work here. The proof of this treachery was soon found in the pocket of a French N.C.O. prisoner—a paper with the exact details of the start of the offensive and Rommel's planned direction of attack. The date given was 4th March, in other words the original date. The two days postponement had given the British army commander time to make all his preparations. Since the whole of Rommel's effort was to be based on surprise, and now there could be no question of this, the battle was lost before it had started. But, as usual, this knowledge only became public property at a much later date.

At the tactical headquarters of the 10th Panzer Division, the G.S.O.1, Lieutenant-Colonel Stauffenberg, bent over the reports. "Smoke-throwers," he kept calling, "smoke-throwers." They alone could cause a breach in the enemy artillery ranks. Stauffenberg himself directed the placing of the mortars, a new and effective weapon on African soil, the forerunner of the modern rocket. But on this occasion they were of no use. The three batteries of smoke-throwers of the 71st Regiment were destroyed by fighter-bombers and the tanks remained under devastating fire from the British gunners. At midday fifty-five burnt-out German tanks lay on the battlefield in front of Metameur. The plan of attack had been betrayed. No one at headquarters doubted this any longer.

The accuracy with which the traitor had worked was proved by the behaviour of the British troops against the frontal attack of the 90th Light Division. It had been sent south for the purposes of deception and was to pin down British forces. Montgomery, however, withdrew his troops from the front of the 90th Light so that the German attack progressed into the blue. He was obviously not in the least worried that a serious attack could threaten him from this quarter. Who was the traitor? In many circles after the war suspicions were voiced that that the treachery stemmed from an officer of the Italian High Command. I do not propose to go any further into this sinister story. . . .

On the afternoon of the 6th March, at about 16.00 hours, it was obvious to Rommel and his commanders that it was no longer possible to win the Medenine–Metameur battle. General Cramer suggested breaking off the attack and Rommel agreed. The last full-scale attack of the Axis Panzer Army was over. Now the tragic end of the African campaign was clearly in sight.

Three days after this battle, on the 9th March, 1943, Field-Marshal Rommel left Africa. He flew to Rome and then on to the Führer's headquarters in a final attempt to organise the evacuation of the two armies of the Army Group Afrika. But Hitler was deaf to all argument. Rommel was ordered to go off immediately and "take a cure."

34

THE AFRIKA KORPS SIGNS OFF

The task of leading to the bitter end the Tunisian army and the Desert Foxes fell upon Colonel-General von Arnim as C-in-C Army Group. General Gause remained chief of staff and the indefatigable Colonel Pomtow became G.S.O.1. The 5th Panzer Army was taken over by General von Vaerst, the former commander of the famous 15th Panzer Division. His Chief of Staff was General von Quast.

The Prussian nobleman, von Arnim, "one of the last knights of the Old School," as Pomtow wrote to me in a letter, fulfilled his task with a consideration, courage and humanity, which neither his own soldiers nor the enemy have forgotten.

Here is an example that is worth while recording in the annals of the African war. Off Tunis in the roadstead of La

Goulette on the first days in May, lay the Italian supply ship *Belluno* with seven hundred British and American prisoners-of-war on board. R.A.F. bombers attacked the ship. The Italian crew abandoned her; the harbour Captain, Keller, rang up the Army Group staff asking for fighter protection for the *Belluno*. But where could protection be found for Allied prisoners-of-war against their own bombers, when there were none to protect his own troops? Captain Keller implored Colonel Pomtow to do something and the staff officer explained the situation to von Arnim. "Send a message to Alexander to stop bombing his own people," was the reply. Von Arnim gave his order to his G.S.O.3, Major Moll. A message in clear went from Army Group Afrika to the British C-in-C in Tunisia, Eisenhower's deputy, General Alexander. "Stop the air attack on Tunis harbour. The ship has seven hundred P-O-Ws on board." Alexander reacted promptly and the British bombers were recalled.

Later, when von Arnim went into captivity and was received by Alexander—General Eisenhower refused to meet any German Army Commanders—he was asked "Have you any wishes, General?" Arnim replied: "Give me my quid pro quo for the seven hundred Tommies and let me send seven hundred seriously wounded Germans in a hospital ship to Italy." Alexander hesitated for a moment and then nodded. "I will do as you ask," he said. The General's wish was carried out.

But it was two months from the battle of Medenine to his captivity. These two months are a dramatic and tragic chapter in the final phase of the North African war. The courage of the officers and men during those months was all the more admirable since they had no hope of victory but only the harsh and bitter duty of bringing a pointless campaign to a decent close. After the battle of Medenine von Arnim's staff and the troops knew perfectly well that it was the beginning of the end. The enemy was so vastly superior in men and materials to the Axis troops that it was now merely a question as to how long the resistance could last on African soil. The Allied air supremacy was complete.

The Army Group had a front of about five hundred miles to defend. To do this it had two armies with a total strength of about three hundred thousand men, a third of whom were Germans. If we deduct the personnel of the supply organizations, which in the case of the Italians was very large, there remained a fighting force of about a hundred and fifty thousand. With this number of troops, five hundred miles of front could not be defended even in favourable terrain or on the lines of the previous conduct of the war in Africa. Whole stretches could only be defended by a few isolated posts. How thin this front actually looked is illustrated by an amazing story which von Arnim himself told me.

Colonel Heigl, the economic expert on Arnim's staff, suddenly announced that the prices on the black market had risen. The reason for this was large-scale purchases by the Arab peasants. The wares were removed from Tunis in long donkey caravans. Strangely enough the Arabs paid in dollars or English pound notes. For the German troops this meant not only an increase in the price of land produce such as wine, fruit and corn but a general shortage. It was a serious problem in view of the shocking supply position. No wonder Heigl took a closer look at the Arab transports. His astonishment can be imagined when beneath the burnous of an Arab donkey driver he discovered a pair of British military boots, and on closer inspection a real live British sergeant appeared. The solution was easy: the British, with special commandos, were buying on the black market in Tunisia and taking the produce by caravan to the British–American front. It was a very strange theatre of war.

To the lack of troops was added the difficulty of obtaining provisions. There was never enough to eat, never enough ammunition or fuel. Rastenburg and Rome were no longer in a position to supply the Army Group with its minimum needs for existence. Only small ships up to three thousand tons arrived in Tunis harbour. Siebel ferries were introduced, but these utility craft could only transport twenty tons, a trifle out of a monthly requirement of seventy-five thousand tons. Nor could supplies by air bring any improvement. Kesselring would have had to use powerful fleets of Junkers and giant transports which he did not posses. Those he sent were shot down over the Mediterranean. Von Arnim said to me with military brevity: "Even without the Allied offensive I should have had to capitulate by the 1st of June at the latest because we had no more to eat."

On 18th March German air reconnaissance reported that a mighty force of three thousand British vehicles was making its way through the desert to do what every commander had feared for weeks—to encircle the Mareth Line. Montgomery rolled forward to the north with a New Zealand division, an Army Tank Brigade and the 1st British Armoured Division, and attacked the Mareth Line frontally and on the flanks.

An attack by the Guards Brigade was beaten off on 16th March by the 361st Infantry Regiment together with a battalion of the 47th. On 20th March the Guards again made an abortive attack on Hill 151; but in the centre of the front the 50th British Infantry Division broke through the positions of the Zigzaghou Wadi, crossing trenches which were six feet deep and twelve feet wide. Before the Tommies could bring up their anti-tank weapons they were subjected to a counterattack by the 15th Panzer Division. In fierce hand-to-hand fighting the British were repulsed. Hundreds of British dead lay in the Zigzaghou Wadi.

On 22nd March the British encircling army attacked the Italian flank beyond the mountain. The 21st Panzer Division still held the front. But now, farther north, the Americans attacked from Gafsa against the El Guettar defiles, held by the Centauro Division and the Imperiali Brigade. This was a simultaneous attack against the front, flanks and rear. In the face of this situation von Arnim ordered the evacuation of the Mareth Line. The Messe army fought its way back.

The new positions were in the Chott or Akarit line, a defile between the salt pans and the Gulf of Gabes. Now a dramatic race began. On 26th March, in a sandstorm, the New Zealanders broke through Messe's outer flank as far as the artillery positions. The moon was high in the sky. The New Zealanders pressed on in the direction of El Hamma to the coast. Had they got through, the entire Messe army would have been cut off and annihilated. The Army Group had no reserves left to prevent this disaster. At this critical moment General Borowitz put his 15th Panzer Division about and, despite his inferiority, attacked the New Zealanders on their south flank. Surprised, the Maoris were diverted from their objective to grapple with the unexpected enemy. The 164th Light and the 21st Panzer Divisions were thus able to build a ring round El Hamma and to hold the British attack until Messe's infantry had taken up its positions in the new Akarit region.

But now blow followed blow.

The American 2nd Army Corps from Gafsa attacked the Italian defences to the rear of Messe's new position. There was the threat of a break-through to the sea. A desperate counter-attack by the 10th Panzer Division was halted by enemy artillery fire. At the same time Eisenhower's troops from the west went over to the attack in the Maknassy gorges. They, too, were trying to reach the sea. A few Tigers appeared. Colonel Lang had to rush up a scratch detachment to the north consisting of a battalion of the 69th and 86th Regiments and a few 88 mm. batteries. For hours on end it was a case of a few battalions against divisions at Maknassy.

In the El Leben wadi Major Freidrich Wilhelm Voss with his reconnaissance unit held the 1st American Armoured Division. On the Maknassy Pass the tragedy was in progress. It was reminiscent of the Spartan, Leonidas, holding the Pass of Thermopylae. Rommel's former bodyguard, under Major Medicus, managed to hold the Pass for over a week against the attacks of one and a half American divisions. Eighty men, half a column of sappers and a headquarters staff fought under Lieutenant Brennert like the bands of Andreas Hofer. They rolled boulders down from the slopes on the advancing tanks and threw stones.

On the 26th March the 21st Panzer Division still had twenty-five tanks left. The 15th had another three. They combined together with the survivors of the Centauro Division at Guettar to counter the resolute Allied attacks.

In the north, Cap Serat fell into British hands. Everything crumbled and no supplies arrived. Special units distilled fuel spirit from Tunisian wine. It was bankruptcy.

The Chott position could not be held. How could such a position stand a seige? They had no frowning walls and no roof against the round-the-clock attacks of the Allied air forces.

Monty continued to attack. His 51st Highland Division took the blood-drenched Jebel Roumana and Hill 175. Once more the 361st and 200th Infantry Regiments threw back the enemy. But then the Italian front broke. On the 6th April the retreat was sounded. The troops fell back to the Enfidaville position, far to the north in the Gulf of Hammamet.

It was one of the ironies of the ideological war that the men of the 1st Regiment of the 999th "Probation" Division, in Colonel Fullriede's combat group, held the defiles near

Pichon–Fondouk for six days against more than two divisions. They destroyed sixty American tanks and covered the retreat to the positions which were reached on the 13th April.

Another episode gives us a glimpse of the irony of human destiny. Lieutenant-Colonel Graf Stauffenberg advanced, standing in his armoured truck. A British fighter-bomber dived. Its machine-guns rattled and Stauffenberg collapsed, badly wounded. Fortunately an ambulance was at hand and the Lieutenant-Colonel was taken aboard. The men of the 90th Panzer Artillery Regiment who saw the episode did not suspect that the British machine-gun had been guided by the hand of Destiny, for Count Stauffenberg had to leave Africa. It would have been better for him had he been captured.

In the history of a war there are as many successful retreats as there are bold advances. The retreat of Army Group Afrika to the Enfidaville position was a masterpiece of the art of war and of the application of troop experience in battle. When the final battle in Tunisia began in the middle of April, Eisenhower entered the fray with fifteen British and five fully equipped American divisions. In addition to this he had at his disposal a French Army Corps, an air fleet and special units for intelligence, supplies and sapper duties.

Against these von Arnim had nine exhausted German divisions, most of which were only up to two-fifths in strength. The six Italian divisions had very little fighting value. In addition to these there were special units bearing the title, brigade, regiment or combat group but which, in reality, were only battalions. This ratio of strength tells the whole story.

Reinforcements fared badly. Sergeant Weinzheimer of the famous 15th Motorised Infantry Battalion was flown to Tunis during those last days in Italian transport machines with elements of an infantry company. The planes crashed. The pilots were killed. Weinzheimer with the rest of his men was taken prisoner from a machine which had force-landed. A few weeks before a reserve battalion of the 104th Panzer Regiment at war strength, under Lieutenant-Colonel Reinhold May, who had fought in 1941 and 1942 at Sidi Rezegh, was shipped in three Italian destroyers to Tunis. The destroyers were sunk. Only six men of the whole battalion were rescued because a high sea was running.

General Alexander, who had regrouped his forces, assembled strong detachments on the central front, and with British troops formed an offensive group of six infantry and two armoured divisions for the main attack on Tunis. His advance route led through the Medjerda Valley, and along the road via Massicault. In the south too, in the Pont du Fahs area, the French prepared to attack. They were supported by three British divisions.

Between the 20th April and the 5th May, Alexander's attacks lashed against the thin lines of the Axis front. In the north the Barenthin Regiment which, after the wounding of its commander was led by Major Baier, retired step by step to the old Jefna position. On the 1st May a threatened breakthrough forced a further withdrawal of the front to the west of Mateur.

At the same time elements of the 334th Infantry Division and the 47th Infantry Regiment fought against the 2nd American Corps for Hill 609 which was lost on the 1st May. At Mateur the remains of the division and the 47th once more formed a front.

At the bitterly contested Longstop Hill the 78th British Division attacked a battalion of the 334th. The bloody height was ploughed up with shells. Since Christmas it had been in German hands. It was lost on the 24th April. With this the defence line around Tunis was broken.

On the Camel Mountain, the 6th British Armoured Division wrested the position from the Hermann Goering Division. Grenadiers of the 10th Panzer Division recaptured it—only to lose it again.

Between the 28th April and the 1st May it was constant attack and counter-attack. On the road to Massicault, at French farm, the fighting was at its fiercest. Here fought the grenadiers of the 15th Panzer Division. Colonel Irkens kept rushing with his remaining tanks to the support of threatened positions. The surviving 88 mm. guns of the 20th Flak Division went on fighting against renewed attacks by British armour. The 8/52 motorised troops of this Division gave a final farewell performance with their trusted 88s. North of Mateur, two guns of Lieutenant Happach's battery shot thirteen American tanks out of an armoured brigade. It was a fiery salute from Sergeant-Major Voigt in honour of the 88 mm. The second section of the 190th Artillery Regiment, which had now shrunk to a single battery under Captain Seidl, had its last duel with the American armour on the 5th

May. Here, too, it was more a question of defiance than useful purpose.

During the night of the 5/6th May, the enemy artillery fire rose to barrage dimensions. Ceaselessly the Allied air forces bombed the German positions. On a three-mile front two British infantry divisions, supported by armour, attacked two weak regiments of the 334th Infantry Division and the remains of the Hermann Goering Division. They put up a stout defence. Machine-gun and anti-tank gunfire met the attackers. It was a final display but it was useless. The front was crumbling. Slowly the Allied attack gnawed away to the east, and at sunset reached the outskirts of Massicault.

The bravery shown by Colonel Irkens with the last remaining tanks of the 15th Panzer Division was of no avail. Nor was the bravery of the Kleinschmid Parachute Column at Hill 530, south of Mateur. Though admirable and gallant it was quite senseless.

Early on the 7th May, after relieving their front-line infantry, the British renewed the attack. In despair, and filled with rage, Colonel Irkens sent his last tanks into the battle. In vain. By midday Montgomery's 11th Hussars were at the gates of Tunis. At the same moment the Americans occupied evacuated Bizerta. The Army Group Afrika had been utterly defeated. The 5th Panzer Army now consisted of a few fighting units. General von Vaerst, its commander, had fought his way back with his last two tanks and a few hundred infantrymen to the coast at Porto Farina. On the Jebel Achkel, north of Mateur, small fighting units still held out. The survivors of the Hermann Goering Division and the Koch Regiment went on fighting on the Miliana River. Here General Franz took up a defence position with the remains of his 19th Flak Division, battalions of the former Ramcke Parachute Brigade and a few 88 mm. guns. The 4th Indian Division was beaten off once more.

The army's fate was sealed by an order from Rastenburg. It read: "To the Army Group Afrika—The German people expect you to fight to the last bullet."

Colonel-General von Arnim was not the man to disobey orders lightly. But had this order any sense? Stalingrad was in everyone's mind. Was Tunisia to become an African Stalingrad? The general asked his staff: "What does the last bullet mean in a modern war?" There was no difference of opinion and so von Arnim informed the troops that by "the last bullet" in a tank attack, the last shell was meant. The weapons were then to be destroyed and the division would surrender to the enemy.

The 10th Panzer Division had dug in its last seven tanks, since it had no more petrol. An American attack with tanks was beaten off with the last shells at midday on the 11th May.

The men sat grimly at their guns. One more and another and now the last one. Good-night! Tanks and guns were blown up. The divisions signed off. "Ammunition expended, weapons and equipment destroyed."

On the Jebel Zaghouan, on the night of the 11/12th May, the Free French attacked in an attempt to force a break-through. The covering units of the Hermann Goering Division were wiped out. No one could explain why this sudden glow of white-hot rage flared up, but on the Jebel Zaghouan there was a final hand-to-hand battle with revolvers, knives, hand grenades and bayonets. It was the last bloody encounter in Africa.

On midday of the 12th Colonel-General von Arnim capitulated on behalf of the two staffs of the Army Group Afrika and the Afrika Korps. General Cramer, the last commander of the Afrika Korps, sent his final message. "To the German High Command—Munitions expended, weapons and war equipment destroyed. The Afrika Korps has fought to a standstill as ordered. The German Afrika Korps must rise again, Cramer."

In the south, too, the end came for the German-Italian Panzer Army of Colonel-General Messe, for the Desert Foxes, the old divisions of Rommel's desert army. On the 10th May the 6th British Armoured Division broke through at Hammam Lif and encircled the Messe Army from the south. The Young Fascist Division and the 90th Light fought together against the advancing British armour. They held out for two days. On the 12th May the dam broke. The guns of the southern army fired their last shells at the 8th Army and the 6th British Armoured Division. Then there was silence. The war in Africa was over.

On the 12th May at 18.00 hours the 90th Light Division capitulated.

On the 13th May at 11.00 hours the last fighting unit, the 164th Light Afrika Division, laid down its arms.

Thirteen thousand German soldiers marched into captivity; 18,594 remained in Africa. They lie forever in Egypt, Libya and Tunisia. More than 3,400 were missing.

No one can estimate the number of German dead that lie on the bottom of the sea from their journey or flight across the Mediterranean.

The Italian dead in the North African theatre of war were officially estimated at 13,748. In addition to this 8,821 were missing.

The British War Graves Commission at the end of April 1958 announced that the British Commonwealth Forces in North Africa had to mourn 35,476 dead.

The American War Graves Commission gave the total dead of all American units in North Africa as 16,500.

If one includes the number of French casualties for which there are no accurate figures, the bloody bill in North Africa was over 100,000 dead.

Evacuated to Sicily in the last naval unit with a special commando of the Brandenburg Division—with secret equipment, specialists and general staff officers and commanders destined for the Eastern front after the fall of Tunisia—sat Achmed el Bedoiu, a completely unknown Arab. He had been batman to Lieutenant Dr. Wagner, the former leader of the Brandenburger Coastal Jaegers, who had recently been killed. Achmed was one of the many who had set his hopes on Germany. He did not wish to remain in Africa, and travelled with his new commander, Captain Kuhlmann, to the storm-racked Continent of Europe. He made the long journey with his German comrades via Palermo, Naples, Rome and Athens. He fought with them in the Aegean, in Corfu and in the Dodecanese. He was awarded the German Infantry Medal and the Iron Cross. He was still with them when the company marched into captivity. The slips of paper with the news which he smuggled into his commander in hospital were addressed: "Mon Pére, mon Commandant." Later Achmed stood trial before a French War Crimes Tribunal which condemned him to death by hanging as a French citizen. His last note, written a few hours before his execution, was signed as usual: "ton fils."

His name is engraved on no memorial.

No Fatherland remembers its servant.

What better commentary on the futility of war?